Lineages
of the
Literary

Lineages of the Literary

Tibetan Buddhist

Polymaths of

Socialist China

Nicole Willock

Columbia University Press

New York

Columbia University Press
Publishers Since 1893
New York   Chichester, West Sussex
cup.columbia.edu

Library of Congress Cataloging-in-Publication Data
Names: Willock, Nicole D., author.
Title: Lineages of the literary : Tibetan Buddhist polymaths of
socialist China / Nicole Willock.
Description: New York : Columbia University Press, [2021] |
Includes bibliographical references and index.
Identifiers: LCCN 2020038974 (print) | LCCN 2020038975 (ebook) |
ISBN 9780231197069 (hardback) | ISBN 9780231197076 (trade paperback) |
ISBN 9780231551960 (ebook)
Subjects: LCSH: Tibet Region—Civilization. | China—Intellectual life—1949– |
Tshe-tan Zhabs-drung, 1910 or 1911–1986. | Bsam-gtan, Dmu-dge. |
Blo-bzang-'phrin-las, Dung-dkar, 1927–1997. | Buddhism—China—
Tibet Autonomous Region—History—20th century.
Classification: LCC DS786 .W493 2021 (print) | LCC DS786 (ebook) |
DDC 951/.3050922—dc23
LC record available at https://lccn.loc.gov/2020038974
LC ebook record available at https://lccn.loc.gov/2020038975

Columbia University Press books are printed
on permanent and durable acid-free paper.
Printed in the United States of America

COVER IMAGES: Ngangwa Gyeltsen

To Gen Rabsal-la:

*Like a lamp through the darkness, you patiently guided me
through the reading of Tibetan texts. Your generosity as a mentor
and compassion as friend are immeasurable. With gratitude for
opening up my world, I dedicate this work to you.*

*In memory of Professor Elliot Sperling (1951–2017),
without whose stalwart support as Doctorvater and
Mensch this book would not have been possible.*

Contents

Notes on Transcription, Transliteration, and Naming Practices

Tibetan terms are transcribed phonetically throughout this book. The transcription method accords with a modified form of "THL Simplified Phonetic Transcription of Standard Tibetan" developed by David Germano and Nicolas Tournadre. For example, I rendered syllables that end with the vowel "*-e*" with "*-é*" (e-acute) to denote /e/ rather than a schwa, e.g., Tséten (Tshe tan) or Géluk (Dge lugs). I also retained the final consonant of Wylie transliteration in terms such as "*Zhabdrung*" (*zhabs drung*) and "Jigmé" (*'jigs med*) in order to accord as much as possible with Tibetan spellings. These slight modifications are aimed to make the pronunciation and readability of Tibetan more accessible to general readers.

On most occasions, the first occurrence of Tibetan proper nouns (e.g., personal names) and important terms appears with the Wylie transliteration following in parentheses. All foreign terms given in parentheses are the Wylie transliteration of Tibetan unless otherwise indicated. Sanskrit terms are marked by (Skt.) according to the International Alphabet of Sanskrit Transliteration (IAST). Chinese (Ch.) terms are given according to pinyin followed by simplified characters. Mongolian terms (Mong.) follow Christopher Atwood's transcriptions as given in his *Encyclopedia of Mongolia and the Mongol Empire* (2004). Proper nouns are listed in the index according to the phonetics followed by Wylie transliterations. Throughout the main body of the text, Tibetan terms are transcribed phonetically; however, Wylie transliteration is used in notes and sources. When citing sources, I retain previously published renderings of Tibetan names and terms, e.g., Arjia Rinpoche. Unless otherwise noted, all translations found in this book are my own.

Acknowledgments

Śāntideva wrote that this precious human life is as rare as a sea turtle who, when rising up for a breath of air, sticks her head momentarily through a yoke in the middle of a vast ocean. The myriad of causes and conditions that manifested in this book are as inimitable as such an occurrence. As I write these words of acknowledgment, we find ourselves, all sentient beings, linked together on this planet amid a global pandemic. This has forced me, like so many others, to question what really matters in our short time in this world. I am humbled and immensely grateful to have had the rare and precious opportunity to spend my life on various aspects of this book project. I am immensely grateful to institutions and people who supported me as I translated, researched, and wrote what has become *Lineages of the Literary: Tibetan Buddhist Polymaths of Socialist China*.

The final phase of research and writing was assisted by a research fellowship in 2017 from The Robert H. N. Ho Family Foundation Program in Buddhist Studies, administered by the American Council of Learned Societies. I am grateful to the administrators at Old Dominion University for granting me research leave and for start-up funds that supported a crucial phase of this project. To the chair of the Philosophy and Religious Studies Department at that time, Dr. Yvette Pearson, and to all my colleagues, especially Dylan Wittkower and Kristian Petersen, thank you for your support. Earlier phases of this research were conducted with the support of the Fulbright-Hays Doctoral Dissertation Research Abroad Fellowship and dissertation fellowships from Indiana University. This research would not have been possible without the support of Qinghai Nationalities University and the assistance of Professor Tsewang Dorjee. I am also very grateful to the Library of Tibetan Works and Archives, especially

Ven. Geshe Lhakdor, Lobsang Shastri, and Sonam Topgyal; and Columbia University's C. V. Starr East Asian Library, especially Tibetan Studies Librarian Lauran Hartley. I thank Kristina Dy-Liacco, Pema Bhum, and Tenzin Gelek, co-founders of the Latse Project, a new nonprofit organization that works to promote Tibetan language use and literacy, and formerly of the Latse Library in New York City (which unfortunately closed in 2020). I am grateful to Tsadra Foundation for supporting workshops such as the Lotsawa Conference that aided in the development of this project. I express my sincere thanks to the editorial team at Columbia University Press, especially to Lowell Frye and Leslie Kriesel for their extraordinary editorial skills and guidance in bringing this book into the world. This work benefited from the feedback from anonymous reviewers.

I also wish to extend my immense gratitude to many individuals who contributed to making this book possible. Foremost among them is Gen-la Gedun Rabsal, senior lecturer at Indiana University, who first introduced me to the writings of the Tséten Zhabdrung, Mugé Samten, and Dungkar Lozang Trinlé. To you, I dedicate this book. To his spouse, Yangkey, and their girls, Palzom and Kunga, I am grateful beyond words. Without their support, I don't know how I would have finished my PhD, a crucial stage of this project.

The immeasurable feeling of gratitude for my doctoral dissertation committee is beyond words. My *Doktorvater*, Professor Elliot Sperling was a steadfast supporter until his untimely death in January 2017. He not only instructed me in the language and research skills necessary for taking on such a project but also modeled a sense of ethics and integrity, *Menschlichkeit*—virtues that remain a source of inspiration. Likewise, Professor Rebecca Manring continues to inspire me to be intellectually rigorous. She is an exemplary model of bringing hard-earned linguistic skills to larger conversations on culture and religion in the academy. Without her unfailing support and encouragement, I would not have the confidence to be the woman professor that I am today. I am grateful to Aaron Stalnaker for his instruction and guidance during my PhD examinations in religious studies. Professor Rick Nance enthusiastically joined my dissertation committee in his first year at Indiana University. He provided me with clarity and guidance in navigating the final years of graduate school and my entryway into the profession. Like a shining star, Professor Christopher Atwood guided me through Mongol-Tibetan history, and his advice at so many turning points set my work in motion. Professor Gray Tuttle's scholarship and mentorship are only exceeded by his ethics. His influence has been so foundational and instrumental in this work, during graduate school and after, that I can't imagine this book would be the way it is without him.

My focus on the lives of three Tibetan scholars emerged at least in part because my professors have left such indelible impressions on me and the way I chose to live my life. In addition to those mentioned above, I need to express gratitude to other lights on the path. For the first taste of this profession, I am immensely grateful to Professors Colin Jeffcott and Bill Jenner of Australian National University, who put up with me as an undergraduate and instilled in me a love of Chinese history and translation. I still have a letter from Professor Jenner that found me at Beijing Film Academy in fall 1992 that sternly told me that I could not write an undergraduate thesis on Tibetan culture in China without learning the Tibetan language first. After I finished my BA in Chinese studies, I took it to heart to study Tibetan. This work was only possible after years and years of studying the Tibetan language (a never-ending endeavor) with many teachers. At the University of Hamburg, I am especially grateful to Professors Dorji Wangchuk, Jan-Ulrich Sobisch, and David Jackson for support during those first few years of Tibetan language instruction. Professor Michael Friedrich in Sinology encouraged me to painstakingly research cultural references and read texts through a historical-cultural lens. I am also grateful to Susan Whitfield and Sam van Schaik for their assistance during an internship at the International Dunhuang Project while doing my *Magistra Artium*. While at Indiana University, I benefited from graduate classes with Professor Robert Ford Campany, a class on Chinese history with Professor Jeffrey Wasserstrom, and a graduate seminar with Professor Jan Nattier. I remain grateful to Professor David Brakke, who encouraged me to join the Department of Religious Studies as a graduate student.

The bulk of research for this work was conducted in China on the Fulbright-Hays Doctoral Dissertation Research Abroad Fellowship. During that fellowship, I had the opportunity to work with incredible young talent as research assistants: Huatse Gyal, Gangri, and Khyungdrik. For their guidance and assistance, I am most thankful. I am especially grateful to Huatse for his help facilitating interviews and meticulous transcription work. On my return visit in 2015, my colleague at Old Dominion University, Professor Qiu Jin Hailstork, facilitated connections with Minzu University—thank you. Thanks also to Dr. Catherine Hardie for facilitating and interpreting two interviews.

To Jigmé Chöphak and the Yang family, I am grateful beyond words. I am also immensely thankful to Dawa Lodrö, Pu Wencheng, Gao Rui, Pema Bhum, Lugyel Bhum, Rebkong Dorje Khar, Gyalmo Drukpa, Gartso Kyi, Jigmé Samdrup, the late Sanggé Gyel, and the late Jamyang Drakpa for sharing their stories. I am grateful to the talented young artist Ngangwa Gyeltsen, who generously donated his drawings for the cover art.

My thanks go to senior colleagues whose conversations, scholarship, words of advice, and/or leadership inspired this work at crucial stages. I am grateful to Roberto Vitali; Tashi Tsering of the Amnye Machen Institute; Professors Heather Stoddard, Tsering Shakya, Françoise Robin, Hildegard Diemberger, Robert Barnett, Kurtis Schaeffer, Andrew Quintman, Leonard van der Kuijp, Jake Dalton, Frances Garrett, Paul Nietupski, Carole McGranahan, Roger Jackson, José Cabezón, Vesna Wallace, and Mark Unno; and especially to Dr. Lauran Hartley. I remain ever grateful to the late E. Gene Smith for opening up a new world of Tibetan texts to me and his encouragement when I returned from the field. An immense sense of gratitude and special thank you go to Professor Janet Gyatso, whose writings, words of advice, and generous feedback remain a constant stream of inspiration.

My deep appreciation goes out to the friends and colleagues made on this path. Thanks to Ulan (Lan Wu), Brenton Sullivan, Benno Weiner, Xenia de Heering, Stacey Van Vleet, Jowita Kruper, Chen Chun (Catherine), Jane Lewis, Biyun, Shawn Ellmers, Daniel Ho, Alice Grünfelder, Marc des Jardins, Eveline Washul, Michael Sheehy, Brandon Dotson, Karl Debreczeny, Annabella Pitkin, Dominique Townsend, Carl Yamomoto, Lara Braitstein, Antonio Terrone, Sarah Jacoby, Jann Ronis, Katie and Mike, Kate Johnston, Kristie Combs, Sandy Belth, Frederica Venturi, Ron Sela, Robin Charpentier, Gil Raz, Judith Hertog, Filiz Çiçek, Sandrine Catris, Erik Hammerstrom, Aimee Hamilton, Nicole Karapangiotis, Amy Holmes-Tagchungdarpa, Michael Stanley Baker, Jonathan Petit and Yuhua, Sarah Conrad, Liz Monson, Lowell Cook, Jue Liang, Amelia Hall, Leigh Miller, and the late André Alexander. I am especially grateful to Holly Gayley and Padma'tsho for their meaningful conversations and inspirational feedback. To Nancy, Markus and Kai, and Liese Hilgeman, may we all enjoy many more meals and conversations together! Thanks again to Nancy and her sister, Linda, for valuable editorial advice that made this a much stronger work. Amikolé, young until we die! Thank you, Steve Marshall and Jaffa Elias, who both first introduced me to the richness of Tibetan cultural life in Lhasa in 1993—the seeds for this project were planted in those conversations at the Yak Hotel so long ago!

Thanks to my family for all their life lessons and love. All of that complex mix helped me become who I am. Thanks to my parents, Wendy Jayvanti and Joe Willock, for giving me this precious life and for their constant love and support. To my stepmother, Jean Willock, thanks for always being there with love and kindness. Thanks to my loving family for sharing their joy and love of life: Abe, Kate, Gavin, Ellen, Chris, Avery, Austin, Christine, Lukas, Matt, Lynn, Natalie, and Jack; Ken and Marie and the Myles cousins; Carol, John, and Dylan Draut; and the Donnelly family. With gratitude to my aunt and talented artist, Leslie Gifford. To my sweet Miriam: thanks for putting up with an overworked mom and forgive me that your first written word at age six was "d-i-s-e-r-t-a-s-i-o-n." You bring immeasurable love and joy to my world. I am so proud of who you are.

Now I turn to disclose a few notes on this manuscript. Due to the intense political pressures facing Tibetan monastics in China, I have redacted the names of all monks whom I interviewed for this project. I'd like to acknowledge that sections of this book build upon ideas in my dissertation and in an article "Rekindling Ashes of the Dharma and the Formation of Modern Tibetan Studies: The Busy Life of Alak Tseten Zhabdrung," in Trace Foundation's *Latse Library Newsletter* 6. Some of the ideas in chapter 5 were initially developed in "The Revival of the Tulku Institution in Modern China: Narratives and Practices," *Revue d'Etudes Tibétaines* 38 (Février 2017); and chapter 3 expands upon ideas and translations that appear in "Tibetan Buddhist Scholars and the Cultural Revolution: Narratives of Spiritual Achievement and Supporting Tibetan Culture" in *Conflicting Memories: Tibetan History under Mao Retold*, ed. Robert Barnett, Francoise Robin, and Benno Weiner (Leiden: Brill, 2020).

Lastly, the perspectives presented throughout this manuscript are my own, as are any errors that I may have unwittingly made. May we all delight in the literary, historical, and philosophical texts that Tséten Zhabdrung, Dungkar Rinpoché, and Mugé Samten have bequeathed to us!

Introduction

In the tenth century, Dentik (Dan tig) Monastery became a place of refuge for three Buddhist polymaths renowned for saving Tibet's monastic tradition from near extinction. Surrounded by vertiginous peaks and conglomerate rock formations, Dentik Monastery today has an air of majestic sanctity reminiscent of Santa Maria de Montserrat, near Barcelona. The first time I visited the mountain retreat in May 2008, I trekked for three hours from our rustic accommodations in a nearby village with an entourage of my two-year-old daughter, Tibetan friends, and two research assistants. During the course of the hike, I noticed young children and their family members appearing from distant footpaths to converge at the same dirt road leading over the most accessible pass. As we walked down the other side of the mountain, monastic buildings and cave complexes came into view. The scene was made all the more striking by the brilliant azure blue sky on that day. We arrived to celebrate the annual showing of *Anyé Lugyel* (A mnye glu rgyal), the *naga* or water-serpent deity that blesses children. The Anyé Lugyel Festival also includes a yearly ritual display of sacred objects originally from Central Tibet, prayer ceremonies, and, of course, feasting. The day's events began with the ritual circumambulation of the complex.

We followed the clockwise circuit of Buddhist pilgrimage. I occasionally paused in amazement to stare at the ancient murals painted high on crags. In single file, we entered the narrow caves built into cliffs, similar to the Mogao Grottoes at Dunhuang. We assembled at one of the larger sites called the Cave of Buddhist Adepts (*sgom chen*), where we listened to a monk whom I will call Jigmé[1] narrate the heroic story of the "Three Polymaths" (*mkhas pa mi gsum*) and how they safeguarded Buddhist monasticism in Tibet a millennium ago.

FIGURE INT.1 Temple of Great Accomplishments, meditation place of Third Dalai Lama, Dentik Monastery, September 2008

Photograph by Nicole Willock

Jigmé expounded a history retold in many Tibetan texts, such as *Butön's Religious History*, *The Blue Annals*, and *The Oceanic Annals: A Religious History of Domé*. These sources emphasize the vital role of the Three Polymaths in saving the monastic tradition at a perilous time. In the ninth century, when the Tibetan emperor Udum-tsen ('U dum btsan), posthumously known as Langdarma (Glang dar ma, d. 842), persecuted Buddhism in Central Tibet, three men escaped. The so-called "Three Polymaths," Mar Shakyamuni, Yo Géjung, and Tsang Rabsel, carried Buddhist scriptures with them. After traveling for some time, they sought refuge at Dentik Monastery, where they ordained a boy in the *Mūlasarvāstivāda-vinaya*, preventing their lineage from extinction. As an adult, he became known as Lachen (bla chen) "the Great Lama" Gongpa Rabsel (Dgongs pa rab gsal)[2] and further transmitted this monastic ordination lineage to ten men from Central Tibet, including Lumé (Klu mes), whose return to Central Tibet marked a new period of Buddhist time, the Later Diffusion of Buddhism.[3] According to oral tradition at Dentik, the Cave of Buddhist Adepts was the site of these ordinations. Historians recognize that the actual dates for the Three Polymaths and Lachen Gongpa Rabsel may never be known because the historical record is so fragmented.[4]

As I listened to this history retold at the cave, the significance of the interplay between storytelling, devotional practices, and communal identity crystallized. The retelling of the Three Polymaths' history imbued this place with the sanctity of a pilgrimage site, thereby reinvigorating the community with a shared past that ignored other worldly concerns, such as the state government of the People's Republic of China (PRC). While the state's presence was not immediately seen at Dentik, its power was felt because of increased military troops and public security personnel on the roads approaching the vicinity—a result of the demonstrations and protests taking place throughout the Tibetan plateau in 2008.

After I returned to my research base in Xining, several monks requested that I translate a guidebook to Dentik Monastery into English, which they later self-published.[5] Their work was based on oral history and on *A Catalogue of Dentik Monastery*,[6] a text by one of the late incarnate lamas of Dentik, the Sixth Tséten Zhabdrung, Jigmé Rigpé Lodrö (Tshe tan zhabs drung 'Jigs med rig pa'i blo gros, 1910–1985); hereafter, Tséten Zhabdrung. I began to see parallels between the retelling of the Three Polymaths' story and the reestablishment of Dentik Monastery's sacred festivals (including the Anyé Lugyel) with themes that emerged in my interviews with former disciples and students of Tséten Zhabdrung. There was a symbolic connection between the Three Polymaths' heroic

FIGURE INT.2 Cave of Buddhist Adepts at Dentik Monastery, site where the first Three Polymaths ordained Lachen Gongpa Rabsel, according to local history

Photograph by Nicole Willock

FIGURE INT.3 Lachen Gongpa Rabsel statue in the Cave of Buddhist Adepts

Dan dou si jian shi [A brief history of Dentik monastery]

efforts to save Buddhism in the first millennium and the survival of Tibetan Buddhist culture in twentieth-century China.

In the early 1980s, as monastery after monastery reopened, the title of the "Three Polymaths" (*mkhas pa mi gsum*) started to recirculate;[7] however, it no longer only referred to the monks of the prior millennium. The title was passed on to a set of three scholars of the twentieth century, including the incarnate lama of Dentik Monastery and historian Tséten Zhabdrung. He and Mugé Samten Gyatso (Dmu dge bsam gtan rgya mtsho, 1914–1993); hereafter, Mugé Samten, and Dungkar Lozang Trinlé (Dung dkar blo bzang 'phrin las), a.k.a. Dungkar Rinpoché (1927–1997), were also called the Three Polymaths. This title represented their efforts to restore Buddhist practices and Tibetan studies in the People's Republic of China after the Maoist period, an epoch characterized by destruction similar to that of a thousand years earlier. The twentieth-century polymaths ensured the survival and continuance of Tibetan Buddhist culture within the PRC.

FIGURE INT. 4   Maitreya Buddha cloth *thangka* at Dentik Monastery, May 2008

Photograph by Nicole Willock

THREE BUDDHIST POLYMATHS OF SOCIALIST CHINA

This book tells the story of how three Tibetan scholars—Tséten Zhabdrung, Mugé Samten, and Dungkar Rinpoché—alternately safeguarded, taught, adapted, celebrated, and discarded Buddhist epistemes, practices, and institutions in China in the aftermath of the Cultural Revolution. This study of their lives and works counters a common presumption that Tibetan leaders active in the People's Republic of China were mere political "collaborators." Frequently, in the Western imagination, it seems as if the leading Tibetan players in China could only be playing the role of either "collaborator" or "resistance fighter."[8] This binary model fails to account for the variety of repertoires, choices, and types of knowledge employed by these intellectuals in their subject positions as teachers, scholars, and writers in both Buddhist monastic and secular state institutions.

In order to understand how Tséten Zhabdrung, Mugé Samten, and Dungkar Rinpoché contributed to both the formation of Tibetan studies as an academic discipline and the revitalization of Tibetan Buddhism after 1979, I build on the notion of "moral agency" as employed by Saba Mahmood. In this work, the concept of "moral agency" signifies the capacities and skills needed for performing particular types of moral actions as bound to historically and culturally specific disciplines of subject formation. As I elaborate below, this conceptualization is particularly helpful to move beyond a binary model of agency as either enacting or subverting norms, the premise underlying the "collaborator"-"resistance fighter" dichotomy. I draw upon moral agency as historically and culturally disciplined capacities of action and skills in order to question what sorts of conditions enable intellectuals to express their ethical values, to promote institutions, and to uphold religious practices even under political restraints. In this case study, I detail how disciplines of subject formation are embedded in Géluk (dge lugs) Buddhist texts, practices, and embodied knowledge thereof, what I refer to as "religious epistemes." I ask how as scholars we can recognize articulations of specific epistemic values and acts of religiosity at particular historical moments.

The story of modern Tibet has yet to be told from the perspective of Buddhist scholars who remained in China after the exile of His Holiness the Fourteenth Dalai Lama, Tenzin Gyatso (b. 1935), in 1959 and the subsequent exodus of about one hundred thousand Tibetan refugees. Following the death of Mao Zedong (1893–1976), the founding father of the People's Republic of China, Euro-American research tells us that a religious "revival" took place in Tibetan areas of China. However, as the former U.S. State Department official and pioneering scholar in the field of Chinese religions, Holmes Welch, counseled in his reflections on the title of his seminal work, *The Buddhist Revival in China*, "the very term 'revival' may turn out to be inappropriate" and "it is the most convenient and customary way of referring to the varied developments that took place in Chinese Buddhism during the second half of the nineteenth century and first half of the twentieth."[9] Although studying a different time period, Melvyn Goldstein similarly employed the term in his ground-breaking volume coedited with Matthew Kapstein—*Buddhism in Contemporary Tibet: Religious Revival and Cultural Identity*.[10]

Like Welch, Goldstein critiqued the notion of "revival," especially in the sense of denoting a return to an original Tibetan way of life. He assessed that once the sluice of Chinese control was raised, the outpouring of religious activity in the post-Mao era was not the same as that prior to the 1950s. Although the sudden resurgence of Tibetan religious life after the lifting of restrictions gives the illusion of a "revival," Goldstein astutely pointed out, "the matrix of beliefs and practices that comprise Tibetan Buddhism have not been restored to their original state. . . . Some individual cultural traits have reemerged identical with the past, but others have reappeared somewhat changed, and still others have not emerged at all."[11] In other words, "revival," if we are to use that term for convenience's sake, was neither homogenous nor monolithic across Tibetan areas of China.

As I discuss in detail in the next chapter, many Tibetan intellectuals construct a new era of Buddhist historiography for this time period. They characterize the post-Mao epoch as *"yang-dar"* which means "a rediffusion of Buddhism."[12] What is being described then is not a return to an original state, but an ongoing dialectic between the Chinese state and local actors involving dynamic processes of adaptation that was and continues to be dependent on various political, social, and local conditions. This study focuses on the lives of three monastic scholars who were a part of these Sino-Tibetan interactions.

The ways that Tséten Zhabdrung, Mugé Samten, and Dungkar Lozang Trinlé—the Three Polymaths—navigated between the discursive territories of Géluk scholasticism and state discourse might be conceived of as viewing Sino-Tibetan relations through a new lens. This book relies on select texts by each of the Three Polymaths as maps that take us on a new path through PRC state formation. Their biographical lives and their writings bring new perspectives on this time period and illuminate hopes, strategies, and compromises for Tibetans living in China. I also discuss the literary and social contexts that permitted the writings of these Buddhist scholars to emerge in the post-Mao era and how their contributions still hold sway to this day.

Lineages of the Literary: Tibetan Buddhist Polymaths of Socialist China presents an alternative view of mid-twentieth-century history based on Tibetan-language autobiographies, poetry, and essays written and published within the People's Republic of China. Unlike many accounts of modern Tibet, such as Shakabpa's *Political History*, Melvyn Goldstein's *A History of Modern Tibet*, and Tsering Shakya's *Dragon in the Land of Snows*, Tséten Zhabdrung, Mugé Samten, and Dungkar Lozang Trinlé did not focus on the political status of Tibet in their writings. Nonetheless, as will become clear, their lives were deeply intertwined with the social and political changes of the twentieth century.

The Lives and Times of "Three Polymaths"

This brief overview illustrates how the lives of Tséten Zhabdrung, Mugé Samten, and Dungkar Lozang Trinlé were entangled with the political vicissitudes that came with the establishment of the People's Republic of China in 1949. Unless otherwise noted, the biographical information presented here comes from the respective autobiographies written by Tséten Zhabdrung and Mugé

Samten, and the biographies on Dungkar Rinpoché; all sources are detailed further in chapter 1. Prior to 1949, the lives of each of the Three Polymaths centered on local affairs, especially on their educations at Géluk Buddhist monasteries near their birthplaces.

China was wracked by civil war in 1946. Although some Tibetans living in Sichuan Province and Qinghai Province were affected by the turmoil of civil war, the winds of major social change had not yet arrived to alter the course of events for Tséten Zhabdrung, Mugé Samten, or Dungkar Lozang Trinlé. Each of the three scholars lived at his local monastic center.

In the Fire Dog year of the Tibetan calendar (1946), both Dungkar Rinpoché and Mugé Samten were awarded the prestigious geshé (dge bshes) degree, the culmination of years of academic study in Buddhist scholasticism. Dungkar Rinpoché, a reincarnate lama or tülku (sprul sku) from the Kongpo region of southeastern Central Tibet, had excelled at his studies at Sera Monastery and received the degree during the Great Prayer Festival in Lhasa. Mugé Samten received his geshé degree from Labrang Tashikyil (Bla brang bkra shis 'kyil), a large monastic complex on the far eastern edge of Amdo, the Tibetan name for a large area encompassing the eastern Tibetan cultural realm. In this region, Mongols, Han Chinese, Hui and Salar Muslims, and Tibetans shared and vied over land and resources. Buddhist life at Labrang Tashikyil Monastery, located in a multilingual and multicultural zone, was occasionally interrupted by fighting between the Nationalists, Communists, and local warlords.[13] About eighty miles away, Tséten Zhabdrung, a recognized tülku and rising star among Géluk (dge lugs) scholars, was busy tending to his ill teacher, Jigmé Damchö Gyatso ('Jigs med dam chos rgya mtsho, a.k.a. Mar nang rdo rje 'chang, 1898–1946), who passed away at Karing Monastery. Their lives for the time being were intimately woven into the fabric of the traditional monastic system with its various obligations and rewards.

This was not the case for a few monastic colleagues who were advocating for social change. One was Geshé Sherab Gyatso (Shes rab rgya mtsho, 1884–1968), who played a major role in the social and political lives of Mugé Samten and Tséten Zhabdrung. Geshé Sherab Gyatso's long involvement with progressive intellectuals and his vision of Buddhist-Marxist cooperation offer a counterexample to the notion that "religion" was a "homogenous force in Tibetan politics" whereby monks of this era were conservative supporters of the established socioeconomic system.[14] Geshé Sherab Gyatso's strong personality and unique vision for Buddhist-Marxist coexistence influenced many throughout his career. To understand how this came be, it is necessary to go back another decade.

In 1937, Geshé Sherab Gyatso quit his high-ranking position as a master teacher at Gomang College of Drepung Monastery in Central Tibet for Nanjing via Kalimpong and Calcutta. In India, he was briefly reunited with his former student, the brilliant savant Gendün Chöpel (Dge 'dun chos 'phel, 1903–1951).[15] Although teacher and student fiercely debated with each other, they agreed that Tibet needed to change. To those ends, they each pursued a different path. Gendün Chöpel remained in India until 1946. When he returned to Tibet, he was arrested by the Lhasa government and died five years later, having served between two to three years in prison. His prolific and insightful writings earned him the reputation of being Tibet's first modern scholar posthumously.[16] His teacher, Geshé Sherab Gyatso, left India for China, where among other projects, he edited and assisted in translating a Chinese-Tibetan bilingual abridged version of Sun Yatsen's *Three Principles of the People*[17] with his disciple, Yang Zhifu. As a member of the Guomindang Central Organization Department, Yang first met Geshé Sherab Gyatso at Drepung Monastery during a group tour of Central Tibet in 1935.[18] This translation project championed Geshé Sherab Gyatso's dream of reform for Tibet. To achieve his goals, he took up various political positions under the Nationalists, but he soon became disillusioned and his allegiance shifted toward the Communists.

After the establishment of the People's Republic of China in 1949, some Tibetan leaders, such as Geshé Sherab Gyatso and all Three Polymaths, among others, were recruited to work in the state bureaucratic system. When Tibetans became an officially recognized "ethnic nationality" or *minzu* (*mi rigs*; Ch. *mínzú* 民族), three government institutions became paramount: 1) the State Ethnic Affairs Commission;[19] 2) the United Front Work Department,[20] which is under the Chinese Communist Party's Central Committee; and 3) the State Administration for Religious Affairs,[21] formerly referred to as the Religious Affairs Bureau, under the administration of the State Council.[22] The State Ethnic Affairs Commission directs official policy for China's fifty-six officially designated *minzu*, comprising the Han majority and fifty-five "minority" (Ch. *shǎoshù* 少数) *minzu*.

In the PRC, the concept of *minzu* blurs "ethnicity" (as in *shǎoshù mínzú* identified in the state ethnic classification project) and "nationality" (in the sense of the affiliation between a person and the political state to which she belongs, e.g., in the Chinese term *zhōnghuá mínzú*).[23] To reflect this particular construct, I translate *minzu* as "ethnic nationality," use the related term "ethnic minority," or leave it untranslated. Since 2016, the ongoing debates on this policy and relevant terminologies resulted in the renaming of related state institutions. For example, the so-called "nationalities institutes/universities" (*mi rigs slob grwa chen mo*; Ch. *mínzú xuéyuàn/dàxué*) were renamed "minzu universities,"[24] which are administered under the State Ethnic Affairs Commission (formerly translated as "Nationalities Commission"). In this way the Central University for Nationalities (krung dbyang mi rigs slob grwa chen mo; Ch. zhōngyāng mínzú dàxué 中央民族大学) became known as Minzu University of China.[25] Throughout this work, although anachronistic in regard to the time period under investigation, I adopt the state-designated official names for minzu universities, leaving *minzu* untranslated. The one exception is Qinghai Nationalities University (mtsho sngon mi rigs slob grwa chen mo; Ch. Qīnghǎi mínzú dàxué 青海民族大学), which according to its website in Chinese and English has retained "Nationalities" in the English translation of its name.[26]

A corollary of China's policy on ethnic nationalities, despite its many drawbacks and problems,[27] is that a large body of Tibetan-language texts are published in China for a global readership.[28] Most of the primary sources utilized for this work were printed at one of the minzu presses. Founded in the early 1950s, the central office in Beijing, the Minzu Publishing House (Ch: Mínzú Chūbǎnshè 民族出版社), and provincial publishing houses are the main outlets for Tibetan-language academic publishing in China.[29] The publishing houses alongside the minzu universities are under the direction of the State Ethnic Affairs Commission, which is responsible for relations between the state and recognized ethnic nationalities. In other words, the ideological framework of the ethnic nationality policy in tandem with its institutional apparatus ensured the Three Polymaths' legacy in two different state organizations: 1) minzu presses, through the printing of their *Collected Works* (as well as other individual texts); and 2) minzu universities, supporting their teaching endeavors.

Throughout the 1950s and into the early 1960s, each of the three scholars—Tséten Zhabdrung, Mugé Samten, and Dungkar Lozang Trinlé—contributed to state-building projects to some degree. Mugé Samten was the first to be recruited by the state. He traveled to Beijing for the first time with Geshé Sherab Gyatso and began working in the propaganda division of the State Ethnic Affairs Commission in spring 1950.[30] Mugé Samten was residing in the nation's capital when Geshé Sherab Gyatso announced the forthcoming "Peaceful Liberation" of Tibet on the radio in May 1950.[31] In October of that year, the Tibetan Army under the command of Ngapö Ngawang Jigmé, an official of Lhasa's Ganden Podrang government, capitulated to the People's Liberation Army (PLA) in Chamdo.[32] Ngapö Ngawang Jigmé then became the main spokesperson between the Lhasa government and Beijing on the treaty that would become known as the Seventeen Point Agreement. In the meantime, others in the Ganden Podrang government tried to secure international help.[33] At the age of fifteen,

His Holiness the Fourteenth Dalai Lama, Tenzin Gyatso, was officially enthroned as the temporal leader of Tibet in a ceremony held on November 17, 1950, at his residential park compound, the Norbulingka.[34] As tensions escalated, His Holiness fled to the border near India in January, but returned to Lhasa in the middle of August 1951 after his cohort failed to gain international support for Tibet. Ngapö Ngawang Jigmé and other signatories arrived in Beijing in April and signed the Seventeen Point Agreement on May 23, 1951; this formally recognized China's sovereignty over Tibet.[35] Mugé Samten proofread the Tibetan version and Chinese translation of the agreement.

A new era of Sino-Tibetan relations began in October 1951, after the Dalai Lama sent a telegram to Mao Zedong confirming acceptance of the Seventeen Point Agreement. Over the next few months, PLA troops arrived in Lhasa.[36] At the same time, the corporatist central government led by the Chinese Communist Party (CCP) consolidated its rule, established policies, and implemented a new social, political, and economic system. Despite the CCP's ideological rejection of religion, its more immediate objective was to establish CCP control and get rid of any opposition; therefore, it adopted a "strategy to reinforce friendly elements within each religious community."[37] Members of the cooperative "religious sector" (Ch. *zōngjiào jiè* 宗教界) were appointed to political positions in such bodies as the Chinese People's Political Consultative Conference (mi dmangs tshogs pa; Ch. rénmín zhèngxié 人民政协) at the local, provincial, or national level.[38] At this time, the state defined the parameters of religion and under the guidance of CCP leaders (especially Zhou Enlai), five patriotic religious associations were formed. The Buddhist Association of China (BAC),[39] established in spring 1953, facilitated official dialogue between the United Front Work Department and Buddhist groups. Although nominally independent, these associations in fact operated under the authority of the State Administration for Religious Affairs.[40] In the 1950s, before the BAC disbanded during the Cultural Revolution (1966), the membership was disproportionately ethnic minorities; twenty-nine of its total ninety-three members were Tibetans.[41] Geshé Sherab Gyatso led the Buddhist Association of China as president from 1953 to 1964.[42] During his tenure, despite the ideological position of the CCP toward religion, he staunchly advocated for the compatibility of Tibetan culture, Buddhist values, and Marxism.[43]

Tséten Zhabdrung's first foray into politics was in 1953. His bilingual skills were needed to translate Chinese state documents into Tibetan for the Qinghai Provincial Translation Committee. In the same year, he was appointed by Zhou Enlai as vice chairman of the recently established Qinghai Provincial Political Consultative Conference, an office he shared with Geshé Sherab Gyatso.[44] Soon thereafter, he was assigned to work in Beijing on the Tibetan translation team for the 1954 PRC Constitution. Toward the end of his four-month stay in the nation's capital, he participated in the celebrations surrounding its promulgation. At that point he had an opportunity to meet with His Holiness the Fourteenth Dalai Lama, who had been invited to Beijing alongside the Tenth Panchen Lama, Chökyi Gyeltsen (Chos kyi rgyal mtshan, 1938–1989), to outline the plans for the establishment of the Tibetan Autonomous Region (TAR). After Tséten Zhabdrung returned to Xining, he was asked to teach at the newly founded Qinghai Nationalities University.

Although Dungkar Rinpoché was a member of the Tibetan traditional elite like Tséten Zhabdrung, his political outlook was more akin to that of the progressive Geshé Sherab Gyatso. In 1954, he was appointed disciplinarian of Gyüto Tantric College in Lhasa. A few years thereafter (1956/7), he also became vice director of the Dakkong (Dakpo and Kongpo counties) branch of the Buddhist Association of China (BAC). In 1959, he moved from his county-level position to the Tibetan regional division of BAC.[45] He excelled scholastically within the Géluk hierarchy and was one of the sixteen chief debate examiners during His Holiness the Fourteenth Dalai Lama's *geshé lharampa* examinations at the annual Great Prayer Festival (Monlam Chenmo) in 1959. Soon thereafter, he went to teach in a town in the Yarlung River valley. He was residing about 120 miles to the southeast of Lhasa when another chapter of Sino-Tibetan history began. A popular uprising that had been fomenting for the previous two years erupted in Tibet's capital, Lhasa. From March 10 to March 23, 1959, Tibetans rose up in revolt while Chinese troops launched attacks. Fearing for his life, His Holiness was forced to leave Tibet in disguise on March 17. On March 23rd, the five-star Red flag was hoisted at the Potala Palace, marking the end of what Tsering Shakya called "the era of uneasy co-existence" in Sino-Tibetan relations.[46] By mid-1960, Dungkar Rinpoché had relinquished his monastic vows and was on his way to Beijing to take up a professorial position at Minzu University of China.

In the eastern Tibetan cultural areas outside the control of the Lhasa-based Ganden Podrang government, the CCP had abandoned its attempts at gradual assimilation and pluralistic approach for ethnic nationalities in the mid-to-late 1950s. The first steps toward land reforms at Tséten Zhabdrung's monastic estates occurred in 1954 with the redistribution of properties. In 1958, Tséten Khenpo (1910–1958), the co-throne holder of his monastic estates,[47] was murdered and Tséten Monastery was turned into a commune. Tséten Zhabdrung was not residing at his monasteries at this time. In 1959, Mugé Samten joined Tséten Zhabdrung to work on the Minzu Publishing House's Tibetan translation of Mao Zedong's *Collected Works*. The two shared quarters for the duration of this project.[48] After they returned to their respective home provinces, the political tides moved further to the left at the cost of all Tibetans, especially the educated monastics and members of the aristocracy.

Although all three scholars had contributed to state-building projects throughout the 1950s, by the mid-1960s, Tséten Zhabdrung, Mugé Samten, and Dungkar Lozang Trinlé became targets for having traditional knowledge, considered a crime at that time. The first to suffer was Tséten Zhabdrung. He was arrested and incarcerated in Xining's Nantan Prison from December 1965 until July 1976. The next was Mugé Samten, who was struggled against and arrested at the government office where he had been working in October 1966. In early 1967, he was moved to a labor camp near Barkham in Sichuan Province until his release in 1973. Although left-leaning, Dungkar Rinpoché was sent back to Lhasa in 1965 and publicly humiliated by being made to wear a dunce hat during a so-called "struggle session" circa 1967. He was never arrested, but was forced to do reform through labor in the Second Village to the north of Lhasa. Following Mao Zedong's death in 1976, the political tides turned again.

After the Third Plenum of the Eleventh Chinese Communist Party Congress in Beijing in December 1978, state policies gradually shifted under the leadership of Deng Xiaoping with the introduction of economic and social reforms. By the early 1980s, a more pluralistic approach permitting the expression of ethnic-nationality cultural identity prompted many surviving Tibetan intellectuals, both monastic and lay, to urgently restore Tibetan culture that had been prohibited in some areas since the mid-to-late 1950s.

As will become clear throughout this work, in the post-Mao era, not only did the life paths of Tséten Zhabdrung, Mugé Samten, and Dungkar Lozang Trinlé cross, but the men also became associated through the title of the "Three Polymaths" as heroes who saved Tibetan culture in her darkest hour. With the introduction of reforms, all three were given positions at the political consultative conferences. Although representatives do not hold any real power, the job is politically prestigious.[49] In October 1977, Mugé Samten was elected to the working committee of the fourth meeting of Sichuan Province's Consultative Conference.[50] At around this time, Dungkar Rinpoché was awarded a position at the national level as a Tibetan representative at the Chinese People's Political Consultative Conference (CPPCC), similar to the female incarnate lama Samding Dorjé Phagmo.[51] Tséten Zhabdrung served as vice president of Gansu Province's Buddhist Association, as a committee member of the Gansu provincial-level Political Consultative Conference, and as a director of China's Ethnic Nationalities Language Commission (mi rigs skad yig slob tshogs).

Alongside such political activities, all three scholars took appointments as professors at newly reopened universities and also returned to their home areas to give Buddhist teachings and raise funds to rebuild monasteries. Dungkar Lozang Trinlé rejoined Minzu University as a professor in Beijing in 1978 for the next seven years. In 1983, he made the centerfold of a national magazine, photographed listening to Tséten Zhabdrung giving teachings at Minzu University, as I detail in chapter 5. In 1985, Dungkar Rinpoché returned to Lhasa to take up a professorial post at Tibet University, where he remained until his retirement in 1996; he still frequented Beijing as vice-director of the China Tibetology Research Center, established in 1986. In 1978, Tséten Zhabdrung became a professor at Northwest Minzu University in Gansu Province, but also lectured in Lhasa and in Beijing. Mugé Samten did not have a permanent professorial position. He lectured at Southwest Minzu University, Northwest Minzu University, and Qinghai Nationalities University. His successful efforts at lobbying against grammatical changes made to simplify Tibetan in line with Chinese language policy were acknowledged by Dungkar Rinpoché in a letter. A photo that circulated on the digital platform WeChat shows Tséten Zhabdrung

FIGURE INT.5 Monastic scholars in the 1980s. Back row: Tséten Zhabdrung, Mugé Samten, and Nyenshul Khyenrab Osel; front row: Réchung Sherab Gyatso, Zenkar Rinpoché, and Mani Drayang Legshé Gyatso

and Mugé Samten with other teachers and scholars—Nyenshul Khyenrab Osel, Réchung Sherab Gyatso, Zenkar Rinpoché, and Mani Drayang Legshé Gyatso—in the early 1980s. At this time, the trio started to be called by the epithet of "Three Polymaths."[52]

The first generation of Tibetan intellectuals to receive higher education degrees after 1976 plumbed the "Three Polymaths" title from Tibetan annals and began to reinscribe their own history.[53] They linked Tibetan historical memory of the tenth-century Three Polymaths with the present situation. The title symbolized the continuance of Tibetan history, language, and religion after a period of widespread destruction.

With the exception of Tséten Zhabdrung's commentary on poetics, most of the texts that I present here were written by one of the Three Polymaths after 1978. Considering that each volume of their respective *Collected Works* is on average three hundred pages and each scholar has multiple volumes, their prodigious writings are alone monumental achievements; however, all three also contributed to the revitalization of Tibetan studies in university settings mentioned above, and also at Buddhist monasteries.

FIGURE INT.6 Tséten Zhabdrung circa 1984, studio portrait

Courtesy of Jigmé Chöpak

Up until his death at age seventy-five, Tséten Zhabdrung gave Buddhist teachings and empowerments throughout eastern Amdo. He worked with the Tenth Panchen Lama, Chökyi Gyeltsen (1938–1989), Shardong Lozang Shédrup Gyatso (1922–2002), and other important Amdo lamas not only to rebuild the monasteries he was connected to as an incarnate lama but also to reestablish the important sites of Karing Monastery and Jakyung (Bya khyung) Monastery. He passed away peacefully at Labrang Tashikyil Monastery in Gansu Province of natural causes in 1985.

Mugé Samten continued to give Buddhist teachings, write, and lecture well into his seventies. He was active mainly in his native Mugé but also went on pilgrimage in Central Tibet and to Wutaishan, where he gave teachings as well. He passed away of natural causes in 1993.

Dungkar Lozang Trinlé was similarly very active up until his death. Although he was the most politically left of the Three Polymaths, he also gave Buddhist teachings at his monastery in Kongpo in the early 1990s. He was the only one of the scholars who received permission to leave China and travel abroad. He died in 1997 at the age of seventy-two in Los Angeles after battling cancer.

The selection of their writings that appears in this book shares their stories about how they remember their experiences of this tumultuous era of modern Tibetan history. It also highlights their efforts to revitalize dynamic aspects of Tibetan Buddhist values and epistemes in the post-Mao era.

ON AGENCY AND RELIGIOUS EPISTEMES— METHODOLOGY

In taking up this project on modern Tibetan Buddhist figures within China, I faced an immediate conundrum: how to study this subject matter without undue influence from polarized accounts of Sino-Tibetan historiography. The voices of exiled Tibetans emphasize Chinese destruction of Tibetan culture and curtailments of religious freedom, while mouthpieces of the CCP laud the state's role in supporting Tibetan institutions (especially financially) within the motherland. Despite their importance, both viewpoints have failed to acknowledge the tremendous contributions of Tibetan Buddhist scholars in China. As I read and translated texts by Tséten Zhabdrung, Dungkar Lozang Trinlé, and Mugé Samten, it was immediately clear that they offered alternative perspectives on this politically divided history. The inadequacies of the prevalent binary framework have been recognized by many scholars, especially in the fields of modern Tibetan literature[54] and anthropology.[55] However, a study on the role of Tibetan religious figures in the history of modern China required a new lens for analysis.

Interdisciplinary scholarship from religious studies, China studies, anthropology, history, and critical theory has aided in the development of a theoretical framework that makes sense of the complex subject positioning of the Three Polymaths and their roles in modern Sino-Tibetan history.[56] The approach adapted here ties together strands of scholarship that emerged out of Talal Asad's theoretical corpus with studies by theorists in religious studies, such as Robert Ford Campany. Drawing from postcolonial and poststructuralist theories, Asad brought attention to how the modern category of "religion" became synonymous with individual belief through the dynamic processes of nation-state formation in Europe.[57] Asad's anthropology of secularism prompted scholars working in different areas of the world to explore aspects of these theories in their specific regions.

One such upshot is found in the intersection of religious studies and modern China studies, where scholars examined the genealogy of "religion" in China as well as the resurgence of many forms of religious practice alongside state secularization in the post-Mao era. For example, Ashiwa and Wank, building on Asad's contributions, looked for an alternative to what they identified as the dominant hegemonic framework whereby studies in the domain of "religion" in China were restricted "to the forceful exercise of state power."[58] Instead they suggested an institutional framework that researched how local actors shape religious discourse within state-sanctioned and unsanctioned institutional bodies in China. Their thesis focused on how the politics of religion in modern China are negotiated by multiple actors—state officials, religious adherents, intellectuals, etc. As they stated, "Religions can accommodate the state institutions as modern 'religion' in order to ensure their existence in the new order while the presence of religion in state institutions shows that the state is a modern, enlightened state that acknowledges religion."[59] Extending this observation to the case of the Three Polymaths is useful insofar as it provides an analytical framework that can include Tibetan Buddhist leaders in China who were vested in ensuring the continued existence of their religious institutions within the state and also explains how they might be perceived as aiding the state in modernization projects.

However, this approach falls short in explaining how they could negotiate between CCP discourse and a host of interlinked concerns that they had as Tibetan Buddhist leaders in the post-Mao era, including such diverse issues as Tibetan identity, revitalization of the Tibetan language, Buddhist ethics, and cultural values in the rebuilding of Tibetan monastic institutions. In order to make sense of these processes, it was necessary to turn to another scholar influenced by Talal Asad's contributions—Saba Mahmood, who pioneered the move to locate agency within the ethics of subject making.[60]

Delinking agency from progressive politics, Saba Mahmood resisted offering a definitive theory of agency and insisted that "the meaning of agency must be explored within the grammar of concepts within which it resides."[61] Similar to Ashiwa and Wank's move, Mahmood's understanding of agency aided me in conceptualizing Tibetan monastic scholars active in China in a nuanced light. They need not be viewed in stark contrasts as either "collaborator" or "resistance fighter." In order to move agency outside the binary model of either conforming to or subverting normative powers, Mahmood turned to Foucault's ideas on ethical formation, suggesting, "Instead of limiting agency to those acts that disrupt existing power relations, Foucault's work encourages us to think of agency: (a) in terms of the capacities and skills required to undertake particular kinds of moral actions and (b) as ineluctably bound up with the historically and culturally specific disciplines through which a subject is formed."[62] Mahmood looked to the relationships among performativity, embodiment, and agency in her study of a piety movement in Egypt. Similarly, Orit Avishai highlights the making of religious subjecthood through religiosity as performed within the grammar of one's religion and in a dialogic relationship with a secularizing other.[63]

For this study, I take "moral agency" as a capacity for action bound by historically and culturally specific disciplines of subject formation performed in relationship with a secularizing other. The sites of these cultural resources and disciplines are grounded in the Géluk Buddhist scholastic tradition of Tibet. All three scholars—Tséten Zhabdrung, Dungkar Lozang Trinlé, and Mugé Samten—drew upon their polymathic knowledge of Géluk Buddhist scholasticism to negotiate the turbulent political tides of twentieth-century China. With that said, it is important not to reify the dynamics of Géluk Buddhist scholasticism, which contains a variety of pedagogies, discursive traditions, and institutional practices that can be deployed in a number of different ways. I refer to these diverse forms of local knowledge, traditions, and practices as "religious epistemes."

These forms of knowledge, epistemes, are "religious" in that they are interpretations of truth based in Géluk Buddhist texts, practices, and institutions, and performed in dialogue with a secular other. In the complex process of Chinese state formation, the three Géluk scholars studied here drew upon differing strategies for action. Similar to how Robert Ford Campany suggests that "religious repertoires" can be viewed as "organized around certain concrete 'scenes or situations of action,'"[64] religious epistemes can be alternately adapted, safeguarded, and sometimes discarded in order to engage with new situations and new types of knowledge found in Chinese Communist discourse. In navigating the dynamic processes of state building, all three Buddhist polymaths were active as writers and teachers and thereby shaped the discursive field of Tibetan studies in China as well as Tibetan religious and cultural identity in the PRC.

Elsewhere, I suggested that by paying attention to the local ethno-linguistic grounds on which the discursive production of "religion" and the "secular" emerges as part of ongoing processes of negotiation in specific historical and geographic contexts, we can productively draw attention to how intellectuals engage with and express ambivalence vis-à-vis emergent categories associated with modernity.[65] Holly Gayley and I labeled this framework as *local articulations of the secular*, building on the concept of "vernacular projects of secularism," which are the boundary-making practices involved in constructing "religion" and the "secular" in different times and places.[66] As Holly Gayley further elaborated in her book on the twentieth-century Tibetan tantric master Tāre Lhamo, "instead of treating ascriptions of agency as assertions to be judged by the epistemic parameters of secular history, it may be more profitable to view them as representational strategies that intersect with culturally specific conventions related to literary genres or oral frames of reference."[67] Unlike Tāre Lhamo, who was dually positioned as both subaltern and elite depending on the different state and local contexts, the Three Polymaths were at the nexus of Sino-Tibetan relations.

Tséten Zhabdrung, Dungkar Lozang Trinlé, and Mugé Samten were active as Buddhist lamas, university teachers, and prolific writers. They pioneered the academic study of Tibetan language, history, and culture at state-run universities, while simultaneously rebuilding their respective monastic institutions and teaching the next generation of monks, nuns, and laypeople. The culturally specific disciplines and religious epistemes that they accessed in their unique subject positions as male Géluk Buddhist elites allowed them, unlike many other leaders in post-Mao China, to cross state-imposed divides between secular and religious institutions that might otherwise have been impossible to bridge. Their embodiment of the scholarly, a "*khé-pa*" (*mkhas pa*), in the intellectual ethos and education system referred to as Buddhist scholasticism or Indo-Tibetan scholasticism[68] provided each of them with a variety of strategies to navigate the complex sociopolitical terrain of twentieth-century China.

Géluk Religious Epistemes

Subject formation for the "Three Polymaths" relied on training in a knowledge system found in the Géluk school of Tibetan Buddhism. Similar to the three other principal traditions (Nyingma, Sakya, and Kagyu), the Géluk school was founded on a system of knowledge referred to as Indo-Tibetan scholasticism, first introduced into Tibet in the thirteenth century.

The seminal text, the *Gateway to Learning* (Mkhas pa 'jug pa'i sgo) by the great luminary Sakya Paṇḍita, set the Tibetan ideals for scholarship and moral cultivation for the next eight hundred years. Jonathan Gold suggests that the original audience for *Gateway to Learning* was the most determined of Tibetan monastic scholars, who were concerned with comprehending scriptures that contained an array of doctrines and practices.[69] Although the hermeneutic struggles of the Three Polymaths of the twentieth century differed vastly from those of their thirteenth-century predecessors, they shared similar values in the sense that as Buddhist scholars, they respected the sophisticated views of learning on a wide range of philosophical issues, including Buddhist doctrinal issues, language, translation, interpretation, and education, all covered in the *Gateway to Learning*.

Sakya Paṇḍita's scholarly ideal consisted of a broad mastery of human knowledge, a regime of disciplines, texts, and practices. This enduring contribution inspired generations of Tibetan scholars, including Mugé Samten, Dungkar Rinpoché, and Tséten Zhabdrung, to embody what it meant to be a "scholar" or "learned one" (*mkhas pa*; Sanskrit: *paṇḍita*). Similar to other medieval scholars, such as al-Ghazali in Persia and Zhu Xi in China, Sakya Paṇḍita organized these domains of human knowledge into a comprehensive system.[70] Knowledge was arranged into five major *rikné* (*rigs gnas lnga*; Sanskrit: *pañca-vidyāsthāna*), alternately translated as "sciences," "fields of knowledge," or "fields of learning."

The major set of five *rikné* are: 1) the science of language (*sgra'i rig pa*, Sanskrit: *śabdavidyā*); 2) the science of medicine (*gso ba'i rig pa*; Skt. *cikitsāvidyā*); 3) the science of artistic skills and craftsmanship (*bzo rig pa*; Skt. *śilpakarmasthānavidyā*); 4) the science of logic and epistemology (*gtan tshigs rig pa*; Skt. *hetuvidyā*); and 5) the "inner science," i.e., Buddhism (*nang rig pa*; Skt. *adhyātmavidyā*). Most of the five minor domains of *rikné* concern aspects of the literary arts such as "mellifluous words" or "poetics" (*snyan ngag*; Skt. *kāvya*); metrics (*sdeb sbyor*; Skt. *chanda*); kennings (*mngon brjod*; Skt. *kośa* or *abhidhāna*); and drama (*zlos gar*; Skt. *nāṭaka*). The fifth minor science, astrology (*rtsis*; Skt. *gaṇita*), involves mathematics and astronomical calculations.[71] As will become clear throughout this book, the Three Polymaths specialized in and adapted aspects of these fields of learning, especially language, poetics, and Buddhism, in their own writings and teachings after the Cultural Revolution. Their commitments contrast greatly with the original purposes of this epistemic system.

According to Sakya Paṇḍita, the scholar's ultimate lofty goal was omniscience. Jonathan Gold explains, "Thus the *Gateway* as a key to the five sciences is a crucial step in attaining omniscience; it is a '*Gateway*' to omniscience, which is in itself an essential characteristic of the bodhisattva path."[72] Interpreted in this light, training in the five *rikné* became an essential part of Buddhist theory and practice, which also involved esoteric methods such as meditation and incantations. These polymathic ideals influenced scholastic learning across the greater Tibetan plateau, even as the curriculum at local monasteries didn't necessarily follow prescriptions outlined in the *Gateway* itself. Quotidian learning for monastics depended on the particular institution and the sect of Buddhism practiced by its adherents.

Tséten Zhabdrung, Dungkar Lozang Trinlé, and Mugé Samten received their monastic training within the Géluk sect of Buddhism. This meant as novice Géluk monks, they began their career with an exoteric course of studies often referred to as "logical philosophy" in English. This translation of the Tibetan term *tsen nyi* (*mtshan nyid*), literally, "defining characteristics," is somewhat misleading because this course of study also contains non-philosophical material, such as the study of texts on monastic discipline. "Logical philosophy" required mastering five main branches of non-Tantric Buddhist canonical literature, including epistemology (*tshad ma*; Skt.: *pramāṇa*); the doctrine of universal emptiness known as the Perfection of Wisdom (*phar phyin*; Skt.: *prajñāpāramitā*); the doctrine of the Middle Way (*dbu ma*; Skt.: *madhyamaka*) as taught by Nāgārjuna and his heirs; the "Treasury of Philosophical Notions" (*mngon chos mdzod*; Skt.: *abhidharmakośa*); and monastic discipline (*'dul ba*; Skt.: *vinaya*).[73] Monks debated in the courtyard of the monastery as a way to integrate the knowledge of the Five Great Treatises (*gzhung chen bka' pod lnga*), which all Géluk monks must memorize and study.[74] "Logical philosophy" as a course of study incorporates an analytical approach that requires a line of philosophical inquiry that is cognitive—involving rote memorization and logical recall of prescribed texts—and it is distinguished from content that is esoteric and supposed to be kept secret, *tantra* (*sngag*).[75]

After mastering the exoteric content of "logical philosophy" and requisite debate skills and fulfilling the needed cultural and ritual norms of the particular Géluk monastery, a *karampa* (*bka' rams pa*), i.e., one who passed the examinations for logical philosophy or *tsen nyi*, could go on to take examinations for a

higher degree. Both Mugé Samten and Dungkar Rinpoché received the penultimate degree: *geshé* (*dge ba'i bshes gnyen*, Skt: *kalyāṇamitra*). As the translation of
the title, "spiritual friend who is meritorious," signals, this was the culmination
of years of arduous study and cultivation of personal relationships within the
monastery. As Georges Dreyfus points out in his seminal work on Géluk scholastic training, the time it took to complete the degree varied. It could be twenty
to thirty years because Géluk scholars would frequently have to wait sometimes
five to ten years after finishing the curriculum before being allowed to take the
exam.[76]

When the Three Polymaths inherited these scholarly and religious ideals in
the early twentieth century, Sakya Paṇḍita's *Gateway* had become foundational
to Tibetan Buddhist epistemes. Monastic curriculums had become institutionalized with intricate bureaucracies and networks of affiliation. Therefore, the
social and political circumstances of monastic learning were contingent on local
contexts in historical time. Yet, the abstract ideal—the value inherit in pursuing
a comprehensive Buddhist education—remains a common goal among many
Tibetan Buddhist monastics, monks and nuns, well into the twenty-first century. Gold observed that Sakya Paṇḍita and his colleagues did not so much
invent a scholastic tradition as "they needed to discover and comprehend it as a
properly comprehensive scholastic unity, and then translate and reconfigure it
for their Tibetan contemporaries. It is this project that we might call their building the fortifying walls, and training the gatekeepers, of the proper Buddhist
intellectual tradition."[77] These ideals of the "proper Buddhist intellectual tradition" resonate in the writings of the Three Polymaths. Their concern, however,
was not how to interpret Buddhist texts from Sanskrit, but how to revive aspects
of these religious epistemes from the ashes of their destruction. To these ends,
each of the Three Polymaths wrote prolifically.

LITERARY PRECEDENTS AND NEW GENRES— SOURCE MATERIALS

In selecting texts for this study, I chose writings by Tséten Zhabdrung, Mugé
Samten, and Dungkar Rinpoché that represent a range of literary styles and subject matters to underscore their polymathic contributions to Tibetan studies
and diverse approaches to the revitalization of Tibetan cultural and religious
practices in the post-Mao era. These source materials sometimes fit and sometimes transgress the larger category of classical Tibetan literature. By way of

introducing them, I reflect on the ways the texts navigated between Tibetan literary precedents and new discursive territory in the People's Republic of China.

Almost unknown only fifty years ago, translations of Tibetan literature, broadly construed, have flooded the English-reading world. Scores of once inaccessible Buddhist texts are now readily available. In their pioneering study, José Cabezón and Roger Jackson bring the emic category of *rikné* (Wylie: *rig gnas*; Sanskrit: *vidyāstāna*), discussed above as "fields of learning" or "science," into conversation with Western literary theory proposing varying typologies for "Classical Tibetan literature."[78] I am not concerned with creating literary typologies, but I take a similar approach insofar as I draw attention to the emic descriptions of the primary sources studied here. By doing so, I suggest ways writings by Tséten Zhabdrung, Mugé Samten, and Dungkar Rinpoché sometimes engage with and sometimes depart from well-established literary precedents. Likewise, the way their texts were gathered and published serves as a starting to point to show how their writings align with and diverge from earlier methods of textual production.

Each scholar has multivolume "*sung-bum*," the Tibetan pronunciation of the word for "Collected Works" (*gsung 'bum*). The first print edition of Tséten Zhabdrung's is in five volumes (Qinghai Minzu Press, 1987) and the second in thirteen volumes (Beijing Minzu Press, 2007); Mugé Samten's is in six volumes (Qinghai Minzu Press, 1997); and Dungkar Rinpoché's is in eight volumes (Beijing Minzu Press, 2004).[79] With a few exceptions, the Tibetan primary source materials studied here are found within these volumes. A few notable standalone works, such as their treatises on poetics, language, and history, were published during the lifetime of the respective author, thus prior to their inclusion in the posthumously printed collections. The fact that Tséten Zhabdrung's, Mugé Samten's, and Dungkar Rinpoché's writings were gathered posthumously by their former students (from both monastic and secular academic institutions) indicates their esteemed status, joining the ranks of many previous Tibetan luminaries with *sung-bum*, including savants such as Butön Rinchen Drup (1290–1364), Tsongkhapa (1357–1419), and the Fifth Dalai Lama (1617–1682). The Three Polymaths' *Collected Works* resemble these earlier literary models, but they depart from past classics by dint of their publication venues and the range of literary genres and styles explored in each *sung-bum*.

Each collection was published at a provincial minzu press or "publishing house" (*dpe skrun khang*, Ch. *chubanshe*). Prior to the establishment of these state-run presses equipped with modern print technology, *sung-bum* were hand-printed from carved woodblocks that were stored at a local monastic printery (*par khang*).[80] One edition of Tséten Zhabdrung's *Collected Works* was completed in the carved woodblock traditional method in the early 1980s and can still be "ransomed"—a euphemism for "printed for a fee"—at the small woodblock printery of Tuwa (Mthu ba) Monastery. All of Tséten Zhabdrung's writings in the woodblock edition and the earlier five-volume set were reprinted in the 2007 edition, making it the most complete.[81] The method of collecting woodblock prints and reprinting them with modern technology at minzu presses, especially *Collected Works* of Tibetan Buddhist scholars of all sects, has since the 1990s become ubiquitous. Tséten Zhabdrung's 1987 version was one of the first such collections to appear in the post-Mao era. Analogous to how the recent publication of *sung-bum* operated between past literary conventions and also became a new one, the writings studied here demonstrate both a reliance on previous literary models and a self-conscious creation of new ones.

Although the construct of genre is bound by linguistic and cultural contexts,[82] I use the term here to highlight emic literary categories employed by the authors themselves in order to demonstrate how their writings both access literary precedents and pave the way for new ones. Most works studied here contain a designation within the title indicating what might be conceived of as the literary genre or form.[83] Sometimes these literary indicators have precedents in earlier models; other times, the author self-consciously fashions a new genre type.

The texts written by the Three Polymaths represent a range of Tibetan literary forms. Two types of writing adapt earlier literary precedents: 1) a type of autobiographical life writing called *jungwa jöpa* (*byung ba brjod pa*) and 2) poetics, i.e., both belletristic verse and literary criticism, frequently referred to by its Sanskrit name, *kāvya*. Other texts represent innovations in Tibetan writings such as 3) encyclopedia (*tshig mdzod*) and 4) the academic essay (*dpyad rtsom*). In making this selection, I highlight the diversity of aesthetic styles, authorial voices, and rhetorical choices that each of these scholars mastered. This also reflects their polymathic contributions to Tibetan Buddhist studies. Below I discuss the particular sources in light of these emic literary descriptions and analyze how the authors sometimes adopt earlier literary models and sometimes forge new ones.

On Life Writing: "A Telling of What Happened"
(byung ba brjod pa)

The academic study of Tibetan life writing received a boon with Janet Gyatso's pioneering study of Jigmé Lingpa's secret autobiography, *Apparitions of the Self*

(1999). Since then, Kurtis Schaeffer (2004), Hildegard Diemberger (2007), Sarah Jacoby (2014), Andrew Quintman (2014), and Holly Gayley (2017) have added to this growing body of scholarship. The booming field of scholarly works alongside the increasing number of translations of Tibetan-language auto/biographies indicates how diverse the life writing genre is in the Tibetan context.[84] Kurtis Schaeffer brought attention to the fact that as the genre emerged in the Land of Snows, Tibetan scholars were equally committed to literary criticism.[85] In bringing these diverse works to the West, Quintman reflected upon the different shades of the emic term *namtar* (*rnam thar*) with its various English iterations including: "sacred biography," "religious biography," "liberative life story," "liberation tale," "life story," and "biography." Further, he aptly pointed out that *namtar* are "neither homogenous nor monolithic and allow for a wide range of literary structures and narrative content."[86] What has gone under the radar so far, however, is the range of registers within the larger Tibetan life writing genre and how Tibetan authors distinguished between differing subtypes of life writing.

As I detail in chapter 2, the autobiographers Tséten Zhabdrung and Mugé Samten self-consciously chose not to label their respective life writings as *namtar*. The third member of the trio, Dungkar Rinpoché, did not write a full-length autobiography, and therefore is not discussed here. Tséten Zhabdrung and Mugé Samten identified their autobiographies as *jungwa jöpa* (*byung ba brjod pa*), which I translate here as "a telling of what happened." They differentiated this type of life writing from two other genres, *namtar* and *tok-jö-d* (*rtogs brjod*); the latter is better known by its Sanskrit iteration, *avadāna*. Tséten Zhabdrung and Mugé Samten chose *jungwa jöpa* because of its role in Tibetan literary history based on previous exemplary autobiographies. Since the publication of their two autobiographies as *jungwa jöpa,* many texts have appeared with this literary designation. For example, Tubten Khétsun's autobiography, published in English as *Memories of Life in Lhasa Under Chinese Rule*, belongs to the genre of *jungwa jöpa*: literally the Tibetan title translates as "A Telling of What Happened: Difficulties and Sufferings" (*Dka' sdug 'og gi byung ba brjod pa*).[87]

Tséten Zhabdrung's autobiography, *Acoustic Ambrosia: A Truthful Telling of What Happened by Jigmé Rikpé Lodrö, a Disciple of the Powerful, Matchless Shākya* (*Mnyam med shākya'i dbang bo'i rjes zhugs pa 'jigs med rigs pa'i blo gros rang gi byung ba brjod pa bden gtam rna ba'i bdud rtsi*), hereafter *Acoustic Ambrosia*, details the experiences of its main protagonist, whose full ordination name was Jigmé Rikpé Lodrö. Tséten Zhabdrung penned this work with scribal assistance from his cousin Alak Mani Jigmé Lekshé Drayang (A lags Ma ṇi 'Jigs med legs bshad sgra dbyangs) from September 1977 to August 1978.[88] The manuscript was based on notes of a version started in 1962, a few years before the author was imprisoned.[89] Based on my interviews with a monk who worked on this project with Tséten Zhabdrung, the woodblock print was started in the early 1980s while Tséten Zhabdrung was still alive. It did not circulate widely until it was included in the 1987 edition of his *Collected Works*, which was sponsored by the Tenth Panchen Lama.[90] I translated the majority of the 1987 publication of his three-hundred-page autobiography and plan to complete it. In comparison, Mugé Samten's *The Luminous Mirror: The Author's Own Telling of What Happened* (*Rtsom pa po rang gi byung ba brjod pa rang sal A dar sha*),[91] hereafter *Luminous Mirror,* is relatively short, at one hundred seventy pages. I have read this piece and chosen to translate select passages for this work. Each author has his own distinct voice and rhetorical strategies; therefore, each autobiography is stylistically unique. The select passages presented in this book shed light on the previously unknown world of Tibetan Buddhist scholars in China for the first time in English. For the ease of readability, I chose to italicize the titles of both autobiographies even though they appear within *Collected Works*. Readers of literary Tibetan can refer to the notes for full citation information.

Both autobiographies meet the expectations of the life writing genre as found in classical Tibetan literature and also transgress those literary boundaries. Among that heterogeneous motley of Tibetan texts, one feature of Buddhist life writings stands out as primary—that is how texts serve as both "model of and model for" leading a religious life, to apply Clifford Geertz's terminology.[92] In the Tibetan context, the ultimate model of and for a religious life was the Buddha's life story; over time this became the paradigm for life writing within the Tibetan context.[93] As Gene Smith aptly observed for *namtar* within the Nyingma tradition:

> Yet while there is often much in a *rnam thar* [*nam-tar*] that is of biographical nature, a *rnam thar* has for the Buddhist a considerably greater significance. Tibetan Buddhism, especially the Rnying ma pa [Nyingma] form, is a highly pragmatic approach toward the development of total awareness of ultimate reality, toward the achievement of results that flow naturally from the unitary resolution of all dualities. The guru is ultimately a standard, a yardstick with which one can measure and test the authenticity of one's psychological insights.[94]

Similar to this description, Mugé Samten's and Tséten Zhabdrung's accounts perceive the nature of reality from a Buddhist perspective. In doing so they

highlight the methods to achieve those insights based on their authors' polymathic training in the Géluk scholastic curriculum and tantric meditation
practices.

Another key religious aspect of these texts is the role of faith in the teacher-
disciple relationship. For example, writing in verse, Tséten Zhabdrung compared his students' incessant requests to write an autobiography to being beaten
on his eardrum with a stick. Their emphatic drumming on his ear represented
their faith in him like a persistent cadence as he playfully acquiesced to their
requests:

> My students of pure faith and vows strike
> my eardrum with paddles of determination.
> I couldn't bear it, so from my throat's citadel
> roar a hundred sounds to tell what happened.[95]

Their show of faith and determination highlights how Tséten Zhabdrung's
Acoustic Ambrosia fits this goal of the life writing project in a Tibetan context,
one shared with *namtar* more generally—to inspire disciples to practice.

However, unlike past writers of *namtar*, these Buddhist authors survived
twenty years of political chaos. During this time a whole generation was denied
training in all forms of Buddhist practice and education in Tibetan literary
culture. Written in the sociopolitical context of the post-Cultural Revolution
era, their life stories become didactic pieces, teaching the scholastic curriculum, aspects of tantric meditation, Tibetan history, and Tibetan cultural values
to those who had been deprived of access to these various forms of knowledge.
Their unmediated accounts shine Buddhist perspectives on the disturbing and
tumultuous times through which these authors lived. Both autobiographies
were written in a mixture of prose and poetics.

Of Mellifluous Words

"Mellifluous words" is my translation of the Tibetan term *nyen-ngak* (*snyan
ngag*), which perhaps is more commonly known by the Sanskrit term *kāvya*. In
the Tibetan context, "mellifluous words" refers to both "poetry" and "poetics."
Depending on the context, "mellifluous words" can be considered a genre, a style
of writing, and one of the five *rikné*. In this book, I translate poems as well as
sections from poetic commentaries. The treatises written by Tséten Zhabdrung

and Dungkar Rinpoché could be considered works of literary criticism. Although Mugé Samten also wrote such poetic commentaries, these are not studied in detail here. By the twentieth century, "mellifluous words" in the Tibetan context referred to not only belletristic verse but also literary aesthetics.[96]

The cornerstone for this art form was laid with the Tibetan translation of Daṇḍin's *Mirror of Poetics* (Sanskrit: *Kāvyadarśa*) in the late thirteenth century. Tséten Zhabdrung, Mugé Samten, and Dungkar Rinpoché composed poetry in this style and also wrote poetic treatises that expanded, adapted, and altered traditional forms for new purposes in the twentieth century.[97] The Sanskrit version of Daṇḍin's *Mirror of Poetics*, Tibetan translations thereof, and subsequent commentaries follow the chapter divisions of the Urtext.

The first chapter defines "mellifluous words" and literary aesthetics. The next two chapters provide examples of literary devices, *alaṅkāra*, which was translated into Tibetan as *gyen* (*rgyan*) and means ornamentation or adornment. Similar to how jewelry or fine clothing beautifies a body, poetic language becomes more beautiful through adornment in one of two ways—semantically or phonetically.[98] Poetic adornments based on thirty-five rhetorical devices (*don rgyan*; Skt. *arthālaṅkāra*), i.e., figures of speech, such as metaphors and simile, compose the second chapter. Wordplay, the ultimate literary beauty, is the focus of the third and final chapter on phonetically based literary devices (*sgra rgyan*; Skt. *śabdālaṅkāra*). In the Tibetan context, this developed into an exquisitely beautiful and technical art form. A prime example of a phonetically "difficult" (*bya dka' ba*) poem is the "supremely beautiful wheel" (*kun bzang 'khor lo*) in the form of a complex chessboard pattern that can be read acrostically in multiple directions. Such poems were frequently painted as murals on the walls of monasteries.

When Tséten Zhabdrung and the other two polymaths wrote their respective poetic treatises, they claimed that this literary art form had become thoroughly Tibetanized. As I discuss in chapters 3 and 5, Tséten Zhabdrung and Dungkar Lozang Trinlé appropriated and expounded upon aspects of literary theories articulated in Daṇḍin's *Mirror of Poetics,* which had had long-lasting influence. In doing so, their texts served various discursive functions ranging from didactically introducing students to literary techniques to providing a medium for expressing affective states otherwise unavailable to Buddhist monks, and to bringing new content, including CCP propaganda, into Tibetan discourse.

Tséten Zhabdrung's *Thoughts on the Art of Proper Composition: A General Commentary on the* Mirror of Poetics (*Snyan ngag me long gi spyi don sdeb legs rig pa'i 'char sgo*); hereafter *A General Commentary on Poetics* (*Snyan ngag spyi don*), serves as important source material for this book. Interestingly, this is also one of the few texts by any of the three scholars to be translated in its entirety into Chinese.[99] Tséten Zhabdrung lists, interprets, and comments on a system of poetic techniques and aesthetics that he suggests became distinctly Tibetan. The clarity of his literary theory underscores the importance of paying attention to Tibetan literary criticism.

A General Commentary on Poetics is not the only source for Tséten Zhabdrung's poetry. Some of his verses translated here are also interspersed throughout his autobiography, *Acoustic Ambrosia*, in which this literary art expresses ineffable aspects of the human condition, as we will see in chapter 3. He also wrote a twenty-page poem, "*Avadāna* of Silver Flowers" (*Rtogs brjod dngul gyi me tog*), verses of which are translated in chapters 3 and 5.[100] Drawing upon literary models from one of the earliest forms of Buddhist literature, this piece falls within many of the expected conventions in terms of his use of *kāvya* and subject matter. A characteristic of this literary genre is to emulate the meaning of the term *avadāna,* which denotes pure comportment in the sense of being selfless, devotional, compassionate, and generous.[101] As I detail in chapter 5, his "*Avadāna* of Silver Flowers" commemorates the visit of the highest Géluk teacher in Tibet, the Tenth Panchen Lama, Chökyi Gyeltsen, to their shared homeland in eastern Tibet, south of the Ma Chu River.[102] An excerpt from this poem was published in one of China's premier Tibetan-language literary magazines, *Spring Rain* (Sbrang char), in 1985, the year of the author's death.[103]

Tséten Zhabdrung, Dungkar Rinpoché, and Mugé Samten simplified aesthetic styles and included new topics for the purpose of teaching Tibetan literary arts at state-run universities. The first edition of Tséten Zhabdrung's *A General Commentary on Poetics* (1957) was written as a textbook to teach Tibetan language at the newly founded Qinghai Nationalities University in Xining. Likewise, Dungkar Rinpoché's *Gateway to the Art of Literary Figures for Writing Poetry* (*Snyan ngag la 'jug tshul tshig rgyan rig pa'i sgo 'byed*) was based on his class lectures from the early 1960s at Beijing's Minzu University. The earliest extant copy of Dungkar's text dates to 1981; it is presumed that earlier editions were destroyed during the Cultural Revolution.

All Three Polymaths expand the sixteen traditional subjects of poetry outlined in the Urtext to include new topics. A prime example of this is "Ode to a Telephone," found in Mugé Samten's *Entryway to a Clear Mind: On Tibetan Writing* (*Bod kyi yi ge'i spyi rnam blo gsal 'jug ngogs*); hereafter *Entryway to a Clear Mind*.[104] First published as a monograph in 1981, Mugé Samten's book is not a commentary or a textbook on poetics per se (although he did write one, it is not studied here). This book can best be described as a literary history but stylistically mixes prose and verse. The poems follow the prescription of "mellifluous words" but use new content. The author also outlines major achievements in the history of Tibetan literary language and includes verses that illustrate certain stylistic themes. Like other poems of the times, "An Ode to a Telephone" praises technology, one of the "Four Modernizations" of state policy, in a simplified *kāvya* style.

In sum, the source materials on poetry and literary aesthetics analyzed for this study come from the following individual texts, all of which also appear in each author's respective *Collected Works*: Tséten Zhabdrung's *A General Commentary on Poetics* and "*Avadāna* of Silver Flowers," Dungkar Rinpoché's *Gateway to the Art of Literary Figures for Writing Poetry*, and Mugé Samten's *Entryway to a Clear Mind: On Tibetan Writing*.[105]

New Genres: Reference Works and Academic Essays

In addition to classical Tibetan poetics and autobiography, this study is also based on writings by the Three Polymaths that were influenced by more secular forces. In particular, I draw upon selections from the *Dungkar Encyclopedia* and Dungkar Rinpoché's academic essays (*dbyad rtsom*).

The *Dungkar Encyclopedia* (*Dung dkar tshig mdzod chen mo*) quantitatively and qualitatively differs from many other state-sponsored reference works, such as the *Tibetan-Chinese Dictionary* (*Bod rgya tshig mdzod chen mo*). This is primarily due to the *Dungkar Encyclopedia*'s monolingual use of Tibetan for all entries (with the exception of a few glosses in Chinese), the vast number of Tibetan-language sources accessed in its production, and its massive breadth of topics. The Tibetan term *tsig-dzö* (Wylie: *tshig mdzod*) means "treasury of terms," and can be alternately translated as "dictionary" or "encyclopedia," depending on the length and purpose of individual entries. With over 14,800 detailed entries, the *Dungkar Encyclopedia* contains a treasure trove of historical information and remains a valuable reference work. The editorial note in the preface explains that the encyclopedia incorporated terms on an array of topics such as famous people in Tibetan history; the political situation between successive Chinese emperors and the local Tibetan government; the legal system of ancient Tibet; the structure of the Tibetan government; an introduction to ancient knowledge, customs, and religion; the five major and five minor fields of learning, i.e., *rikné*, and explanations of difficult terms.[106] This editorial note also lists all Tibetan historical source materials and a few Chinese histories (*tongshi*) accessed for its compilation.

The idea for the encyclopedia emerged at a time when very few Tibetan-language reference works existed. In the 1950s, reference works, especially bilingual dictionaries, were integral to Chinese Communist administrative and ideological control over Tibet,[107] yet only a handful of Tibetan dictionaries existed. There was Geshé Chödrak's dictionary (1957) and Tséten Zhabdrung's bilingual orthography, *Thonmi's Mind Ornament* (*Dag yig thon mi'i dgongs rgyan*, 1957). The *Dungkar Encyclopedia* began as a collection of terms for Dungkar Rinpoché's courses at Beijing's Minzu University in the early 1960s. The project was abandoned during the Cultural Revolution, but Dungkar Rinpoché's research resumed in 1976. It took another ten years for the project to gain the recognition it needed to be published. After the founding of the China Tibetology Research Center (Krung go'i bod rig pa zhib 'jug lte gnas,; Ch. Zhongguo zangxue yanjiu zhongxin, 中国藏学研究中心) in Beijing in May 1986, Dungkar Rinpoché was appointed as its vice general director (*spyi khyabs las 'dzin sku gzhon*) under Dorjé Tséten (Rdo rje tshe brtan) as the general director.

Under their leadership, plans for editing and publishing the encyclopedia were laid out. Dungkar Rinpoché took the helm. The project started up again in 1988. With assistants hired, the work continued. After Dungkar Rinpoché's death in 1997, another few years passed before its completion in April 1999. Finally it was published in 2002 through the China Tibetology Research Center Press.[108]

In addition to long, detailed descriptions of key terms and people in Tibetan history, it contains an editorial preface, a biography of Dungkar Rinpoché, and an appendix called "A Clear Mirror: A Chronology" (*lo tshigs dwangs shel me long*). The contemporary scholar Gedun Rabsal convincingly argues that this is mainly based on Tséten Zhabdrung's historical chronology.[109] An interesting feature of the appendix is that when a significant event occurred in Dungkar Rinpoché's life (1927–1997), autobiographical jottings are added. The biographical information on Dungkar Lozang Trinlé included in this book comes from this source as well as other biographies written by his students and colleagues contained in his *Collected Works* (2004). His book *The Merging of Religious and Secular Rule in Tibet* was the only one of any of the Three Polymaths' works to be translated into English during their respective lifetimes.

In chapter 4, I retranslate sections of *The Merging of Religious and Secular Rule in Tibet* and another academic monograph called "An Explanation of Select Major Terminologies in '*The Red Annals*'" (*Deb ther dmar po'i nang gi gal che'i tshig 'grel gnad bsdus*) to show how Dungkar Rinpoché contributes to the writing of Tibetan history as an alternative to both traditional Buddhist accounts and Chinese national history. Mugé Samten and Tséten Zhabdrung also wrote essays for academic audiences. Unlike the life writings of *namtar* or *jungwa jöpa*, the literary indicators of academic essays are not found in "classical Tibetan literature." Terms such as "an explanation" (*bshad pa*) or "discussion" (*gleng ba*) indicate that these are of a new genre type—the academic essay. One of Mugé Samten's most acclaimed works has been translated into English by Sangye Tendar as *A History of Traditional Fields of Learning: A Concise History of Dissemination of Traditional Fields of Learning in Tibet* (*Bod du rig gnas dar tshul mdo bsdus bshad pa*).[110] The Tibetan title, like Dungkar Rinpoché's essay, comprises the term "explanation" (*bshad pa*). This fifty-page essay provides a brief overview of Tibetan intellectual history, with a special focus on Géluk scholars.

Taken as a whole, these varying source materials shed light on aspects of Tibetan history, culture, language, and ethical values prized by each of the Three Polymaths. Their writings together highlight the ways they adapt and disregard religious epistemes for the purposes of revitalizing Tibetan culture in their own fashion. As will become clear, their writings do not highlight the social-political contexts of their lives. What emerges instead is how Buddhist epistemes are strategically deployed to impart varying visions of Tibetan culture in the post-Mao era. All Three Polymaths agree on the value of Tibet's language and long literary heritage. Throughout this work, I compare their writings with other sources, including interviews with their former students and Buddhist disciples, Chinese-language Buddhist journals and newspapers, and relevant English-language secondary sources.

OVERVIEW

With this foundation laid, I turn to address this book's central concern: how three Buddhist monastics moved across state-imposed boundaries between religious and secular domains to advocate for Buddhist epistemic values, to continue Tibetan Buddhist institutions, and to secularize Tibetan studies within the People's Republic of China. Chapter 1, "Three Polymaths: Past and Present," shares the story of how the Tibetan historical title "Three Polymaths" (*mkhas pa mi gsum*) was resurrected in the post-Mao era. When the post-Cultural Revolution generation of students enrolled in Tibetan studies programs at select minzu universities in China looked to their own history, they found that their teachers Tséten Zhabdrung, Dungkar Lozang Trinlé, and Mugé Samten shared certain qualities with the historical "Three Polymaths," Buddhist scholar-adepts who saved Tibetan Buddhism from obliteration under the rule of the anti-Buddhist King Langdarma in the ninth century. The Three Polymaths of the twentieth century survived a similarly horrific period in Tibetan Buddhist history, the Cultural Revolution. This chapter presents biographical overviews of the "Three Polymaths" after the Cultural Revolution. Their polymathic training and achievements as Géluk Buddhist scholars prior to the Maoist period were central factors in their being labeled with this honorific epithet in the 1980s.

The next two chapters focus on Mugé Samten's *Luminous Mirror* and Tséten Zhabdrung's *Acoustic Ambrosia* and how the autobiographers championed Buddhist epistemes in remembering the first two decades of Chinese rule. Chapter 2, "Telling What Happened: Buddhist Recollections of the 1950s," details Mugé Samten's and Tséten Zhabdrung's authorial choices regarding the genre of "telling what happened" in penning their respective life stories and how they edify the value of spiritual friendship and *bodhicitta,* an altruistic, awakened mind, in service of the state. In the last section of this chapter, I bring the two autobiographies into conversation with a literary political piece, the Fourteenth Dalai Lama's "*Monlam* to Mao" (1954) in order to cast the political changes between the pre- and post-Mao era into sharp relief while also highlighting the continuity of Tibetan discursive practices.

Chapter 3, "Mellifluous Words on the Human Condition: The Maoist Years," looks at poetry written about the twenty years of authoritarian rule in Tibetan areas of China through the lens of poetic theory and Buddhist philosophy. The mellifluous words in belletristic verses serve to reinterpret the collective trauma of twenty years of relentless persecution of Tibetan culture through Buddhist ontologies. Unlike standard histories of this period, which tend to document the persecution of Tibetans under Chinese rule, poems by Tséten Zhabdrung and Mugé Samten remap their sufferings as opportunities for spiritual realization. I analyze their poetic remembrances of the Maoist years through the lens of "doing religion." To understand their rhetorical framing, I turn to aspects of Tibetan literary theory as laid out in commentaries on Daṇḍin's *Mirror of Poetics* (Skt.: *Kāvyadarśa*) by Tséten Zhabdrung and Dungkar Rinpoché. This brings Buddhist perceptions on the human condition to the fore in a mode of writing that gives voice to the ineffable experiences of human suffering and spiritual realization. These two chapters serve to highlight how Mugé Samten and Tséten Zhabdrung carried select Buddhist epistemes into the post-Mao era.

Chapters 4 and 5 focus on the strategies employed by all Three Polymaths to revive Tibetan history and Tibetan-language education, and safeguard Buddhist institutions in the post-Mao era. Chapter 4, "Dungkar Rinpoché on the Contested Ground of Tibetan History," focuses on this scholar's contributions in developing the academic study of Tibetan history distinct from its Buddhist roots. Dungkar Rinpoché, both a Marxist theorist and Buddhist scholar, forged a secular past for Tibet and redefined the construct of "religion" in Tibetan-language discourse, thereby ensuring the survival and continuance of Tibetan history in this new era.

Chapter 5, "Diverging Lineages," brings attention to Géluk Buddhist authority in two key institutions in the post-Mao era: the *tülku* institution and academic institutions. A *tülku* or reincarnate lama is a Buddhist teacher who took a vow to help all other sentient beings throughout the continuous wheel of rebirths known as *samsāra*, and is understood to have gained thereby the esoteric mastery necessary to project their consciousness to be reborn in the next life after their body dies. After the thirteenth century, this spiritual ideal became institutionalized, and *tülku* began to inherit land and wealth from their predecessors. Now the institution is a hallmark of Tibetan Buddhism; the most famous *tülku* are the Panchen Lama and the Dalai Lama. There are many *tülku* in Tibet, such as Tséten Zhabdrung and Dungkar Rinpoché.

Tséten Zhabdrung's autobiography, *Acoustic Ambrosia,* presages the precarious reinstatement of the *tülku* institution in the post-Mao era. Neither he nor his main supporter in this endeavor, the Tenth Panchen Lama, lived long enough to see the recognition of new *tülku* at this time. Although their attempts to revive this Tibetan Buddhist institution failed, other endeavors were more successful. All three scholars—Tséten Zhabdrung, Mugé Samten, and Dungkar Rinpoché—played pivotal roles in adapting Tibetan language and literature for secular academic purposes.

Taken together, these chapters present an alternative history of Sino-Tibetan relations from circa 1950 to the death of Dungkar Rinpoche, the last of the Three Polymaths to pass away, in 1997. This history is based on my translations and interpretations of select writings by these three influential Tibetan savants who navigated between their training in Géluk Buddhist scholasticism and the dictates of the socialist state of the People's Republic of China. The boundary-breaching acts between the religious and secular through diverse writings and educational efforts in some ways seem to have ended with the deaths of this generation of scholars as the Chinese state increases its control over the domain of religion. The simultaneous secularization of Tibetan studies is such that it seems impossible for an incarnate lama or *geshé* to also serve as a university professor in the People's Republic of China today.

By prioritizing these select writings, I show how the Three Polymaths acted as moral agents by strategically accessing Buddhist epistemes amid dire political constraints. While this is the first monograph devoted to the writings of any of them, it is nonetheless limited in scope because it does not represent their full literary corpus or all their various achievements. With that said, I hope this book inspires others to delve into the rich world of Tibetan literature, history, and culture.

I

Three Polymaths

Past and Present

Who were the Tibetan heroes remaining in China after the Fourteenth Dalai Lama and some one hundred thousand refugees fled from the invading People's Liberation Army? This question preoccupied me from my first visit to Lhasa, the capital of the Tibetan Autonomous Region, during Losar (Tibetan New Year) in 1993. Many years later, this line of inquiry led me to Dentik Monastery where, as detailed in the previous chapter, I visited the cave in which the first set of "Three Polymaths" ordained Gongpa Rabsel, thereby preserving Buddhist teaching lineages from the wrath of tyrannical king Langdarma one millennium ago. This line of questioning also prompted my research and interviews with leading Tibetan scholars, writers, and intellectuals living in China, the United States, and India. As I gathered information from various sources—oral histories (Dentik local history and interviews) and texts (Tséten Zhabdrung's autobiography and his *Guide to Dentik Monastery,* among others), I came to understand that Tséten Zhabdrung, Mugé Samten, and Dungkar Rinpoché not only were heroes to many Tibetans in China but also had become cultural icons, symbolizing both the survival and the continuance of Tibetan culture in the post-Mao era.

As I listened to my Tibetan interlocutors casually refer to "Three Polymaths after the Cultural Revolution," I began to reflect on the contemporary symbolic value of this designation and how normative it had become for Tibetan monastics and educated laypeople. I then began to ask: When culture (in this case, the symbolic value of the Three Polymaths title) merges with life (i.e., the normative use of this title) in such a way as to become nearly invisible, how do I as a scholar begin to recognize and describe the ways that certain people use cultural and religious materials, appropriating some and discarding others, at different historical moments?[1]

One such moment came in 2017 when I read an article titled "Tibet's Three Polymaths of the *Yang-dar* Era."[2] Circulating on the digital platform Weixin and in an online journal, *Tibet.CN*, this Tibetan language article intertwined the biographical lives of the three twentieth-century scholars, Tséten Zhabdrung, Mugé Samten, and Dungkar Lozang Trinlé, in no uncertain terms. Like their tenth-century predecessors, they were charged with saving Tibetan Buddhism at a pivotal time. Additionally, their efforts to preserve Buddhism, similar to those of the historical monastics, marked a new timeline for Tibetan Buddhist history. This new era is signified in the title of the article. The "*Yang-dar* Era" (*bstan pa yang dar skabs*) refers to a third epoch in the historical development of Tibetan Buddhism. The "Three Polymaths" title emblematically connected the efforts of three monastic scholars of the first millennium to their twentieth-century counterparts, attributing agency and symbolic meaning to efforts to preserve and continue Tibetan Buddhist culture.

Translated as the "Era of the Dharma's Rediffusion," the "*Yang-dar* Era" orders time in a way that ignores the standard historical sequencing of events as determined either by the death of China's founder, Mao Zedong, in 1976, or by the socioeconomic reforms initiated by Deng Xiaoping in 1978. The concept and term *yang-dar*[3] finds its foothold in two earlier divisions of Tibetan Buddhist history: the "Earlier Diffusion of the Dharma" (*bstan pa snga dar*) between the seventh and ninth century and the "Later Diffusion of the Dharma" (*bstan pa phyi dar*) beginning in the eleventh century.

Similar to the article, I bring the biographies of these three scholars into the same discursive space. Then I attempt to uncover how, why, and to whom the twentieth-century "Three Polymaths" became cultural symbols. This chapter lays a foundation necessary for realizing the larger goals of this book. That is, in brief, to discover how the writings and activities of the Three Polymaths—Tséten Zhabdrung, Dungkar Lozang Trinlé, and Mugé Samten—shaped the discursive formation of aspects of Tibetan culture in both secular and religious institutions in China at a critical historical juncture.

BIOGRAPHICAL LIVES

Tséten Zhabdrung

Alak Tséten Zhabdrung Jigmé Rigpé Lodrö (A lags Tshe tan Zhabs drung 'Jigs med rig pa'i blo gros, 1910–1985), i.e., Tséten Zhabdrung, is credited with

FIGURE 1.1 Tséten Zhabdrung

Illustration by Ngangwa Gyeltsen

regenerating many aspects of Tibetan culture at a time of unprecedented socio-political change. "Alak" is an honorific title for a *tülku* or reincarnate lama in Amdo dialect; my Tibetan interlocutors often referred to him as "Alak-tsang" or "Alak Tséten Zhabdrung-tsang." Despite enduring nearly twelve years in prison, Alak Tséten Zhabdrung energetically reclaimed his Géluk scholastic education after the Cultural Revolution to further transmit nearly all the traditional fields of learning, including language, poetry, history, astronomy, calligraphy, and Buddhist philosophy.

Tséten Zhabdrung's virtues lay in his steadfast commitment to the creative tradition of Tibetan scholarship rooted in the work of Sakya Paṇḍita Kunga Gyeltsen (Sa skya Paṇḍita Kun dga' rgyal mtshan, 1182–1251) and Butön (Bu ston, 1290–1364), and continued to change and innovate with the works of Jamgön Kongtrul ('Jam mgon Kong sprul, 1813–1899) and Ju Mipham ('Ju Mi pham, 1846–1912), among many others. Alak Tséten Zhabdrung's *Collected Works* contains a treasure trove of information on almost every aspect of traditional Tibetan Buddhist scholarship. Throughout his autobiography he emphasizes the core value to strive for: "virtue" (*yon tan*). As I detail in chapter 5, *yon-tan*, for him, was synonymous with intellectual pursuits because these provide the gateway to developing the most virtuous deed: to increase one's knowledge of discernment, i.e,. to take up behaviors that fit with Buddhist teachings and to abandon actions that do not support the Dharma.

Tséten Zhabdrung's autobiography, the title abbreviated as *Acoustic Ambrosia* here, documents his life and serves as the main source for this brief biography. Written in a style that mixes traditional literary techniques with colloquialisms, Tséten Zhabdrung's autobiography was praised by Dawa Lodrö (Zla ba blo gros), the head editor of *Spring Rain*, a premier Tibetan-language literary journal published in China, as one of the most influential pieces of Tibetan biographical literature that he has ever read.[4]

According to *Acoustic Ambrosia*, its author was born on the twenty-second day of the fourth month of the Iron Dog year in the fifteenth *rabjung* (*rab byung*) cycle of the Tibetan calendar.[5] The roughly equivalent Western calendrical date of May 31, 1910, is not provided in the life narrative.[6] He was the second youngest of eight children. His father had names in both Chinese (G.yang tshe; Ch. Yang Cai 杨才) and Tibetan (Lozang Tashi; Blo bzang bkra shis). His mother was called Lhamotar (Lha mo thar).[7] His birthplace of Yadzi (Ya rdzi) is more commonly known today by its Chinese name, Jishi Town (Ch. Jishi zhen 积石镇) in today's Xunhua Salar Autonomous County of Qinghai Province.

In describing his ethnic identity, Tséten Zhabdrung drew upon classification factors that had been used in state projects to demarcate groups of ethnic nationalities (Ch. *minzu*), characteristics that had been adapted from Stalin's "Four Commonalities." Tséten Zhabdrung identified himself as Tibetan based on language, culture, and territory.[8] His mixed ethnic background led to some controversy concerning his recognition as an incarnate lama or *tülku*.

Despite initial disputes about his inclusion in the pool of three possible *tülku* candidates, Amdo Zhamar Paṇḍita Gendün Tenzin Gyatso (A mdo Zhwa dmar paṇḍita Dge 'dun bstan 'dzin rgya mtsho, 1852–1912)[9] of Dītsa Monastery (Lde tsha)[10] recognized him as the reincarnation of the Fifth Tséten Zhabdrung, a minor Géluk lineage. The young Sixth Tséten Zhabdrung took charge of his own monastic estate as well as six other monasteries that he shared with Tséten Khenpo (Tshe tan mkhan po)[11] at age six. Tséten (Tshe tan) is a place name; whereas *zhabdrung* (*zhabs drung*) and *khenpo* (*mkhan po*) are titles of high incarnate lamas.[12] His initial enthronement at the Six Encampment (Sgar ba kha drug) monasteries was embroiled in further controversy because his ceremony took place before his fellow throne holder, Tséten Khenpo. The *khenpo's* position was considered to be superior because his past incarnation had been the original founder of the estates and reincarnation lineage.

They shared the Six Encampment monasteries, now located in far eastern Hualong and western Minhe counties of Qinghai Province: Tséten Monastery (Tshe tan; Ch. xìng'er 杏儿 or cáidàn 才旦), Tuwa Monastery (Mthu ba; Ch. tǔwa 土哇), Chenpuk Monastery (Gcan phug; Ch. zhàomùchuān 赵木川), Katung Monastery (Ka thung; Ch. gǎdòng 尕洞), Gongkya Monastery (Kong skya; Ch. gōngshénjiā 工什加), and Dentik Monastery (Dan tig; Ch. dāndòu 丹斗).[13] The history of both incarnation lineages, including bygone rivalries, is addressed in Tséten Zhabdrung's autobiography as well as his local history, *A Catalogue of Dentik Monastery*.[14] As young adults, the two incarnate lamas resolved childhood tensions at the behest of their mutual teacher, the great Amdo lama Jigmé Damchö Gyatso, a.k.a. Marnang Dorjé chang (Mar nang Rdo rje 'chang, 'Jigs med dam chos rgya mtsho, 1898–1946).

Tséten Zhabdrung received an excellent monastic education under the tutelage of some of the brightest Géluk scholars in Amdo. He received novice monastic vows in the Fire Dragon year (1916) from the fifth Seri Mani Paṇḍita Gendün Tenzin Gyeltsen (Gser ri'i Ma ṇi paṇḍita Dge 'dun bstan 'dzin rgyal mtshan, 1896–1944)[15] at Tuwa Monastery, and was given the name Gendun Shédrup Gyatso (Dge 'dun bshad sgrub rgya mtsho). He learned to read from a second cousin at around this time. By age ten, he began training in the "Collected Topics" (*bsdus grwa*)[16] of the Géluk curriculum with Jigmé Damchö Gyatso, who later brought him before Giteng Rinpoché Yongzin Paṇḍita Lozang Peldan (Sgis steng Rin po che Yongs 'dzin paṇḍita Blo bzang dpal ldan,

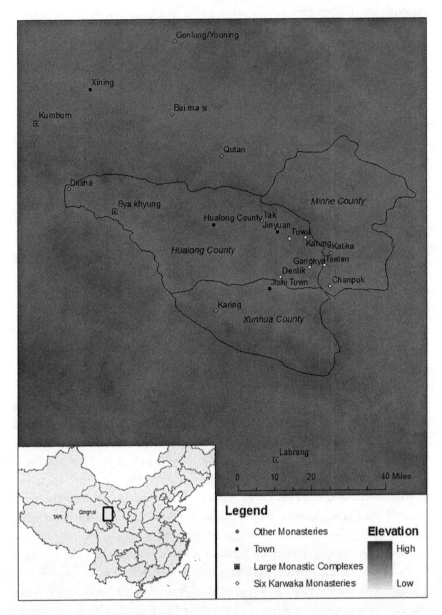

FIGURE 1.2 Map of Six Encampment (Garwaka/Karwaka) monasteries

Map by Nicole Willock

1880/1–1944).[17] The latter instructed him in Tibetan classical poetry, starting at age fourteen. He completed his monastic studies under their supervision at age eighteen, in the Earth Dragon year (1928). He took full vows and received the ordination name Jigmé Rigpé Lodrö in the presence of his two main teachers.

At age twenty-four in the Wood Dog year (1934), Tséten Zhabdrung worked on the publication of Jigmé Damchö Gyatso's *Collected Works*. He not only compiled and edited these fifteen volumes but also raised funds for the construction of a printing house at Tuwa Monastery to print them.[18] Jigmé Damchö Gyatso's commentary, *The Essence of Eloquence on the Interpretive and Definitive Teachings* (*Drang nges legs bshad snying po*), is reportedly highly acclaimed and widely read by Géluk scholars today, including by His Holiness the Dalai Lama. The woodblocks for these tomes were recarved and the printing house rebuilt in the 1980s, after being burned to the ground in late 1965.[19] The woodblocks were kept in the printing house until the early 2000s, when they were moved to Rongbo Monastery in Repgong, where they are currently located.

Tséten Zhabdrung's autobiography details his impressive monastic, tantric, and scholastic training. He received and then further transmitted so many tantric initiations, reading transmissions, and empowerments that they are too numerous to repeat here; but it is important that although he was a Géluk lama, he was well versed in teachings from multiple sects of Tibetan Buddhism and familiar with Bön teachings too. For example, in addition to receiving transmissions in the Géluk tantric practices of Chakrasaṃvara (*bde mchog*) and Yamāntaka (*rdo rje 'jigs byed*), he also received full instruction in the Sarvavid Vairocana cycle (*kun rig rnam par snang mdzad*).[20] He also praises Bön-po literature. According to the customs of the tantric communities in the Six Encampments region, he initiated the monastic constitutions (*bca' yig*) and led prayers according to the Nyingma tradition.[21] As a Géluk lama, he was vested in maintaining his *vinaya* vows, especially that of celibacy, even though he was forced to wear Mao suits during the leftist political periods.[22] Tséten Zhabdrung also instructed on the necessity of upholding the *vinaya* or monastic discipline.[23]

The most recent edition of Tséten Zhabdrung's *Collected Works* (2007) comprises many volumes dedicated to his commentaries on Buddhist practice and philosophy, including liturgical texts such as "taking refuge" (in volume 6), explanations of the "gradual path to enlightenment (*lam rim*)" in no fewer than three volumes (9, 10, and 11), and information on several tantric cycles (12 and 13).

Besides excelling in the training in the standard monastic curriculum, Tséten Zhabdrung was intrigued by mathematics and methodologies in the calculation of historical dates. In addition to mastering Chinese astronomy (*rgya rtsis*), he wrote many essays comparing systems and methods of calculating dates according to various Tibetan scholars. These essays were first published by Tséten Zhabdrung's nephew Jigmé Chöpak ('Jigs med chos 'phags) in *A Useful Collection of Essays by the Great Scholar Tséten Zhabdrung* (*Mkhas dbang Tshe tan zhabs drung gi dpyad rtsom mkho bsdus*).[24] Similar to the iconoclastic Amdo scholar Gendün Chöpel, Tséten Zhabdrung instructed readers on basic geographical and cosmological knowledge, such as heliocentricity and the scientific reasons for an eclipse.[25]

As I detail in chapters 2 and 3, Tséten Zhabdrung barely mentions political events throughout his autobiography. On the founding of the People's Republic of China, he wrote, "At that time, with a thundering roar proclaiming the liberation of Qinghai Province, a great change occurred throughout the vast empire (*rgyal khams*)."[26] In the first decade of Chinese Communist rule he published many books;[27] two original prints are known to be still extant: a manual on letter writing (*'Phrin yig spel tshul lhag bsam padmo 'dzum pa'i nyin byed*)[28] and the first edition of his *General Commentary on Poetics*.[29] He wrote this while teaching at the Qinghai Nationalities University in order to fill the need for a textbook on poetry that "accorded with modern times."[30] Tséten Zhabdrung's dictionary *Thonmi's Mind Ornament: An Orthography*, republished in India in 1969, was first written in the early 1950s.[31] He also wrote a treatise on Tibetan grammar, including a brief history of the Tibetan language called the *Thonmi's Counsel* (*Thon mi'i zhal lung*)[32] which is also used as a textbook. Additionally, Alak Tséten Zhabdrung mastered different styles of calligraphy and created new scripts. His unparalleled skills as a calligrapher can be seen in volume 8 of his *Collected Works* (2007), which reprinted several calligraphy pamphlets, all written in different styles in his own hand.

His fate was to be the same as that of the majority of Tibetan religious leaders who remained in China. Alak Tséten Zhabdrung was arrested in late 1965 and confined at Nantan (南滩) prison in Xining for almost twelve years.[33] After his release in July 1976, he spent two years recuperating.[34] In the spring of 1978, Ngawang Chödar (Ngag dbang chos dar), then director of the Tibetan Studies Department at Northwest Minzu University in Lanzhou, Gansu Province, invited Tséten Zhabdrung to join the staff of the Tibetan Studies Department.[35]

It was there that Tséten Zhabdrung trained the next generation of Tibetan historians, scholars, and translators. His former students comprise some of the most important people in Tibetan studies today. His graduate students (*zhib 'jug slob ma*, Ch. *yanjiu xuesheng* 研究学生) included Pu Wencheng (蒲文成), a prominent historian and translator; Dawa Lodrö (Zla ba blo gros; Ch.: Dawa

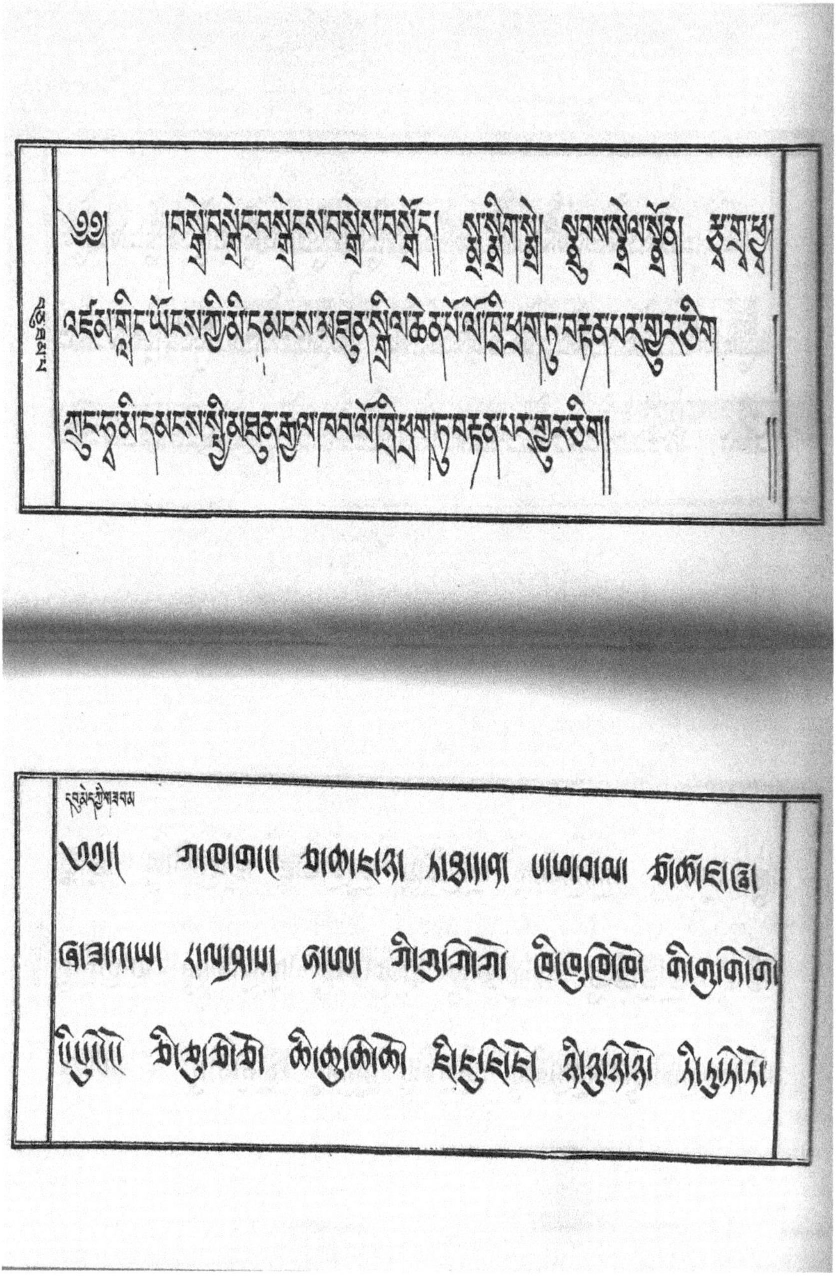

FIGURE 1.3 Calligraphy by Tséten Zhabdrung

FIGURE 1.4 Tséten Zhabdrung with PhD students Pu Wencheng, Dawa Lodrö, and Gao Rui, and monks, Ganden Monastery, 1981

Courtesy of Jigmé Chöpak

Luozhi 达哇洛智), literary critic and head editor of *Spring Rain*; and Gao Rui (Gnya' gong dkon mchog tshe brtan, Ch. 高瑞), an administrator at Northwest Minzu University. This select group of graduate students accompanied Tséten Zhabdrung on pilgrimage to Lhasa, where he gave lectures in the summer of 1981.

A few undergraduate students in the Tibetan Studies Department in Lanzhou were permitted to attend Tséten Zhabdrung's graduate classes in that first year, due to their high level of Tibetan. This group included Pema Bhum (Pad ma 'bum, Ch. Wanma Ben 万马奔). At Tséten Zhabdrung's behest, Pema Bhum continued at Northwest Minzu University to pursue his graduate work. From his undergraduate days until Tséten Zhabdrung's death, Pema Bhum was a research assistant for Tséten Zhabdrung.[36] Other well-known graduate students include the national translator Repgong Dorjékhar (Reb gong rdo rje mkhar) and the writer Chabga Dorjé Tsering (Chab 'gag rdo rje tshe ring). Many others sat in on his lectures, studying with him informally.

Besides all of this, Tséten Zhabdrung contributed to the revitalization of Tibetan culture in two other significant ways. After he was rehabilitated by the government, he was given compensation. He used this as seed money to start a scholarship fund for talented Tibetan studies undergraduates with financial need at Northwest Minzu University.[37] This fund still exists and has been expanded to include scholarships for high school students in the Tibetan Studies Middle School in Xunhua.[38]

Up until his death in 1985, Tséten Zhabdrung continued to give Dharma teachings and empowerments throughout eastern Amdo. As I detail in chapter 5, he also worked with the Tenth Panchen Lama as well as Shardong Rinpoché, one of his main disciples, to rebuild all of the Six Encampment monasteries in addition to his own monastic seat at Tak Monastery, Karing (Ka ring) Monastery, and Jakyung (Bya khyung) Monastery.[39] He passed away peacefully at Labrang Tashikyil of natural causes. A cremation ceremony at Labrang followed, which drew thousands of mourners.[40] His main reliquary *stūpa* is located within his compound at Dentik Monastery. Tséten Zhabdrung's legacy lives on in his writings, his scholarship fund, and the monasteries that he helped rebuild, and foremost in the hearts and minds of those he inspired.

After a twenty-year vacuum, Alak Tséten Zhabdrung Jigmé Rigpé Lodrö played a crucial role in the revitalization of Tibetan culture and language both inside and outside of monastic settings. By transmitting his classical knowledge in new, innovative ways (some of which are detailed throughout this work), he effectively bridged two worlds. His contributions to Tibetology, especially his writings and the generation of scholars that he trained, continue to teach and inspire students in Tibetan studies around the world.

Mugé Samten

Similar to Tséten Zhabdrung, Mugé Samten Gyatso (Dmu dge bsam gtan rgya mtsho, 1914–1993) contributed to the revitalization of Tibetan education in Buddhist monastic and secular institutions as a writer and a teacher. Whereas Tséten Zhabdrung's writings span three decades, with four major works published in the 1950s, all of Mugé Samten's texts were written after 1978. His most influential works were in the field of Tibetan literary history and language. Beyond these contributions, Mugé Samten gained a reputation as a fierce advocate for Tibetan language education and reform.

FIGURE 1.5 Mugé Samten

Illustration by Ngangwa Gyeltsen

Unlike Tséten Zhabdrung and Dungkar Rinpoché, Mugé Samten was never recognized as a reincarnate lama. He rose to prominence among the Géluk elite due to his family's support, educational achievements, and intellectual acumen. In the 1980s and 1990s, his activities crossed state-imposed religious and secular divides, revitalizing Tibetan language studies in both Buddhist monastic institutions and state-run universities.

"Mugé Samten" is an appellation partly derived from his birthplace. He was born in the village of Mugé (Dmu dge), also spelled "Mogé" (dmod dge),[41] in today's Songpan County (Zung chu rdzong) of Sichuan Province during the waxing moon of the eleventh month of the Wood Tiger year, i.e., in late December 1914.[42] Like Tséten Zhabdrung, he penned his own autobiography. This work, its title abbreviated here as *Luminous Mirror*, was written in 1992–1993 and is included in the first volume of his *Collected Works*, following a biography devoted to his root lama.

Luminous Mirror serves as the main source material accessed for this study; however, three English-language biographies exist. Two of them are very brief: one is on the *Treasury of Lives* website, and another is in the introduction to *A History of Traditional Fields of Learning*, the only essay from Mugé Samten's corpus to be translated in its entirety. Recently, Dhondup Tashi completed his MA thesis on Mugé Samten, "A Monastic Scholar Under China's Occupation of Tibet: Mugé Samten's Autobiography and His Role as a Vernacular Intellectual."[43]

In my reading of *Luminous Mirror,* the straightforward prose lacks the literary flourishes in Tséten Zhabdrung's autobiography. Mugé Samten was adept at verse, but few poems are found within his life narrative. It details his family life, education, arrest during the Cultural Revolution, Dharma activities, and lecturing positions at multiple universities. The majority is dedicated to recounting the numerous teachings he gave both in Buddhist monastic settings and at nationality universities from 1984 until his death in 1993.

The beginning of the autobiography focuses on his early family life and his parents' support of his education. The household supported themselves on pastoral-agricultural livelihood and were "neither very rich nor very poor."[44] Unlike Tséten Zhabdrung, who frequently paraphrased and cited other Buddhist texts, Mugé Samten seldom used this technique. One rare instance is when he attributes the following saying to the fourth-century Buddhist philosopher, Nāgārjuna (dpal mgon 'phags pa klu sgrub): "May you be born to a family of middling means! May you be born in a household of neither great poverty nor great wealth!"[45] He considered his family to be fortunate because they were middle class. His family residence was called Gyongmé Khorlo (gyong smad 'khor lo tshang) because it was located on a riverbank near a prayer wheel (*khor-lo*) spun by water.[46]

His family prioritized his education within the Géluk scholastic system. His father, Gendün Kyab (Dge 'dun skyabs), affectionately called "A-gen" (A dgen), was from a well-educated family with many learned *geshé* among them. His mother, Atshe (A tshe), was the daughter of one of two sisters of a famous *geshé* called Thel Lama Lozang Chödan Pel Zangpo (dge bshes thal bla ma blo bzang chos ldan dpal bzang po). Both sisters were married to Sodar (bsod dar), Mugé Samten's maternal grandfather, who was the nephew of a *tülku* at Gyalrong Monastery (rgyal rong sgom chen pa) called Khétsang Lama Jamyang Khédrup Gyatso (Khe tshang bla ma 'jam dbyangs mkhas grub rgya mtsho).[47] Mugé Samten learned to read and write with his father and his maternal great-uncle, Geshé Thel Lama Lozang Chödan Pel Zangpo. Both men, especially his great-uncle Geshé Thel Lama, supervised his education.

With this family support and his prodigious intellect, Mugé Samten excelled at the Géluk scholastic curriculum and received the highest degree after completing his foundational studies at the local monastery. At age eleven, he received novice ordination vows and a new name, Lozang Samten (Blo bzang bsam gtan), formally entering Mugé's Tashi Khorlo Monastery (Dmu dge bkra shis 'khor lo).[48] Mugé Samten digresses briefly from the narrative focus on his own education to provide the history of how Tashi Khorlo Monastery became a branch of Labrang Tashikyil, the largest Buddhist university in eastern Tibet, when it was gifted to Labrang's highest-ranking incarnate lama, Jamyang Zhépa, Konchok Jigmé Wangpo ('Jam dbyangs bzhad pa dkon mchog 'jigs med dbang po, 1728–1791).[49]

From age eleven onward, his maternal great-uncle Geshe Thel Lama and a renowned scholar by the name of Geshé Konchok Gendün (Dkon mchog dge 'dun) taught him reading and gave him permission to study various Buddhist rituals, such as White Mañjuśrī and the Three Wrathful Deities (*drag po gsum*). Also under their instruction, he studied the standard texts of the Géluk scholastic curriculum, including the Collected Topics, the root texts of the Four Philosophical Schools (*grub mtha' rtsa ba*), and the Stages and Paths of the Bodhisattva (*sa lam rnam bzhag*), especially the commentary by the Second Jamyang Zhépa, as well as Perfection of Wisdom (*Prajñāpāramitā*) literature.[50]

Maintaining close ties with his family, Mugé Samten continued to advance in his monastic career after moving to Labrang Tashikyil at age twenty. Seven years later, he became a fully ordained monk. After he had been at Labrang for a total of nine years, his father became ill, and he broke off his studies to return to

Mugé for eight months. When he came back to Labrang, he did an intensive retreat on White Sarasvatī (Dbyangs can ma dkar mo) and studied commentaries on grammar, poetics, and Sanskrit with Paṇḍita Jamyang Lekshé ('Jam dbyangs legs bshad). He also wrote his first poetry at this time.[51] At thirty-two, he and several monks were commissioned to go to Amchok (A mchog) Monastery to decorate the assembly hall with *lantsa*-style calligraphy, an ancient letterform of Sanskrit frequently used for writing mantras on pillars or beams in Tibetan temples. During his stay, he studied Chinese astrology with a local monk by the name of Jamyang Ngatrük (A khu 'Jam dbyangs rnga phrug).[52] After that, annually he calculated and drew the lunar calendar with the days, months, and eclipses, which was used for ritual purposes.

In 1946, shortly after the Fifth Jamyang Zhépa, Lozang Yéshé Tenpé Gyeltsen ('Jam dbyangs bzhad pa sku phreng lnga pa Blo bzang 'jam dbyangs ye shes bstan pa'i rgyal mtshan, 1916–1947) returned to Labrang Tashikyil, Mugé Samten achieved the highest of Géluk accolades—the *geshé dorampa* degree. He was then appointed as a teacher at a modern school established within Jamyang Zhépa's residential compound, called Labrang Tubten Podrang (Bla brang thub bstan pho brang). Mugé Samten taught language and grammar classes there for a few years.[53]

Almost immediately after the People's Liberation Army (PLA) entered Xiahe (the town adjacent to Labrang Tashikyil), monastics were invited to visit China on study tours. To discuss this prospect, the Sixth Gungthang Rinpoché, Jigmé Tenpé Wanchuk ('Jigs med bstan pa'i dbang phyug, 1926–2000) met with Mugé Samten in nearby Lanzhou. Mugé Samten had been requested to go to the city by monk officials and the leaders of Xiahe; presumably among this group was Apa Alo, the local leader of Xiahe, who in October 1949 led twenty thousand Tibetans to meet the PLA five kilometers outside of the town. Traveling to greet a visiting party is a Tibetan custom to show good will.[54] Yet these events are barely mentioned by Mugé Samten, who, similar to Tséten Zhabdrung, does not highlight political events in his autobiography.

Mugé Samten writes about the recognition procedures of the reincarnation of the late Fifth Jamyang Zhépa, who had died in 1947.[55] Meanwhile, Gungtang Rinpoché, who was about ten years younger than Mugé Samten, requested instruction on aspects of Tibetan history (*lo rgyus*) and culture (*rig gnas*).[56] Gungtang Rinpoché appointed Mugé Samten to the rank of secretary (*drung chen*) and asked if he wished to go to western Tibet or to China in that capacity. Mugé Samten declined the offer to go to western Tibet and agreed to go to China (rgya yul) as Gungtang Rinpoché's representative.[57] The future leader of the Buddhist Association of China, Geshé Sherab Gyatso, became a traveling companion and mentor at this time. Mugé Samten and Geshé Sherab Gyatso arrived in Beijing in the spring of 1950.

Although Mugé Samten claimed "to have known nothing about politics,"[58] his career straddled political and Buddhist domains for the rest of his life. Like his mentor, Geshé Sherab Gyatso, he seems to have been committed to both CCP propaganda work and teaching Buddhist philosophy.[59] Soon after arriving in Beijing, he began work at the State Ethnic Affairs Commission (Mi rigs don byed U yon lhan khan) with others such as Dorje Tséten (Rdo rje tshe brtan), Phuntsok Tashi (Phun tshogs bkra shis), and Sonam Gyatso (Bsod nams rgya mtsho), translating and editing the *People's Pictorial (Mi dmangs brnyan dpar)*, a propaganda journal showcasing nationalistic achievements. When representatives from Lhasa arrived in Beijing in 1951 for the signing of the Seventeen Point Agreement, Mugé Samten was requested to proofread the document for accuracy in translation.[60] This treaty, the Agreement of the Central People's Government and the Local Government of Tibet on Measures for the Peaceful Liberation of Tibet, affirmed China's sovereignty over Tibet.

After residing for two years in the nation's capital, Mugé Samten returned to his home region in 1952, due to illness.[61] In Sichuan Province, he assisted in starting up Songpan County's Chinese Community Party committee (tang gi U yon lhan khan) for the Autonomous Government of Mugé (Dmu dge'i rang skyong srid gzhung).[62] In 1953, he received a directive from the office of the Sixth Jamyang Zhépa, Lozang Jigmé Tubten Gyatso Chökyi Nyima Pelzangpo (Blo bzang 'jigs med thub bstan rgya mtsho chos kyi nyi ma dpal bzang po, b. 1948), appointing him and Geshe Lharamapa Konchog Tenzin (Lha rams pa Dkon mchog bstan 'dzin) as teachers of Buddhist philosophy (*mtshan nyid*) at Tashi Khorlo Monastery in Mugé.[63] In 1955, he became an editor at the office of the *Minjiang People's Paper* (Ming kya'ang gsar 'gyur) and assistant head of the Cultural Office of the Lhagyel Regional Government.[64] In 1958, he relocated to Barkham ('Bar khams) after the regional government had moved from Lhagyel (Lha rgyal gling).[65]

In May 1959, he was recruited by the Minzu Press[66] to join Tséten Zhabdrung on a team responsible for translating and editing the Tibetan-language version of Mao Zedong's *Collected Works (Ma'o tse tung gig sung rtsom gces bsdus)*.[67] At this time, new language policy reforms or "Essential Points" (*gnad bsdus*) were implemented. These followed nationwide attempts to simplify language, especially to align literary and colloquial languages and introduce simplified Chinese characters. The Tibetan "Essential Points" did not accord with established literary conventions or Tibetan grammar rules, causing great confusion for

Tibetan language readers. Nonetheless, all Tibetan-language publications had to implement these guidelines.[68] Mugé Samten petitioned to get rid of this policy in the 1980s.[69]

As the political situation grew increasingly tense, Mugé Samten was forced to wear lay clothes, but he remained committed to his monastic vows. Despite their outward appearance dressed in Mao suits, Mugé Samten and Tséten Zhabdrung maintained their vows. Adherence to the *vinaya,* in particular the vow of celibacy, as a way of life for Mugé Samten and Tséten Zhabdrung indicated their perseverance in upholding the values of Géluk monasticism.

In 1966, Mugé Samten was arrested at his workplace in a government office and then struggled against, enduring torture and public humiliation. He was then forced to do reform through labor.[70] In 1974, he returned to Mugé in Ngaba (Rnga ba, Ch. Aba 阿坝) Prefecture to recover. A year later he went to Chengdu to work as an editor on the *Tibetan-Chinese Dictionary* (*Bod rgya tshig mdzod chen mo*), a large project that involved Dungkar Rinpoché and many other scholars as well. In October 1977, Mugé Samten was elected to the working committee of the fourth meeting of Sichuan Province's Consultative Conference (Zi khron zhing chen srid gros skabs bzhi pa'i rgyun las U yon).[71]

In early winter 1978, Mugé Samten wrote one of his most influential works, *Entryway to a Clear Mind: On Tibetan Writing.*[72] As I detail in chapter 5, this book filled a desperate need in Tibetan language education. It was popular among many young Tibetans who had not been granted the opportunity to study Tibetan language in their youth due to the policies during the Cultural Revolution. This generation included present-day Buddhist luminaries such as Khenchen Tsultrim Lodrö (b. 1966), who read this work as a teenager and now serves as a director of the largest Buddhist community in China, called Larung Gar.[73] *Entryway to a Clear Mind* didactically introduces Tibetan literary history and aesthetics. Mugé Samten's own poems, such as "Ode to the Magic of Generating Electricity" and "Ode to a Telephone," exemplify how he adapted modern subject matter to traditional poetic forms.[74] For him, modernizing Tibetan language education was key to reviving Tibetan culture. He took it upon himself to teach language and grammar. He also established local schools in his home region of Ngaba Prefecture in northern Sichuan.[75]

Unlike Tséten Zhabdrung and Dungkar Rinpoché, Mugé Samten never held a permanent professorial position. However, he traveled widely and lectured at many Tibetan studies programs in China, including at Northwest Minzu University in Lanzhou, Qinghai Nationalities University in Xining, Southwest Minzu University in Chengdu, and Minzu University of China in Beijing. From the early 1980s onward, he wrote Buddhist commentarial pieces, especially on logic and epistemology (volume 2 of his *Collected Works*) and essays on grammar, poetry, and Sanskrit (volume 4). In July 1982, he flew to Lhasa for China's Astronomy and Astrology Conference (Krung go gnam rig skar rtsis kyi tshogs 'du) and was nominated as vice-chairman of the Astrological Council (Skar rtsis mthun tshogs). He then went on a four-month pilgrimage throughout the region, including Tsang and southern Tibet. He met with the Tenth Panchen Lama during his tour.[76] In 1983, he spent three months in Beijing at Minzu University, where he taught poetics based on his book *Treasury of Clear Illumination: A Commentary on Kāvya (Snyan 'grel yang gsal snang mdzod).*[77] He went on pilgrimage to Chengde and Wutaishan after his sojourn in the capital.[78] On the return trip, he taught at many monasteries throughout Amdo, including Kirti Monastery, Labrang Tashikyil, and Kumbum.

The tone and mode of writing in the last section of *Luminous Mirror* shifts slightly. It is written in terse snippets that list the author's numerous Dharma activities from 1984 onward until shortly before his death in his eightieth year, by Tibetan calculations, the Water Bird year of 1993.[79] He documents numerous Buddhist activities such as tantric retreats, Dharma teachings, sutra recitations, and ordinations at various monasteries throughout Amdo.[80] His political duties lessened somewhat, but he still attended various important events, such as the local Barkham Political Consultative Conference.[81] The autobiographical narrative ends shortly before his death. An addendum to *Luminous Mirror* explains how funds were collected for a memorial service and reliquary stupa at the end of the fifth lunar month of 1993.[82]

Dungkar Rinpoché

The third member of the trio who came to be collectively known as the Three Polymaths was Dungkar Lozang Trinlé (Dung dkar blo bzang 'phrin las, 1927–1997), a.k.a. Dungkar Rinpoché. Unlike Tséten Zhabdrung and Mugé Samten, who penned their own life stories, the scant autobiographical details on Dungkar Lozang Trinlé are jotted in the chronological tables at the end of the *Dungkar Encyclopedia*. Other sources for his life are Tibetan-language biographies including "An Introduction to the Author" found in the *Dungkar Encyclopedia* and life narratives written by his former students located within his *Collected Works*.[83] The most comprehensive biography on Dungkar Lozang Trinlé to appear in English was written by Pema Bhum for *Latse Library Newsletter*.[84]

FIGURE 1.6 Dungkar Rinpoché

Illustration by Ngangwa Gyeltsen

Another biography written by his son, Dungkar Jigmé, offers a personal perspective on his family life.[85] Tenzin Gelek, a scholar and translator at the Latse Project, wrote a piece remembering his interactions with the scholar toward the end of his life.[86]

Unfortunately, the chronologies in these biographies do not always accord with one another. Some important dates provided in his son's biography are inconsistent with other sources, such as the year of his recognition as an incarnate lama. This brief overview of Dungkar Rinpoché's life takes these inconsistencies into consideration and aims to present an accurate chronology based on all of the information.

All sources agree that the child later recognized as Dungkar Rinpoché was born in 1927. According to Dungkar Rinpoché's son Jigmé, their family came from the village of Jomo (Jo mo) under the jurisdiction of Jomo County (Jomo rdzong) in the Nyingtri region of Tibet (Bod ljongs Nying khri sa khul). The prefecture is known in Chinese as Linzhi (林芝市) and is located in the southeast Tibetan Autonomous Region, near the border with Arunachal Pradesh.

The future Dungkar Rinpoché was given the name Dawa (Zla ba) shortly after his birth. His father was Tsering Wangdu (Tshe ring dbang 'dus) and his mother was Tashi Tsomo (bkra shis mtsho mo), the oldest of three sisters. It was said that on the day of his birth, it snowed and the trumpeting sound of a white conch shell (*dung dkar*) pervaded the entire village, which were taken as auspicious signs.[87] In the Iron Sheep year of 1931, he was recognized as the reincarnation (*yang srid*) of the seventh Dungkar incarnation lineage by the Thirteenth Dalai Lama.[88] He began learning to read aloud under his parents' care.[89] In 1935, he took the throne at Kongpo's Tashi Chöling Monastery (Bkra shis chos gling dgon) as the Eighth Dungkar incarnation. The famous Tibetan Géluk scholar Pabongka (Pha bong kha) gave him the Dharma name (*chos ming*) of Lozang Kelden Trinlé Gyatso (Blo bzang skal ldan 'phrin las rgya mtsho).

Dungkar Rinpoché then studied Tibetan language and religious texts with *ācārya* (*slob dpon*) Ngawang Yonten Gyatso (Ngag dbang yon tan rgya mtsho), a scholar specializing in monastic discipline texts (*vinaya*) at Kongpo's regional division of Sera-mé (Ser ra smad) monastic college. According to "A Brief Introduction to the Author" in the *Dungkar Encyclopedia*, he was a child prodigy. He memorized the entire monastic assembly recitations and over two hundred commentaries and the root texts of the so-called "Five Great Treatises" (*gzhung chen po lnga*), which are the five main topics of the Géluk scholastic tradition: Perfection of Wisdom, the Middle Way, Valid Cognition, Phenomenology, and Monastic Discipline.[90]

From the Fire Mouse year of 1936 until late 1945, he resided at Kongpo's regional division of Sera-mé Monastic College (*grwa tshang*) at Sera Monastery near Lhasa. There he studied with Geshé Ngawang Gendün (dge bshes gnyen chen po Ngag dbang dge 'dun) for ten years. At Losar ushering in the Fire Dog year (1946), he received the *geshé lharampa* title (*dge shes lha ram pa*) during the Great Prayer Festival in Lhasa.

Throughout most of the 1950s, he continued to practice Buddhism and received teachings from many of Tibet's Buddhist luminaries, but by the end of the decade he gave up his monastic vows. Soon after receiving the prestigious *geshé lharampa*, he resided at the Upper Tantric College (Rgyud stod grwa tshang) in Lhasa. He established a Dharma connection with Ganden Tri Rinpoché Lundrup Tsondru (Dga' ldan khri rin po che Lhun 'grub brtson 'gru) as a spiritual teacher. In the Iron Tiger year (1950), he received the position of second ranking Vajrayana master (*sngags rams pa Ang gnyis pa*). In 1954, he was appointed as disciplinarian (*dge bskos*) at the Upper Tantric College. During the Wood Sheep year (1955), he was active studying Tibetan Buddhism whenever the opportunity arose. He also established Dharma connections with high-ranking lamas such as Ling Rinpoché (Gling rin po che) and Trijang Rinpoché (Khri byang rin po che). In front of the venerable Khéwang Tsatrul Rinpoché (Mkhas dbang Tsha sprul rin po che), he received lessons on all aspects of *kāvya* (*snyan ngag*) and grammar (*sum rtags*). From the venerable Khéwang Nyemo Yeshe Chophel (Mkhas dbang Snye mo ye shes chos 'phel) he received instruction on several chapters of astrology.[91]

Around the same time in the mid-1950s, Dungkar Rinpoché also became involved with Chinese Communists. This came about five years after that of the other two polymaths—Mugé Samten and Tséten Zhabdrung. In 1956 he was appointed as the vice-director of Dak-kong (Dakpo and Kongpo) counties, the local branch of the State Administration for Religious Affairs. This office is responsible for both implementing the state's religion policies and enforcing official regulations as directed by the State Council and dictated through the United Front Work Department of the Party.

According to the biography by Pema Bhum, Dungkar Lozang Trinlé was one of sixteen *geshé* to serve as an examination debater when the Fourteenth Dalai Lama took his *geshé lharampa* examination in early 1959. In March 1959, Dungkar Rinpoché was teaching poetry and grammar in the Yarlung River Valley in Chonggye, so he didn't participate in the uprising following the Dalai Lama's exile into India. In that year, he was also appointed director (*las 'dzin*) of Tibet's Regional Division of the Buddhist Association of China.

While it remains unclear whether Dungkar Rinpoché chose to give up his monastic vows or was coerced into marrying at this time of upheaval in Central Tibet, according to two biographies he arrived in Beijing in 1960 with his first wife.[92] At this time Dungkar Rinpoché launched his teaching career that spanned four decades. In September 1960, at the behest of Zhou Enlai, he was recruited as a professor for the graduate program specializing in Tibetan studies (Bod yig zhib 'jug 'dzin grwa) within the Department of Ethnic-Nationalities Languages (Mi rigs skad yig tshan khag) at Minzu University of China, formerly called Central Nationalities Institute. For five years, he taught many courses on Tibetan grammar, poetics, history, and Buddhism.

Similar to Tséten Zhabdrung, he wrote a textbook-commentary on Tibetan poetics as part of the secular curriculum for Tibetan-language programs at universities in China. Copies of the 1957 print of Tséten Zhabdrung's treatise on *kāvya* still exist, but pre-Cultural Revolution publications of Dungkar Rinpoché's *Gateway to the Art of Literary Figures for Writing Poetry* did not survive that tumultuous time when many books were burned in public assemblies.

As a professor in Beijing in the early 1960s, Dungkar Rinpoché began collecting terms that were included in his most ambitious work, the encyclopedia that bears his name, the *Dungkar Encyclopedia*.[93] According to his autobiographical jottings in the *Dungkar Encyclopedia*'s "A Clear Mirror: A Chronology," he returned to Lhasa from Beijing in 1965.[94] This source also mentions that for several months, he was assigned to a work team (*las don ru khag*) for education (*slob gso chen po*) in Shigatse (Gshis rtse) and Gyantse (Rgyal rtse). This was part of the political movement known as the Socialist Education Campaign, which had started in 1962 and spread through Tibet between 1964 and 1966, whereby students and professors were tasked with promoting socialist thought.

Due to his social status, Dungkar Rinpoché was sentenced to undergo "reform through labor" (*ngal rtsol bsgyur bkod;* Ch. *láodòng gǎizào,* 劳动改造) from 1966 to 1973. He was assigned to the Second Neighborhood Committee in Lhasa's northern area of Khrin-kon chu (Ch. *Chéngguān qū,* 城关区).[95] Dungkar Jigmé recalled seeing his father "wearing a hat" in a public struggle session, shortly after the launch of the Cultural Revolution. He reported that after they had returned home, the hat inscribed with "annihilate bad people" (*mi ngan pa rtsa med du gtong*) was placed underneath the bed (*mal khri*).[96]

According to Tibetologist Heather Stoddard, who met frequently with Dungkar Rinpoché in Lhasa in the 1980s and early 1990s, he had told her that he was forced to work on roads at this time.[97] Although the Cultural Revolution was not over in 1973, after that, Dungkar Lozang Trinlé no longer had to do any hard labor. His erudition and political leanings made him a choice candidate for historical and cultural projects. For example, in 1974 he was put to work in the Tibetan Autonomous Region's (TAR) Archives and on the TAR Revolutionary Exhibition Hall (Bod rang skyong ljong gsar brje 'grems ston khang). In 1975 he was assigned, along with Mugé Samten, to assist Zhang Yisun's editorial team in Chengdu on the *Tibetan-Chinese Dictionary (Bod rgya tshig mdzod chen mo)*. In 1976, when he was placed at the TAR Cultural Relics Supervisory Office (Bod rang skyong ljong rig dngos bdag gnyer khang), he resided in a room at the Norbulingka, the former summer residence of the Dalai Lama in Lhasa.[98] Here, his son recalled, he was permitted to read whichever Tibetan book or *pe-cha* he wished, which he loved. This position gave him unfettered access to rare texts, which he used as sources for his many essays, such as one on the history of the Potala, the grand palace at the heart of Lhasa and former residence of the Dalai Lamas.

After Mao Zedong's death in 1976 and the official ending of the Cultural Revolution, he regained his earlier posts. He was also rehabilitated, and similar to Tséten Zhabdrung and Mugé Samten, received the State Council's special compensation fund. He then went on to hold numerous high-ranking positions for the rest of his life. He was appointed by the Tibetan Autonomous Region People's Government as honorary leader of the TAR's Academy of Social Science and as vice-director of the China Tibetology Research Center. He was reinstated in the Buddhist Association of China and served as a standing committee member of the Tibetan Autonomous Region's branch regional council; he was a Tibetan Autonomous Region representative committee member (srid gros U yon) for the fourth through sixth National Conferences (rgyal yongs srid gros). Due to his high political positions, he was the only one of the three scholars to travel abroad for international conferences.[99]

In 1978, Dungkar Rinpoché was invited back to Minzu University in Beijing. He was a professor there for the next seven years. In 1985, he returned to Lhasa to take up a professorial post at Tibet University (Bod ljongs slob grwa chen mo), where he remained until his retirement in 1996. He still traveled to Beijing during this time as vice-director of the China Tibetology Research Center.

In the course of Dungkar Rinpoché's professorial life, he guided the career of many famous students, including Döndrup Gyel (Don 'grub rgyal), regarded by many as the first modern Tibetan writer; the great Tibetologist Lhakpa Puntsok, who began his studies with Dungkar Lozang Trinlé in Beijing in the 1960s; the head of the Tibetology Research Center in Gansu and author of many

histories of Amdo, Drukthar ('Brug-thar); the eminent historian Chen Qingying (Khrin chen dbying); and many others.

Dungkar Rinpoché's son Jigmé remembered his father as a kind and compassionate person who had encouraged him to be a good person and reminded him
of the necessity of embracing humility. Dungkar Jigmé further observed that his
father diligently completed projects close to his heart: "He wrote essays and
books with great diligence and always encouraged me to be industrious in whatever I did."[100] Dungkar Lozang Trinlé's legacy lives on in his prodigious array of
Tibetan-language historical texts and important commentaries on religious subjects included in his *Collected Works*.

In chapter 4, I examine his controversial work *Merging of Religious and the
Secular in Tibet* (*Bod kyi chos srid zung 'brel skor bshad pa*), comparing the Tibetan
text with its Beijing-official English translation. Commissioned by the United
Front Work Department, it views the history of Tibet through a Marxist lens.
In this book, I do not look at many of Dungkar Rinpoché essays, including "An
Exposition of Religious Sects" (Grub mtha' rnam bshad), the abovementioned
"A Concise History of the Potala Palace and Lhasa's Jokhang Temple" (Pho
brang po ta la dang lha sa'i gtsug lag khang gi lo rgyus mdor bsdud), and "The
Development of Tibetan Education" (Bod kyi slob gso rig pa), among others.

Although mainly known as a secular university professor and Marxist
scholar, Dungkar Rinpoché bestowed some Dharma teachings in the mid-
1990s. His activities were not as widespread as those of Tséten Zhabdrung and
Mugé Samten, both of whom traveled extensively giving many empowerments,
teachings, and conferrals of ordination vows. Nonetheless, Dungkar Rinpoché
returned to his native Kongpo to resume his throne as an incarnate lama in
1992, according to Pema Bhum's biography and photos courtesy of Thubten
Trinlé (Thub bstan 'phrin las). Dungkar Rinpoché gave Buddhist teachings at
Tashi Chöling Monastery at that time, donning the traditional Géluk yellow
hat and wearing laymen's clothes.[101] On July 21, 1997, Dungkar Lozang Trinlé
passed away at the age of seventy-two in Los Angeles after battling cancer.
Obituaries appeared in English, such as those published by the UK's *Independent*[102] and Tibet Information Network.[103] On the twentieth anniversary of
the scholar's death, the College for Higher Tibetan Studies (CHTS) at Sarah
in India held a conference commemorating his contributions to Tibetan history and language.[104]

The biographical lives presented above provide an overview of how each
scholar was educated in the Géluk Buddhist scholastic tradition and applied
their trainings in very distinct ways to contribute to the revitalization of Tibetan
language, culture, history, and Buddhism in the post-Mao era.

REINVENTING THE "THREE POLYMATHS"

Now to return to my claim at the onset of this chapter that through the title of the "Three Polymaths," Tséten Zhabdrung, Mugé Samten, and Dungkar Rinpoché became representatives and symbols of both the survival and the continuance, i.e., "survivance," of Tibetan culture in China. Anishinaabe literary theorist Gerald Vizenor coined this term by combining "survival" and "continuance" in order to describe an active state of presence of Native American stories within the United States that renounces political domination and victimhood.[105] Although the three Tibetan scholars studied here were active in very different historical and political contexts than those addressed by Vizenor, the construct of "survivance" serves to emphasize the dynamic endurance of lived cultural traditions amid political and social oppression. I trace aspects of the discursive formation of the "Three Polymaths" title as signifying survivance.

In other words, I look at how this title became a cultural symbol in the context of twentieth-century Tibet. Ann Swidler's research queries how people use culture, appropriating some symbols and discarding others, in different situations:[106]

> Trying to understand how people selectively appropriate and use cultural meanings can lead to the ability to ask why in some situations cultural symbols lose their force or plausibility while in others they remain vibrant and persuasive; or why people sometimes invest beliefs, rituals, and symbols with ever increasing meaning, while at other times they live with great gaps between culture and experience.[107]

This line of inquiry inspired me to investigate how the "Three Polymaths" title became applied to these three scholars. The discursive interplay between "Three Polymaths" past and present shows how a fragmented historical record was transformed into a cogent narrative of Tibetan cultural survivance.

I now turn to writings by these three historians to investigate how each wrote about the first set of Three Polymaths of a millennium ago. It seems that Tséten Zhabdrung predominantly, and Mugé Samten to a lesser extent, transformed the historical Three Polymaths into cultural symbols of Tibetan survivance. Tséten Zhabdrung looks to Tibet's literary past to shape the symbolic value of the Three Polymaths in his local history on Dentik. Mugé Samten, in contrast, promotes the longevity of Tibetan Buddhist culture embellishing the story of Gongpa Rabsel to highlight how Tibetan epistemes survived persecution in the past. Dungkar Lozang Trinlé does not promote the symbolic value of the title in his writings on the historical Three Polymaths.

The Historical Three Polymaths

Unlike the well-documented social contexts, biographical information, and literary writings of the twentieth-century trio of scholars, scant historical evidence is extant on the first set of Three Polymaths (*mkhas pa mi gsum*).[108] Their names, Mar Shakyamuni (Dmar shākya mu ni), Yo Géjung (G.yo dge ba'i 'byung gnas), and Tsang Rabsel (Gtsang rab gsal), appear in Tibetan histories, such as *Butön's Religious History* (*Bu ston chos 'byung*) by Butön Rinchen Drub and *The Blue Annals* (*Deb ther sngon po*) by Go Lotsāwa Zhonnupel ('Gos lo tsā ba gzhon nu dpal, 1392–1481).[109] These texts provide their names and information on their roles in ordaining Gongpa Rabsel, who kept the lineage intact through further transmissions. However, many discrepancies exist in the historical record. Basic facts, such as when they lived and whether they actually were responsible for the lineage transmissions that led to the Buddhist renaissance in the eleventh century, remain unconfirmed.

The lack of a coherent historical record is due to the fact that the first set of Three Polymaths lived at a time when three major Asian empires were in decline. The Chinese Tang Dynasty crumbled from the 840s to its official collapse in 907. The Uighur state fell in 840, and the Tibetan empire tumbled around this time as well. Similar to the works of other Tibetologists, such as Petech (2005), Iwasaki (1993), Davidson (2005), and Stoddard (2004), Tséten Zhabdrung's writings reveal a deep concern for resolving discrepancies in the chronology of this period. His local history, *Zither of Meaningful Words: A Catalogue of Domé's Sacred Place: Dentik, the Crystal Mountain and Its Branch Monasteries* (*Mdo smad grub pa'i gnas chen dan tig shel gyi ri bo le lag dang bcas pa'i dkar chag don ldan ngag gyi rgyud mngas*), abbreviated here as *A Catalogue of Dentik Monastery*, attempted to clarify the long gap between the fall of the empire in the mid-ninth century and the Three Polymaths' ordination of Gongpa Rabsel in the tenth century by examining the chronology of key events, including the dates of Gongpa Rabsel's life, in various histories.

For example, according to the *Blue Annals*, Gongpa Rabsel was born in the Water Mouse year 892 in a village near Dentik, and in his forty-ninth year went to the mountain retreat to be ordained. He lived there for another thirty-five

FIGURE 1.7   Main assembly hall and stupa at Dentik, May 2008

Photograph by Nicole Willock

years and passed away in the Wood Hog year 975.[110] Tséten Zhabdrung's *A Catalogue of Dentik Monastery* follows a different chronology. He argues that the dates given in the *Blue Annals* are off by one full sixty-year cycle, and concludes that Gongpa Rabsel must have lived from 953 to 1035.[111] Although he pieced together a complex historical mosaic to make sense of this period, the great Tibetologist Luciano Petech observed, the lack of a unified empire meant that the historical narrative has never been standardized.[112] My goal is not to weigh in on this fragmented historical record but to examine how a certain historical trope on the survivance of Tibetan Buddhist culture in the tenth century came to take on new life in the twentieth century.

In addition to writing about early Tibetan historiography, Tséten Zhabdrung wrote about the past Three Polymaths in his autobiography. He directly and indirectly intertwines the historical story with the notion of Buddhist survival after a period of persecution under authoritarian rule and the importance of the ritual landscape of Dentik in that narrative, blurring past and present. His life experiences show how he connected the history of the Three Polymaths with the sacred space of Dentik. In the early 1920s Tséten Zhabdrung's teacher Geshé Ngawang Tsültrim (Ngag dbang tshul khrim) taught him about the activities of the Three Polymaths. His teacher had returned from Central Tibet to Dentik with many precious objects, including a *thangka* painting with the

Thirteenth Dalai Lama's handprints on its verso. Tséten Zhabdrung's autobiography, *Acoustic Ambrosia,* tells us:

> In the spring of that year [1921], when Dentik's *geshé lharampa* Ngawang Tsültrim brought many precious objects from Central Tibet to our monastery, I requested to have a good look at them. When I served tea to the honorable *lharampa,* I asked him about the so-called "Three Polymaths," who they were, etc. He told me, "They were Tsang Rabsel, Yo Géjung, and Mar Shakyamuni." I happily held this in my heart.[113]

Shortly after this event, Geshé Ngawang Tsültrim initiated the Anyé Lugyel Festival, during which these items are displayed.[114] All were visible when I attended in 2008. Miraculously the precious objects carried from Central Tibet in the 1920s survived the Maoist years at Dentik.

This was not the case for nearby monasteries and their sacred relics, such as Tséten Monastery (Tshe tan dgon), which was almost completely gutted in 1958.[115] A stanza in a longer poem within Tséten Zhabdrung's autobiography, translated in its entirety in chapter 3, serves as historical allusion. Tséten Zhabdrung laments the horrors of the leftist political pogroms of 1958 through historical references:

> Oh my!
> I am trembling with fear! The holy texts,
> volumes that dispel ignorance,
> are fastened to the soles of shoes, a nightmare
> never even conjured by Langdarma![116]

This documents the author's horror at witnessing or perhaps being forced to participate in sacrilegious acts like the stitching of sacred Buddhist scriptures onto cloth shoes. The reference to King Langdarma (803–842 or 863–906) was likely transparent for Tséten Zhabdrung's intended Tibetan audience. Even this anti-Buddhist king who oppressed Buddhists and sent the Three Polymaths out of Central Tibet could not have dreamed of the violent acts instigated by his suggested historical counterpart, Mao Zedong. Yet, despite suffering and persecution, all was not lost in tenth-century Tibet or a millennium later.

Tséten Zhabdrung was instrumental in reinstating the rituals of the Anyé Lugyel Festival when Dentik Monastery reopened after being shut down for over twenty years (ca. 1958–1980). The historical Three Polymaths were part of the ritual landscape at Dentik Monastery, as the cave where these ordinations took place was part of the pilgrimage circuit. They were thus remembered as key figures in the survival and continuance of Buddhism at a crucial point in historical time, safeguarding Buddhist scriptures and transmitting the Mūlasarvāstivāda-vinaya ordination, keeping the lineage intact. Recognizing the interconnectedness between history and ritual practice, Toni Huber suggests that Tibetan "né" (gnas) or "sacred spaces" differ from mundane spaces because of the relationship formed between exalted Buddhist masters, ritual objects, and specific geographic location:

> Tibetan pilgrimage has primarily to do with persons forming certain relationships with a gnas, which can also have a rten (object, building, human body, etc.) as its basis, and which is physically located on the earth's surface and is assigned a particular ontological value. It is about Tibetan conceptions of the inherent power of certain places in relation to a given ontology, and how people can become involved with and capitalize on that.[117]

Tséten Zhabdrung's Catalogue of Dentik Monastery claims that "Many superior beings—erudite scholars and accomplished practitioners, blessed these craggy cliffs."[118] The first section of this text is organized around the activities of three "superior beings." They are: Bodhisattva Arthasiddhi from the sūtra of the same name, who purportedly resided at Dentik;[119] Gongpa Rabsel, which includes the efforts of the historical Three Polymaths; and the Third Dalai Lama, Sonam Gyatso (Bsod rams rgya mtsho, 1543–1588).[120] Dentik became a power place because of their Dharma activities.

For Tséten Zhabdrung, authority and agency were fused in order to establish a place as sacred. Since his death, his reliquary stupa has been included in the ritual circumambulation route. The monastic community at Dentik weaved together various strands of Buddhist historiography, biography, and historical writings by this exalted master to continue ritual practice that imbues their geographic location with esoteric power. Because Tséten Zhabdrung was recognized as one of the main incarnate lamas of Dentik Monastery, the story of the first set of Three Polymaths held more meaning for him personally than for Mugé Samten and Dungkar Rinpoché.

Mugé Samten's A History of Traditional Fields of Learning similarly remembers the legacy of the historical Three Polymaths for the purposes of the present; however, it is not concerned with correcting a fractured Tibetan historiography or reviving rituals. Other than adopting the dates for Lachen Gongpa Rabsel (953–1035) proposed by Tséten Zhabdrung, his work reiterates the standard historical account in the *Blue Annals*.[121] In fact, Mugé Samten exaggerated his accomplishments, claiming that he studied all the traditional fields of learning or *rikné*: "Meanwhile a talented boy named Muzu Salwar [i.e, the future Lachen Gongpa Rabsel] was born in Tsongkha Dekham. As he grew older, he studied the traditional fields of learning such as the Tibetan language, grammar, and astrology and eventually became a learned man."[122] While Tibetan histories report that the Gongpa Rabsel studied texts such as the *vinaya* and *Abhidharma*, it is generally understood that traditional fields of learning or *rikné* were not introduced into Tibet until the thirteenth century with Sakya Pandita, so Mugé Samten's claim is anachronistic.

Dungkar Rinpoché only briefly mentions the names of the first set of Three Polymaths in his encyclopedia, alongside another set of three great scholars in the Nyingma tradition.[123] His other work studied here, the *Merging of Religious and Secular Rule in Tibet*, mentions Gongpa Rabsel's role in transmitting the *vinaya* to Lumé, whose four disciples are considered the "Four Pillars." These four men were responsible for founding monasteries in Central Tibet in the eleventh and early twelfth century.[124] Dungkar Rinpoché's focus is on the historical record, and he only tersely mentions the past Three Polymaths.

The Twentieth-Century Three Polymaths

The symbolic value of the "Three Polymaths" title as representing Tibetan cultural survivance seems to have gained traction in both religious and secular settings after the death of Tséten Zhabdrung, when monastic disciples at Dentik began to use it. At around the same time, the next generation of Tibetan intellectuals, those trained by one of the twentieth-century Three Polymaths at secular universities, intertwined the historical epithet with the agency of the modern teachers. Sometime thereafter, a new timeline of Tibetan Buddhist history, the "Era of Dharma's Rediffusion" (*yang-dar*), began. There is clear evidence for this from the early 2000s, but it seems that the notion of the *yang-dar* era began to circulate earlier. By 2017 a published article merged the Three Polymaths with a new Tibetan Buddhist historiography, emphasizing the significance of the survival of Tibetan culture on its own terms.

In the 1980s, the relative political and cultural liberalization under the new leadership of Deng Xiaoping brought acknowledgment of the utter decimation of all aspects of Tibetan traditional life and also led to a renaissance of Tibetan culture within China. Writings by Tséten Zhabdrung, Mugé Samten, and Dungkar Rinpoché were published, Dentik Monastery reopened, the Anyé Lugyel Festival restarted, and universities opened their doors for young Tibetans to study their history. It was at this time that the past and present Three Polymaths were symbolically connected.

The young Tibetan intellectuals of the 1980s drew upon their knowledge of Tibetan history, adapting this title to suit the needs of the day. The twentieth-century Three Polymaths—Tséten Zhabdrung, Mugé Samten, and Dungkar Rinpoché—and several other important scholars whose lives are not studied here, including Nyenshul Khyenrab Ösel (Nyan shul mkhyen rab 'od gsal) and Zenkar Rinpoché (Gzan dkar sprul sku), became mentors and teachers to the next generation of Tibetan scholars.

Pema Bhum (Pad ma 'bum), cofounder of the Latse Project and director of Latse Contemporary Tibetan Cultural Library in New York until it closed in June 2020, reflected, "Many Tibetan intellectuals consider that the impact of the destruction of Tibetan culture during the Cultural Revolution was the same as that of Langdarma's destruction of Buddhism in Tibet some thousand years earlier, and thus the achievements of the three modern scholars can be compared to those of the three earlier scholars."[125] The cultural framework in Pema Bhum's assessment mirrors that expressed in the "Tibet's Three Polymaths of the *Yangdar* Era" article cited at the beginning of this chapter. The history of the epithet and the biographical lives of Tséten Zhabdrung, Dungkar Lozang Trinlé, and Mugé Samten merge naturally. In this discursive space, the disempowering Chinese-state narratives of Tibet as "feudal" or "backward" are silenced while narratives of Tibetan history are brought to the fore to emphasize cultural survivance.[126]

The trio of twentieth-century scholars earned the epithet of *khé-pa mi-sum* (*mkhas pa mi gsum*) or "Three Polymaths" because of their contributions to Tibetan studies as an academic discipline in China and their equal influence in the revival of Géluk Buddhist monastic life in the 1980s for Tséten Zhabdrung, and into the 1990s for Mugé Samten and Dungkar Rinpoché. In one sense, they were literally *khé-pa* or "polymaths," an honorific designation for someone who demonstrated mastery of the comprehensive system of Buddhist education. However, this title gained further symbolic meaning because these three men took up the charge of transmitting Buddhist knowledge after a period of tyranny and destruction, similar to their historical predecessors. In the early 1980s, the reinstatement of the ritual practices at Dentik Monastery occurred at around the same time as the symbolic title "Three Polymaths" began to circulate among the educated secular students at universities. From that point onward, the Three Polymaths became cultural symbols representing survivance, dynamic efforts to keep Tibetan Buddhist culture alive despite political oppression.

When exactly the notion of the *yang-dar*, "Era of the Dharma's Rediffusion," emerged is unclear. I found no evidence of this term in any of the writings by Tséten Zhabdrung, Mugé Samten, Dungkar Rinpoché, or the Tenth Panchen Lama that I was able to read. When I conducted my fieldwork and interviewed Tibetan scholars in 2008 and 2015, the notion of *yang-dar* frequently emerged in conversations about the Three Polymaths, especially Tséten Zhabdrung. According to some intellectuals, the "Later Diffusion" ended in 1959 with the Dalai Lama's exile to India and the "Rediffusion" (*yang-dar*) began in the late 1970s–early 1980s.[127] *Yang-dar* signifies the placement of Tibetan Buddhism at the center of the historiographical narrative.

Ethnographic research conducted by Charlene Makley between 2007 and 2011 confirms that the notion of *yang-dar* circulated in eastern Tibet. In her study it was particularly associated with the Panchen Lama's activities at Rongbo Monastery in Repgong, not with any of the Three Polymaths. Translating *yang-dar* as "Buddhist restoration," Makley drew attention to how Tibetans engaged in processes of "counterdevelopment" in the post-Mao era, whereby the contentious "battle for fortune" relied on much older notions to create specifically Tibetan modernities.[128] In the rebuilding and improvements undertaken at the large complex of Rongbo Monastery in Qinghai Province, Makley highlighted the Panchen Lama's role in "advocating *yang dar* (Buddhist restoration) as a new era of Tibetan Buddhist counter-development embedded in modern time spaces."[129] Although it remains unclear whether the term *yang-dar* was actually used by the Panchen Lama in his speeches,[130] it is evident that Makley's interlocutors viewed the activities of the Panchen Lama as the signifier for *yang-dar*. In many ways this dovetails with the evidence that I found. It was the next generation that assigned agency to incarnate lamas (*trulku* or *tülku*), such as Panchen Lama, Tséten Zhabdrung, or Dungkar Rinpoché, for the rediffusion of the Dharma. As Makley pointed out, the idea of *yang-dar* is not a matter of "revival." The stakes are much higher. Historiography no longer belongs to the nation-state, but to Tibetan Buddhist history makers.

In the complex matrix of diverse modernities in China, the Three Polymaths of the twentieth century—Tséten Zhabdrung, Mugé Samten, and Dungkar Rinpoché—have become symbols within Tibetan Buddhist cultural framings of history and time. Tséten Zhabdrung's close association with Dentik Monastery and the history of the original Three Polymaths along with its potent theme of Buddhist survivance laid the groundwork for the selective appropriation of this cultural symbol in the post-Mao era. As we will see in the subsequent chapters, Tséten Zhabdrung and Mugé Samten interweave their life stories, Tibetan history, Buddhist values, religious practices, and Tibetan identity to inspire the next generation of future secular scholars and Buddhist practitioners. Dungkar Rinpoché, however, seems to have been less concerned with promoting religious-cultural symbols and concentrated his efforts on how to reformulate Tibetan history for secular academic purposes in the post-Mao era.

2

"Telling What Happened"

Buddhist Recollections of the 1950s

s I reflect on my journeys from Qinghai's provincial capital of Xining to Tséten Zhabdrung's ancestral home, I recall a passage from *Acoustic Ambrosia* in which the author describes his birth-place in a way that sharply contrasts with my travel experiences. I remember stopping at a famous cave, Martsang Drak, about thirty miles outside of Xining, marked by a Maitreya Buddha carved into the cliff. The name "Mar-tsang" refers to two of the three historical polymaths, and according to one Géluk scholar, Tukwan Lozang Chokyi Nyima (1727–1802), Lachen Gongpa Rabsel's reliquary stupa rested inside the cave complex.[1] I didn't observe any other Tibetan Buddhist sites along this route. As I approached Tséten Zhabdrung's hometown of Yadzi (Ch. Jinshi), Middle Eastern-style minarets towered above the skyline and diminished the static presence of functional white-tiled build-ings and concrete apartment blocks that are so familiar in any Chinese cityscape. The mosques belong mainly to the Salar people, a Turkic ethnic minority of China, after whom the Xunhua Salar Autonomous County is named.

In contrast to my observations, Tséten Zhabdrung autobiographically imbued this landscape, especially his hometown in the Xunhua Salar Autono-mous County, with Buddhist sanctity. Due to the natural geography of moun-tains and waterways, Yadzi on the southern shore of the Ma Chu,[2] the Tibetan tributary of the Yellow River, is an important stopping point on this thorough-fare. A Tibetan Buddhist scholar called Shangtön Tenpa Gyatso (1825–1897) poetically lamented that the area along this route was, from a Buddhist perspec-tive, a spiritual wasteland. Shangtön was on his way from his monastery, Labrang Tashikyil, in the east, now in Gansu Province, to visit his teacher at Gönlung

Monastery, north of Xining. Setting up a literary debate, Tséten Zhabdrung cites Shangtön's verse:[3]

> The road from Labrang [Tashikyil] to the north, arduous as the narrow *bardo* pass.
> Arid plains devoid of water and grass; many barbarian towns en route.
> Like *torma*, mountains red of blood and flesh; people as poor as hungry ghosts.
> A hell realm compared to my birthplace of Tsézhung with its verdant fields.[4]

Building on Shangtön's claim that traveling this road was as difficult as traversing the *bardo*, the liminal state between death and rebirth, Tséten Zhabdrung creates a literary straw man in order to argue with the long deceased author about the sanctity of his birthplace.

In his retort, Tséten Zhabdrung transforms Shangtön's barren land into a Buddhist holy mountain and adds a verse to counter the insult in the second couplet:

> Mountains appearing devoid of verdant pasture,
> resemble, to me, a relative of Jalandhara,[5]
> a natural coral in color, without applied tempera,
> radiates yogic inner heat of *tummo*: a sacred site.
>
> From outside, the town appears poor to the eye,
> but inside, it's as rich as the nagas' king's.
> Food and clothing appear meager, but real fortune
> lies in the search for the path to awakening![6]

This literary exchange exemplifies how Tibetan poets philosophically sparred with one another. Tséten Zhabdrung builds on Shangtön's verse to put forth his own argument.

For Tséten Zhabdrung, the illusion of poverty dissipates when true wealth is recognized. Real fortune comes with the opportunity to practice "the path to awakening," i.e., a Buddhist path. Tséten Zhabdrung challenges Shangtön because Yadzi was where he was born and according to Buddhist ontology, the possibility for awakening requires taking a human birth.

Similar to how an analysis of this interchange illuminates Buddhist cultural values and Tibetan discursive practices, this chapter examines how Tséten

Zhabdrung and Mugé Samten adapt traditional literary genres, craft opening verses, and deftly weave wordplay in their life narratives. The third polymath, Dungkar Lozang Trinlé, did not write an autobiography, so his writings are not studied in this chapter nor the next. Select passages from their autobiographies, *Acoustic Ambrosia* and *Luminous Mirror,* completed in 1978 and 1993 respectively, take the 1950s as a formative period and uphold specific Buddhist values. Sections from Mugé Samten's *Luminous Mirror* and Tséten Zhabdrung's *Acoustic Ambrosia* remember the decade in which momentous life-altering political policies were implemented. Comparisons between their autobiographical accounts and "A *Monlam* to Mao," a literary artifact dated to 1954, serve to highlight discursive continuities between the 1950s and the 1980s despite political changes..

In interesting parallels, other scholars see connections between the 1950s and the post-Mao era. Lama Jabb draws attention to the historical endurance of style, language, and metrics in the development of modern Tibetan literature.[7] Lauran Hartley shows that "the projects of the 1950s maintained a critical thread of continuity from the pre-Communist era, laying the foundation for later literary negotiation."[8] Perry Link observes strong connections between literary establishments in Chinese urban scenes of the 1950s and their resurgence in the late 1970s and the 1980s after the breakdown of the Chinese socialist literary system during the Cultural Revolution era.[9] Matthew Akester draws connections between the 1950s and 1980s in his identification of three phases of Communist rule in Tibet: Liberal, 1950–1958; Maoist, 1959–1979; and Liberal, 1980–1989.[10] In this chronology, these two decades are connected by a liberal political atmosphere. The connections that Mugé Samten and Tséten Zhabdrung forge between the 1950s and the post-Mao era in their autobiographies emphasize literary continuity and prioritize the endurance of Tibetan Buddhist morals and societal values. Their writings are indicative of the relatively liberal political atmosphere during Deng Xiaoping's governance, but also signal how much political influence Géluk leaders had lost since the first decade of the PRC.

One indicator of this change in political status materialized when I discovered a historical photo at Tséten Zhabdrung's familial residence and birthplace in Yadzi. After I had passed through the outer gate of the family home, one of Tséten Zhabdrung's nephews guided me to the late master's former quarters, preserved like a museum. I approached the dais in the middle of the main room and paid my respects by placing a *katag* alongside other white silk scarves in front of Tséten Zhabdrung's photo, which was positioned carefully on the throne's yellow brocade. I looked to the wall above to see photos of his main teachers, Jigmé Damchö Gyatso and Giteng Rinpoché Lozang Pelden. As I circumambulated the rooms among Buddhist statues, a beautiful portrait of Tséten Zhabdrung's mother, and other family photos, I noticed a black-and-white photo that stopped me in my tracks.

Faces of Chinese dignitaries popped out as I stepped closer. To my amazement, I recognized many of the former political leaders of China seated in the middle of the front row: Zhou Enlai, Mao Zedong, and Deng Xiaoping, who was flanked by the Buddhist Marxist lama, Geshé Sherab Gyatso, on the one side, and Tséten Zhabdrung on the other. I couldn't identify many others in the undated photo taken in front of a brick building with curved terracotta eaves. Tséten Zhabdrung's nephew was unaware of the photo's provenance other than

FIGURE 2.1 Historical photo, circa 1954: front row middle from left to right: Zhou Enlai, Mao Zedong, unidentified figure, Geshé Sherab Gyatso, Deng Xiaoping, Tséten Zhabdrung, unidentified figures

Courtesy of Jigmé Chöpak

that it was definitely taken in Beijing during the 1950s. He thought it likely that it was honoring those who participated in the translation of the PRC Constitution in 1954. Awed to be in the private residence of Tséten Zhabdrung, I asked the family for permission to take photographs of the space, including a snapshot of the photo of Tséten Zhabdrung with the highest echelon of Chinese political dignitaries.

Analogous to how a photo can remind us of a forgotten historical moment, I bring an important historical literary piece—the Fourteenth Dalai Lama's "*Monlam* to Mao"—into conversation with the autobiographical texts in order to spotlight the political changes between the 1950s and the post-1976 era, while also highlighting the continuity of Tibetan discursive practices between the same time periods. The two autobiographies and the Dalai Lama's prayer-poem impart literary qualities emblematic of Tibet's biographical culture.[11] Internal textual evidence and its publication in a periodical of the Buddhist Association of China dated to 1954 indicate that the Dalai Lama's "*Monlam* to Mao" expressed hopes and aspirations for state protection of Buddhist institutions. As I detail later in this chapter, bringing these pieces together provides insight into the significance of remembering the 1950s with a focus on Buddhist ethical values. "*Monlam* to Mao" reminds us that during the 1950s, Géluk hierarchs, including the autobiographers themselves, were involved in state-building projects because they believed that the newly founded People's Republic of China would uphold the promise of protecting Tibetan Buddhist institutions. The autobiographers rekindle this potential in a new and cautious way in the 1980s while adapting and continuing well-established discursive practices through their life writings. By examining Tséten Zhabdrung's and Mugé Samten's autobiographies through a literary-historical lens, I aim to contextualize their life writings in light of Tibet's literary culture and to add new perspectives on Sino-Tibetan relations. I begin by looking at how these two polymaths adapt established literary precedents to write their life stories.

LIFE WRITING GENRES IN TIBET

Both autobiographers, Mugé Samten and Tséten Zhabdrung, shift the historical spotlight away from the nation-state to focus their life narratives on Buddhist ethical values and Tibetan epistemes. Each author only vaguely mentions his involvement in major state-building projects that defined Sino-Tibetan relations in the People's Republic of China during its first decade, such as the translation of the major Sino-Tibetan treaty, the Seventeen Point Agreement; the translation and promulgation of the 1954 Chinese Constitution; and the translation of Mao Zedong's works into Tibetan.

Their autobiographies, similar to Tséten Zhabdrung's literary sparring with Shangtön, are located within a sphere of Tibetan Buddhist knowledge production, discursive practices, and ethical values on which this work seeks to shed light. Literary theorist Paul John Eakin encourages us "to approach autobiography in the spirit of a cultural anthropologist, *asking what such texts can teach us about the ways in which individuals in a particular culture experience their sense of being 'I'*—and, in some instructive cases that prove the rule, their sense of not being an 'I.'"[12] Inspired by this theoretical insight, in my analysis of these autobiographies, I ask: What cultural resources did Mugé Samten and Tséten Zhabdrung draw upon to write about their lives? What was at stake in writing about the past in the way that they did? Examining the discursive practices as well as religious and ethical values of these two Tibetan Buddhist monks, I focus on how they self-reflexively chose a Tibetan autobiographical genre that honored Tibet's life writing tradition and simultaneously adapted normative life writing practices due to political changes.[13]

"Telling What Happened"

Tséten Zhabdrung and Mugé Samten draw upon the emic literary category "telling what happened" (*byung ba brjod pa*) in order to place their autobiographies near to, but also distinct from other types of life writing that venerate Buddhist luminaries for religious purposes. They distinguish "telling what happened" from two other genres in particular: *namtar* and *tok-jö* (Skt.: *avadāna*). *Namtar* abbreviates *nampar tarpa* (*rnam par thar pa*; Skt.: *vimokśa*)[14] and can be translated as "complete liberation." This term refers to biographies of Tibetan luminaries and is sometimes translated as "hagiography," i.e., stories of holy people.[15] *Tok-jö* (*rtogs brjod*) or "realization story" is more commonly known by its Sanskrit iteration, *avadāna*, and frequently refers to Buddhist canonical literature that tells the "past lives of Bodhisattva."[16] Tibetan scholar Gedun Rabsal notes that the term *tok-jö* (*rtogs pa brjod pa*) appears as early as the late eighth to early ninth century in Zhang Yeshé Dé's translation of *The Story of Sūkarika* (*Phag mo'i rtogs pa brjod pa*; Skt.: *Sūkarika-avadāna-namasūtra*).[17] By the eighteenth century, *avadāna* in the Tibetan context developed so as to become synonymous with *namtar*; however, as Gedun Rabsal explains, *namtar* tend to mix prose and verse, whereas *avadāna* generally are written in verse, although this is not a hard rule. A prime example of *tok-jö* in verse is Janet Gyatso's translation of the secret autobiography of Nyingma Buddhist luminary Jigmé Lingpa (1729–1789).[18] Mugé Samten and Tséten Zhabdrung distance their writings from both *namtar* and *avadāna* by choosing a biographical form that is much rarer in Tibetan literary history—"telling what happened."

I suggest that their authorial choices can be viewed as exemplifying a kind of modernist reflexivity. Similar to Eakin's observation that "makers themselves, autobiographers are primed to recognize the constructed nature of the past,"[19] textual evidence suggests that Tséten Zhabdrung and Mugé Samten viewed their writings as a reflective performative recovery of the past for certain purposes. Their life stories are not only told to instruct their immediate monastic disciples, as expected of traditional Tibetan life writing. They position their texts within Tibetan discursive traditions while making subtle distinctions within those practices in order to emphasize Tibetan ethical values at a particular historical juncture. The importance of their subjective viewpoints for historical analysis is a point clearly articulated by Mugé Samten.

The strongest evidence that both Mugé Samten and Tséten Zhabdrung intentionally distinguish between the varying registers of Tibetan life writing comes from passages within their respective autobiographies. I highlight Mugé Samten's and Tséten Zhabdrung's use of the emic term "telling what happened," and interchange my own use of the term with "autobiography."[20] In referring to their life writings as "autobiographies," I follow Philippe Lejeune's "Autobiographical Pact," which distinguishes autobiography from novel based on an understanding among the author, reader, and publisher that the authorial signature and the narrator are the same person, whose life is situated in time and place.[21] The texts by Mugé Samten and Tséten Zhabdrung fit this description.

Tséten Zhabdrung's opening poem in his autobiography, *Acoustic Ambrosia*, highlights the usage of the literary descriptor "telling what happened." Two of the thirteen stanzas (the seventh and eighth) indicate how the author makes a case for distinguishing between genre types. The opening verse, translated in its entirety here, repeats "telling what happened" thrice, thereby underscoring the author's literary choice:

> To the great Buddha Shākyamuni,
>   who knew what to accept and what to discard,
>   and instructed with the power of compassion,
>   I bow a hundred times by faith's three doors.

A remedy: equal heaps of the doctrine,
antidote to eighty-four thousand *kleshas*,
in the Holy Buddhist Jewels, the revered
Kanjur, Tenjur and their commentaries.

A plane of respect for monks assembled, wearing
belts of the *pong-dun* vow,[22] a supreme group
with a wealth of knowledge, mastery of the baskets
of Sūtra, Vinaya, and Abhidharma.

To him, who protects the Three Jewels assembled,
whose mere recollection grants prosperity
in this life and the next, to that glorious guru,
bearer of Dharmic kindness on earth, I bow.

My students of pure faith and vows strike
my eardrum with paddles of determination.
I couldn't bear it, so from my throat's citadel
roar a hundred sounds to **tell what happened**.

The defining feature of everyday people
is their lack of oral teachings and realizations,
performing joys and sufferings on the electric stages
of *samsara*—a waste of ink and paper.

As unexalted as a clod of *samsaric* mud,
so unworthy of a *namtar*.
I am as realized as a rabbit is horned,
so how can this be a realization story, an *avadāna*?

I cannot claim "to have nothing to say,"
nor will I pretend to have much to expound.
Instead, I will express my own life genuinely,
and label this writing as **"telling what happened."**

Taking Buddhist teachings as a whole,
it is near impossible to leave family behind,
to take vows, prostrate at the feet of a friend
of the Mahāyāna, to learn the complete Dharma.

It is said that "Sentient beings sometimes come
into good merit and wisdom; yet as rarely
achieve enlightenment with Buddha's blessings
as a thunderbolt unveils night-dark clouds."

But this breathtaking image strikes me as
completely unsuitable for my life.
And yet, I can't deny there's no one else
quite like me in all of my hometown.

I am alone, afloat in the Ocean of Dharma,
drifting in the emptied boat of study,
pondering my renunciant's life. How rare now,
when scholars are fixed on materialism!

So, wearing on my face a mask
thick with all of these reasons, I shout forth,
holding back nothing, to all my students
this string of words to **tell what happened.**[23]

    This verse makes clear distinctions among three categories of life writing in the Tibetan context: *namtar*, *avadāna*, and "telling what happened." The author clearly labels his writing (*rtsom*) as the latter, using repetition for emphasis. However, in what ways does this distinction matter? Is it in name only?

    In analyzing this choice, I suggest that drawing attention to these differences signifies the author's move to both ground his life writing within the continuity of Tibetan discursive traditions and recognize the societal changes that have altered these practices. This creative refashioning of Tibetan discursive traditions in the "era of Dharma's rediffusion," i.e., "the *yang-dar* era," is emblematic of the significance of the Three Polymaths' contributions more generally.

    The authors distinguish between registers of life writing in the Tibetan context in order to show the survivance of Tibetan discursive traditions and to recognize political change. On one hand, both Tséten Zhabdrung and Mugé Samten uphold cultural norms regarding expected levels of diffidence when positioning their works within the Tibetan literary tradition. On the other hand, their authorial choices indicate a type of self-reflexivity beyond that of the normative parameters of life writing in Tibet, i.e., as a means for a devotee to

venerate the guru-protagonist on the Buddhist path. As will become clear, Tséten Zhabdrung and Mugé Samten self-reflectively observe the role of the life
writing project as socially constructed in making their respective authorial deci-
sions, and Mugé Samten also stakes a claim that his subjective perspective holds
historical value.

In many ways, Tséten Zhabdrung's opening poem exemplifies expected
cultural norms for the Tibetan life writing project. Following the normative
patterns of "'auspicious words'" (*shis brjod*) that contain poetical writings of
eulogy and homage,[24] *Acoustic Ambrosia* opens with four stanzas praising each
of the Four Jewels of Tibetan Buddhism respectively: the Buddha, the Dharma
(Teachings), the Sangha (the community), and the Guru. The fifth stanza
illustrates another expected literary trope in the Tibetan context—the
request. The pact between Tibetan monastic authors and their devotee-readers
with "paddles of determination" relies on a request to write an autobiography,[25]
similar to how a disciple will entreat a guru to give a particular teaching or
empowerment.

In the sixth, seventh, and eighth stanzas of the opening poem, the tone shifts
away from the normative eulogy to an authorial reflection that no longer fits
neatly within a typical praise poem. While the seventh stanza meets one of the
well-identified cultural expectations of Tibetan life writings—that of humility—it also does something new by bringing attention to different categories of
life writing. Janet Gyatso observes that "Due to powerful constraints in Tibetan
linguistic convention on how one should talk about oneself, [autobiography]
typically exhibits a studied diffidence,"[26] and Tséten Zhabdrung humbly dis-
avows his spiritual accomplishments. However, he also does so in a way that
makes comparisons between his story and other life writing genres, *namtar* and
avadāna:

> As unexalted as a clod of *samsaric* mud,
> so unworthy of a *namtar*.
> I am as realized as a rabbit is horned,
> so how can this be a realization story, an *avadāna*?

He claims that his life is not worthy of the praise of *namtar* but mired in samsara. Tséten Zhabdrung stresses the impossibility of his spiritual realization,
similar to the unlikelihood of a horned rabbit. This expresses humility by
rebuffing his religious accomplishments, but it also serves to highlight varying
registers of Tibetan life writing in a new way.

The purpose of these comparisons is made more overt in the following stanza, when the author both cites the Great Fifth Dalai Lama in his claim to "have nothing to say" and also labels or "fastens" (*gdags*) his writing (*rtsom*) to the genre of "telling what happened":

> I cannot claim "to have nothing to say,"
> nor will I pretend to have much to expound.
> Instead, I will express my own life genuinely,
> and label this writing as *"telling what happened."*[27]

With an anticipated diffident register, Tséten Zhabdrung cleverly distinguishes between three forms of Tibetan life writing—complete liberation or *namtar*, the realization story or *avadāna*, and "telling what happened" (*jungwa jöpa*). He claims the latter as the most suitable form for his own work. This seems to highlight the type of content the reader should expect.

In Tibetan literary theory, "telling what happened" can be considered as "a base" (*khyad gzhi*), the Tibetan term for "genre" in this context. Tibetan literary theorist and scholar Pema Bhum explains:

> I would suggest there are two components [to Tibetan literary titles]: a "base" (*khyad gzhi*) and "attributes" (*khyad chos*). For example, in the case of the Fifth Dalai Lama's *Annals: Song of the Queen of Spring* (*Deb ther dpyid kyi rgyal mo'i glu dbyangs*), "Annals" (*deb ther*) is the base, "*Song of the Queen of Spring*" (*dpyid kyi rgyal mo'i glu dbyangs*) the attributes. [. . .] The base component shows the type of contents of the literary work; the attributes component indicates, for the most part, how the contents of the work, and its mode of expression, will benefit the reader.[28]

Pema Bhum's analysis demonstrates how Tibetan literary theorists understand the functions of titles in the Tibetan context. The "genre" or "base" indicates the type of contents expected of a literary work. Titles can be applied by later editors, but this was not the case for the autobiographies by Tséten Zhabdrung and Mugé Samten. Their innovative move to use this genre or "base" designation to indicate how they view the content of their texts becomes clear when we look at the historical usage of this term.

Only a few pre-1950 Tibetan autobiographical works contain the genre component "telling what happened." For example, in the Tibetan Library of Works and Archives Catalogue on historical biographies (1983), 621 biographical works have *namtar* in the title, but only two are labeled as "telling what happened."[29] These two texts are also self-narrated autobiographies. One was written by the great Buddhist polymath of the nonsectarian or *rimé* movement in eastern Tibet, Jamgön Kongtrul Thaye (1813–1899).[30] The other, by Dokhar Tsering Wangyel (1697–1763), is considered the first Tibetan autobiography by a layperson. This text is commonly known as *Avadāna of a Cabinet Minister* (*Bka' blon rtogs brjod*); however, as Lauran Hartley has pointed out, that title is not found in the text; the base component is "telling what happened."[31] The rarity of this term in the tradition of life writing shows how Mugé Samten and Tséten Zhabdrung mined historical genres in order to position the content of their self-penned texts.

Similar to how jazz musicians play and improvise off of one another, these authors display their talents in an interplay between literary tradition and innovation that celebrates registers of life writing. This is significant to our understanding because it indicates how self-consciously they positioned their works within Tibetan literary discourse. Adapting the genre designation from autobiographical writings by the great luminaries Jamgön Kongtrul Thaye and Dokhar Tsering Wangyel can be viewed an expression of confidence. This then might be viewed as uncharacteristic of life writing that shows "a studied diffidence."[32] This type of confidence is also exhibited in the sixth stanza of Tséten Zhabdrung's opening poem, in which the author sets his own life writing apart from the "joys and sufferings on electric stages." Such stories merely repeat the endless cycle of birth, death, and rebirth in samsara, and therefore are not worth "ink and paper." This shows his confidence in sharing his unique story. This idea is reiterated throughout the last stanzas of the opening poem and summed up with the phrase, "there is no one else quite like me in my hometown."

On the other hand, the very fact that both Tséten Zhabdrung and Mugé Samten label their works as "telling what happened" shows a certain level of diffidence, albeit on an elite literary spectrum. After all, this genre is not on the same level as *namtar* or *avadāna* (*rtogs brjod*). The latter genre title can be found in one of Tibet's most celebrated life writings, the Fifth Dalai Lama's autobiography: *A Fine Silken Dress: Writing in the Style of Avadāna, the Illusive Play of Zahor Bande Ngawang Lozang Gyatso* (*Za hor gyi ban dhe ngag dbang blo bzang rgya mtsho'i 'di snang 'khrul ba'i rol rtsed rtogs brjod kyi tshul du bkod pa dukūla'i gos bzang*). This long title has many attributes but only one genre component, the Tibetan translation of the Sanskrit term *avadāna* (*rtogs brjod*).[33] Both Mugé Samten and Tséten Zhabdrung cite from the Fifth Dalai

Lama's literary classic while also laying claim to their works as "telling what happened."

Tséten Zhabdrung and Mugé Samten draw upon the Fifth Dalai Lama's model of life writing, which involves explaining authorial intent. The Great Fifth clarifies various modes of life writing in the first chapter of his *Fine Silken Dress*, "Requests to Write an Autobiography." He distances himself from life writing in the mode of hagiography, in which telling the life story of a holy person exaggerates reality. In a model later adopted by both authors, the Great Fifth calls for a realistic approach based on his own memory of events. He asserts, "My activities are not secret, but are transparent, therefore like this drama between pleasure and pain; the three doors of body, speech, and mind are free of deceitful words that make claims when there is **nothing to say** [emphasis mine] or say nothing when there is something to say."[34] Tséten Zhabdrung cleverly plays with the short syncopated speech of the Fifth Dalai Lama's "nothing to say" (*med la yod ces*) in the first couplet of the seventh stanza, when he also claims "to have nothing to say" (*med la yod ces*). This is quickly followed by the labeling of his writing as "*telling what happened.*"[35] Mugé Samten likewise makes reference to the Great Fifth's classic.

Mugé Samten, like Tséten Zhabdrung, begins his autobiography with auspicious words of eulogy and homage. His opening stanzas reference not only the Fifth Dalai Lama's work but that of others as well, such as Yungtön Dorjé Pelzang (G.yung ston rdo rje dpal bzang, 1284–1365), a disciple of the Third Karmapa. Although Mugé Samten must have been influenced by Tséten Zhabdrung's work, he does not cite it. He poetically expresses his gratitude toward the Tenth Panchen Lama Chökyi Gyeltsen, the sponsor of the first edition of Tséten Zhabdrung's *Collected Works* (1987),[36] who encouraged Mugé Samten to write his autobiography without exaggeration.[37] At the end of his four-page preamble, Mugé Samten cites a section of the Great Fifth's autobiography and then discloses why he chose to label his text "telling what happened." In this way, he also writes with an expected level of humility and simultaneously breaches traditional literary expectations.

In a show of diffidence, Mugé Samten cites an introductory section of the Fifth Dalai Lama's *A Fine Silken Dress* (folio 5–11), a kind of apologia for writing about oneself. Samten Karmay's beautiful translation of the Great Fifth's autobiography does not include this passage because "it is embedded with clusters of words and expressions of poetic imagery that are almost impossible to render faithfully into English."[38] Mugé Samten cites a verse from this introductory apology for the arrogance in writing about "I":

The Omniscient Great Fifth penned:

Heaps of impure, exaggerated talk in a literary work
bring together word and meaning, poetically becoming a precious
ornament.
To express with babbling tongue, transforming the drama of falsehoods,
how, at the heart, is conceit not the result of this jewel?[39]

Here cultural expectations of writing about oneself are laid bare as conceit, whereas "falsehoods" can be interpreted as false perceptions of reality from a Buddhist perspective. I take this to refer to the drama of daily life, similar to the "joys and sufferings on electric stages" mentioned by Tséten Zhabdrung above. Mugé Samten, like Tséten Zhabdrung, recognizes the cultural expectation of diffidence and chooses to cite a verse that cuts to the chase on how boastful it is to write about oneself.

Mugé Samten's more interesting rhetorical move comes directly after this citation when he explains why he used the genre component in the title of his autobiography, *Luminous Mirror: The Author's Own Telling of What Happened* (*Rtsom pa po rang gi byung ba brjod pa rang sal A dar sha*).[40] Mugé Samten cleverly puns the two disyllabic words that make up the term "telling what happened." In a creative act of wordplay, he imbeds the syllables that make up this phrase within a sentence, as he claims, "I **told what happened** and the worldly changes of these times, so that later, when historical analysis is conducted, it **tells** something about the nature of samsara at an important time."[41] The bold type highlights the Tibetan syllables of the genre designation, "telling" (*brjod pa*) "what happened" (*byung ba*); in the original Tibetan these words do not require inflection. Mugé Samten clarifies that he views this work as important to the historical record. He predicts that when historical analysis (*lo rgyus brtag dpyad*) is conducted, his subjective perspective on these events will be considered important. He clarifies that he views his autobiography as not only edifying his monastic disciples but also as telling history (*lo rgyus*).

Both authors draw upon the expectations of autobiographies in the contemporary sense as accurate representations of historical facts from their own subjective viewpoints. They develop a historically attested emic literary category by comparing it with other like genres (*namtar* and *avadāna*). This indicates how their writings fit within the tradition of Tibetan life writing. They didn't invent a neologism or draw upon one from Chinese discourse but mined and advanced "telling what happened" from their literary heritage. At the same time, the application of this literary description to their own works signifies changes to the discursive practices associated with the writing of one's life in the Tibetan context. Their accounts lack hyperbolic stories of miracles or otherworldly spiritual feats. As Tséten Zhabdrung notes, his work is expressed genuinely, that is, without artifice and exaggeration. Mugé Samten makes explicit that he believes his subjective viewpoints are relevant to history. As autobiographers, they claim to have something to say for the sake of remembering the past in a certain way.

Before diving into what their texts say about the 1950s, an important distinction needs to be made between how the autobiographers themselves position their self-written texts as "telling what happened" and how readers of those same texts label them. These texts often are read as *namtar*, the honorific term for life writing in the Tibetan context. The revered status of the central religious figure of the life story influences relational reading practices of Tibetan biographical culture.

For example, Dawa Lodrö, a literary critic and head editor of *Spring Rain* (*Brang char*), the premier Tibetan-language literary magazine in China, was well aware that Tséten Zhabdrung's autobiography is labeled "telling what happened" because when I interviewed him, we discussed Tibetan biographical categories at length. He also extolled this work: "Tséten Zhabdrung's *namtar* was extraordinary" and an "important read."[42] In that conversation, Dawa Lodrö referred to Tséten Zhabdrung's autobiography as a *namtar* out of respect for his former teacher. This was often the case when I spoke to other scholars about Mugé Samten's and Tséten Zhabdrung's autobiographies. This example speaks to the relationship between author and reader as an important aspect of Tibetan biographical culture.[43]

The choice by Mugé Samten and Tséten Zhabdrung to pen their works as "telling what happened" is significant for several reasons. This designation positions the autobiographies within the discursive tradition of Tibetan Buddhist life writing while also distinguishing between *namtar* and *avadāna,* which was relevant to their historically situated lives. This indicates that the authors viewed their works as not only relevant for their disciples but also genuinely telling what happened for the purposes of later historical analysis. Mugé Samten and Tséten Zhabdrung turn to this genre in remembering the 1950s as a time when Buddhist values, such as spiritual friendships, were still honored. By telling what happened, they make sense of the sometimes conflicting forces that they had to negotiate.

Both self-narrated life stories frame the world from a Buddhist perspective. The narratives do not depict the founding of the People's Republic of China as a political rupture. There are no epistemic breaks, no looming authoritarian politicians, no army, and few references to technology. In short, little mention is made of modern nation-state formation despite their decisive roles in many state projects. Rather, their writings on this formative decade of the 1950s share common Buddhist cultural themes—the value of spiritual friendship and the altruistic vow to help all sentient beings as motivation for worldly work.

CULTURAL REPERTOIRES IN THEIR "TELLING WHAT HAPPENED"

In their telling of what happened, Mugé Samten and Tséten Zhabdrung highlight Tibetan epistemes, i.e., forms of knowledge, championed by her past philosophical and literary savants, such as the Fifth Dalai Lama, Ngawang Lozang Gyatso (Ngag dbang blo bzang rgya mtsho, 1617–1682), and Cangkya Rolpé Dorjé (Lcang skya rol pa'i rdo rje, 1716–1786) in order to espouse Buddhist ethical values. Throughout their autobiographies, the value of human life is a constantly recurring theme. This is not only a reminder of Buddhist truth but also a recognition of the devastating loss of lives during the Maoist years.[44]

Prevalent Buddhist themes that emerge from their writings on the 1950s include a reverence for spiritual friendship and an interpretation of political work in terms of benefiting all sentient beings. Mugé Samten highlights Géluk social hierarchies and uses the voices of his teachers to position his worldly work within Buddhist frameworks of benefiting others. Tséten Zhabdrung's autobiography promotes an ethos of spiritual friendship by rooting this value in the resolution of a historical conflict against the backdrop of the implementation of Land Reform in the mid-1950s and by praising one of his main teachers who had passed away in 1946. Their memories of the 1950s, first and foremost, edify their readership in Buddhist moral values that prevailed prior to the extreme secularist agenda of the Maoist years.[45]

Spiritual Friendship

In a parable from the *Samyutta Nikaya* (45.2) of the Pali Canon, Ānanda went to the Buddha and paid his respects by bowing. Then he sat to one side and commented, "This is half of the holy life, lord: having admirable people as friends, companions, and colleagues." The Buddha responded, "Don't say that, Ānanda. Having admirable people as friends, companions, and colleagues is actually the whole of the holy life. When a monk has admirable people as friends, companions, and colleagues, he can be expected to develop and pursue the noble eightfold path."[46] The importance of spiritual friendship on the Buddhist path[47] is also expounded upon in Nāgārjuna's *Letter to a Friend* (Sanskrit: *Suhṛllekha*), a text cited by both Mugé Samten and Tséten Zhabdrung in their respective life narratives:[48]

> The virtuous friend in whom to place your trust
> Has brought pure conduct to perfection
> So follow holy beings, many are they
> Who relied upon the Buddha and found peace.[49]

As these canonical texts indicate, spiritual friendships can be interpreted bidirectionally: as vertical, i.e., between teacher and disciple as indicated by the comportment between Buddha and Ānanda in the sutra, and as horizontal, i.e., between friends, companions on the path to enlightenment.[50]

In the Tibetan context, Patrul Rinpoché explains the bidirectionality of spiritual friendship while also stressing the role of the guru: "Ordinary people like us are, for the most part, easily influenced by the people and circumstances around us. That is why we should always follow a teacher, a spiritual friend."[51] The notion of a spiritual friend takes on particular importance for Géluk practitioners, as the term is identical with the title for the penultimate degree awarded after years of monastic study—the *geshé* degree (Tibetan: *dge ba'i bshes gnyen*).[52] The Tibetan term translates as "a friend" (*bshes gnyen*) who has "virtue" (*dge ba*) and carries with it great prestige. Therefore, in Tibet, spiritual friendship not only represents the bidirectional relationships between sangha members and between the student and her teacher but also involves Buddhist practice and education.

In bringing attention to the ethics of spiritual friendship as a theme in their autobiographical remembering of this formative period of Sino-Tibetan relations, Mugé Samten and Tséten Zhabdrung harken back to a time when the relationships (both vertical and horizontal) between sangha members were based on a social ordering of mutual respect. This is significant because they wrote their autobiographies on the heels of twenty years of societal chaos when all social relationships were turned upside down during class struggles associated with the leftist policies of Maoism. In the early 1980s, the few remaining Tibetan Buddhist leaders in China took steps to revive the ethical values in monastic communities. For example, when Khenpo Jigmé Phuntsok, the founder of Larung Gar (now one of the largest Tibetan Buddhist monastic communities in the world), began trying to revive Nyingma monastic traditions in the early 1980s, one of his first moves was to advocate for ethical reform and purification to correct many of the depravities among the monastic community.[53] Similar to Khenpo Jigmé Phuntsok's efforts at ethical reform, when Mugé Samten and Tséten Zhabdrung highlight the ethos of spiritual friendship, they not only tell their readers about their lives at a time when social relationships among Buddhist sangha members were built on established traditions but also model those relationships.

Mugé Samten's Luminous Mirror

Mugé Samten's entryway into the events of the 1950s is through his relationships with his teachers, his spiritual friends. *Luminous Mirror* tells how his monastic education served him in good stead when following his spiritual guide's advice to altruistically aid others. There is no explicit mention of the establishment of the People's Republic of China. Dates are provided according to the Tibetan lunar calendar. In some cases, the Western calendrical date follows in parentheses. The chronological organization of the autobiography allows a readership familiar with the historical timeline to be aware of various CCP campaigns, even though state policies or campaigns are rarely mentioned explicitly. The narrative focus remains on spiritual relationships, including the value of the monastic community within which he received his *geshé* degree. Mugé Samten frequently uses direct speech in *Luminous Mirror*, as if his autobiographical voice speaks through the mouthpieces of his teachers.

One of the most significant events in Mugé Samten's life was when he obtained his degree in Tibetan scholasticism called the *geshé dorampa*.[54] Before looking at how he discusses this achievement through his teacher's voice in *Luminous Mirror*, some background information is necessary to understand its importance. Georges Dreyfus's firsthand account of the Géluk scholastic system based on his knowledge and experience of obtaining the *geshé lharampa* degree, the first Westerner to do so, tells us that there are four types of *geshé* depending on the type of examination monastic candidates undergo.[55] Dreyfus also explains that the *lharampa* title is usually considered the most prestigious; however, this doesn't always equate with scholarly excellence.[56] One distinct feature of the traditional *geshé lharampa* degree in Tibet is that it was only awarded after a monk succeeded in a series of intense exams. The first one was at the summer residence of the Dalai Lama, the Norbulingka, with the Dalai Lama or his assistant as examiner; the second examination was at the home monastery, one of the "Three Seats" or main Géluk institutions of Ganden, Drepung, and Sera; and the penultimate exam was at the spiritual center of Tibet, the famous Jokhang Temple in central Lhasa, during the Great Prayer Festival that took place at Losar, the Tibetan New Year.[57] In contrast, a *do-ram* degree is given at a local monastery. *Do-ram* refers to the ritual space where the examination takes place, i.e., on the monastery's stone platform or *do (rdo)*. At Labrang Tashikyil, the largest monastery in Amdo, where Mugé Samten achieved the *geshé dorampa*, the exams and title were extremely competitive because of restrictions placed on how many degrees could be awarded in a year.

Yontan Gyatso's *Chronicle of Labrang Monastery* describes the *geshé do-ram* examination process as follows:

> One waits for years to take this exam. It is similar to the title of *lharampa* in Central Tibet (*yul dbus*), but it is also different. Particularly, it is necessary to defend each of the five esoteric texts for study on a different day: day one is Epistemology (*tshad ma; pramāṇa*); day two is Monastic Discipline (*'dul ba;* Sanskrit: *vinaya*); day three is Perfection of Wisdom (*phar phyin; prajñāpāramitā*); day four is Treasury of Philosophical Notions (*mngon chos mdzod;* Sanskrit: *abhidharmakośa*); and day five is the Doctrine of the Middle Way (*dbu ma; madhyamaka*). Only one out of all the candidates is awarded the title, and no others. Out of the class of *karampa* [*bka' rams pa*, scholars who passed the highest examination in a philosophical college], the majority are *rig-lung (rigs lung)*, and below that are the *dröleng (bgro gleng)*. This makes the awarding of the *geshé "do-ram"* title very special.[58]

In Lhasa, the *geshé* exams took place during the New Year festivities, whereas at Labrang Tashikyil the exams took place twice a year, with only one *geshé doram* awarded at the end of each exam period. This meant that only two *geshé do-ram* titles were awarded annually, making it extremely competitive. Exactly which of the two degrees is more competitive is hard to assess without clear data on how many monks sat for the *geshé* annually.

Thirty pages of Mugé Samten's autobiography detail his education, including how he passed the grueling exams outlined above.[59] His narrative does not use his own voice to detail how he was awarded the *geshé dorampa*. Rather, the autobiographer quotes words of praise that he received from his teacher, the Fifth Jamyang Zhépa, Lozang Jamyang Yéshé Tenpé Gyeltsen, who was the main incarnate lama of Labrang Tashikyil. After returning from Central Tibet, the Fifth Jamyang Zhépa opened a school attached to his own residential compound (*labrang*) with the vision of providing new educational opportunities and enhancing local culture. This modern school for young monks and Buddhist laypeople offered a variety of new subjects, including music, craft skills, science, and Chinese, as well as Tibetan language classes.[60] Mugé Samten was appointed as a Tibetan teacher in this school upon conferral of his *geshé dorampa* degree.

Through Jamyang Zhépa's voice, Mugé Samten refers to himself in the third person as "A-khu," a polite address for "monk" in Amdo dialect. Mugé Samten recounts: "The Venerable Omniscient One [i.e., Jamyang Zhépa] gave a speech at an assembly . . . where he said, 'Because of A-khu Samten's prodigious intellect in both Dharma and the secular world (*'jig rten*), I am appointing him a teacher [of my new school]. It is vital that you honor and respect him.'"[61] Making use of Jamyang Zhépa's voice to highlight his own achievements seems to draw on a rhetorical technique that Sarah Jacoby identified as autobiographical ventriloquy, whereby an author speaks her intentions, hopes, or thoughts through the mouthpiece of her guru.[62] In her study of the famous female Nyingma treasure revealer Sera Khandro's autobiography, Jacoby views this technique as means to deflect praise.[63] Mugé Samten exhibits a similar show of diffidence by citing Jamyang Zhépa's direct speech instead of writing in the first person about his success. This same technique also reinforces a sense of authority and legitimacy that underscores Mugé Samten's erudition. On one level, the rhetorical mode suggests a diffident way to show pride in the author's scholastic successes within culturally accepted norms. However, it also seems to have a different discursive purpose from that in the autobiography of the Nyingma treasure revealer: to highlight Géluk male hierarchies of transmission of knowledge.

This authority is reinforced when Mugé Samten's potential readership is addressed in the phrase, "It is vital that you honor and respect him." Through the mouthpiece of Jamyang Zhépa, Géluk authority and status are stressed. The reader is reminded that Mugé Samten is a *geshé dorampa,* an authentic holder of Géluk teachings, and that he received this recognition from one of the highest ranking Géluk hierarchs, the Fifth Jamyang Zhépa, shortly before the latter's death in 1947. This use of autobiographical ventriloquy also serves to admonish the reader to be respectful.

Through the voice of Jamyang Zhépa, Mugé Samten underscores the importance of respecting spiritual friends, here in the vertical sense of honoring one's teacher and lineage. This seems likely a way of reestablishing authority. Throughout the Maoist era, intellectuals, Buddhist and non-Buddhist, were often the target of verbal and physical abuse in so-called "struggle sessions," large public gatherings in which the victim was publicly humiliated.[64] Dungkar Rinpoché directly cites this passage from Mugé Samten's autobiography in his encyclopedia.[65] This similarly indicates the importance placed on reestablishing traditional hierarchies and social relationships in the post-Mao era. As *Luminous*

Mirror moves forward chronologically, a similar rhetorical technique is used when Mugé Samten explains his rationale for taking employment at PRC government agencies, such as the Ethnic Affairs Commission.

Mugé Samten's Altruistic Motivations for Worldly Work

The notion that worldly actions should benefit the teachings and sentient beings (*bstan 'gro don*) lies at the heart of Mahāyāna teachings. The core tenet of bodhicitta (*byang chub kyi sems*), or "the mind of awakening," involves altruistically serving all sentient beings on the path to realization. Cultivating and maintaining this mind of awakening are the subjects of core chapters of Tsongkhapa's *The Great Treatise on the Stages of Enlightenment* (*Lam rim chen mo*),[66] one of the most renowned works of Buddhist philosophy and a central text of the Géluk Buddhist tradition. The idea of committing to actions that benefit the Dharma and sentient beings can be interpreted in a number of different ways. One approach for Mugé Samten, characteristic of Buddhist modernists such as the Chinese Buddhist reformer Taixu (1890–1947), meant serving others by taking action in the world, not retreating from it.[67]

When Mugé Samten details his government positions, he gives his reasons for taking up civil duties within the Buddhist philosophical framework of bodhicitta. He explains that not only were these worldly activities within the monastery motivated by benefiting others, but so was his work for the nation-state. Mugé Samten held positions in government offices essential for this formative period of Sino-Tibetan relations. He was among the first Tibetans to be recruited to work at the State Ethnic Affairs Commission.[68] Other sources inform us that this organization was crucial for communication between Lhasa and Beijing and also played a decisive role in the ethnic classification project, literally defining the nation's fifty-six ethnic groups.[69] Standard histories on Sino-Tibetan relations scantly mention the role of Tibetan monastic scholars in these government offices, yet the fact that they staffed the State Ethnic Affairs Commission and other offices,[70] such as translation bureaus, is prominent in both Mugé Samten's and Tséten Zhabdrung's memories of the 1950s. Some historians might categorize such Tibetans as members of the "patriotic upper strata," a term for ethnic minority leaders who were integral to the CCP's policy of cooperation in the 1950s. However, Mugé Samten presents his motivations for taking up government employment as following the instructions of his spiritual friend, his teacher, in order to serve all sentient beings.

As if to emphasize the importance of Géluk social hierarchies and authority, Mugé Samten again draws upon the voice of one of Labrang Tashikyil's religious teachers, in this case the Sixth Gungtang Rinpoché, to explain how he received his first appointment in Beijing. Mugé Samten describes that as the People's Liberation Army moved into the area around Labrang Tashikyil in the late summer and early fall of 1949, unrest broke out, so he and other monastic officials moved to the nearby city of Lanzhou.[71] There he met with the Sixth Gungtang Rinpoché, Jigmé Tenpé Wangchuk (Gung thang 'Jigs med bstan pa'i dbang phyug, 1926–2000). The short biographies available for Gungtang Rinpoché tell how he became an important religious leader at Labrang Tashikyil after the death of the Fifth Jamyang Zhépa in 1947. A few years after taking his throne at Labrang Tashikyil, however, like many other high lamas, he was removed for political reasons and then imprisoned for two decades, from circa 1958 until 1979.[72]

According to *Luminous Mirror*, Gungtang Rinpoché instructed Mugé Samten to go to China as his representative during their meeting in 1949. As Mugé Samten narrates:

> At that time, Gungtang Rinpoché exhorted me with requests for public and personal reasons. He asked me to explain aspects of history and culture to him. On the topic of going to China, he summoned me and said, that, "As secretary, you belong to our entourage and you are the rank of 'abbot' (*mkhan po*); if you don't want to do this, it is possible for you go to Western Tibet instead." I didn't want to go to Western Tibet and requested permission to go to China. He said that, "If you go to Beijing, it would be beneficial. As my representative, you should respectfully bow to the Commander-in-Chief, Chairman Mao and make observations. All expenses will be paid by me." Then we discussed that it was necessary for me to go to my root lama to ask permission to do this.[73]

Making use of direct speech in his narrative, Mugé Samten explains in a straightforward tone, characteristic of his autobiography, how he first ended up going to China. He was not compelled to do so for political reasons; agreed to Gungtang Rinpoché's request and then they both followed Géluk social etiquette. Gungtang Rinpoché was superior in rank within the monastic hierarchy; however, he did not dictate to Mugé Samten what to do. They both followed cultural norms by obtaining permission from Mugé Samten's root guru first. This sense of mutual respect among spiritual friends pervades the narrative.

Through the mouthpiece of a third senior religious teacher, Geshé Sherab Gyatso (1884–1968), we again are reminded of the importance placed on benefiting the Dharma. In this way, Mugé Samten's reasons for accepting positions at the Ethnic Affairs Commission and as translator emerge through another use of autobiographical ventriloquy. Due to Gungtang Rinpoché's request to travel to Beijing as his representative, Mugé Samten resigned from his position as secretary (*drung chen mkhan po*) at Labrang Tashikyil Monastery. He flew to the nation's capital with another senior Buddhist colleague, Geshé Sherab Gyatso.

As mentioned in the introduction, Geshé Sherab Gyatso was a Buddhist monk and important politician who advocated for the compatibility of Buddhism and Marxism. He served as vice president and then president of the Buddhist Association of China from 1953 until it was disbanded in 1966.[74] Through Geshé Sherab Gyatso's voice, Mugé Samten explains how he agrees to work at the Ethnic Affairs Commission:

> The head of the Ethnic Affairs Commission, Yang Jinren,[75] needed us as civil servants. At that point in time, Sichuan, a few areas, and Tibetan territory[76] had not yet been liberated and so it was said that work in Tibetan language was very important. Geshé (Sherab Gyatso) Rinpoché certainly approved, saying, "it was necessary to do whatever is in one's power to benefit the teachings and sentient beings," and so I agreed to do this.[77]

Writing frankly, Mugé Samten provides pragmatic reasons for joining this government office. At the same time, the driving force to this narrative is his testimony that he followed expected social and cultural obligations and obeyed his monastic superiors. The use of direct speech imparts the authoritative voices of his teachers. In this use of autobiographical ventriloquy, there is no sense of deflecting praise. The words of his senior Buddhist colleague, Geshé Sherab Gyatso, similar to the authoritative voices of Gungtang Rinpoché and the Fifth Jamyang Zhepa, are used to instruct and to reinforce the importance of the hierarchical dimension of spiritual friendship. At the same time, the ethical message communicates the importance of benefiting the Buddha-Dharma and all sentient beings, thereby fulfilling his vows as a Géluk Buddhist monastic.

Mugé Samten briefly mentions his involvement in important state projects of the early 1950s. While at the Ethnic Affairs Commission, he was involved in translation and planning.[78] In this capacity, he worked as an editor for Tibetan-language translations of the *China's Pictorial* (*Mi dbangs brnyan dpar;* Chi. Renmin huabao 人民画报). In 1951, he proofread the Seventeen Point Agreement on the Peaceful Liberation of Tibet (Bod zhi ba'i bcings 'grol gyi chings yig don tshan bcu bdun pa thag bcad), the official treaty that arranged Tibet's incorporation into the People's Republic of China.[79] Mugé Samten's *Luminous Mirror*

sketches his work for government offices without much detail, in a straightforward matter-of-fact style.

Written in 1992–93, at the end of his life, Mugé Samten's memories of the
early 1950s call attention to traditional Tibetan social norms and hierarchies,
especially by highlighting Buddhist education and the need to show deference
to one's teachers and following their directives. Similarly, Tséten Zhabdrung
draws attention to the importance of Géluk social relationships; however, unlike
Mugé Samten, he doesn't use the technique of autobiographical ventriloquy.

Tséten Zhabdrung's Acoustic Ambrosia *Remembers 1954*

The Sixth Tséten Zhabdrung, Jigmé Rigpé Lodrö, edifies his readers on the
value of spiritual friendship through his relationship with his co-throne holder,

FIGURE 2.2   Tséten Zhabdrung, circa 1954, studio portrait

Courtesy of Jigmé Chöpak

Tséten Khenpo, and his audience with the Dalai Lama and Panchen Lama. Both of these events occurred in the Wood Horse year of the Tibetan calendar. The Western calendrical year 1954 is not provided; for that information one has to search charts that provide equivalents. This was a pivotal year in Sino-Tibetan relations for many reasons. It is when the Dalai Lama and the Panchen Lama visited Beijing and met Mao Zedong. For Tséten Zhabdrung, an incarnate lama in charge (either solely or jointly) of seven monastic estates, that was the year he was first impacted directly by Land Reform. This policy created by the CCP appropriated lands from the traditionally privileged classes and redistributed them.

The implementation of Land Reform took place at different times in ethnically Tibetan areas and eventually led to the dismantling of all monastic estates, the hubs for social and economic life prior to Chinese political interference. As Tsering Shakya points out:

> Tibetans saw the reforms first and foremost as an attack on their value system; whether rich or poor, they were united in their belief in Buddhism and in their support of religious institutions and could not envisage any reform that would mark the end of these religious institutions, which formed the center of their world view. . . . Despite the inequality and exploitation that existed in Tibetan society, there was no peasant uprising against the injustice that prevailed in the traditional system.[80]

When core Buddhist institutions were demolished, Tibetans viewed this as violence against Tibetan values. Tséten Zhabdrung's autobiography doesn't describe how ordinary Tibetans viewed Land Reforms; nor does *Acoustic Ambrosia* mention this political policy. Tséten Zhabdrung draws attention to the forgotten history of the Six Encampments (sgar ba kha drug).

Before diving into how and why he writes about this history in his autobiography, some background information is necessary. Six Encampments is the collective name for six monastic estates shared between two incarnate lamas, Tséten Khenpo and Tséten Zhabdrung. The sharing of this throne holder position started in 1623 with the establishment of Tséten Monastery and then ceased in 1958, when the Eighth Tséten Khenpo, Jigmé Rigpé Nyingpo ('Jigs med rigs pa'i snying po), was murdered during the collectivization of Tséten monastery.[81] During the Maoist era, the Six Encampment monasteries did not function and were partly destroyed. When they reopened, our autobiographer, the Sixth Tséten Zhabdrung, was their sole leader as well as that of his own monastery until his death in 1985. Similar to Mugé Samten's autobiographical account, such political realities recede into the background as Tséten Zhabdrung reminisces about the history of the Six Encampments and the sometimes conflicted relationship with Tséten Khenpo.

SPIRITUAL FRIENDSHIP AMID LAND REFORM, 1954

In the spring of the Wood-Horse year, the Venerable Tséten Khenpo who had been residing at Labrang Tashikyil for the past two years, was requested by the government through proxies to leave immediately and return to our monasteries in the Six Encampments area. I was working in Xining and so he came to stay at my place first. We had long flowing conversations on various topics and were overjoyed with happiness. After ironing out details in discussions on the work in the Six Encampments area, uncle and nephew, i.e., Tséten Khenpo and myself, set forth to Tséten Monastery directly. The Three Supports [for Buddhist practice, i.e., texts, stupas, and statues] and other things were divided out based on the records of each appointed caretaker and according to the estate taxes of Tséten, Göngar, Dentik, and Tuwa, etc. A new system was established whereby each caretaker was placed under the direct command of each of us. The best of endeavors are "good waters, happy fish"; rankings were accomplished. At the same time, at Tséten Monastery and Prince's Cave, my corresponding encampments were laid out based on the buildings at each place.[82]

When I first read the above passage, I experienced an ebullient feeling, conjuring that sensation of a reunion with a dear friend—the long, flowing conversations, perhaps until late at night, discussing past adventures and future plans. Yet something nagged at me about this passage too. It was describing more than the reunion of two dear friends. The circumstances surrounding this jubilant moment were not joyful at all. The reasons for their meeting are revealed through a code of phrases "requested by the government" and "rankings accomplished," suggesting that there was more going on here. This description of their happy reunion hid the long and frequently marred history of the Tséten co-throne holders and the sudden implementation of Land Reform, and also foreshadowed a tragedy. This interpretation became apparent after reflecting on this in light of other sections of Tséten Zhabdrung's autobiography as well as his *Catalogue of Dentik Monastery*.

Acoustic Ambrosia tells a redemption story of how a troubled relationship between two incarnate lineages was resolved. Tséten Zhabdrung explains that in the early history, "Uncle and nephew were of one heart and mind"; however:

Over time, unfortunately the servants around them lacked the essence of the Dharma by not paying heed to the teachings, instead they latched onto the worldly existence of this lifetime. Since they had polluted minds, they would arrogantly stir up trouble causing mental attachment and aversion, and the flame of bias regarding the names of the young and old lamas would rise up to the deep heavens. This did not quiet down for several generations.[83]

The animosity between the two factions heated up in the mid-nineteenth century and took its toll on the relationships between the two throne holders over multiple generations of incarnations. Tséten Zhabdrung details that due to disagreements between the Fourth Tséten Zhabdrung, Jigmé Tubten Norbu (1804–1861), a.k.a. "Chubby" Zhabdrung, and the Sixth Tséten Khenpo, Jasag Ngawang Jamyang Dondrup (Ja sag Ngag dbang 'jam dbyangs don grub, 1782–1842), the Sixth Khenpo left the Six Encampments to return to his native Chuzang (in today's Huzhu County, Qinghai Province), where he passed away. When the local Buddhist hierarch of Chuzang refused to return his remains, Chubby Zhabdrung led a small army to forcibly seize them (only to be punished by the Qing courts after the fact). The next Khenpo incarnation was born in Chuzang but passed away young, and the Fifth Tséten Zhabdrung, known as Nan Tāzhin, also fought in the military, this time on the side of the Qing.

So it came to pass that the author, the Sixth Tséten Zhabdrung, and the Eighth Tséten Khenpo, Jigmé Rigpé Nyingpo were born in the same year (1910) instead of being a generation apart to recognize each other as uncle and nephew. These familial terms do not indicate a blood relation. In the Géluk Buddhist tradition, "the uncle and nephew" positions articulate the close nature of the relationship between incarnation lines to recognize one another across generations. The Tséten Khenpo incarnation lineage preceded that of the Tséten Zhabdrung and so was deemed slightly higher in status. In his autobiography, the Sixth Tséten Zhabdrung explains that when he took the throne first, it was considered to be a breach of etiquette because the Tséten Khenpo lineage had a longer history. So the jealously and hostility between the two camps repeated itself in the twentieth century. This came to a head around 1920, when the two boys, around ten years old, got into a physical fistfight at Tséten Monastery. In their teens, Tséten Zhabdrung explains, they reconciled their differences due to the interventions of their mutual teacher, Géluk scholar Jigmé Damchö Gyatso.[84]

Tséten Zhabdrung's autobiography depicts this reunion in 1954 as a joyous occasion because they had become genuine friends through the resolution of past hostilities and due to the mutual respect created through the reconciliation process. Although *Acoustic Ambrosia* never states this explicitly, from the context it seems that the reason for the reunion with Tséten Khenpo was the implementation of Land Reform. Euphemistically, the text states that Khenpo "was *requested* by the *government* [emphasis mine] through proxies" to return to the Six Encampments, which likely meant that his monastic homecoming had been mandated.

Other sources tell us that that the process of implementing Land Reform was deliberately calculated to involve the local population. The initial stages involved assessing property and assigning class ranks to each person, so that the wealth could be divided evenly. The cooperation of the local populace was necessary for the effective implementation of this policy and also involved identifying anyone who was deemed to be against this policy, a so-called "counter-revolutionary." June Dreyer points out that a common propaganda slogan at this time was "the army is the fish and the people are the water."[85] This indicates how important and pervasive the army was in forcing the local people to accomplish this socio-economic restructuring. Tséten Zhabdrung signposts this Chinese slogan by writing, "good waters, happy fish" and "rankings were accomplished" (*rim pa can zhig bsgrubs*) in the same sentence. In this context, I read the latter phrase as "assigning" class rank in accord with the early stages of implementing Land Reform, which at the beginning allowed for the upper class stratum to retain some of their property. The intended readership could likely pick up on the historical allusion without the autobiographer having to explicitly mention the reasons for divvying up property. Sadly, this redemption story also signals a tragedy to come. Based on my reading of *Acoustic Ambrosia*, this may have been the last meeting between the two Tséten incarnations. Within a few years, Tséten Khenpo would be killed.

Tséten Khenpo's tragic death is not explicitly stated in *Acoustic Ambrosia*. We only learn about it from Tséten Zhabdrung's local history, *A Catalogue of Dentik Monastery*, which details the Tséten Khenpo incarnation lineage. Here the author notes that the death of his co-throne holder was in 1958.[86] From interviews that I conducted in 2008 and 2015, I learned that Tséten Khenpo chose to stay on at Tséten Monastery to oversee the Six Encampments after the first stages of implementation of Land Reform. When they were mandated to collectivize in 1958, he was murdered, but the circumstances are unclear. The accounts I heard were that either he was killed at Tséten Monastery by the army because he resisted or that he died en route to Nantan Prison in Xining. Tséten Zhabdrung was not at the Six Encampments at that time. We learn more about this in the next chapter. For Tséten Zhabdrung, 1954 was a time characterized by precious opportunities to meet spiritual friends.

TSÉTEN ZHABDRUNG ON PRECIOUS OPPORTUNITIES,
BEIJING 1954

Similar to Mugé Samten's remembrances of the 1950s, Tséten Zhabdrung
extols the value of spiritual friendship. Unlike Mugé Samten's narrative, Tséten Zhabdrung's does not rely heavily on direct speech in the authoritative
voices of his teachers. In addition to addressing spiritual friendship through
the telling of local history, he details his audience with the Dalai Lama and the
Panchen Lama, and thereby tells of his achievements in publishing his teacher's works. Tséten Zhabdrung was also involved in critical state-building
projects, such as being a member of the committee responsible for translating
the 1954 PRC Constitution into Tibetan, but he only tersely mentions these
facts.

Other sources tell us that as the autumnal equinox of 1954 drew near, hundreds of thousands of Chinese citizens took to the streets of Beijing to celebrate
the fifth anniversary of the nation and the promulgation of the Chinese Constitution. One of the most significant pieces of legislation in national history, the
Constitution of the People's Republic of China was adopted on September 20,
1954, by the first National People's Congress (NPC).[87] Hundreds of distinguished delegates came from all over the consolidated territories of the PRC,
including members from Tibet. After traveling over a thousand miles from the
Tibetan capital city of Lhasa to Beijing, the Fourteenth Dalai Lama, Tenzin
Gyatso, along with his entourage, joined the Tenth Panchen Lama, Chökyi
Gyeltsen's party in Xining to proceed to the capital together.[88] During their six-
month stay, they met with many figureheads, such as the Great Helmsman, Mao
Zedong, and Zhou Enlai. Images of the Dalai Lama, Panchen Lama, and Mao
Zedong cordially greeting one another can still be viewed in extant newspapers
and newsreel recordings.[89] Such images, like the photograph on the wall of Tséten Zhabdrung's family residence in Yadzi, record a formative period in modern
Sino-Tibetan relations when the Dalai Lama and other well-respected Buddhist
hierarchs had the unique opportunity to share the same space as high-ranking
politicians of the Chinese Communist Party. Although Tséten Zhabdrung met
both Mao Zedong and the Dalai Lama in Beijing in 1954, he is evasive about
politics. His narrative, similar to Mugé Samten's *Luminous Mirror*, is focused
on the ethical value of spiritual friendships, especially in regard to the transmission of his teacher's life works.

Acoustic Ambrosia vividly recounts the audience with His Holiness the Fourteenth Dalai Lama and the Tenth Panchen Lama in Beijing in 1954. Tséten
Zhabdrung describes the teachings he received from His Holiness the Dalai

Lama as a "taste of the essence of the Dharma." Metaphors of the senses—gustatory and auditory—feature prominently in his autobiography as its title *Acoustic Ambrosia*, which the literal translation "Nectar for the Ears" (*Rna ba'i bdud rtsi*) reveals more blatantly. This essence, nectar, or ambrosia—all of which serve to translate the Tibetan term *dü-tsi*—is another metaphor frequently employed in Tibetan Buddhist literature to suggest nourishment, especially for spiritual well-being. The Dalai Lama's teachings took place at the Yonghegong or Yonghe Temple in Beijing, a historically significant site for Qing-Manchu-Tibetan Buddhist activities. Originally an imperial Buddhist monastery sponsored by the Manchu Qianlong Emperor, the site in the 1950s seems to have still served its historical purpose as a center for Buddhist teachings by high Géluk lamas.[90] Tséten Zhabdrung describes enjoying the "taste of the Dharma" at the Yonghegong as follows:

> At the end of the summer, I went to Beijing to translate the new National Constitution. For several months I worked with a group of translators. At this time I met the Two Protectors of all Sentient Beings and tasted a small bit of the essence of the Dharma. On the anniversary of the birth of the nation [October 1], the majestic sovereignty of the Great Helmsman became an object of my senses; I freely enjoyed various activities and festivities among top-ranked officials. On the twenty-second day of the eighth month of the Tibetan calendar in the Tsongkhapa Chapel of Yonghegong,[91] His Holiness provided a general explanation on the *Gradual Path to Enlightenment*, and gave reading transmissions on *Hundred Deities of Tusita*,[92] *The Three Essential Points of the Path* by Tsongkhapa,[93] *The Ground of Good Qualities*,[94] and *All Victorious Ones*.[95] In his chambers, His Holiness happily gave further reading transmissions on *Hundred Deities of Tusita* and *Taking Refuge*.[96] He also provided extensive oral transmissions on *Victorious Siddhis Long-life Empowerments*.[97]

Like a banquet of Dharma teachings, the spiritual nourishment he receives gushes from the narrative. Similar to how Tséten Zhabdrung evades the political circumstances of the ebullient meeting with his co-throne holder Tséten Khenpo earlier in 1954, he does not mention politics here. The autobiographer highlights his audience with the "Protectors of all Sentient Beings," epithets for the Dalai Lama and Panchen Lama, on a specified date in the Tibetan calendar, which according to conversion tables was October 16, 1954.[98]

During the course of that day, Tséten Zhabdrung also explains that he had the opportunity to converse with His Holiness's tutor, Trijang Rinpoché Lozang Yéshé Tenzin Gyatso (Khri byang rin po che blo bzang ye shes bstan 'dzin rgya mtsho, 1901–1981), who praised the erudition of Tséten Zhabdrung's root lama, Jigmé Damchö Gyatso. In particular, Trijang Rinpoché lauded Jigmé Damchö Gyatso's commentary on Tsongkhapa's text on *The Essence of Eloquent Speech on the Definitive and Interpretable* (*Drang nges dka' 'grel chen mo*) and offered the necessary funds to procure a print of Jigmé Damchö Gyatso's *Collected Works*.

Later sections of *Acoustic Ambrosia* explain that after Tséten Zhabdrung returned to eastern Tibet, with this new funding, he was able to realize his dream of printing his teacher's *Collected Works*. He explains that his root guru's early death in 1946 due to illness left him in charge of the editorial duties and printing obligations of a project that had begun in the 1930s. The printing house at Tuwa Monastery was constructed for the sole purpose of printing this work.[99] From my fieldwork in 2008, I learned that the printing house still stands today, although it no longer houses the woodblocks for Jigmé Damchö Gyatso's *Collected Works*; it is now used for the printing the xylographic edition of Tséten Zhabdrung's *Collected Works*. The Tuwa Monastery publishing house first printed Jigmé Damchö Gyatso's *Collected Works* in 1955, as Tséten Zhabdrung details in *Acoustic Ambrosia*: "At this time, it was evident that the finely engraved woodblocks for the fifteen volumes of [Jigmé Damchö Gyatso's] *Collected Works*, lasting in duration for twenty-one years, were complete. On the first day of the tenth month a large ceremony marked this achievement. The expenses totaled 10,343 silver coins."[100] In the Fire Monkey year (1956/7), Tséten Zhabdrung details how he sent a letter to Trijang Rinpoché in Lhasa requesting a dedication prayer from His Holiness the Dalai Lama for this multivolume tome. This wish was granted.

The Dalai Lama's belletristic verse, included as a foreword in the woodblock print of the *Collected Works*,[101] praises Jigmé Damchö Gyatso:

> Om Sarasvatī!
> I heap respect onto the sublime youth with Sarasvatī mind
>   whose pure karma and aspirations ripened at the perfect time;
>   the holder of the magic key of exposition, debate, and composition to
>   open the door to the jeweled treasury of the two benefits,
>   the great Dharmakośa of the holy Buddha with the four
>   fearlessnesses.[102]

The Dalai Lama describes Jigmé Damchö Gyatso—the sublime youth—as possessing the mind of Sarasvatī, the goddess of scholars and poets. This type of poetic figure does not simply compare the savant with Sarasvatī but rather uses a type of parallelism to express their equivalence. In other words, it intimates that the Dalai Lama perceives Jigmé Damchö Gyatso as an emanation of Sarasvatī and his *Collected Works* as a jeweled treasury. The poem (five folio pages long) continues to laud this work and Tséten Zhabdrung's erudition by association.

Acoustic Ambrosia recalls that at the beginning of the summer of 1957, Tséten Zhabdrung sent the fifteen volumes of Jigmé Damchö Gyatso's *Collected Works* along with many offerings to Lhasa via a person called Kelzang (Skal bzang). Kelzang was from Karing Monastery, near the Tenth Panchen Lama's birthplace, which is not far from Yadzi, Tséten Zhabdrung's hometown.[103] According to an interview with a close associate of Tséten Zhabdrung in 2008, members of the monastic community believe that this multivolume work reached Lhasa before the Dalai Lama went into exile in 1959.

Mugé Samten and Tséten Zhabdrung as Spiritual Friends

As the decade came to a close, Tséten Zhabdrung and Mugé Samten had an opportunity to spend time together in Beijing. The political assignment that was the impetus for their meeting is not detailed in either autobiography. Chinese sources inform us that they translated Mao Zedong's *Collected Works* into Tibetan. In *Acoustic Ambrosia* and *Luminous Mirror,* each author respectively recalls meeting the other and speaks of their spiritual friendship on equal terms. Their narratives evoke similar themes of respect, kindness, and erudition, but the autobiographers differ in their approach to remembering the types of sites that they visited.

Tséten Zhabdrung's narrative recalls visiting the Buddhist landscape of Beijing and the nearby Fragrant Hills. They went to places associated with the great Géluk Buddhist polymath Cangkya Rolpé Dorjé, an advisor to the Qing emperor Qianlong.[104] As Tséten Zhabdrung remembers:

> When I was in my fiftieth year, in the Earth Pig [1959] year, I was invited to Beijing by the Minzu Publishing House in order to take up the task of editing and doing translations of important works. Here I shared a room with the great scholar from Labrang, Mugé Samten, for three months. Because he was so knowledgeable and kind, the time passed full of meaningful conversations. At this time we did whatever sightseeing we wanted to do. We visited the Fragrant Hills (Zhang hran < Ch. Xiang Shan) and the surrounding area. We visited the site where Cangkya Rolpé Dorjé wrote his *Treatise on Philosophical Systems*

(*Grubs mtha'i rnam gzhang*). We went to a temple with a reclining Buddha and a temple with five hundred Arhats and a temple with a tooth relic of the Buddha and relic of Tang Seng (Thang sang, Ch. 唐僧).[105]

When Tséten Zhabdrung recollects that the Minzu Publishing House invited him to Beijing to translate important works, he does not even mention that he was on the translation team for Mao Zedong's *Collected Works*. Chinese language sources, such as *The Hualong County Gazetteer,* emphasize the importance of his involvement in the translations of Mao's writings in particular.[106] As in other passages of *Acoustic Ambrosia*, the political circumstances for their meeting recede into the background.

The authorial choice involved in this glaring omission signals a way Tséten Zhabdrung expresses his moral agency as a Buddhist savant through his life narrative. Similar to how he turned away from the politically charged topic of Land Reforms to spotlight his spiritual friendship with Tséten Khenpo, here he again focuses on Buddhist epistemes. In the above passage, he evokes the ethos of spiritual friendship and remembers visiting sites associated with Buddhist history in the nation's capital. Absent from the narrative are references to any of the political places at the nation's capital, e.g., Tian'anmen Square, where Mao Zedong held massive rallies at that time. According to *Acoustic Ambrosia*, he and Mugé Samten busied themselves in the Buddhist landscape of Beijing and surrounding areas. Tséten Zhabdrung reminds his readers of the activities of the great Géluk polymath Cangkya Rolpé Dorjé, an advisor to the Qianlong emperor and an important ambassador between Tibet and the court. From this description, it seems likely that they visited Songzhu Monastery (嵩祝寺), the residence of the Cangkya incarnations and an important printing house of Tibetan and Mongolian language materials at the capital.[107]

In *Luminous Mirror,* Mugé Samten reiterates the fondness that he had for his spiritual friend, Tséten Zhabdrung. Mugé Samten remembers their shared appreciation of Tibet's own culture (*bod rang gi rig gnas*), but he doesn't highlight visiting the Buddhist landscape of the nation's capital:

> Tséten Zhabdrung arrived in Beijing and we shared a room together. Because his character was very gentle and because he had an intense appreciation for Tibet's own culture, we became good friends. We ate together and went on walks, and got along really well. On September 30th, on the eve of the tenth anniversary of the founding of the nation, we attended a large banquet. On one of those occasions, in the evening, we went to a performance and were distracted by the show.[108]

This intimate portrayal of like-minded friends tells readers of their common appreciation for Tibetan culture without mentioning Buddhism directly. This passage of Mugé Samten's life narrative provides the Western calendrical date, a practice adhered to when the author remembers nation-state events. The mention of festivities associated with the tenth anniversary of the founding of the PRC reveals their participation in the events; he omits visiting the Buddhist landscape of Beijing, but like Tséten Zhabdrung remembers the past in a way that evokes Buddhist values in social relationships.

WIDENING THE HISTORICAL-LITERARY LENS OF ANALYSIS

The autobiographers' espousal of Tibetan cultural values and Buddhist knowledge in their life narratives recalls the 1950s as a time when Tibetan Buddhist institutions with distinctive discursive practices and modes of authority were protected by the state, yet both autobiographers avoid mentioning their important political roles in the dynamic processes of state formation. These passages from *Luminous Mirror* and *Acoustic Ambrosia* indicate that Mugé Samten and Tséten Zhabdrung convey moral agency by tracing their subjective pasts in certain ways for specific purposes. If we observe that "the past is the very ground through which subjectivity and self-understanding of a tradition's adherents are constituted," as suggested by Saba Mahmood,[109] then what was significant about remembering the 1950s in the way that they did and when they did?

The authors of *Luminous Mirror* and *Acoustic Ambrosia* portray a world in which Tibet's own culture is appreciated and Buddhist ethical values prevail. They remind readers of a time when Géluk social relationships were respected, but not in an overly idealistic way, as indicated by Tséten Zhabdrung's sober retelling of the conflicted history between the two Tséten lineages. The importance of remembering key events of the 1950s as immersed in Buddhist ethics, social values, and local history comes into sharper focus when we reevaluate their autobiographies in light of a Tibetan literary prayer written by the most influential Tibetan Buddhist scholar of our time, the Fourteenth Dalai Lama, Tenzin Gyatso, which circulated among members of the Buddhist Association of China in the 1950s.

By bringing the autobiographical memories of the 1950s into conversation with historical evidence from 1954, I aim to shed further light on the complex subject positions of Tibetan Buddhist leaders in China more generally. I will do so in three ways: by showing the continuity of Tibetan discursive traditions from the pre- to the post-Mao era, by spotlighting the loss of political authority held by Tibetan Buddhist leaders in the first decade of the PRC; and by bringing attention to how the Dalai Lama and other Buddhists overtly expressed hoped for state protection of Buddhist institutions prior to 1959, and how Mugé Samten and Tséten Zhabdrung rekindled this optimism tenuously in their autobiographies.

Continuing Discursive Traditions: The Dalai Lama's "Monlam to Mao"

The Fourteenth Dalai Lama wrote *"Monlam* to Mao," an aspirational prayer, in a letter to Mao Zedong, but it was not a private epistle. The authorial signature of Tenzin Gyatso, the Fourteenth Dalai Lama, matches with events that the author himself lived through, and in that sense is autobiographical.[110] Internal textual evidence indicates that he wrote this piece in the summer of 1954 at his summer residence in Lhasa, the Norbulingka or "Garden of Jewels," prior to his visit to the nation's capital.[111] Its publication in Chinese in the official journal of the Buddhist Association of China indicates that it circulated among Buddhist clergy at that time.

The Dalai Lama's *"Monlam* to Mao" has been translated in its entirety from Tibetan into English and into Chinese by a Chinese publisher.[112] The English title found in that publication, *A Collection of the Historical Archives of Tibet,* is "Ode to Mao." In my translation, I have chosen to retain the emic Tibetan genre, *monlam,* found in the colophon of the Tibetan text. *Monlam* is a type of aspirational prayer in esoteric Buddhist literature.[113] The following select stanzas from "*Monlam* to Mao" exemplify Tibetan discursive techniques:

> Om Sarasvatī.
> The Three Jewels yield abundant showers upon the
> glorious world, all virtuous excellences;
> protect us always with your auspicious sacred
> countenance, everlasting and unparalleled!
>
> You, the people's leader, with countless good deeds,
> equal in glory to Mahāsammata, the King of Universal Respect,
> and to Brahma, the Creator of the World,
> resemble the sun shining upon earth!

May the almighty Chairman Mao,
whose knowledge extends to the horizon
like ocean waves,
live in this world forever!

People regard you as a mother who protects us
and enthusiastically inscribe your image;
May you live forever to show us the good path of peace,
through friendship free of bias and strife!

Upon completely loosening all fetters of ignorance
that cause suffering to permeate the Yellow Earth,
with the new splendor of your virtuous countenance,
please grant us assurances and happiness!

. . .

May you, fearless Garuḍa, powerfully disseminate
victory over all cunning imperialists,
tricksters, envoys of Māra,
snakes, enemies with writhing tongues.[114]

. . .

Tenzin Gyatso, the Fourteenth Dalai Lama[115]

Rhetorical appeals for the state protection of Buddhist institutions are evident in this poetic prayer. With its literary flourishes, it exemplifies Géluk scholarly practices and overtly calls on Mao Zedong to protect Tibet and Buddhist institutions. The Dalai Lama's capacious use of Tibetan rhetorical and linguistic registers resonates with types of wordplay found in *Acoustic Ambrosia* and *Luminous Mirror*, yet there are also significant differences between these texts.

Similar to the first stanza of the Dalai Lama's praise poem to Jigmé Damchö Gyatso, the opening line calls upon the bodhisattva of speech and poetry, Sarasvatī. Then, like Tséten Zhabdrung's opening poem (and many Buddhist rituals or liturgies), he invokes the Three Jewels (Skt.: *triratna*), Buddha, Dharma, and Sangha, which are the Buddha Śākyamuni, his teachings, and the Buddhist community. Yet as the first stanza segues into the next *śloka* or couplet, the poet blurs the lines between Buddhist invocation and secular eulogy with a grammatical shift that renders the subject unclear. Either the Dalai Lama calls upon the Buddhist teachings to protect the readership or the appeal to "Protect us!" is directed toward Mao Zedong himself.

The next verse signals the latter because Mao Zedong is portrayed as holding
the ethical responsibility of granting Tibetans his protection. Using double metaphors common in Tibetan poetics, Mao Zedong is compared not only with
Mahāsammata (Mang pos bkur pa rgyal po), a sagely king considered a forefa-
ther of the Buddha Śākyamuni,[116] but also with the Indic god Brahma, the cre-
ator of the world. Overt comparisons with judicious and powerful figures from
the subcontinent underscore the Dalai Lama's cultural orientation to India as
the homeland for Buddhist teachings. India frequently looms larger in the literary Tibetan imagination than Tibet's eastern neighbor China.[117] This was also
evident in Tséten Zhabdrung's reference to the legendary place Jalandhara in his
poetic sparring with Shangtön at the beginning of this chapter. Here, the Great
Helmsman, Mao Zedong, is not compared to powerful figures of China's past
but to Buddhicized Indic figures, continuing a tradition of poetry praising lay
rulers of Tibet, Mongolia, and China.[118] Lauran Hartley has shown that political praise poems, such as this one by the Dalai Lama and others by Geshé Sherab
Gyatso, were "accepted discourse at this time" and reveal some of the aspirations
for the future of Sino-Tibetan relations.[119]

The Dalai Lama, similar to Tséten Zhabdrung and Mugé Samten, ties
together social relationships and Buddhist ethical values, as indicated by his
appeal to Mao "to show the good path of peace, through friendship free of bias
and strife!" The Dalai Lama's term for "friendship" (mdza' gcugs) expresses
warmth and congeniality toward Mao Zedong, yet this construct differs from
the idea of spiritual friendship found in the autobiographies. Nonetheless, his
literary choices articulate a harmonious intertwining of Buddhist ideals with
the secular Chinese nation-state.

The Dalai Lama creatively expands Tibetan discourse to accommodate the
new political situation and to shape it in prescriptive ways. The following stanza,
the seventh in his eulogy to Mao, fuses Buddhist-nationalist sentiment with
socialist ideology:

> May you, fearless Garuḍa, powerfully disseminate
> victory over all cunning imperialists,
> tricksters, envoys of Māra,
> snakes, enemies with writhing tongues.[120]

The Garuḍa is a Buddhist protector in the form of a large predatory bird like
an eagle. In this stanza the Garuḍa is a metaphor for the poet's interlocutor,
Mao Zedong. Through this literary comparison, the Dalai Lama stresses the
expectation that the leader of China, the Great Helmsman, will be an ethical

protector of Buddhist teachings. This depiction of Mao as a defender of Buddhism in the form of Garuḍa is further elaborated on using Marxist-socialist ideology when the Dalai Lama calls upon the Garuḍa to destroy his natural born adversary, the metaphorical vipers—imperialists.[121] Here the multiple extended metaphors are peppered with Buddhist imagery and infused with Marxist rhetoric. The Fourteenth Dalai Lama deploys the finest literary skills to craft this poem presenting a vision of Mao as a political leader whose ethos harmoniously matches Buddhist ideals.

Interestingly, although the Fourteenth Dalai Lama frames this poem in the *monlam* genre, the English and Chinese translations (in the *Historical Archives of Tibet* publication) translate this term as a ceremonious "Ode" (Ch. *song*, 颂) and thereby elide the *monlam*'s characteristic of religious devotion.[122] A prime example of this type of omission can be found in the fifth stanza above. The Beijing version is on the left and my new translation on the right:

Though the earth is vast, people struggled for breath in their bondage of darkness and pain. With a new radiance you have dispelled the darkness and "broken the bondage," and people can now breathe freely and enjoy life.	Upon completely "loosening all fetters" of ignorance that cause suffering to permeate the Yellow Earth, with the new splendor of your virtuous countenance, please grant us assurances and happiness![123]

The implied "you," similar to the metaphorical Garuḍa above, is the poet's addressee, Mao Zedong, heroically leading his people away from a dark past and into a bright future. The Chinese publication declared that Mao Zedong had already completed these lofty goals. However, the imperative tense in the phrase "Please grant . . ." (*sbyin 'gyur cig*) signposts this as a wish for the future, as indicated in my translation, "Please grant us assurances and happiness!"[124] This stanza voices an urgency and hope not carried in the English translation in the *Historical Archives of Tibet* publication. The author's brilliant use of wordplay is similarly lacking.

The photographic reproduction of the *"Monlam* to Mao" artifact reveals how the Dalai Lama penned nine syllables (within the second and third stanzas) in red ink in order to highlight "The Great Leader of the Fatherland, Chairman Mao" (*mes, rgyal, gtso, 'dzin, rlabs, chen, ma'o, kru, zhi*).[125] The Fourteenth Dalai Lama, following a tradition of Tibetan literati, embellishes his verse with wordplay uniquely suited to the Tibetan language. Poets, including all Three Polymaths, play with double entendre by highlighting individual syllables embedded within multisyllabic terms. We read an example of this in Mugé Samten's embedding of the term "telling what happened" in a sentence to underscore his choice of autobiographical literary genre, as detailed above.[126] In the Dalai Lama's verse, each syllable of Mao's name is highlighted in ink while at the same time each retains semantic value within a compound word. As we will read in the next chapter, this literary technique can be deployed in a number of different ways to create various rhetorical effects, e.g., to highlight a topic to play with double entendre, or to emphasize the name of a Buddhist master. Sometimes the syllable used in this way would be punctuated with a dot, but in this case, the author used red ink to honor its recipient, Chairman Mao.

The Dalai Lama's *"Monlam* to Mao" exemplifies the capaciousness of Tibetan literary language, with rhetorical techniques common among Tibetan poets. Many of these discursive techniques were also employed by the two autobiographers, Tséten Zhabdrung and Mugé Samten, in their writings dating to the post-Mao era. Similar to how the Dalai Lama clearly stakes a claim in writing this piece, Tséten Zhabdrung poetically sparred with Shangtön to make a philosophical point. Similar to how the Dalai Lama draws upon a genre that is suitable for his writing, both Tséten Zhabdrung and Mugé Samten chose an emic literary category appropriate for their writings. It is precisely this creative refashioning of Tibetan discursive traditions in the new world of post-Mao China that makes the contributions of the Three Polymaths, Tséten Zhabdrung, Mugé Samten, and Dungkar Rinpoché, so wide-reaching. However, the way that the Dalai Lama boldly addresses Mao Zedong and cleverly conveys his aspirations for the state's protection of Buddhist institutions could not be more different from the way the two autobiographers approach writing about their own roles in state-building projects and politics in general in the post-Mao era. This points to something significant about the way the autobiographers remembered the 1950s.

Discontinuities in Political Status and the Reception of "Monlam *to Mao"*

An examination of the publication of the Dalai Lama's *"Monlam* to Mao" serves as a reminder of how much has changed for Tibetan Buddhist leaders since its circulation in the 1950s. *"Monlam* to Mao" was translated into Chinese at a public ceremony of the Buddhist Association of China in 1954 and published in its journal. As explained in the introduction to this work, the Buddhist

Association of China (BAC) was inaugurated in spring 1953 to facilitate official dialogue between the United Front Work Department and Buddhist groups. In the 1950s, prior to the BAC's disbanding during the Cultural Revolution, the membership was disproportionately national minorities, with twenty-nine of the total ninety-three members Tibetans.[127] The September 1954 issue of its journal, *Modern Buddhist Studies* (*Xiàndài fóxúe*, 现代佛学),[128] also published the Dalai Lama's *monlam* in Tibetan script followed by a Chinese translation.[129] This indicates that the poem's hopes for state protection of Buddhist institutions were shared among a larger Buddhist community.

The Tibetan text of "*Monlam to Mao*" in *Modern Buddhist Studies* matches the photographic reproduction of the artifact in *A Collection of Historical Archives of Tibet*,[130] but they are written in different hands. The editor of *Modern Buddhist Studies* adds the following postscript, which I translate from the Chinese here:

> The Dalai Lama recently wrote in his own hand, "An Ode to Mao Zhuxi" (Máo Zhǔxí sòng, 毛主席颂) eulogizing the great deeds of Chairman Mao. At the Buddhist Association of China Meeting, the Venerable Fazun (法尊) was asked to render the original precious Tibetan with its fine literary style and exquisite calligraphy into Chinese, to issue it in our publication, so that our fellow Buddhists can look at it with reverence.[131]

This addendum ends with a comment that Zhang Jianmu wrote up Fazun's text in vernacular Chinese (*yǔ tǐ wén*, 語體文).[132]

A later issue of *Modern Buddhist Studies* (November 1954) reports that the Fourteenth Dalai Lama and the Tenth Panchen Lama visited the headquarters of the Buddhist Association of China located at Guangji Temple in Beijing on September 12, 1954, a week before the promulgation of the PRC Constitution.[133] This short report also states that Fazun acted as interpreter. Fazun, a disciple of the Buddhist modernist Taixu, was an early member of the Buddhist Association of China, a frequent contributor to *Modern Buddhist Studies*, and as noted above, the translator of the Chinese print version of "Ode to Mao Zhuxi" in that publication.[134]

This indicates that the *monlam*'s message was spread by other Buddhists in China. From *Acoustic Ambrosia*, we know that Tséten Zhabdrung was in Beijing at this time. From other sources, such as the *Dungkar Encyclopedia*, we learn that he was a member of the Buddhist Association of China, but it is unclear if his membership was active during this time period. The ideals espoused by "A *Monlam* to Mao"—Buddhist aspirations for social harmony under the direction of a virtuous leader who supports Marxist and Buddhist ideals—were publicly shared in the media, and also in ritual space, in 1954.

Similar to the photo of Tséten Zhabdrung with Chinese dignitaries preserved in his family home, these artifacts remind us of the political status given to high-ranking Tibetan lamas in the early years of the PRC. For this reason, among others, historians such as Melvyn Goldstein and Tsering Shakya characterize Sino-Tibetan relations of the 1950s as "the lull before the storm"[135]—that is, "the storm" of Chinese military occupation, which resulted in profound changes to every aspect of Tibetan life—personal, public, religious, economic, social, political, and cultural. Likewise, Heather Stoddard points out that most of the leading Tibetan intellectuals remained in China with the hope that Seventeen Point Agreement would safeguard Tibetan ways of life:

> Until 1959, many of the contemporary Tibetan scholars whom we know today were still inside Tibet, living in a society that functioned essentially along traditional lines. Except for a few outstanding individuals, such as Lu-khang-ba, there were few in Tibetan government who spoke up in public against the Chinese presence. Society continued, to all intents and purposes, to function as before. The Seventeen Point Agreement, signed on May 23, 1951, guaranteed on paper at least, that this should be so.[136]

In other words, Tibetan hopes or expectations for Chinese state protection of Buddhist institutions were in many ways normative at that time. They did not manifest suddenly in the 1950s; a complex intermix of religion and politics had long undergirded Sino-Tibetan relations.[137] For example, Gray Tuttle's *Tibetan Buddhists in the Making of Modern China* shows how Tibetan and Chinese Buddhists forged relationships based on mutual respect and understanding in the Republican era.[138] Fabienne Jagou highlights the Ninth Panchen Lama's activities in China in the early 1930s to promote world peace.[139] Geshé Sherab Gyatso, a key figure in forging Sino-Tibetan relations during the Republican era, became president of the Buddhist Association of China in 1954. He was also a confidant and friend to Mugé Samten as well as a colleague of Tséten Zhabdrung, and like the young Dalai Lama, Geshé Sherab Gyatso viewed Marxism and Buddhism as compatible.[140] These relations were turned upside down during the Maoist years.

The content and publication of the Dalai Lama's *"Monlam* to Mao" reminds us of how Buddhists envisioned state protection of their institutions in the 1950s. In the post-Mao era, it was glaring how much political authority Tibetan Buddhist leaders had lost since the first decade of the PRC. Many Buddhist hierarchs had followed the Dalai Lama into exile. Those who had stayed in China were subjected to horrific fates, such as Tséten Zhabdrung, who would be imprisoned in 1965, or Mugé Samten, who was forced to do reform through labor in 1966. Most lamas, including Dungkar Rinpoché, were subjected to struggle sessions, trials of public humiliation, and frequently torture. In the next chapter, I look at how Tséten Zhabdrung and Mugé Samten approached remembering the unspeakable atrocities of that time period. Given the hardships that the two autobiographers had lived through, it is unsurprising that they wrote about any involvement in politics with trepidation.

Recognizing how Buddhists envisioned state protection of their institutions in the 1950s helps to deepen our appreciation of the complex lives and subject positions of Tibetan Buddhist leaders in China, such as all of the Three Polymaths, Mugé Samten, Tséten Zhabdrung, and Dungkar Rinpoché. The two autobiographers, Mugé Samten and Tséten Zhabdrung, wrote about their subjective pasts after living through the "lull before the storm" and the Maoist years.

Mugé Samten and Tséten Zhabdrung chose a genre that fits within Tibet's established literary practices but also alters that tradition to "tell what happened" in order to edify their monastic disciples and secular students, and to tell about their lives for the sake of history. They draw upon discursive techniques, especially poetic wordplay, to extol certain virtues and make philosophical points that continue in the tradition of past scholars. The autobiographers recall Tibetan religious epistemes, such as the ethics of spiritual friendship and altruistic motivations for worldly work in order to benefit all sentient beings. They remember discursive traditions and values that were respected and protected by the PRC government in the 1950s; however, they wrote about their own involvement in political affairs with much more caution. Neither author emphasized the national history of the PRC. Rather, they wrote in a literary genre of autobiography that evoked moral values steeped in Buddhist ethics and Géluk philosophy and framed these within the contours of Tibetan literature. They thereby reproduced the conditions of discursive traditions that they simultaneously contributed to and altered at a particular historical juncture, the Deng Xiaoping era of China.

Tséten Zhabdrung's and Mugé Samten's autobiographical focus on Buddhist values during the 1950s rekindles hope for the state protection's thereof. They charge themselves with edifying readers in Buddhist ethos in the *yang-dar* era because any sort of state support for these values and institutions had been denied for a twenty-year period. When they add their voices to an ensemble of past Tibetan masters whose sacred texts carry prized cultural values, they write about the past in a way that creates and constitutes the sensibilities and embodied capacities of Buddhist ethical values to revive Tibetan traditions in the post-Mao era. As I detail in subsequent chapters, despite enduring great personal hardships, all Three Polymaths emerged from the Maoist years to engage in various efforts to preserve and continue Tibetan cultural life in the post-Mao era.

3

Mellifluous Words on the Human Condition

The Maoist Years

The monster of this heartless era
opened its fearsome mouth as wide as
the space between earth and sky.
In this gap, its weapons, teeth and fangs,
gnashed irrevocably and ferociously! Terrifying!
(Literary device of the affective state of fear)[1]

"Avadāna of Silver Flowers," Tséten Zhabdrung

Histories of modern Tibet indicate that any hopes or aspirations for legal protection of Tibetan Buddhist culture were exiled to India with the Dalai Lama in 1959.[2] At around the same time, devastating famines gripped Tibetan areas of western China due to the failed policies of the Great Leap Forward (1958–1962). The next two decades saw the subsequent exodus of approximately eighty thousand Tibetan refugees into India; ten thousand into Nepal; and thousands more into Europe, Canada, and the United States.[3] Chinese historical accounts characterize the Maoist era, delineated here as a twenty-year period from circa 1958 until 1978, by leftist idealism, social chaos, and aberrant violence against all aspects of Tibetan society and culture.[4] Unlike prevailing historical accounts, Tséten Zhabdrung and Mugé Samten do not offer true-to-life exposés of what happened to them during this time period. Rather, as signaled by the verse from "*Avadāna* of Silver Flowers" above, they deftly weave Tibetan literary aesthetics, emotions, and memories into their autobiographical narratives.

In remembering the haunting "monster of this heartless era," the authors of *Acoustic Ambrosia* and *Luminous Mirror* (almost) erase the all-powerful state from their respective life stories. Unlike testimonials that detail violent acts during zealous secularizing campaigns of the Maoist years, the autobiographers mix poetry and prose to express Buddhist truths of impermanence, human suffering, and spiritual realizations. The poetic verses translated throughout this chapter alternately lament the loss of Buddhist teachings, sing of profound spiritual realizations, and call attention to the power of the mind due to the efficacy of Buddhist practice. The poetic mode of articulating what happened during this era indicates that Tséten Zhabdrung's and Mugé Samten's accounts are not intended to depict ordinary lives, despite diffident claims to the contrary, as discussed in the previous chapter. Nowhere else in their autobiographies does it become clearer that their perceptions of reality are extraordinary as in their writings on this period of Sino-Tibetan history.

If these texts are neither testimonials nor ordinary accounts of what happened, then this raises the question of how to read their life narratives. To answer it, I bring autobiographical theory and the notion of "doing religion" to bear on my analysis. Focusing on the performative dimension of their texts brings the religious ideals of a *khédrup*, a scholar-adept, to the fore. I read their telling of what happened during this period of history as a way of exemplifying the Géluk Buddhist ideal of the "scholar-adept" (*khédrup*) in which scholarship and spiritual wisdom are embodied as one. Both autobiographers remember their lives through Buddhist truths and present these memories within well-established discursive parameters of Tibetan language arts to construct their autobiographical selves as living "scholar-adepts." The literary techniques used in their life stories value Buddhist truth and Tibetan literary aesthetics in the same stroke. In this way, these two authors become testimony to the continuity of Tibetan cultural practices throughout the heartless era into the age of the Dharma's rediffusion.

EXPRESSING THE INEFFABLE

Acoustic Ambrosia and *Luminous Mirror* vaguely mention life-changing events caused by Maoist policies. The sparse details on Tséten Zhabdrung's twelve-year imprisonment and Mugé Samten's hard labor sentence render their autobiographies different from historical testimonies of this time period. Standard accounts tend to give harrowing details on how victims of political injustice were mistreated. Neither author describes any acts of torture or violence, which we know from other testimonials they must have endured. What little we learn of their sufferings is alluded to in verse and prose within their respective autobiographies and some poetic verses found in other works. An example of the latter is the epigraph from the *"Avadāna* of Silver Flowers," in which Tséten Zhabdrung laments the loss of Buddhist teachings in a way that does not personalize his sufferings, but characterizes the entire era as a "monster."

Similarly, the twenty-page section of Tséten Zhabdrung's autobiography that details his life during the Maoist years begins with a verse. The seven-stanza poem is dated to 1958, the year his co-throne holder, Tséten Khenpo, was murdered. He does not offer specifics on what happened to him personally, but his grief is palpable when we read, "I suddenly lost the words to express such suffering, a grim memory."[5] "Words" (*tshig*) seems to mean "prose" because Tséten Zhabdrung then recalls the mass destruction of Buddhist culture (that he presumably must have witnessed) in an emotionally jarring poem.

It begins with Buddhist teachings (Buddha-Dharma) represented as the sun setting in the West, a metaphor for death, perhaps in the western Buddhist paradise of Sukhāvatī. This metaphor establishes a sense of the inevitable destruction of Buddhism from the onset of the poem. Like a tsunami, each stanza violently crescendos with waves of atrocities, one after the other relentlessly desecrating various aspects of Buddhist life.

> Kye ma! Alas!
> Who can stop the sun, Treasure
> of Buddhist Teachings for spiritual well-being,
> setting in the west, Varuṇa's lap,[6] when slim strands of merit
> can be found like the tip of a sage's hair?

> Kye ma! Alas!
> Who can rescue the sinking ship,
> bearing the banner of teachings and experience
> when those who ape *śramaṇa* begin to speak
> discordant negative speech against the Buddha?

> Kye ma! Alas!
> Who can save the monasteries from destruction,
> protect those who bear saffron robes,
> when those who stand in the ranks of Dharma holders
> carelessly cast off their vows like chaff?

Kye ma! Alas!
Can anyone still sleep peacefully, knowing
the karmic results of these actions made
with anger and weapons against the three supports,
sites respected by worship and prostrations?

Kye ma! Alas!
Sacred volumes to dispel ignorance
attached to soles of shoes, a nightmare
never even conjured by Langdarma.
Taken up in trembling, quivering hands.

Kye ma! Alas!
How easy is it for those who crave gold
to pass the bardo ridge? The precious grains
placed in the treasury of sutras and shastras
are given to the fire and melted down.

Kye ma! Alas!
Terror! Who can count the highest number,
the number of priceless lives lost, powerless
in this period of merely outward symbols,[7]
forced to wear lay clothes before the world?

These stanzas are a brief reprieve to express how I felt weighed down by
      an unbearable grief at the obscuration of the Buddhist teachings as
      the lamp of existence[8] disappears behind thick dark clouds.[9]

Throughout this poem, Tséten Zhabdrung calls for someone to stop the
onslaught of destruction, but no one answers. Instead this poem becomes his
testimony, the autobiographical memories of sacrilegious acts committed during secularizing campaigns of the Maoist era. We learn of the "discordant
negative speech against the Buddha," forced laicization as monks carelessly
"cast off their vows like chaff," and the wanton destruction of Buddhist objects
known as the "three supports," i.e., statues, scriptures, and reliquary shrines.
Even the anti-Buddhist king, Langdarma, could not have perpetrated the hei-
nous acts committed under the command of the leader alluded to, Mao
Zedong. The author, Tséten Zhabdrung, laconically discloses these unspeakable acts through poetry.

Studies on life narratives that deal with traumatic experiences, such as the Holocaust, sexual abuse, and torture, explain how "narrators struggle to find ways of telling about suffering that defies language and understanding; they struggle to reassemble memories so dreadful they must be repressed for human beings to survive and function in life."[10] Tséten Zhabdrung articulates the ineffable through poetic lament and by remembering religious epistemes, which I detail later in this chapter. Likewise, sections of Mugé Samten's autobiography remember Buddhist ontologies through an evocative use of language. As will become evident throughout this chapter, neither author presents their memories as haunting or disruptive to their autobiographical life. In order to establish a basis for making comparisons between these modes of remembering, I turn briefly to other personal accounts of this time period.

Scar Literature and Tibetan Testimonies on the Trauma of the Maoist Years

A considerable number of testimonies dealing with the experiences of the Cultural Revolution, both fictional and nonfictional, have been published by Han Chinese in China; there are far fewer written by Tibetans.[11] Frequently these accounts emphasize the extremity of the crisis and the victim's ability to survive the traumatic experience.

One such type of writing emerged within Han Chinese intellectual circles around the same time as the Three Polymaths became professors at different nationality universities in the late 1970s and early 1980s. "Scar literature" (伤痕文学; shānghén wénxué) entails fictional stories that present the scars of personal loss as a result of leftist excesses during the Cultural Revolution. In its aftermath, these wounds are healed through the benevolent actions of the Chinese Communist Party. For example, the popular novel Hibiscus Town (Fúróngzhèn) by Gu Hua was published in 1981 and made into a film by the director Xie Jin in 1986. Hibiscus Town presents the Cultural Revolution through the personal losses of Hu Yuyin, the main protagonist. Ultimately the Party prevails in rectifying the injustices caused by the false conviction of her partner, Qin Shutian. In the end, the two live happily ever after as food stall owners. A key feature of this genre is that the corruption, personal losses, and trauma are restricted only to the "ten years of chaos." The Cultural Revolution is therefore construed as a brief aberration in the otherwise just leadership of the CCP.[12] This literary movement never touched on Tibetan identity or the fact that Chinese political campaigns began to alter every aspect of Tibetan society nearly a decade before the launch of the Cultural Revolution in 1966.

Histories of modern Tibet inform us that any special privileges that Mao Zedong had granted Tibetans in the first decade under Chinese rule began to unravel with the implementation of democratic forms of local government in Tibetan areas in the mid-late 1950s, and then ended completely with the launch of the Cultural Revolution. The ideological campaigns in Tibet both up to and after 1966 were in many ways no different from what occurred in other parts of China. Some Tibetans became Red Guards (Chi.: *hóng wèibīng*) and enthusiastically embraced Maoist ideals.[13] However, as Tsering Shakya points out, whereas political factionalism was at the root of the campaigns and counter-campaigns in the mainland, traditional culture became a target in Tibet.[14] From this perspective, the political idealism of the Maoist Revolution was intended to destroy traditional ways of life and force Tibetans to embrace socialist thought.

Various coercive measures were implemented to achieve socialist transformation. For example, one of the primary tasks given to the Red Guards was to rid the country of the "Four Olds"—old ideas, culture, customs, and habits—which were considered remnants of the feudal, exploitative past.[15] Anyone who refused to participate was considered a "counterrevolutionary." Many were subjected to *thamzing* (*'thab 'dzing*), the Tibetan term for a "struggle session."[16] From the state's point of view, struggle sessions were held ostensibly to benefit the target by ridding him or her of all traces of counterrevolutionary or reactionary thinking.[17] These large public gatherings often resulted in the humiliation and torture of the person who was the "target."

There are only a handful of testimonies about the Maoist years written by Tibetans living within Tibet. Two of the most prominent, *Autobiography of Tashi Tsering* and *A Tibetan Revolutionary: The Political Life and Times of Bapa Phüntso Wangye*, were published in the United States. Within the past decade, a couple of books, *Nagtshang Boy* (*Nag tshang zhi lu'i skyid sdug*) and *Rinzang's Serial Notes* (*Rin bzang gi mu 'brel zin tho*), which came out in two volumes: *My Homeland and Peaceful Liberation* (*Nga'i pha yul dang zhi ba'i bcings grol*) and *My Homeland: Listen Carefully* (*Nga'i pha yul dang gzab nyan*), have been published unofficially in China. These testimonies along with popular autobiographies, such as *The Autobiography of a Tibetan Monk* and *Ama Adhe: The Voice That Remembers*, which were cowritten with ghost writers and published for Euro-American markets, have similar modes of presenting the events of Maoist years.[18] They all graphically detail the extreme brutality and injustices characterizing this time period and tell how the main protagonist survived.

The *Autobiography of Tashi Tsering*, was written by a Tibetan living in Lhasa. Tashi Tsering had traveled to India, then studied in the United States at Williams College from 1960 to 1963. He returned to China a few years prior to the start of the Cultural Revolution. In 1967, Tashi Tsering was subjected to a struggle session, a *thamzing*, which he describes as follows:

> They at once put the blackboard around my neck and half-pushed, half-dragged me out to a hall packed tightly with about five hundred students and teachers waiting to struggle against me. This meeting, my second large struggle session, was organized by Chen and Ma Ximei for the purpose of teaching me a lesson for my use of Mao's words.... The meeting started when the student leader yelled out, "Drag in Tashi Tsering the counterrevolutionary." As I was being pushed in, others shouted, "Down with Tashi Tsering's arrogance," "Down with the enemy of the motherland" and so forth.... After a few weeks more, I got so fed up ... something inside me broke.[19]

While Tashi Tsering recalls being broken by the relentless struggle sessions, the ghost-written autobiography of Palden Gyatso recounts how the prison guards tortured him during *thamzing* in a Chinese prison:

> He scolded me as if I were a child. "There is only one road left for you!." He nodded to the cell leader, who raised his fist and shouted, "Eliminate reactionaries!." The other prisoners joined him like a chorus. The guard and the cell leader began to beat me. I cupped my hands in front of my face to protect myself. The beating seemed to go on forever, but it could not have lasted more than twenty minutes.... During that period I must have endured thirty or forty of those beatings. No prisoner was exempt from *thamzing*. And because *thamzing* always involved other prisoners, the Party was absolved of any responsibility.[20]

Similar brutality is documented in an interview in *Rinzang's Serial Notes*. The author, Rinzang, recorded his conversations with elderly survivors of the Maoist years. In the second volume, *My Homeland: Listen Carefully,* a monk called Akhu Yarphel explains how he and another monk called Akhu Kalden were subjected to torture and name-calling in struggle sessions in the late 1950s:

> Akhu Yarphel: Every day, both of us were struggled against. I wore their four "criminal hats." I wore the Hat of Feudalism, the Hat of the Four Kinds of Evil People, the Hat of the Landlord Class, and the Hat of the Exploiters (*bshu gzhog*). Akhu Kaldan had to wear the Hat of the Religious Exploiters. The

people who did the struggle sessions acted like they were completely insane. They tied both of Akhu Kaldan's hands back and twisted them, almost dislocating both of them, but he didn't even flinch. He was really tough! Even the people who were torturing him were amazed. During the struggle sessions they made him put on his monk's robes and both his monk's hat and the paper hat. During the sessions, they put the shoulder-bone and a jaw of an animal in his hands, and forced him to bang on the shoulder blade with the jaw-bone. At the same time as that, he had to criticize himself saying, "Don't copy me! I am an evil person and I committed mistakes like this." After the struggle session, he had to take off his monk's robes. He held them in his hands on the way back home.[21]

This account sheds light on the various types of crimes, the so-called "hats," that victims were charged with. In this respect, it is slightly more detailed than Tashi Tsering's and Palden Gyatso's testimonies. All three testimonials are strikingly similar in the way they remember the past, i.e., through graphic true-to-life descriptions of public humiliation and physical violence. Other testimonials by Tibetan survivors of the Maoist years describe their experiences of this era as confusing and disorienting.[22]

For example, Bapa Phüntso Wangye (Phünwang) underscores the mental anguish caused by solitary confinement and false accusations. His life story shows how the highest ranking Tibetan Communist cadre (from 1951 to 1958) fell out of political favor and ended up spending eighteen years in the Chinese Alcatraz—Qincheng Number One Prison—beginning in 1960, six years before the start of the Cultural Revolution.[23] Phünwang details his imprisonment as follows:

> For almost two years they had called me only by my cell number, and I think I had temporarily forgotten who I was and what my name sounded like. When I realized this, I began to cry. The tears welled up from deep inside and streamed uncontrollably down my cheeks.... The formal interrogations weren't all I had to endure during these first few years. Sometimes, without warning, men would come to my cell at night and beat me. They never gave me a reason; it was simply one of those things they did to break my spirit.[24]

Along with aberrant violence, disorientation and cruelty are poignant themes found in these testimonies of the Maoist era.

Pema Bhum's memoirs of the Cultural Revolution depict another type of disorientation. He remembers how many Tibetans were confused by the jargon of Chinese propaganda. He documents how writings by Tibetan scholars, such as Tséten Zhabdrung, were labeled "poisonous weeds" and that only one book was allowed—*Quotations from Chairman Mao*. Before the "little red book" became the only one available, its title circulated by word of mouth. Pema Bhum gives the following humorous yet jarring description of his experiences at this time:

> The title of this little book arrived before the work itself. It had a Chinese name: Mao Zhuxi Yulu. Not knowing what this was, some Tibetans pronounced it "Ma'o-kru'u-zhi-re'u-lo" which in Tibetan means "Chairman Mao's Baby Goat." In many places throughout Amdo, the book was called "Nanny Goat's Baby" or simply "Baby Goat." As a child, I used to love playing with the kid goats my family kept and these goats were fond of me, as well.... Perhaps this was the reason I myself preferred to call the book, "Chairman Mao's Baby Goat."[25]

Later nomadic children would be forced to learn to recite from this book, the meaning of which often eluded them.[26] The massive lack of understanding underscores how absurd Chinese political jargon must have been to Tibetans at this time.

In another autobiography, Chinese leaders are depicted as completely incompetent. Tubten Khétsun details in *Memories of Life in Lhasa Under Chinese Rule* how he was forced to obey one absurd command after the next. He remembers being compelled to do labor that was incredibly dangerous and for which he had absolutely no training, such as setting dynamite to blow up mountains for road work. His life narrative chronicles how one impossible task after the next fell upon him.[27]

In the acts of remembering the past, the above Tibetan testimonials attend to the grave facts of the Maoist years, documenting torture, death, confusion, and grave injustices. We will not know what happened for many others. For example, although rumors have circulated that Dungkar Lozang Trinlé wrote a diary during the Cultural Revolution, no publication has yet appeared. When we compare Tséten Zhabdrung's poetic lament translated at the beginning of this chapter with the above testimonials, it becomes clear that Tséten Zhabdrung neither documents mental disorientation nor provides graphic details of what happened in personal terms. Mugé Samten's portrayal of his own experience of a struggle session also differs considerably from the depictions of violence or disorientation found in other remembrances of the Maoist years.

Mugé Samten's Song of Realization

Contrary to depictions of the Maoist years as brutal or confusing, Mugé Samten's remembrances of this era are positive, purposeful, and direct. He celebrates what happened to him in a song of spiritual realization. Mixing prose and verse, his autobiographical memories signal another way of perceiving a public struggle session:

> When I was being led around the market square, they forced me to put on my monk's robes and wear the flat hat used for retreat. They made me carry on my back three texts: the *Litany of the Names of Mañjuśrī*; the *Condensed Prajñāpāramitā-sūtra*, and *Aspiration to Good Conduct*. On my shoulders they stuck pages of *The Collected Teachings of the Kadampa,* and in one hand they placed my rosary, and in the other, a section of *The Great Life Story of Jowo Atisha*. Then they pushed me through the streets shouting slogans. In my mind a great happiness was born, and I wished to rejoice by singing a song of realization (*mgur*); whatever came to mind poured out of me:

> > Please dress me in a saffron robe,
> > adorn me in the Kadampa teachings,
> > place the *The Collected Teachings* in my hands
> > put the long, flat hat on my head.
> > Wow, such a joyous time![28]

This portrayal does not align with the political understanding of a struggle session, a technique to turn subjects into good socialists. The *thamzing* is not described as torture. The author rejoiced that it was "a joyous time!"

The four lines of verse are written in a literary style called "*gur*" or "song of realization." Translator Victoria Sujata describes its religious significance:

> *Gur* are a genre of unique importance for understanding the tradition of Tibetan Buddhism. They have religious themes, but are at the same time more direct expressions of personal experience than classic monastic literature.... They are largely sung by recluses in solitude or for other hermit-disciples away from monastic settings; their expression is often less formal and very personal.... Because *gur* are simple expressions of personal religious insights

that aim to appeal to the people in a way that is accessible and pleasing, they fill an essential role in Tibetan Buddhism.[29]

Sujata characterizes *gur* as songs of personal realizations performed in reclusive settings. This description contrasts sharply with the backdrop for Mugé Samten's *gur*. He carols a song of spiritual insight in the midst of a public *thamzing* struggle session.

Mugé Samten does not present his memories of what happened to him in a way that recalls historical accounts of the name-calling and beating that accompanied being "led through a market square" during a *thamzing*. He sings a *gur*. Although it is sung outside of the normative retreat setting, the *gur* serves to voice Mugé Samten's realizations of Buddhist truths. For him, this struggle session is viewed as joyous because of the spiritual insights he gained through the experience. This exemplifies an approach to remembering the Maoist years used by both autobiographers. Mugé Samten and Tséten Zhabdrung write about their lived experiences within the parameters of Buddhist truth and the Tibetan literary arts.

SCHOLAR-ADEPTS ON KARMA AND THE HUMAN CONDITION

Considering that both autobiographers were Géluk Buddhist monks, it is unsurprising that their life narratives construct their autobiographical selves through Buddhist ontology. What is novel and extraordinary are the circumstances through which they survived. The authors of *Luminous Mirror* and *Acoustic Ambrosia* do not present themselves as victims of tyranny. They remember their lives in terms of Buddhist truths.

For example, Tséten Zhabdrung views *saṃsāra,* the never-ending cycle of birth, death, and rebirth, as fueled by karma, actions that feed the causes and conditions of suffering. As he explains:

> As for the nature of *saṃsāra*, there is no beginning for the chain of rebirths from time immemorial till now. Regardless which form of the six types of sentient beings is taken, countless bad deeds and sins are accumulated, unless these are countered by powerful measures. When causes collect in karmic maturation, it is like the body and its shadow together. All negative consequences must be experienced even if you don't want them; this is irreversible.[30]

This didactic explanation of the nature of reality from a Buddhist perspective is not abstract for him. It is grounded in this-worldly observations that are simultaneously poetic. He compares the notion of karma and its effects with the body as inseparable from its shadow. Self-reflectively, the author applies the irrevocability of this moving truth to his own personal situation.

Tséten Zhabdrung reveals that he understands that negative acts committed in his former life resulted in his imprisonment:

> By dint of the fact that I and my previous incarnation Nan Tāzhin have one consciousness, because he followed the emperor's orders and suppressed local chieftains in the Hui wars and as the ruling military official brought several hundred men to court, then these impure actions from that life fall upon me in this life. I have contemplated the law of karmic results based on several works.[31]

By this account, Tséten Zhabdrung does not blame the state for his arrest. He places accountability on himself based on his actions in a past life. He draws upon the integral link between *saṃsāra* and *karma* to interpret his incarceration as an inevitable outcome of misdeeds in a former life. In this way, he unequivocally ties karmic effect to the actions of his predecessor, the Fifth Tséten Zhabdrung.[32]

We know from other sections of his autobiography that the earlier incarnation, Jigmé Thupten Gyatso ('Jigs med thub bstan rgya mtsho), alias Nan Tāzhin (Nan ta' zhin, 1863–1908), renounced his monastic vows during the 1895/6 siege of his hometown and led an army on the side of the Qing in order to defend the garrison of Yadzi during a Muslim uprising.[33] Because of his role in the military, he was responsible for the punishments, even death sentences, of the men he brought to court. These misdeeds caused the karmic effect of imprisonment in this life.

After establishing the karmic basis for his arrest, the narrator moves on to talk about the arrest. It is the only factual information we learn about his imprisonment in all of *Acoustic Ambrosia*. He writes:

> Because of this [i.e., negative karmic effects], from my fifty-sixth year to my sixty-seventh year, that is from the anniversary of Tsongkhapa's death on the 25th day of the tenth month in the Wood-Snake year [December 1965] until the thirteenth day of the sixth month in the Fire-Dragon year [July 1976]; for a period of [almost] twelve years, the punishment of the ruler, the Gyelpo (rgyal po), the terror of karma, fell upon me. I tied together the inner confines with the outer confines, as I had to make prison my place of residence.[34]

Even this memory is written with literary flourishes, as Tséten Zhabdrung uses a poetic term for prison (*khri mon*). He does not refer to the state but uses a more archaic term for "ruler," *gyelpo*, which is more commonly translated as "king." Stylistically this is similar to other passages in the sense of the author's use of a kind of rhetorical ellipses whereby factual details, such as the name and location of the jail in this case, are omitted.

Before reading more from their autobiographies and discussing in more detail the literary devices they used to remember this time period, it might be helpful to pause and reflect on why these authors might frame a struggle session as a spiritual experience or claim karma as the real reason for a twelve-year prison sentence.

Writing the Self as a Scholar-Adept

Tséten Zhabdrung's ascription of karmic effect as the reason for his imprisonment provides fertile ground for analysis. It might be argued that such an interpretation of *saṃsāra* and karma blames the victim for the atrocities of state violence. Such a reading, however, would frame agency in terms of power structures. This sets up a dichotomous positioning of the subject as either a victim of the state or a collaborator with the state. Yet the authors of *Acoustic Ambrosia* and *Luminous Mirror* write about their lives in ways that almost completely ignore state power. For this reason alone, interpreting these autobiographical accounts through the lens of power is not particularly helpful. Theorists in both literature and religious studies point in another analytical direction: toward the historical and cultural contexts within which autobiographies are produced.

Sidonie Smith and Julia Watson remind us, "The complexity of autobiographical texts requires reading practices that reflect on the narrative tropes, sociocultural contexts, rhetorical aims and narrative shifts within the historical or chronological trajectory."[35] Paul John Eakin explains that when we approach autobiography, "we may not necessarily recognize another culture's practice of identity narrative as such."[36] He proposes that we attend to the "relational" aspects of identity formation, which include "environmental" factors such as social institutions as well as personal relationships, which have a decisive impact on the autobiographer.[37] If we attend to the sociocultural context, rhetorical aims, and environmental factors of these autobiographies, it becomes clear from the readings thus far that they are grounded in Géluk knowledge, i.e., epistemes,

and Buddhist practices. Similarly, the notion of "doing religion" brings attention to the cultural context and performative dimension of subjecthood, of how
identity is shaped through actions. Orit Avishai argues that "Doing religion is
associated with a search for authentic religious subject-hood and that religiosity
is shaped in accordance with the logics of one's religion, and in the context of
controlling messages about threatened symbolic boundaries and cultural Others."[38] Interpreted within the grammar of Géluk Buddhist epistemes, Mugé
Samten's and Tséten Zhabdrung's autobiographical writings serve to bring
Tibetan scholasticism and Buddhist practices to the fore.

This aligns well with the fact that both scholars, along with Dungkar
Rinpoché, were referred to as "polymaths" (*mkhas pa*). The notion of a Buddhist polymath, i.e., *khépa* (*mkhas pa*), is understood here within a system of
Tibetan scholasticism, which involves mastering the five "major *rikné*," as
explained in the introduction and chapter 1. Tséten Zhabdrung's *A General
Commentary on Poetics* (1957) underscores the mastery of the language arts as
integral to being a "polymath":

> The sites of activities for polymaths are the five fields of knowledge (*rikné*): lan-
> guage arts, logic, crafts, medicine, and Buddhism. Within the branch of lan-
> guage arts:
>
> > If you know literary devices, then you master poetics;
> > If you know kennings, then you master word choice;
> > If you know metrics, then you master verse;
> > If you know drama, then you master language;
> > If you know arithmetic, then you master counting.[39]

Language arts includes various skills in the use of literary devices, kennings,
rules of composition, drama, and math.[40] Comprehensive knowledge of these
skills plays a crucial role in the subject formation of a scholar. Interestingly, in
the verse above, the verb "to master" (*mkhas*) shares the same root as the nominalized "polymath" (*mkhas pa*). "Mastering" these skills, especially composition
and literary techniques, lies at the heart of what it means to be a "polymath"
in the Tibetan cultural context. This model of scholarship frequently blurs the
lines between the religious scholar and the secular specialist in a given
subject.[41]

Another etymologically related word is important to our understanding of
why Mugé Samten's and Tséten Zhabdrung's autobiographies might highlight
both Buddhist scholasticism and practices. That term is *khédrup* (*mkhas grub*), a

"scholar-adept." This can serve as a title for highly revered lamas. For Géluk practitioners, for example, it has particular relevance because it serves as the name and title of one of Tsongkhapa's closest disciples, Khédrup-je (Mkhas grub rje, 1385–1438).[42] This title reflects an important ethos for Tibetan Buddhists that combines two excellences as one: scholarly achievement and spiritual realization. Mugé Samten's and Tséten Zhabdrung's autobiographical writings mirror this cultural value.

The way that Mugé Samten and Tséten Zhabdrung engage in remembering involves a level of performativity that serves to construct their autobiographical selves in a relational environment deeply embedded within the "doing" of Géluk Buddhist epistemes. The act of "telling what happened" exemplifies Buddhist scholasticism and practices even under the most extreme secular circumstances. They become *khédrup* in their retelling of the Maoist years.

When Tséten Zhabdrung cites karmic effects as the reason for his imprisonment, he removes the state from the narrative and places himself in an autobiographical relational environment grounded in Buddhist notions of karma. By this self-ascription of karma, no matter how horrific the outside circumstances, he returns to "the inner confines." His remembering and creating subjectivity in this way stakes an important claim. Regardless of what the state does or the degree to which power is abused, the protagonist's mind remains unharmed due to the efficacious results of Buddhist practice. Mugé Samten explicitly brings this point out in the following passage:

> In the male Fire-Horse year, 1966, in the sixth month [of the Tibetan calendar], when I was fifty-three years old, the great calamity known as the Cultural Revolution began. In the tenth month of that year, the so-called "Red Guards" arrested five people including myself from our work at a local government office. They seized all of our things, led us around the market, and struggled against us. However, this didn't harm my mind. I thought this was the natural state of *saṃsāra*[43]

The terms "Cultural Revolution," "Red Guards," and "struggle session" all indicate that Mugé Samten must have been attacked by leftist zealots, friends, or former colleagues. Yet here again the reader is left to imagine the details of what happened. The narrative erases the outer conditions, leaving an inner subjective reality framed by mental acuity.

Unlike Tashi Tsering and Phünwang in their testimonial accounts of disorientation and violence, Mugé Samten and Tséten Zhabdrung set the discursive and ethical boundaries of their own autobiographical lives. Unlike Akhu Yarphel and Palden Gyatso, neither author identifies himself with a political position, such as "reactionary" or as a "member of the exploitative class." Tséten Zhabdrung only refers to prison with a poetic term.

As *khédrup*, both Mugé Samten and Tséten Zhabdrung self-reflectively write about their scholarly understandings of Buddhist philosophical truths, and their accounts also serve to demonstrate their capacity for embodied awareness that comes with Buddhist practice. Mugé Samten alludes to the notion of a *khédrup* (scholar-adept) by connecting his scholarly training with a deeper insight gained through embodied meditative experience: "Earlier in my life I had pretended to meditate on the inherent flaws of *saṃsāra* and impermanence and I read a few books, such as *The Great Treatise on the Stages of the Path to Enlightenment* and *Mind Training,* but then in the struggle session, I became well acquainted with the truth of suffering."[44] The struggle session became a site for him to deepen his spiritual insights. The two texts mentioned here, Tsongkhapa's *Lam Rim Chenmo* or *The Great Treatise on the Stages of the Path to Enlightenment,* abbreviated as *Stages of the Path,* and *Mind Training,* are foundational for Géluk training in both philosophy and meditation.

Mugé Samten reports that when he had studied the *Stages of the Path* earlier in his life, he had only pretended to grasp its concepts. This tells us that he meditated upon its lessons, such as *saṃsāra* and impermanence, in his training as a young monk. Tsongkhapa's *Stages of the Path* is a magnum opus of the Géluk Buddhist tradition. It is an extended commentary on Atisha Dipamkara's *A Lamp for the Path to Awakening* (Skt. *Bodhipathapradīpa*), the foundational text for the Lam Rim tradition, which reconciles varying commentarial and doctrinal interpretations and outlines the entire Buddhist path according to the capacity of the practitioner. Lam Rim serves as a guide for Mugé Samten's practices, as it does for many Buddhist practitioners.

One technique found within the Lam Rim texts is to recognize the inherent flaws of *saṃsāra* or cyclic existence. This cognitive meditation as outlined in *Stages of the Path* urges students to develop stronger motivations for spiritual practice. Tsongkhapa explains, "Unless you develop a determination to reject cyclic existence through meditating on its faults, you will not seek relief from suffering.[45] As Géluk monks, Mugé Samten and Tséten Zhabdrung would have been required to memorize and to practice the steps explained in *Stages of the Path.*

Mind Training, the other text mentioned by Mugé Samten, is more difficult to identify precisely because there are several versions and commentaries. The foundational mind training teaching is attributed to Atisha Dipamkara, the eleventh-century Bengali master, who authored the foundational text, *A*

Lamp for the Path to Awakening. The Tibetan term for mind training is *lojong*, wherein *lo* (*blo*) refers to conceptual mind, thought, or attitudes and *jong* (*sbyong*) connotes training, acquiring a skill, mastering a field of knowledge, or cultivating specific mental qualities. Thupten Jinpa describes the efficacy of this meditative practice in transforming one's conceptual habits "from the ordinary deluded state whose modus operandi is self-centeredness to a fundamentally changed perspective of enlightened other-centeredness."[46] After the codification of Atisha's teachings on mind training a century after his death, the teaching was organized into a seven-point approach, which is the most common form today.[47]

Similar to how Mugé Samten recalls receiving the opportunity to practice mind training in a public struggle session, Tséten Zhabdrung writes about practicing mind training during his incarceration. Tséten Zhabdrung explicitly refers to one particular aspect, the third of the seven points of mind training. This involves a spiritual exercise that cognitively remaps negativity into opportunities for enlightenment, referred to as *tonglen* (taking and giving). The verse from the translation of Chekawa Yeshé Dorjé's *Seven-Point Mind Training* is as follows:

> III. Taking adverse conditions on the path to enlightenment
> When the world and its inhabitants boil with negativity,
> Transform adverse conditions into the path of enlightenment.
> Banish all blames to the single source.
> Toward all beings contemplate their great kindness.[48]

When Tséten Zhabdrung and Mugé Samten studied this point in their monastic training, they would have received detailed meditation instructions accompanying the text even though they are not mentioned overtly in their life narratives. Both autobiographers present meditative and cognitive techniques accompanying textual studies as efficacious. Tséten Zhabdrung writes about his daily *tonglen* practice while in prison as follows: "I didn't forget even for a day, even in my imagination, to meditate well on *tonglen* (*gtong len*) and on directing one's thoughts to the practice of bodhicitta based on verses from *Mind Training* and prayers to the venerable guru."[49] Bodhicitta refers to the mind of awakening motivated by compassion and empathy for all sentient beings. Whereas most prisoners describe torture and imprisonment as disorienting, Tséten Zhabdrung and Mugé Samten remember their actions with clarity. Eakin reminds us that "relational identity confounds our literary and ethical categories; both need to be stretched to accommodate the fluidity of selves and lives."[50] Their clarity of mind, we are given to understand, comes from their disciplined training as Géluk monks.

Because Mugé Samten could interpret the negative conditions brought by the Cultural Revolution (struggle sessions, starvation, and imprisonment) and mentally remap them as an opportunities, he reports experiencing happiness, as his testimony above attests: "Then they pushed me through the streets noisily shouting slogans. In my mind a great happiness was born."[51] This euphoria arose due to spiritual insights into the nature of the human condition. These accounts become testimony that Mugé Samten and Tséten Zhabdrung are carrying Buddhist epistemes and practices into the post-Mao era. Their autobiographies provide several more examples of how they embody the ideals of scholar-adepts, especially by documenting their dreams and practices under conditions that must have been horrifying.

Dreams and Spiritual Realizations

The authors of *Luminous Mirror* and *Acoustic Ambrosia* interpret the ineffable suffering of the Maoist years as integral to the human condition according to a Buddhist worldview. Therefore, this time was replete with opportunities for spiritual practice. Each autobiographer reports intensifying his commitment to daily practice. Tséten Zhabdrung remembers:

> During this time [i.e., in prison], I mentally created Cloud Offerings[52] filling the sky, and I increased my daily practice without stopping, my tongue recited slowly, alternating between the practices of the Hundred Torma Offerings, Taking Refuge and Arousing Bodhicitta, the Offering to the Lama, the Aiming at Loving-Kindness Prayer, the Supplication Prayer to the Lama, the Ritual to Yamāntaka, the Medicine Prayer, the Ocean of Clouds of Praise Pleasing to Mañjuśrī, the Twelve Prayers of Sutra and Tantra, Torma Offerings, and the Verses of Praise to Tara.[53]

The reader again is left to imagine the circumstances in which he recited these prayers. I learned from interviews with Tséten Zhabdrung's former colleagues that he was jailed in Xining's Nantan Prison, a fact corroborated in the *Dungkar Encyclopedia*.[54] Inmates during the Cultural Revolution were presumably forbidden to carry out any religious practices. They probably were not allowed to perform rituals, such as the practice of offering cakes, *torma* in Tibetan. Yet we would never know this from Tséten Zhabdrung's description of his daily ritual life.

He must have recited these prayers in silence, while wearing a Mao suit, with no prayer beads in hand, and with only imaginary *torma*. His reframing of his prison environment presents this experience as an opportunity to practice, almost erasing the state out of the narrative. There is no mention of embracing socialist thought or details of prison life as in Palden Gyatso's testimony. Their autobiographies center their spiritual lives and commitments to Buddhist training as of foremost importance. As in Mugé Samten's account above, Tséten Zhabdrung's work describes an embodied awareness of doctrinal concepts such as cyclic existence (*saṃsāra*), karma, and impermanence.

Their autobiographies also convey such spiritual insights through the narration of dream sequences, which imply that they achieved their soteriological goals of spiritual advancement. While in prison, Tséten Zhabdrung reports having a vision of Amitābha Buddha, who resides in the western Pure Land, Sukhāvatī:

> One night in a dream, Amitābha Buddha, which was the same size as the surface of the mountain, appeared vividly in the sky in front of Drakar (Brag dkar) Mountain near Rama Denma (Ra ma 'dan ma). The beautiful image of Amitābha was standing erect, wearing monks' robes. His feet were covered by clouds, which were in the style of Chinese painting. His face looked toward the east and his clothes were flapping gently in the wind. Nearby stood my friend, Geshé Nyenkong Gendün Chödrak (Dge bshes gnyen khong Dge 'dun chos grags). Both of us were looking at his face and recited lines from the Threefold Training in ethical conduct, meditative insight, and wisdom (*tshul khrims, ting nge 'dzin*, and *shes rab*). The next day, this dream was very vivid in my mind. For days after, the blissful feeling this generated did not disappear.[55]

Tséten Zhabdrung remembers a visualization of Amitābha Buddha appearing as large as the precipitous Drakmar Mountain, located near his main monastery. In this dream, he recites prayers with a friend, about whom I was unable to find any further information. The circumstances must have been dire, but we don't know any details. He was in prison, and Amitābha is frequently associated with dissolution practices at the time of death. Yet the author reports this as an auspicious omen, bringing him an extraordinary sense of bliss.

Similarly, Mugé Samten remembers dreams demonstrating the efficacy of Buddhist practice. From the larger textual context, it is clear that the following dream sequence reported in his autobiography took place when he was doing "reform through labor" (Ch. *láodòng gǎizào*, 劳动改造), i.e., a punishment that involved penal labor. The following translation conveys Mugé Samten's prayers to Tārā, a female tantric deity who embodies compassion and offers protection to those who call upon her:

> I had a dream that that my teacher Lopön Rinpoché (slob dpon rin po che) marked with an OM was sitting on my bed. I asked him, "What does the fate of us Tibetans hold?" He answered, "In the long run everything will be fine." I then asked, "In the short term compared to what you say is the long term, will there be any more struggle sessions?" He answered, "Tārā Tārā." At that moment, I woke up and I didn't understand the meaning, but the long final suffix -ā indicated that the goddess Drolma, i.e., Tārā was meant; therefore I chanted to her. After that there were a lot of tense moments, but because of praying to precious Tārā, I didn't have any problems.[56]

The narrative focuses on the verbal utterances of the Sanskrit name, Tārā, which is integral to the practice of evoking a deity. Such affirmations of the efficacy of Buddhist prayers are one way these authors place Buddhist narratives at the center of their memories of the Maoist era.

So far this discussion has focused on comparing what Tséten Zhabdrung's and Mugé Samten's autobiographies say about the Maoist years and comparing them to other accounts of this time period. Now I turn to the literary aesthetic qualities of their writings. The penultimate verse in this section of Tséten Zhabdrung's autobiography offers a starting point to understand key aspects of Tibetan literary aesthetics and discursive practices that will shed further interpretive light on the presence of Buddhist poetry in these two life narratives.

*Spiritual Experiences (*Nyams*)*

Tséten Zhabdrung's memories of the Maoist years culminate in a belletristic verse highlighting his spiritual experiences. As in other passages, the setting of the Chinese prison fades into the background as the narrative focuses on his spiritual realizations. According to charts that convert the Tibetan dates to Gregorian calendrical ones, this poem covers a month-long period from late December 1970 through the end of January 1971.[57] The author had been jailed for about five years at this point. The fact that he remembers the dates attests to his mental clarity, as he must have only had an opportunity to write this down after his release from prison. Although Tséten Zhabdrung remained incarcerated for another six years, we learn nothing about that time period. His autobiographical memories of the Maoist years end with this poem:

> Crystal snow mountains circle like a rosary,
> Bhod-ta, Tibet, magnified by images of letters;
> gratitude to the Great Illuminator, Thonmi,
> beyond measure, at the end of time.

> In my sixty-first year, on (the twenty-eighth) day of (the eleventh) month.

> Expositions replete with a treasury of splendid teachings,
> debate as vast as the ocean of logic,
> compositions as melodious as Sarasvatī's lute;
> Hurray! The marvelous three activities of a polymath.

> In my sixty-first year, on (the seventh day) of (the twelfth) month.

> Noble Ones master the profound scriptures of the Buddha,
> adopting experiences of Truth to discipline lower conceptions of self,
> an ethical tradition subduing the fox of unwholesome thoughts;
> Atisha's religious precepts surpass anything else.

> In my sixty-first year, on (the nineteenth) day of (the twelfth) month.

> The View, E-wam, union set with a seal,
> meditation, special insights embellished with exalted wisdom,
> comportment adorned by the ambrosia of the Four Merits of Six
>   Perfections,
> Jamgön Tsongkhapa's doctrinal system cannot be matched!

> In my sixty-first year, on (the twenty-third) day of (the twelfth) month.[58]

Tséten Zhabdrung's "Sixty-first Year" poem echoes the Géluk ideals of the *khé-drup*, the scholar-adept. The first stanza paints the Himalayas with letters of the Tibetan alphabet, invented by Thonmi Sambhota, illuminating the snow-covered peaks like sky lanterns. On this foundation, the poet praises the three activities of the polymathic *paṇḍita*: exposition, debate, and composition. The third stanza focuses on the practices of ethical comportment, correct views, and meditation found in the writings of Atisha, the founder of the Lam Rim tradition, among other scriptures that help tame the "fox" or deceived mind of the lower self. The final stanza gives words to the ineffable beauty experienced by the meditator in a state of nonduality, the union of compassion and wisdom. Taken together, these verses celebrate the activities of *khédrup*.

By reading Tséten Zhabdrung's commentary on poetics, it is easy to deduce that this verse is crafted using "difficult" (*bya dka' ba*) ornamentations, so called because they make poetry beautiful through "ornaments" (*rgyan*; Skt.: *alaṃkāra*) that stretch the literary imagination. This wordplay technique is also used in the Dalai Lama's highlighting of the syllables of Mao Zedong's name within the verses of "*Monlam* to Mao" and in Mugé Samten's emphasis on the syllables for "telling what happened"; both underscore authorial choices. This type of wordplay can involve many other techniques, such as acrostics, whereby each line starts with a letter of the Tibetan alphabet; or zig-zag "cow's piss" (*ba lang gcin*) poems; or using each letter of the Tibetan alphabet, as we find in "Sixty-first Year."[59]

The most obvious wordplay in the poem is its repetitive refrain, "in my sixty-first year (month) and (date)," which is marked by dots. Underneath these dots, different months and days are penned in to show the time frame. I use parentheses in my translation to mark this textual feature. Another literary feature is the addition of dots underneath ten syllables in the poem. By stringing these syllables together, the author creates an additional phrase that similarly highlights the activities of scholar-adepts: "exposition (*'chad*), debate (*rtsod*), composition (*rtsom*), polymath or master (*mkhas*), ethical comportment (*btsun bzang*), the right view (*lta*), and meditation (*sgom*)."[60] In my translation of the poem, I underline these words to represent the dots in Tibetan. As mentioned previously, the verb for "master" (*mkhas*) can be nominalized as "polymath."

In the prelude to this poem, Tséten Zhabdrung explains the context for its composition: "At the end of my sixty-first year, I had powerful 'mind experiences' (*sem kyi nyams*) in the middle of several nights when I couldn't sleep. I composed several stanzas in my head using the entire alphabet of thirty letters while my head lay on a pillow."[61] The term used for "experiences" is *nyams*, which has a range of nuanced meanings and applications in contemplative practice.[62] Janet Gyatso explains the significance of *nyams* experience as involving nonduality:

Perhaps most importantly, the tendency for subject and object to reflect each other and thereby to become blurred in salient, absorbed states of meditation serves to link *nyams* experiences with the highest goal of Tibetan Buddhist meditative traditions, namely, the collapse of all subject-object dualism altogether. This in turn explains, or so I would argue, why these traditions were so interested in cultivating *nyams* experiences in the first place.[63]

Tséten Zhabdrung claims that this poem was the result of a *nyams* experience. The final stanza enigmatically addresses this nondual state as, "The View, E-wam, union set with a seal, meditation, special insights embellished with exalted wisdom." In the stanzas leading up to this the required knowledge, comportment, and integration of mind-body practices culminate over a series of nights in these "experiences of Truth" (*thos don nyams bzhes*). I understand this to mean that Tséten Zhabdrung describes experiencing an embodied meditative understanding of the nature of reality from a Buddhist perspective.

This verse and other poems interspersed in their life narratives indicate that poetry is an important literary mode of expression for these autobiographers. Prompted by this observation, I turn to look at a few technical aspects of Tibetan literary theory because, as will become evident, the capaciousness of Tibetan poetics offers a means by which to embrace the varying dimensions of these autobiographical representations of the Maoist years, ranging from affective states of grief and joy to dreams and spiritual realizations and to Buddhist ontology.

LITERARY TECHNIQUES TO EXPRESS THE INEFFABLE

When Tséten Zhabdrung and Mugé Samten pepper their life narratives with poetry, they tap into literary techniques that awaken the playful, the sublime, the contemplative, and proud scions of Tibet's literary heritage, including Longchenpa (1308–1363), Tsongkhapa (1357–1419), the Fifth Dalai Lama (1617–1682), Jigmé Lingpa (1729–1798), and Zhuchen Tsultrim Rinchen (1677–1744), among others. It is not hyperbole to state that most of Tibet's great literary savants have written in verse, drawing upon the rules of Tibetan literary aesthetics, often referred to by its Sanskrit name, *kāvya*. Much of *kāvya* literary theory is found in Tibetan commentaries of Daṇḍin's Urtext (c. 700), the *Mirror of Poetics* (Skt. *Kāvyādarśa*), as discussed in the introductory chapter.

One particular aspect of *kāvya* will aid in contextualizing the writing practices of these polymathic authors. It will also give us new ways of reading the
autobiographical verses based on aesthetic values from within Tibetan literary
discourse. The particular aspect of Tibetan literary theory relevant here is a
homonym of *nyams* in the sense of mind "experience" in Tséten Zhabdrung's
"Sixty-first Year" poem above. In the *kāvya* context, *nyams* translates the Sanskrit term *rasa*, which means "taste" as in something aesthetically pleasing, what
we might describe today as "delicious."

Daṇḍin's *Kāvyādarśa* describes *rasa* in three distinct ways: 1) as a general
term for tasteful poetry; 2) as a term for any sophisticated language, and 3) as a
technical term for various affective dimensions of literary expression.[64] This
range of connotations is also reflected in Tibetan; as Dan Martin noted, *rasa* has
been translated into Tibetan in at least five different ways.[65] In Tséten Zhabdrung's and Dungkar Rinpoché's commentaries to Daṇḍin's *Kāvyādarśa*, two
terms are used: *nyam"* and the compound *nyams-'gyur*.

Tséten Zhabdrung underscores the importance of *nyams* within the *kāvya*
tradition when he cites two of its great scholars: the tenth-century Kashmiri
poet Kṣemendra and the fifteenth-century Géluk savant Tsongkhapa:

> Kṣemendra's *Wish-fulfilling Vine* (*Dpag bsam 'khri shing*) [Skt.: *Avadānakalpalatā*]
> states, "Without scholars, wisdom would diminish and human livelihood would
> be purposeless; without nonpareil poems, scholars would be akin to mimicking
> parrots." As expressed here, if compositions do not possess poetic *rasa* (*snyan ngag
> gi nyams*), then no matter how much expertise one has in any given subject, the
> poet would not surpass a mimicking parrot. Keeping that in mind, the great
> Tsongkhapa wrote:

>> Analytical minds perfectly differentiate methods of reasoning,
>> practices that manifest scriptures as instructions,
>> glorious words of experts in composition,
>> all three appear as jewels on this earth.
>> Sublime words transmitting perfect compositions are valued as one of
>>   the earth's jewels.[66]

Tséten Zhabdrung didactically points out that *nyams* or *rasa* is nothing less
than accomplishing poetic excellence. In order for a poet to achieve their own
delicious style, they must develop *nyams*.

Like Tséten Zhabdrung, Dungkar Rinpoché urges new poets to develop
their own flair. He addresses his potential audience directly: "Beginners of

poetry, after grasping the foundations of writings, you can start to practice. Gradually, you will become experts in writing all sorts of compositions infused with *rasa* (*nyams 'gyur*)."[67] This indicates that developing one's own *rasa*, "taste," or style is important in writing anything. In other word, mastering *nyams* is integral to the craft of writing. This is made clear in Tséten Zhabdrung's commentary when he argues that *kāvya* (*snyan ngag*) theory is used for all sorts of discursive purposes:

> Furthermore, it is far too narrow to understand *kāvya* (*snyan ngag*) as only literature composed in verse, prose, or mixed verse and prose. Besides that, poetics is [1)] for presenting meaningful lectures to a circle of scholars gathered together; [2)] for teaching texts based on scriptures to a crowd of many laypeople; [3)] for textual instruction to students who are motivated; [4)] for debating an opponent through examination and refutation; [5)] for teasing and satirizing (*zur za*) in order to direct one's attention to an important topic; and [6)] for chatting and discussing in order to express the motive of friendship.[68]

This is important to consider in reading Tséten Zhabdrung's *Acoustic Ambrosia* and Mugé Samten's *Luminous Mirror*, as it draws our attention to the cultural expectations placed on these Tibetan polymaths; their compositions are expected to possess a delicious aesthetic quality.

Another technical aspect of *nyams* is even more interesting to consider, as this sheds light on the affective dimensions of Tséten Zhabdrung's and Mugé Samten's verses that might not otherwise be clear from the translations above. Verse offers a discursive mode for these monk-authors to write about "emotions" or "affect" (terms used warily) in a way that not only displays their polymathic talents but also allows for the expression of affective states within the parameters of Buddhist truths about the mind and impermanence. We learn from Dungkar Rinpoché's and Tséten Zhabdrung's commentaries that "taste" or *rasa* (*nyams 'gyur*) involves a dialogic relationship between arousing emotions and physiological responses.

Both Tséten Zhabdrung and Dungkar Rinpoché break down the two syllables in *nyams-'gyur* to explain the relationship between emotions and their physical manifestation in this context. Emotion or *gyur-ba* (*'gyur ba*) is to be understood as a temporary aroused state of mind. Tséten Zhabdrung explains, "Agitating arousals of the *yid*-mind (*yid kyi kun slong g.yos*), such as happiness and anger, are not expressed outwardly—in speech or in the body; such a state is *emotion* (*'gyur ba*)."[69] He goes on to explain that the moment this inner arousal intensifies to the point that one cannot help to express it in the outer world, it becomes an embodied physical response, which is *nyams* or *rasa*, "taste." Dungkar Rinpoché explains: "When this *emotion* (*'gyur-ba*) increases and arises in speech and in the body, for example, as an angry expression or a smile, then this is *nyams* (*rasa*)."[70] Tséten Zhabdrung states that "By increasing *nyams*, poetry becomes particularly exceptional."[71] This aesthetic quality to writing involves psycho-physiological arousals, but they are understood as temporary because they take place in the *yid*-mind, according to these two *kāvya* theorists.

This is significant because it indicates that Dungkar Rinpoché's and Tséten Zhabdrung's explanations of *nyams-'gyur* within *kāvya* theory fit with the Buddhist Abhidharmic understanding of mental faculties or emotions as transitory. Any arousals of the *yid*-mind (happiness or sadness or other emotions) are described as *'gyur ba,* which can translate as both "emotion" and "changing." This choice of terminology reflects these literary theorists' understanding of Buddhist ideas on the transitory nature of the *yid*-mind. Georges Dreyfus explains, "Buddhist epistemologists do not believe in an ontology of substances, but argue that reality is made of things consisting of a succession of evanescent moments. Thus, mental and material events interact in a constantly on-going fluctuating process."[72] According to Abhidharmic philosophy, disturbances of the mind that cause restlessness and unease are "afflictions" (*nyon mongs*; Skt. *kleśa*). Whether these disturbing mental factors such as passion, delusion, etc. can be called "emotions" is debatable, as Dreyfus points out.[73] Poetics as a mode of writing offers a culturally acceptable way to talk about affect, which might otherwise be considered taboo in a Buddhist context.

Until recently Tibetans did not have a word that corresponded to "emotion" or "affect" in the Euro-American psychological discursive use of the term. The Tibetan neologism for "emotion" (*tshor myong*) was created through interactions between Tibetan lamas and Euro-Americans.[74] For this reason, I use the term "emotion" with some hesitation. Nonetheless, it is a convenient and useful term as long as we keep in mind that, as Catherine Lutz observes, "Regardless of the key category used or the tradition invoked, these overlapping academic explorations [of affect/emotion] concern themselves with what moves and matters in human life."[75] Unsurprisingly, neither Tséten Zhabdrung nor Dungkar Rinpoché uses the neologism *tshor-myong*, nor do they describe these transitory states of arousal as "afflictions" (*nyon mongs*). Rather, they describe a dialogic relationship between *nyams* and *gyur* (*'gyur*) that glorifies Tibetan literary aesthetic qualities.

In India, *rasa* formed a core component of audience response theory. For example, Sheldon Pollock's translation of the *Treatise on Drama*, *Nāṭyaśāstra*, dating to the first centuries of the Common Era, explains, "Emotion (*bhāva*) is also so called because it serves to 'bring into being' (*bhāvayan*) the poet's inner emotion (*bhāva*) by means of the four registers of acting: verbal, physical, psychophysical, and scenic."[76] In the Tibetan context the relationship between the poet's inner emotion and that of the audience is unclear. However, building on earlier Tibetan translations of the *Kāvyadarśa* and presumably the eight *bhāva* found in *Nāṭyaśāstra*, Tséten Zhabdrung explains that eight transitory mental states align with eight psychophysical responses as outlined in the following chart designed by Lauran Hartley:[77]

Affective state/Vicissitude of emotion ('gyur, Skt. bhāva)	Psychophysical response/aesthetic experience (nyams, Skt. rasa)
1. love (*dga' ba*)	gestures that express amusement (*rtsed 'jo*) or alluringness (*sgeg pa*)
2. humor (*dgod bro ba*)	laughing (*bzhad gad*), smiling (*gad mo dgod*)
3. sorrow (*mya ngan*)	solemn face (*bzhin mdangs*) or sympathy (*snying rje ba*)
4. anger (*khro ba*)	the crinkling of the brow in a fierce way (*drag shul lam smin ma bsdus pa*)
5. confidence (*sems kyi gzengs mtho*)	gestures that are courageous (*spobs pa che*) and heroic (*dpa' ba*)
6. horror (*skrag pa*)	gestures that demonstrate timidity (*bag 'khums pa*) and fear (*'jigs*)
7. disgust (*skyug bro ba*)	gestures of nausea (*zhe mer*) and repulsion (*mi sdug pa*)
8. amazement (*ngo mtshar ba*)	gestures of being surprised (*rngam pa*) and amazed (*rmad byung*)

These need to be understood as guidelines for Tibetan writers to be rhetorically effective in their craft. A good example of how this works is found in the stanza from "*Avadāna* of Silver Flowers" by Tséten Zhabdrung cited at the beginning of this chapter:

> The monster of this heartless era
> opened its fearsome mouth as wide as

the space between earth and sky.

In this gap, its weapons, teeth and fangs,

gnashed irrevocably and ferociously! Terrifying![78]

In an uncommon move, Tséten Zhabdrung records the type of literary device that he uses after each stanza of "*Avadāna* of Silver Flowers." The device used in the above verse is the "ornament of the emotion (*rasa*) of fear" ('*jigs rung gyi nyams gyi rgyan*). Neither Tséten Zhabdrung nor Dungkar Rinpoché details whether this theory refers to the poet's embodied mental state and psychophysical response at the time of writing or is intended as a technique to elicit a certain response from the audience.

Although much still needs to be understood about Tibetan poetics and aestheticism, this taste of literary theory helps us appreciate the wide range of discursive practices available to Tséten Zhabdrung and Mugé Samten when they penned their autobiographies. Tséten Zhabdrung and Dungkar Rinpoché as literary theorists viewed a dialogic relation between temporary affective states and poetry interpreted through Buddhist lenses. This literary-aesthetic theory is capaciousness enough to encompass Buddhist cultural values, including interpretations of transitory affective states and experiences of the ultimate goal of nondualism, as in Tséten Zhabdrung's "Sixty-first Year" poem.

Perhaps similar to how Zen kōans use language paradoxically to elicit spiritual insights, the enigmatic quality of Tibetan poetics heightens religious expression. The autobiographical verses studied here express affective states of Buddhist monks in socially accepted ways that underscore Buddhist truths of impermanence and inevitable change. This adds another layer to the autobiographical verses that might not otherwise be visible without an understanding of the discursive range of *nyams*. The capaciousness of Tibetan poetic theory allows authors to draw upon a range of discursive practices, such as wordplay techniques, expressions of joy or sadness, and appreciating a Buddhist perspective on the fleeting yet haunting memories of the Maoist years. As Ottone M. Riccio proposes, "In the final analysis, *recognizing poetry* is dependent on 'the feel'—a knowing at a deeper than usual level that *one is in the presence of poetry*; that poetry is language in living action as complex as life itself; that is directional and non-directional, particular and universal at the same instant."[79] For Mugé Samten and Tséten Zhabdrung, the Tibetan literary language serves as a vehicle for expressing the unsayable higher truth of the human condition.

In this chapter, we have looked at how Mugé Samten and Tséten Zhabdrung frame their memories of the Maoist years within a relational environment grounded in Géluk Buddhist epistemes. As Paul John Eakin suggests, autobiographical subjectivity operates within a nexus of societal expectations about how to talk about the extended self. That is the autobiographical self constructed through a myriad of culturally, psychologically, dependent relational factors.[80] We read in the previous chapter how these two autobiographers carefully drew upon the parameters of Tibetan life writing discourse to prioritize Buddhist ethical values and aspirations. Here their writings convey Buddhist truths that place each author at the center of his narrative.

Autobiographical memory serves to re-create history through Buddhist values. Holly Gayley points this out in her study of Khandro Tāre Lhamo (1938–2002), an important female Nyingma Buddhist master. She played a vital role in reviving Tibetan Buddhist practices in the Golok region of Tibet in the aftermath of the Cultural Revolution. Gayley shows how Khandro Tāre Lhamo's hagiography portrays her role in healing the collective karma of the traumatic Maoist years. Gayley argues that "the hagiographic appropriation of collective karma provides an important mechanism in *Spiraling the Vine of Faith* to decenter Beijing and recenter Tibetans as the principal actors in their own history."[81] Similarly, the autobiographies by Tséten Zhabdrung and Mugé Samten assert Buddhist narratives.

Their particular way of remembering this time period positions Mugé Samten and Tséten Zhabdrung as *khédrup* who enigmatically express spiritual realizations, whether through *gur* or *kāvya* poetics. The use of verse in remembering the Maoist years provides discursive space to express affective dimensions of their experiences, such as horrors and fears, within the grammar of Géluk Buddhist epistemes. This evocative mode of writing speaks of the human condition in Buddhist terms and spiritual experiences in one stroke, reflecting the *khédrup* model of mastering study and practice as one.

After the Cultural Revolution, Mugé Samten and Tséten Zhabdrung were among the very few *khédrup* remaining in China. Carriers of Tibetan Buddhist knowledge and practice were desperately needed after so much destruction and the death or exile of so many Tibetan Buddhist masters. These two polymaths seized the moment of relative liberalization to write their autobiographical memoirs. They remembered the past as indicating the values that they brought with them into the post-Mao era. In this way, their accounts of personal sufferings become much more than a subjective history of this time. For their readers, the autobiographies become testimony to the power and efficacy of Tibetan Buddhist practices, such as *tonglen*, the transformation of adversity into spiritual realization. The authors become living exemplars of the survival and continuance of Tibetan traditions.

The reading and analysis of their autobiographies shed much needed interpretative light on Tibetan Buddhist memories of the first three decades of the People's Republic of China. The authors cannot be viewed as passive pawns or victims of the state; they are *khédrup*. As moral agents, they present a counter-narrative to history as an "evolving unity of the nation."[82] The authors transmit prized ethical and cultural values through their autobiographical writings to contribute to the start of a new era of time, the "Era of Dharma's Re-diffusion" (*bstan pa yang dar skabs*). This was not the only way Mugé Samten and Tséten Zhabdrung participated in the *yang-dar* era. Chapter 5 examines the crucial roles of all Three Polymaths in the reestablishment of Buddhist institutions and Tibetan academic lineages in the post-Mao era.

The next chapter turns to the third member of the trio. Dungkar Lozang Trinlé's famous *An Explanation of the Merging of Religious and Secular Rule in Tibet* was one of the first Tibetan-language texts published in China after the Cultural Revolution. He does not prioritize Géluk epistemes in the same way as Mugé Samten and Tséten Zhabdrung do in their "telling what happened" texts, yet he creates discursive space for expressions of collective Tibetan identity in the domains of "history" and "religion" within state discourse in pioneering ways.

4

Dungkar Rinpoché on the Contested Ground of Tibetan History

The primary debate over Tibet's status is a debate about history.[1]
—Elliot Sperling

T
his and the following chapter examine the ways the Three Polymaths exerted their moral agency as Géluk *khépa* at the intersection of Tibetan Buddhist epistemes, Chinese state ideology and policies, and state-led institutionalization of religion. To this end, this chapter focuses on how Dungkar Rinpoché as a Marxist theorist and Buddhist scholar created a secular past for Tibet and redefined the construct of "religion" in Tibetan language discourse, thereby ensuring the survival and continuance of Tibetan history in the *yang-dar* era.

When CCP leadership took steps to repair some of the damage done to traditional Tibetan institutions, norms, and culture during the Cultural Revolution, the Three Polymaths found themselves actors in a complex enterprise of "post-Mao religious institutionalization," which involved religious leaders, government officials, and scholars.[2] As Buddhist leaders, members of the Buddhist Association of China, and university professors, they became participants in state projects that secularized traditional forms of Tibetan knowledge within the framework of Chinese state policies on ethnic minority culture and the political discursive space of religion. Secularization is understood here as a process of institutional differentiation of the so-called "secular" spheres (economy, science, politics, etc.) from religious institutions and norms.[3] Scholars such as Rebecca Nedostup, Vincent Goossaert, David Palmer, and Mayfair Yang, among others, have traced how the modern Chinese state, in the Republican era and then under CCP rule, has drawn distinctions between the religious and secular domains for its own purposes.[4] Secularization as a historical project is intimately linked with "secularism" as both an ideology and a statecraft principle; as we will read, Dungkar Rinpoché's creation of a Tibetan history links traditional Tibetan ideas of secularism with the CCP's state secularization goals.[5] Yet, as Goossaert and Palmer aptly observe, "China's religious question poses itself precisely because the logic of secularization has been realized only incompletely, and has led to unexpected outcomes."[6] One unforeseen consequence is that Tibetan Buddhist figures engaged with and subverted Chinese state discourse in order to set their own agenda by drawing upon Tibetan religious epistemes.

The Three Polymaths' goals to preserve and continue Tibetan culture in the aftermath of the Cultural Revolution were shared by other prominent Tibetan Buddhist leaders, such as Khenpo Jigmé Phuntsok, the founder of Larung Gar (now one of the largest Tibetan Buddhist monastic communities in the world), and Khandro Tāre Lhamo, one of the most influential Buddhist women teachers and treasure revealers of the modern era.[7] Unlike these Buddhist leaders based in their local communities, all Three Polymaths were active nationally and in the case of Dungkar Rinpoché, internationally. One of the truly remarkable features of the lives of the Three Polymaths is how they crisscrossed religious domains and state-supported secular institutions in China in ways that might be unthinkable today.

In this chapter, I look at Dungkar Rinpoché's contributions to Tibetan history and some of the consequences of his work: the development of Tibetan national identity within the parameters of CCP state discourse and the reinvention of "religion" in Tibetan language discourse. Similar to Tséten Zhabdrung and Mugé Samten, Dungkar Rinpoché wrote and published prolifically in the *yang-dar* era. Whereas they record their autobiographical pasts in ways that focus on doing Buddhist activities in a secular world, he seems at pains to discursively separate the religious and secular domains in the Tibetan context. In doing so, he carves out a new space for Tibetan history that alternately draws upon and departs from both traditional Buddhist historiography and Marxist historical materialism with Chinese characteristics.

This chapter begins by looking at the contested nature of "Tibetan" history and contextualizing how the author wrote *An Explanation of the Merging of Religious and Secular Rule in Tibet* (*Bod kyi chos srid zung 'brel lam lugs skor bshad pa*) between 1977 and 1979. An understanding of how Dungkar Rinpoché pioneered a new kind of Tibetan historiography illuminates moral agency under dire conditions by examining the ways he discursively unifies "Tibet." Despite past regional and sectarian affiliations that thwarted the development of a national identity, his focus on "the merging of religious and secular rule" *(chos srid zung 'brel)*, a concept moored in traditional Tibetan ideas of secularism, creates the discursive space for a secular past for Tibetans while adhering to the CCP's state secularization goals. The few autobiographical reflections that we have from Dungkar Rinpoché reveal how he took advantage of his unique position as a highly educated reincarnate lama with a *geshé* degree, a well-versed Marxist theorist, and a CCP policy adept able to advance bold and original ideas.

Then I turn to how Dungkar Rinpoché addresses a flashpoint in interpretations of Tibet's historical status vis-à-vis China by comparing recensions of his seminal work *An Explanation of the Merging of Religious and Secular Rule in Tibet* with sections from his "An Explanation of Select Major Terminologies in the *Red Annals*" *(Deb ther dmar po'i nang gi gal che'i tshig 'grel gnad bsdus)*, hereafter, "Terminologies in the *Red Annals*." From Beijing's perspective, Sakya-Yuan relations in the thirteenth century represent when Tibet became part of China; some exile Tibetans interpret these historical events as the beginning of Tibetan independence based on the ideal of "the merging of religious and secular rule." By comparing the English language print translated by the Beijing Foreign Languages Press with a Tibetan recension of *An Explanation of the Merging of Religious and Secular Rule in Tibet,* it becomes clear that the Beijing-sanctioned English version was used to promote the state's version of Tibet's historical status for an international audience, whereas the author presented a much more nuanced and detailed history of Tibet (within political constraints) to bolster a national identity for Tibetophone readers of this text and "Terminologies in the *Red Annals*" within the PRC.

At the same time that he creates a secular past for Tibet, Dungkar Rinpoché also redefines the term *chöluk (chos lugs)* to signify "religion" as a modern construct. On one hand, this heuristic move advocated for a separation of religion and politics; on the other, it served to discursively unite the various religious sects as Tibetan. To highlight the different ways Tibetan monastic scholars could exercise moral agency in historiography, I briefly compare *An Explanation of the Merging of Religious and Secular Rule in Tibet* to Mugé Samten's history, *An Explanation of the Fields of Learning in Tibet.* In contrast to Dungkar Rinpoché, who aligns religion within state discourse, Mugé Samten retains "Buddhism" in its traditional home as one of the five major "fields of learning" or *rikné,* thereby securing a place for Tibet's diverse religious traditions within PRC discourse on ethnic minority culture.

Although Dungkar Rinpoché has been charged as a "collaborator" by some Tibetans in exile, he also forged new ways of writing about Tibetan history and transformed Tibetan studies into an academic discipline in China. In order to appreciate his innovative approaches in developing modern Tibetan historiography within China, it is important to understand the historical context within which he wrote, especially in regard to the contested ground of what constituted "Tibet" in the early post-Mao era.

HISTORY AS CONTESTED GROUND

In 1977, when Dungkar Rinpoché was tasked with writing *An Explanation of the Merging of Religious and Secular Rule in Tibet*, the political atmosphere was incredibly tense. The reforms that would be initiated under Deng Xiaoping at the Third Plenum of the Eleventh Chinese Communist Party National Congress in Beijing in December 1978 had not yet come to pass. This was three years prior to Hu Yaobang's speech on May 29, 1980, stating that Tibetans would be allowed "to exercise nationality autonomy in the region fully," a policy shift that paved the way for the revival of Tibetan Buddhism and culture more broadly.[8] Toward the end of the Cultural Revolution in 1976, Dungkar Rinpoché had been assigned to work at the Cultural Relics Office[9] in Lhasa, the capital of the Tibetan Autonomous Region. The office was located within the Dalai Lama's former summer residence, the Norbulingka, and held a vast repository of precious Tibetan documents saved from the ravages of book burning.[10] He received this posting because of his Marxist political views at a time when other incarnate lamas, such as the Tenth Panchen Lama and Tséten Zhabdrung, were still imprisoned. The majority of Tibetans didn't have access to Tibetan texts because such writings had been labeled as "poisonous weeds."[11] Some hadn't even seen works in Tibetan script in decades. This work assignment at the Cultural Relics Office gave Dungkar Rinpoché access to rare Tibetan documents and traditional histories. Unlike many school-age Tibetans in the 1960s and 1970s who were denied education in their native tongue, as a learned *geshé* who received his degree in 1946, he had attained the skills to read and analyze these sources. All of these factors came together for Dungkar Rinpoché to write a comprehensive two-thousand-year history called *An Explanation of the Merging of Religious and Secular Rule in Tibet*.[12]

To talk about a collective Tibetan history was a politically dangerous move at that time. To this day, the political history of "Tibet" vis-à-vis China lies at the crux of the internationalization of the issue and PRC claims of sovereignty over Tibet. After the implementation of economic reforms in 1978, the CCP briefly attempted rapprochement with the Dalai Lama. At that time, how to perceive "Tibet" (politically, ethnically, historically, territorially, etc.) emerged in full force as a primary concern for both exiled Tibetans and those inside China. At the heart of this issue is how to deal with what scholars have identified as "the Tibet Question," which Melvyn Goldstein describes as "the conflict over what should be the political status of Tibet vis-à-vis China."[13] The late historian Elliot Sperling astutely pointed out that many other issues interconnect with perceptions of Tibet's historical status, including territorial integrity, the role of religion in modernity, human rights, political and religious freedom, and emigration and colonization, among others.[14] In China, as in exile, the boundaries of these issues are still being negotiated and fought over. On this contested ground, it was politically challenging to find a way to talk about a collective Tibetan history.

For Dungkar Rinpoché, what counts as Tibet emerged amid sectarian conflict, local identities, and state discourse. Today, Buddhism stands as an emblem of Tibetan national consciousness, especially in the West, so it is hard to imagine a time when sectarian differences precluded a unified "Tibet." Samten Karmay (b. 1936), a leading Tibetan Buddhist historian and translator, explains:

> In the process of awakening national identity there are two governing factors in Tibet's case: the experience of being under foreign occupation, and the close contact with Westerners in foreign countries and in recent years, also in Tibet itself.... With the advent of Buddhism and particularly from the 11th century onward, the national consciousness of the Tibetan people suffered greatly.... If patriotism is the core of nationalism and if it were ever felt, it is often expressed in terms of protecting Buddhist doctrine and institutions, and not the country as a nation or a state.[15]

From this perspective, Tibet prior to Chinese occupation did not have a strong national identity because religious and regional alliances often took precedence over a sense of national unity.

In exile, a lack of an independent state led to Buddhism becoming synonymous with Tibetan national identity. Samten Karmay elucidates this point further:

> Tibet has not even the status of a stateless nation in international legal terms. Consequently, the integrity of its culture is in peril. But its national identity nevertheless remains alive and has been reinforced and highlighted by Chinese repression since 1987. During the last forty years, however, Tibetan

Buddhism, which once worked to counter a strong sense of nationality, now works the other way. . . . Tibetan Buddhism has come to symbolize Tibet's national identity.[16]

The focus placed on Tibetan Buddhism as a core part of Tibetan identity has led some popular writers to idealize Tibet's past. An example of this is John Avedon's classic, *In Exile from the Land of Snows*, in statements such as, "With the collapse of the early empire, the single-minded zeal Tibetans had shown for the pursuits of war turned to those of peace, transmuting the national character to that of a long-forgotten father of the race. The change resulted primarily from Buddhist ideas themselves."[17]

Contrary to such portrayals of an ideal Buddhist past, Dungkar Rinpoché writes about Tibet's history in a nuanced light. He structures his account around the concept of "the merging of religious and secular rule in Tibet" (*bod kyi chos srid zung 'brel*), which, as I will detail below, is steeped in Buddhist historiography, but his narrative is not a Buddhist history that idealizes Tibet as a peaceful Buddhist utopia prior to 1950. Elliot Sperling has often critiqued the attempts to make the current Dalai Lama's view on *ahimsa*, nonviolence, "a Buddhist value that has dominated Tibetan political history and the institution of the Dalai Lama for centuries."[18] Similarly Donald Lopez cautions, "To allow Tibet to circulate in a system of fantastic opposites . . . is to deny Tibet its history, to exclude it from the real world of which it has always been a part, and to deny Tibetans their agency in the creation of a contested quotidian reality."[19] When Dungkar Rinpoché interprets "a system of religious and secular rule in Tibet," he subsumes religious and sectarian differences within Marxist discourse and also discursively creates "Tibet" amid historically strong regional identities.

Many scholars have noted how dispersed regional affiliations have thwarted the development of a Tibetan national identity. For example, regional affiliations precluded the development of a term for a unified "Tibet" because people refer to themselves by their local origin, such as "Amdo-wa" (A mdo ba), i.e., "a person from Amdo."[20] Dungkar Rinpoché compared the thirteenth-century wars between the Sakya-pa tradition in Tsang (Gtsang) and the Drigung Kagyu in Ü (Dbus) to the relationship between "a crow and an owl"—that of bitter enemies.[21] Tsering Shakya makes the case that in exile, the term "Böd-pa" (*bod pa*) usually refers to Tibetans under Chinese rule. He and Heather Stoddard agree that Tibetans historically lacked a single national toponym.[22] Today some Tibetologists, such as Melvyn Goldstein, distinguish between "political Tibet," equivalent to the present-day Tibetan Autonomous Region (TAR), and "ethnic Tibet," which includes areas outside the TAR but within the PRC that have significant Tibetan populations.[23] Sometimes scholars identify a region of "greater Tibet" or a "pan-Tibetan region" (*bod chen po'i rgyal khams*) to connect the eastern reaches of Tibetan-speaking populations in "ethnic" Tibet, i.e., Amdo and Kham in present-day Qinghai, Gansu, Yunnan, and Sichuan provinces, with Central Tibet (Dbus gtsang) or the TAR.[24]

In contrast, Dungkar Lozang Trinlé uses the terms "Böd" (*bod*) for "Tibet" and "Böd region," i.e., "Tibetan region" (*bod sa gnas*). He does not refer to the political borders of Tibetan territory or use the term for the Tibetan Autonomous Region (*bod rang skyong ljongs*) to refer to historical Tibet. "Tibetan region" (*bod sa gnas*) is used frequently as a neutral descriptor but also implicitly refers to Tibet as a regional government (*sa gnas gzhung*) under the central government (*krung dbyang*) of China. As we will read, he frequently makes use of the ambiguity of these terms in his creation of a continuous history of a people and their land, even when the exact geopolitical boundaries are not clearly identified. A striking feature of *An Explanation of the Merging of Religious and Secular Rule in Tibet* is how Dungkar Rinpoché discursively creates "Tibet" (*bod*) historically, and thereby lays the ground for a Tibetan national identity, forging local identities and disparate religious affiliations amid state discourse.

Dungkar Rinpoché's *An Explanation of the Merging of Religious and Secular Rule in Tibet* and Mugé Samten's *A History of Traditional Fields of Learning* were able to use the term "Böd" for Tibet to talk about a collective national identity due to Chinese state discourse on ethnic nationalities. This is what Hu Yaobang referred to in his speech as "nationality autonomy." Despite its many problematic consequences and heuristic entanglements discussed by other scholars, the state policy on ethnic minorities (Ch. *mínzú* 民族), sometimes referred to as "nationalities," allows for markers of ethnic and cultural differences in contradistinction to the Han Chinese majority.[25] The state ethnic classification project started in the 1950s and includes "Tibetans" (Ch. *zàngzú* 藏族) as one of the fifty-six ethnic national minorities of China. When this project began, Chinese social scientists identified ethnic groups according to "nationality characteristics," i.e., variable markers of difference along the lines of Stalin's "four commonalities" (language, territory, psychology, and customs), but did not always strictly adhere to the Stalinist taxonomic measures.[26] Some Tibetan leaders used this policy as a way to advocate for the survivance of Tibetan cultural identity within the PRC.

For example, in the early 1960s, the Tenth Panchen Lama, Chökyi Gyeltsen, drew upon these markers of ethnic difference to emphasize the importance of language and customs distinctive to Tibetan "nationality" identity. In the 70,000 Character Petition, presented to Mao Zedong in 1962 to push back against the democratic reforms sweeping across the Tibetan plateau, he uses this as a political strategy:

> As concerns so-called nationality, people are all the same. Those things which are taken to be differences in nationality arise from individual nationality's area, ethnicity, national culture, language, costume, customs and other such characteristics.... Once a nationality's language, costume [i.e., distinctive clothing], customs and other important characteristics have disappeared, then the nationality itself has disappeared—that is to say, it has turned into another nationality. For example, a person whose ancestors were Tibetan but who himself does not understand the Tibetan language, and who does not have a single Tibetan characteristic, and who is indistinguishable from people of another nationality, although he might say he is Tibetan, is Tibetan in name only.[27]

According to this perspective, not observing "nationality" or ethnic characteristics, i.e., markers of cultural difference, would entail the disappearance of Tibetans as a "nationality" (*mi rigs*; Chi. *minzu*). Mao shot down the petition as "a poison arrow" against the people. Shortly thereafter, zealous Maoists abused the Panchen Lama, torturing and publicly humiliating him during large-scale struggle sessions. He was then imprisoned.[28] The Cultural Revolution was launched in 1966. During this time, the policies supporting ethnic minorities disappeared.

The political tides began to change again in 1978. At the National Committee of the Chinese People's Political Consultative Conference in February, the Panchen Lama appeared in public for the first time since his arrest.[29] By 1980 policies allowing for the right to autonomy gained traction after announcements made at the National People's Congress. Hu Yaobang's speech in May signaled these policy changes.[30] The right to exercise ethnic nationality autonomy opened some political-discursive space to address Tibetans as a people and to relax the draconian restrictions placed on their culture and religion in the Maoist years. Yet this was not without its challenges. One of the major drawbacks was the creation of a kind of "civilizing project"[31] whereby the Han majority are seen as objectively more advanced than other minorities.[32] The resulting "Han paternalism" is deeply intertwined with the Chinese Communist Party's interpretations of Marxist historical materialism and how Tibet's historical status is perceived therein.

In Chinese state versions of history, Tibet is split into two, "old Tibet" and "new Tibet," with the pivot from one to the other being the establishment of the People's Republic of China. The state has created a political-historical timeline that divides pre-1949 "old Tibet," as "feudal" and therefore "backward" (Chi. *luohou* 落后), from a "new," "liberated Tibet" under the paternalistic protection of the motherland. The rhetoric of "backwardness" of Tibetan culture still pervades Chinese state documents, such as the 1992 State Information Office's *White Papers*: "Education in old Tibet was very backward. There were no schools in the modern sense. Before Tibet's peaceful liberation, only some 2,000 monks and children of the nobility studied in government and private schools. The masses of serfs and slaves had no right to receive education."[33] This type of pejorative rhetoric is not only used to justify Chinese rule over Tibet but also deeply embedded within the CCP's ideology toward Tibet. Chinese Marxist historical materialism mixed with the ethnic classification project, starting in the 1950s.[34]

Like images refracting in a hall of mirrors, this ideological mix has distorted the indigenous cultural, linguistic, and religious diversity of pre-1950s China into different directions. On a theoretical level, each ethnic nationality is placed in a stage of historical progression advancing from primitive to slave to feudal to capitalist and eventually socialist modes of production.[35] In the 1950s and again in the late 1970s, the United Front Work Department (of the CCP), one of two major wings of what Goossaert and Palmer identify as the "state corporatist system of religious management," communicated this type of ideology to religious leaders, such as Dungkar Rinpoché. The other wing, known as State Administration for Religious Affairs (formerly the national Religious Affairs Bureau),[36] an agency of the State Council, worked with official religious associations such as the Buddhist Association of China, which included Dungkar Rinpoché and Tséten Zhabdrung as members. In minority areas such as Tibet, the Ethnic Affairs Commission worked closely with the Religious Affairs local offices.[37]

As we will read below, Dungkar Rinpoché's texts carefully legitimize a continuous Tibetan civilization amid Han paternalism that treated "Tibet" as "backward" and as "part of China." When writing about Tibetan history, culture, and language in the post-Mao era, all Three Polymaths were working within the CCP's ideological framework that enmeshed "Buddhism" with "feudalism" and "ethnic minority" issues.[38] Each of the three scholars responded to these policies in different ways. In the previous two chapters, we read how Tséten Zhabdrung and Mugé Samten almost erased the state from their autobiographical narratives. Dungkar Rinpoché took a different route through this political hall of mirrors.

Front matter included in one of the editions of *An Explanation of the Merging of Religious and Secular Rule in Tibet* informs us of its provenance. The preface to *A Collection of Dungkar Lozang Trinlé's Essays* (1997), absent from other editions published in English and in Tibetan,[39] confirms that it was commissioned by the government. Dungkar Rinpoché explains, "In 1977, The Chinese Communist Party of the Tibetan Autonomous Region and the United Front assigned me to write a history about something like the emergence of the system of merging religious and secular rule (*chos srid zung 'brel*) in Tibet."[40] He clearly states his assignment and that the intended audience of this text was members of the CCP. He also signals the political constraints within which he was able to write on Tibetan history. Subsequently, Dungkar Rinpoché was referred to as a collaborator with the Chinese state by some members of the exile community, although this charge has been rescinded by many in the last two decades.

Reception: More on Moral Agency

In many ways, Dungkar Rinpoché's reputation reflects the contested ground of what constitutes "Tibet" in the post-Mao era. Due to his status within the PRC, Dungkar Rinpoché was able to travel abroad in the mid-1980s, a privilege that very few Tibetans in China enjoyed, especially at that time. In order to be able to travel abroad, a Tibetan scholar had to have proven his loyalty to the Chinese Communist Party and have a firm grasp of Marxist-Leninism with Chinese characteristics. It is likely for these reasons that the other two polymaths, Tséten Zhabdrung and Mugé Samten, were never able to go out of the country. Dungkar Rinpoché's first trip abroad was to Munich, Germany, in 1985 for the International Association of Tibetan Studies conference.[41] Dungkar Rinpoché became known for his erudition within the international community of Tibetan scholars at this time. Contemporary Tibetan scholars, such as Tsering Shakya, have recognized his innovative moves in applying Western social scientific methods to the analysis of Tibetan Buddhist texts.[42] Dungkar Rinpoché's work still serves as a major primary source for American Tibetologists. For example, Melvyn Goldstein cites data collected by Dungkar Rinpoché that show the increases in the size of the monastic population between 1694 and 1733 to develop his well-known "mass monasticism" thesis.[43] Dungkar Rinpoché's repute was well-established after his seminal essay was published under its English title, *The Merging of Religious and Secular Rule in Tibet,* in 1991.

The fact that it was published in English by the Beijing Foreign Languages Press indicates that this work met the necessary political standards. Its original publication was commissioned in 1977 by the United Front/CCP. The English edition served as a platform for China's position on Tibet directed to a global audience because Tibet had become an international issue, in part due to the Dalai Lama's being awarded the Nobel Peace Prize in 1989. The fact that this text contains Marxist ideology led to some exile Tibetans identifying Dungkar Rinpoché as a "collaborator."[44]

The late Tsering Gongkatsang (a translator and Tibetan language lecturer at Oxford University) pushed back against the collaborator label. He eloquently summed up two perceptions of Dungkar Rinpoché: "Though some Tibetans will remember Dungkar as a collaborator, for those who knew him better (colleagues, students, and readers), he was a realist who did his best to safeguard Tibetan identity and culture within the new socio-political framework of the People's Republic of China."[45] Tsering Gonkatsang's emphasis on the social and political conditions in which Dungkar Rinpoché was embedded help to make sense of his complex role. This sober assessment dovetails with my suggestion that the dichotomous model of agency vis-à-vis state power (as either collaborator or resistance fighter) is not useful for this study on the Three Polymaths because it forecloses consideration of their numerous achievements.

Dungkar Rinpoché uses different strategies based on his capacities as a learned Buddhist scholar, Marxist theorist, and politically astute person to advocate for the survivance of Tibetan history and culture in shifting political circumstances. For these reasons it is important to look at moral agency in terms of capacity for action bound by historical conditions and by culturally specific disciplines of subject formation. Then we can observe how, even under enormous political constraints, all Three Polymaths acted as moral agents to promote certain ethical and epistemic values at specific points in time, each doing so in different ways. The fact that Dungkar Rinpoché earned the title of one of the Three Polymaths is a reminder that Tibetans within China honor his contributions.

When Dungkar Rinpoché wrote this text at the behest of the CCP in the Tibetan Autonomous Region and the United Front and used Marxist ideology to bear on the analysis of Buddhist governance, his steps were pioneering, especially under the dire political circumstances of 1977. Reflecting on the impact of Dungkar Rinpoché's *An Explanation of the Merging of Religious and Secular Rule in Tibet*, Pema Bhum clarified that this work was widely read by the younger generation of Tibetan intellectuals in China for two main reasons: its comprehensive coverage of nearly two thousand years of Tibetan history up to 1959 and how this information was delivered. Marxist ideas were familiar to this generation: "At the time the book was published—there was a strong trend throughout Tibet and China to consciously and unconsciously examine any and

all concepts through a Marxist lens. As a result, Dungkar Lozang Trinlé's examination of religion and state with a Marxist view was appropriate and suited to
young Tibetans' state of mind at the time."[46] In the context of late 1970s China,
Dungkar Rinpoché created a comprehensive Tibetan history for a public thirsty
for this knowledge in a novel and politically safe way. A few of his autobiographical reflections reveal how he valued scholarly pursuits and was aware of the ideological constraints placed on those who pursue a life of knowledge.

Dungkar Rinpoché's Reflections

Dungkar Rinpoché did not write a full-length autobiography, so we do not have
detailed accounts of his subjective viewpoints like those found in the life narratives by Tséten Zhabdrung and Mugé Samten. Nonetheless, a few of Dungkar
Rinpoché's personal reflections were published in editions of *An Explanation of
the Merging of Religious and Secular Rule in Tibet* and in later interviews. A
comparison of these texts reveals interesting differences and similarities that, at
the end of the day, show both the constraints placed on Dungkar Rinpoché and
his appreciation for an objective pursuit of knowledge.

The following reflective writing at the end of *An Explanation of the Merging
of Religious and Secular Rule in Tibet* can be divided into two parts. In the first
part, the author looks back on his status as an incarnate lama, and in the second,
he reveals his philosophies of education and learning. The Beijing-sanctioned
English print and the original Tibetan text share Marxist framings that underscore the political constraints in which this text was written in the late 1970s.
The philosophies disclosed in the second part align with values that he still held
a few years before his death. The first part of this section published in the Beijing
Foreign Language Press's print reads:

> I have lived under the Tibetan politico-religious system for many years, and was
> entitled "Living Buddha." With the help of the Chinese Communist Party, I
> have participated in revolutionary work and studied the theory of Marxism-
> Leninism as well as social and natural scientific works and ancient Tibetan
> annals. Now I have a better understanding of dialectical materialism and his-
> torical materialism and thus have gained a wider field of vision.[47]

In contrast to the secular Marxist overtones in the above rendition, the Tibetan
text also includes strong references to Buddhist ideas. My retranslation of

Dungkar Rinpoché's closing statement based on the print found within his *Collected Works* (2004) is:

> I lived under Tibet's system of Buddhist governance for many years and was titled *tülku* with the profound karmic residue of the exploitative class of the Buddhist religion. With the compassionate concern of the Chinese Communist Party, I participated in revolutionary work and studied Marx's and Lenin's collected writings and Mao Zedong's collected works. At the same time, I read works from the social sciences and natural sciences as well as many ancient Tibetan historical documents. Through this, I have gained a better understanding of the view of history through the lens of dialectical materialism and my field of vision has expanded.[48]

The most obvious difference between these two translations is the lack of Buddhist ideas in the Beijing edition. The author's references to core Buddhists concepts, such as "karmic residue" (*bag chags*) and "compassionate concern" (*byams brtse'i thugs khur*), even when framed by Marxist ideology, are omitted from the Beijing English translation. The culmination of karma over many lifetimes, or "karmic residue," is missing from the first sentence. It is shortened to "I have lived under the Tibetan politico-religious system for many years, and was entitled 'Living Buddha.'" The Buddhist notion of "compassionate concern" is translated perfunctorily as "help."[49] The term "Living Buddha" comes from the Chinese (Chi. *huofo* 活佛) and not from the Tibetan "*tülku*" (*sprul sku*), literally "emanation body," also known as a reincarnate lama. These translation choices on the part of the Beijing Languages Press censor any mention of Buddhist ideas and thereby reveal the constraints and possibilities for Tibetans writing within the PRC.

Despite this censorship and the Marxist ideas on class exploitation in both versions, Dungkar Rinpoché's attitudes toward the value of analyzing historical documents and material culture are apparent in the second part of this passage. My retranslation does not differ much from the Beijing print:

> The gates of one's mind can be opened by grasping lessons of the past and recognizing modern phenomena through structured analysis and research of past historical manuscripts, historical events, and ancient material culture. Based on all of this, I wrote a candid and true history from my point of view on the emergence of what resembles a system that merges the religious and the secular in Tibet. Readers are asked to give their invaluable advice and suggestions on whatever shortcomings in order to improve this essay.[50]

He underscores the value of peer review as well as a rational-empiricist approach to examining historical documents and material culture in order to assess the past from an objective point of view.

Nearly twenty years later, in the mid-1990s, he gave his philosophical viewpoints more latitude, an opening afforded by the easing of political restrictions (due in parts to policy changes and being abroad). His views emerge in an interview with Tenzin Gelek, a researcher, translator, and cofounder of the Latse Project, a nonprofit organization formed in 2020 that works to promote Tibetan language use and literacy. Signaling how attitudes have changed in exile, this interview from June 1995 was published posthumously in the Tibetan-language proceedings of a conference held on the twentieth anniversary of Dungkar Rinpoché's death in July 2017 at the College for Higher Tibetan Studies at Sarah, in India. In response to a question about whether he considered himself a Marxist-Leninist, Dungkar Rinpoché answered:

You asked what my own view is. My philosophy is to constantly examine the connections between cause and effect and then express these in clear language. Even though we had a tradition of merging religious and secular governance (*chos srid zung 'brel*), as in whatever other matter, think about its successive stages—at the beginning there is cause, that is desire, then successively this develops, and in the end there is the condition of disintegration; think well about that! At this point in time, it is possible to clearly understand this essential feature of reality, and we can amass a lot of evidence to examine this. Fundamentally, it is necessary to look at the causes and effects, however one views reality. It is necessary that the causes and conditions do not contradict one another; scientists and Buddhists do not have any great debates on this. When you conduct historical research, it is important to have a fundamental awareness; a scholar's work is mainly to investigate the truth. It's necessary to view all reality in order to find the truth. The main obstacle to finding truth is a prejudiced mind. From the point of view of a scientist, it is necessary to abandon bias; for a Buddhist practitioner, the essential point is to abandon grasping at the self. The mind of those with biased views can't find the truth; the reason for this is that you can't perceive it from only one side. Likewise, a religious person can't obtain liberation if they can't abandon grasping at self.[51]

Dungkar Rinpoché poignantly reveals his own core values as a scholar. His thoughts are more clearly elucidated than under the political constraints at the time of writing *An Explanation of the Merging of Religious and Secular Rule in*

Tibet. At the same time, his perspectives in many ways align with those expressed in that work, in such statements as "studying and analyzing historical events, annals, and relics and by learning lessons from the past," and "opening the gate to one's mind by looking at the past." Although the intended audience and publishing venues were different, common among these reflections is Dungkar Rinpoché's emphasis on epistemology—how to discern the nature of knowledge and the role of objective analysis in arriving at truth.

In this articulation, he draws connections between scientists and Buddhists, a move that anticipated the dialogues and ongoing research between these two groups. For him, Buddhists and scientists share a common pursuit of truth that is measured by logic—the indisputable relationship between causes and effects. However, he observes that Buddhists and scientists come at this from different perspectives. Each group has to overcome different prejudices; a scientist must reject bias (*phyogs ris*) and a Buddhist practitioner must discard grasping at the ego. As a Buddhist modernist, he discloses a compatibility between Buddhism and science grounded in a rationalist-empiricist approach to epistemological claims.[52]

These autobiographical reflections also point a way out of the political hall of mirrors that Dungkar Rinpoché had to navigate to achieve the difficult goal of writing about Tibetan history with academic integrity in early post-Mao China. He strategically uses the available resources when he wrote *An Explanation of the Merging of Religious and Secular Rule in Tibet* between 1977 and 1979, and another history, "Terminologies in the *Red Annals*," shortly thereafter.

LAYING THE GROUND FOR A SECULAR TIBETAN HISTORY IN THE EARLY POST-MAO ERA

In writing a history of Tibet, Dungkar Rinpoché navigates Chinese state requirements and anchors the narrative on a Tibetan Buddhist concept of governance—*chö-sī zung-drel* (*chos srid zung 'brel*). The Beijing Foreign Language Press translates this concept in the title of his essay as "the merging of religious and secular rule." In this translation choice, *chö* (*chos*) is "religious" and *sī* (*srid*) is "secular"; they are brought together in a "connected pair" (*zung 'brel*), i.e., they "merge." I have followed this previously established translation, but others are available, such as: "the relationship between religion and state," "the conjunction of religious law," and "Buddhist government," among others.[53] Regardless, this concept represents a Tibetan articulation of secularism in that it "entails a theory of what 'religion' is or does."[54] Dungkar Rinpoché's approach to writing history develops a secular past for Tibet at a time when there were few, if any, histories on Tibet within the PRC, especially in Tibetan language.[55]

In the Tibetan context, the importance of the concept *"chö-sī zung-drel"* cannot be overstated. This model of secularism, with varying interpretations and adaptations in different historical circumstances, lies at the center of Inner Asian politics.[56] The historian Dieter Schuh views *chö-sī zung-drel* as a later manifestation of the sacral kingship model of governance, evident in early Tibetan history as far back as the *tsenpo* emperors of the Yarlung Dynasty.[57] Yumiko Ishihama describes this as the basis of Tibetan-Mongol-Manchu diplomatic relations that the Fifth Dalai Lama tried to restrict to the Géluk form of government in the seventeenth century.[58] *Chö-sī zung-drel* can also involve other related concepts, such as that of the "twin temporal and spiritual traditions" (*lugs gnyis*) or the relationship between the lay-ruler-donor (*yon dag*) and his preceptor-officiant (*mchod gnas*).[59] In twentieth-century history, a few years prior to the People's Liberation Army's march into Lhasa, the Ganden Podrang government celebrated this form of governance as humanitarian. In 1946, the same year that Dungkar Rinpoché attained his *geshé* degree, the Tibetan government sent a letter to Chiang Kai-shek that stated, "There are many great nations on this earth who have achieved unprecedented wealth and might, but there is only one nation which is dedicated to the well-being of humanity in the world, that is the religious land of Tibet which cherishes a system of 'joint spiritual and temporal rule' [i.e., *chos srid zung 'brel*]."[60] This type of rhetoric, as explained earlier in this chapter, would become a cornerstone for exile Tibetan national identity. The parameters of *chö-sī zung-drel* are still negotiated among Tibetan scholars and politicians in exile today.[61]

As a learned Buddhist scholar, reincarnate lama, and debate partner in the Fourteenth Dalai Lama's *geshé* exams,[62] Dungkar Rinpoché must have been aware of the valorization of this concept in Tibetan history. He developed his thesis on *chö-sī zung-drel* from the relevant manuscripts and histories at his disposal at the Cultural Relics Office at the Norbulingka to write a diachronic history of Tibet. At the same time, Dungkar Rinpoché employs a term related to *chö* i.e., *chöluk,* for "religion," to forge a Tibetan religious identity within CCP constraints. Given how embedded *chö-sī zung-drel* is in "traditional," "old," "feudal" Tibet, and considering the contested ground of what constituted Tibet in the politicized situation in which Dungkar Rinpoché wrote this text (between 1977 and 1979), it is astounding that he was able to center his narrative on Tibet and the concept of "the merging of religious and secular rule," and to compose this in Tibetan language.

Dungkar Rinpoché turns to Marxist ideas on the separation of church and state as a way to frame *chö-sī zung-drel* within Chinese Communist discourse. A preface to the reprint of his seminal essay in his *Collected Works* (vol. 4, 2004) called "Essential Points Reflecting on Initial Research for the System of Merging the Religious and Secular in Tibet" (*bod kyi chos srid zung 'brel gyi lam lugs la thog ma'i zhib 'jug byas ba'i shes tshor gnad bsdus*) details how he and other "comrades" (*blo mthun*) discussed two interpretations of "the merging of religious and secular rule in Tibet."[63] After reading an essay written by Friedrich Engels, Dungkar Rinpoché refutes the notion that *chö-sī zung-drel* dates to the seventh century when *tsenpo* Songtsen Gampo (Srong btsan sgam po) implemented a legal code based on religious law (*chos khrims*). Dungkar Rinpoché explains that after he read and later edited a Tibetan translation of Engels's famous essay, "Frederick William IV, King of Prussia,"[64] also included in his *Collected Works* (vol. 4, 2004), he realized that this first interpretation could not be correct because *chö-sī zung-drel* is when "the king and preceptor are in one person."[65] This type of governance, Dungkar Rinpoché claims, first happened under the rule of Pakpa ('Phags pa, 1235–1280), whom we will read more about shortly.

Based on his interpretation of *chö-sī zung-drel,* Dungkar Rinpoché divides *An Explanation of the Merging of Religious and Secular Rule in Tibet* into two main parts: "The Struggles Between Religions and the Political Conditions of the Time Prior to the Establishment of a System Merging Religious and Secular Rule in Tibet"[66] and "The Actual Beginning of a System Merging Religious and Secular in Tibet and the Struggles Between the Upper Strata of Religious Sects to Use Religion for Seizing Political Power."[67] A concluding section sums up Dungkar Rinpoché's theories on Buddhist governance and includes his reflections on writing this piece.

A chapter-by-chapter overview indicates how Dungkar Rinpoché blends Chinese Marxist ideology with a comprehensive history of Tibetan Buddhism and applies *chöluk* or "religion" to the names of the various traditions in Tibet. Part 1 has eight chapters with the following titles:1) "Bonpo Religion (*bon po'i chos lugs*) and the Societal Conditions in Tibet Before the Introduction of Buddhism (*sang rgyas chos lugs*) in Tibet (*bod*)"; 2) "The Economic and Political Conditions in Tibet When Buddhism Was Introduced Into Tibet"; 3) "The Struggles Between the Bon Religion and Buddhism"; 4) "The Formation of the Nyingma Religion (*nying ma'i chos lugs*) and the First Buddhist Monastics in Tibet"; 5) "The Transformation of Some Buddhist Monks from Slaveowners to

Landlords of Monastic Estates"; 6) "The Suppression of Buddhism by the King Langdarma and the Causes Thereof"; 7) "The Peasant Uprising in the Tibetan Region (*bod sa gnas*) and the Period of Fragmentation; the Political Situation in Tibet and the Interior (*rgyal nang*)"; and 8) "After the Period of Fragmentation: the Revival of Buddhist Religion and the Causes Thereof."[68] Dungkar Rinpoché weaves together content relating to traditional Tibetan Buddhist historiography, such as the introduction of Buddhism in Tibet and its decline under the anti-Buddhist king Langdarma, with Marxist dialectics that reference stages of historical progression, transitioning from the slave stage to feudalism.

Part 2 similarly forges a new way to write about Tibetan history. It has ten chapters that proceed chronologically from the thirteenth century onward. Each chapter title signals its contents: 1) "Sakya Seize Political Power in the Tibetan Region and the War Between the Sakya and Drigung (*'bri gung pa*) [Kagyu]"; 2) "Pakmodrupa (*phag mo gru pa*) Seize Rule Over the Tibetan Region and the Spread of the Géluk Religion (*dge lugs pa'i chos lugs*)"; 3) "Conflict Within the Ruling Class of the Pakmodrupa"; 4) "Conflict Between the Rinpungpa (*rin spungs pa*) and the Géluk"; 5) "Conflict Between the Regent of Tsang (*gtsang pa sde srid*) and the Géluk"; 6) "Güüshi Khan's (Gu shri han) Annihilation of the Regent of Tsang and the Establishment of the Tibetan Regional Government and the Suppression of an Uprising by the Karma Kagyu Religion (*karma bka' bgyud chos lugs*)"; 7) "Religious Contradictions Between the Nyingma and the Géluk and the Resulting Political Conflicts Among the Upper Classes"; 8) "The Decline of the System Merging Religious and Secular Rule and Struggles for Political Power Among the Ruling Class"; 9) "Forces of Imperialist (*btsan rgyal ring lugs pa*) Aggression Encroach on Tibet and the Reactionary Upper Classes[69] Betray the Fatherland"; 10) "The Reactionary Upper Classes of the Tibetan Region Launch an Armed Rebellion Under the Banner of Religion and Nationalities; the Abrogation of the System of Merging Religious and Secular Rule in Tibet."[70] This last chapter is heavily laden with the Chinese Communist Party's perspectives on recent Tibetan history, and while he was cooperating with the Chinese state in this way, he had to consider the intended audience of CCP cadres. It is not surprising that we find Marxist historical teleological classification terms throughout the narrative.[71] More surprising is that he navigates the parameters afforded by the CCP's Marxist ideological framework to create a *longue durée* of Tibetan governance and Buddhist institutions in the PRC in the late 1970s. We see the significance of this in two instances: the discursive unity of "Tibet" and his deployment of the modern construct of religion (*chos lugs*).

The Historical Status of Tibet

Dungkar Rinpoché's central thesis that *chö-si zung-drel*—the merging of religious and secular rule—began under the rule of the Sakya hierarch Drogön Pakpa happens to also serve as a flashpoint over Tibet's historical status. According to PRC official perspectives on Sino-Tibetan relations, Tibet became part of China during the Yuan Dynasty of the thirteenth century. This remained the dominant narrative until the late 2000s, when the PRC's claim shifted to the beginning of Sino-Tibetan contact, as I will detail later on in this chapter. In contrast, exile Tibetan historians, such as Tsepon Shakabpa, view Sino-Tibetan relations through the lens of Buddhist history. From this perspective, the relationship of the donor, the emperor Qubilai Khan of the Yuan Dynasty, who gave control over Tibetan territories as a gift to his preceptor, Drogön Pakpa, is testimony to Tibetan independence. It is on such points that Tibet's historical status vis-à-vis China, and therefore Tibetan history, becomes a highly politicized and contentious subject.[72] Examining how Dungkar Rinpoché treats Tibet's historical status vis-à-vis China will show how he complicates Chinese state dictates and contextualizes traditional Tibetan Buddhist historical texts. He simultaneously draws upon and departs from both historiographical approaches to forge his own interpretation of Tibetan history that discursively unites "Tibet" despite past regional and sectarian divides that thwarted Tibetan national identity.

Dungkar Rinpoché does not openly challenge the Chinese state on its view of Tibet's historical status. He turns to Tibetan historical texts such as the *Red Annals* to show how Sakya-Mongol-Yuan relations were not equivalent to Sino-Tibetan relations in the People's Republic of China. The importance of this cannot be overstated, as the anachronistic treatment of the PRC as equal to the Yuan dynasty is the basis for the PRC's legitimation of political and territorial claims on Tibet.[73]

For Dungkar Rinpoché, the system of *chö-si zung-drel* began under the rule of Pakpa, a.k.a. Drogön Pakpa Lodrö Gyeltsen ('Gro mgon 'phags pa blo gros rgyal mtshan, 1235–1280), the Fifth Patriarch of the Sakya Tradition and also the Yuan Dynasty's first "Imperial Preceptor" (Ch. *dishi*, 帝师).[74] Dungkar Rinpoché highlights Sakya rule at this time as follows:

The nine Sakya Throne Holders (*sa skya'i khri thog*), from Drogön Pakpa until Dāben Lodrö Gyeltsen (Ta' dben blo gros rgyal mtshan), and the twenty successive Pönchen, from Pönchen Shakya Zangpo to [Pönchen] Wangtsön (Dbang brtson), under the direct orders of the Yuan Central Government (Yon krung dbyang srid gzhung), ruled over both religious and secular [domains] (*chos srid gnyis ka'i dbag po byas*) in the Tibetan region and controlled all of Tibet (*bod yongs*) beginning in 1264, the Wood-Ox year of Tibet's fourth *rab-byung* cycle, until the Wood-Horse year of Tibet's sixth *rab-byung* cycle in 1352, for a period of ninety-one years.[75]

Some key concepts and terms to pay attention to in this passage include the positions of the Sakya hierarchs, the references to Tibet and the Yuan, and the use of reign dates according to the sixty-year cycles of the Tibetan calendrical system, i.e., *rab-byung*, pronounced "*rap-jung*." These are important because they signal to the reader how Dungkar Rinpoché navigates through this contested political minefield. By highlighting the leadership role of Pakpa and other Sakya hierarchs and describing key aspects of Mongol-Tibetan administration, he writes a fact-based (and not ideologically motivated) Tibetan history, as he aspired to do according to his reflections.

In writing about this period of history, Dungkar Rinpoché draws attention to the administrative bureaucratic system of the Sakya-Yuan period. As indicated by the above passage, two of the highest positions were that of the Sakya Throne Holder and the Pönchen, the highest administrative official; both offices were occupied by Tibetans. Other sections of *An Explanation of the Merging of Religious and Secular Rule in Tibet* detail the Sakya administrative apparatus, including those bureaus established by the Yuan court, such as the Tubo Pacification Office (*thu bo shon wu'i si*; Ch. *tubo xuanwei si*, 吐蕃宣威付), and the position of imperial preceptor created by Qubilai Khan and bestowed upon Pakpa in 1270. He also describes other ranks and positions, including those in the military, such as the myriarchs (commanders of 10,000); those at monastic estates, such as the *sol-pön* (*gsol dpon*), attendants in charge of high-ranking monks' daily life; and those in local districts, such as the *dzong-pön* (*rdzong dpon*), an official in charge of a fort, among others. In charge of all this was Pakpa, as Dungkar Rinpoché emphasizes: "Drogön Pakpa was the ruler of the three feudal lords of Tibet at this time."[76] He details the Sakya-Yuan government apparatus and thereby does not anachronistically treat the Sakya-Yuan period as the same as China of the twentieth century.

The Beijing-sanctioned English-language print is censored in such a way as to cover his nuanced rhetorical moves. A good example of this can be found in the following passage from *An Explanation of the Merging of Religious and Secular Rule in Tibet*, which focuses on military campaigns that paved the way for the Mongols to rule over a vast territory that now comprises many countries, such as the People's Republic of China, Mongolia, the Republic of Buryatia, and far eastern Russia.[77] The Beijing Foreign Languages Press's translation of Dungkar Rinpoche's text glosses over this fact:

> In the Iron-Rat year of the fourth cycle of the Tibetan calendar (A.D. 1240), Prince Go-dan [Mongolian: Köten] sent an expeditionary force under General Dor-rta-nag-po's command to Tibetan areas. In the Wood-Dragon year of the fourth cycle of the Tibetan calendar (A.D. 1244), Prince Go-dan of the Yuan Dynasty invited Sa-skya Pandita to the hinterland. In the Water-Rat year of the fourth cycle of the Tibetan calendar (A.D. 1252), Mongke Khan ascended the throne. In the following year, the Water-Ox year (A.D. 1253), he sent troops to Tibet and merged it into China's territory.[78]

The use of the phrase "China's territory" is noteworthy here because it is a clear example of how PRC state historiography simplifies complex political relationships and geographic territory to serve nation-state interests. In the original Tibetan text there is no mention of "China's territory"; the last sentence reads: "In 1253, Möngke Khan, [Emperor] Xianzong of the Yuan Dynasty (yon shan tsung), sent troops and united all of Tibet's territories as one (bod yongs rdzogs gong bu gcig gyur byas)."[79] Dungkar Rinpoche was well aware that the vast territories of the Mongol empire were not part of "China." In the Tibetan version of his text, there is no evidence that he uses the term "China" (krung go) for the Yuan Dynasty. The Beijing translation adds the phrase "China's territory," which anachronistically treats the extent of the Mongol empire as the same as that of the PRC.

The erudite Dungkar Rinpoché (with unfettered access to rare historical documents), similar to other experts of Inner Asian history, such as Christopher Atwood, Elliot Sperling, and Luciano Petech, understood the complex dynamics of thirteenth-century Inner Asia. Dungkar Rinpoché strategically uses historical terms, such as reign titles, to signal these complexities. For example, he refers to Möngke Khan as shan tsung, which is the Tibetan transliteration of the Chinese posthumous reign title Xianzong (憲宗). Other sources explain that Ming dynasty historiographic convention posthumously recognizes Mongol Great Khans, who reigned between Chinggis Khan's coronation in 1206 and the ascension of Qubilai Khan (Kublai, 1215–1294) to the throne, as "emperors" of the Yuan Dynasty.[80] Dungkar Rinpoché' treats the Sakya-Yuan administrative apparatus within its historical context and does not make anachronistic claims.

Dungkar Rinpoché's constant references to the Tibetan calendrical dating system and to Mongol and Tibetan reign titles all serve to illustrate this point.

For example, when Dungkar Rinpoché states, "Drogön Pakpa gained temporal powers for three years beginning in 1264, the Wood-Ox year of Tibet's fourth *rab-byung* cycle, Qubilai Sechen Khan's first year of the Zhi Yuan era (至元),"[81] he refers to Qubilai Khan, the first emperor of the Yuan Dynasty, by his Mongol reign title, Sechen Khan, and uses both Tibet's dating system and the Chinese historiographic convention of splitting Qubilai's reign periods into two based on his ascension to the throne as emperor of the Yuan Dynasty.[82] Other examples of this are peppered throughout the text. Two further examples on the importance of titles come from the block quote on Mongol military incursions above.

Beijing's English translation states that "Prince Go-dan sent an expeditionary force . . . into Tibet." Prince Go-dan was the grandson of Chinggis Khan and one of the sons of the Great Khan, Ögedei (d. 1241). His name in Mongolian transcription is Köten.[83] The Tibetan text refers to the first Mongol military leader to enter Tibet as "*Gyelpo* Köten, emperor of the Yuan Dynasty" (*yon rgyal rabs kyi gong ma go dan rgyal po*). In this case, the Beijing translation of the title is technically correct from the perspective of Mongol history. Köten was a prince because he was never appointed to the position of khan at the *quriltai*, the assembly of Mongol leadership.[84] The *gyelpo* title, which means "ruler" and not prince, is frequent in Tibetan texts because Köten was the first Mongol ruler to make direct contact with Sakya Paṇḍita, the uncle of Pakpa, who established Mongol-Tibetan relations. Tibetan historiographers elevate his position posthumously. Dungkar Rinpoche follows the Tibetan precedent here.

Through nuanced details, Dungkar Rinpoché indicates that "the Yuan Dynasty" cannot be equated with the People's Republic of China, even though he occasionally refers to the Yuan as a Central Government (Yon krung dbyang srid gzhung), a nod to Chinese Communist divisions between central and local polities. He nonetheless treats history with factual information, including references to reign titles, different calendrical systems, and administrative offices. To appreciate how nuanced Dungkar Rinpoché's approach to Tibetan history was, it may be useful to briefly compare it with other descriptions of this historical flashpoint.

As noted above, from the exile Tibetan perspective, Sakya-Mongol relations of the thirteenth century marked an era of Tibetan political independence based on the "donor-preceptor" relationship between Qubilai and Pakpa. Tsepon W.D. Shakabpa's monumental work *Tibet: A Political History* (*Bod kyi srid don rgyal rabs*) served for many years as the seminal history of Tibet in exile. Tsepon Shakabpa (Rtsis dpon dbang phyug bde ldan zhwa sgab pa, 1907–1989), a minister of finance in the Tibetan government, witnessed Chinese troops entering Lhasa and chose to leave Tibet shortly thereafter in 1951. First published in 1967, *Tibet: A Political History* underscores Tibet's historical independence. Derek Maher points out, "Despite the title, this book is not really a general history of all of Tibet. . . . Shakabpa primarily narrates those episodes that contribute to his main agenda of making the historical case for Tibetan independence."[85] According to Shakabpa, Tibet became independent in 1253; both the claim of "independence" and the date are problematic.

Shakabpa's argument centers on the donor-preceptor relationship. He surmises that when Qubilai (1215–1294), the donor, gave Pakpa, the preceptor, the thirteen myriarchies of Tibet, thereby establishing *yön-chöd* (*yon mchod*), i.e., the "donor-preceptor" or "patron-priest" relationship, Tibet became independent. As Shakabpa states, "However, ever since Qubilai Khan presented the three provinces and Ngari to Drogön Chogyel Pakpa in 1253, Tibet has remained completely independent (*rang btsan gtsang ma*). As a result of the preceptor-patron relationship between Tibet and Mongolia, high lamas have gone from Tibet to China and Mongolia."[86] Shakabpa's interpretation of Tibet's historical independence is the main focus of his narrative.

In contrast to this perspective, Western historians have assessed how difficult it is to pinpoint dates for this complex relationship between the Yuan and the Sakya. One fact, however, is clear. The year 1253, given by Shakabpa and found in other Tibetan histories (but not Dungkar's), cannot be correct. Based on his reading of Tibetan and Chinese language histories, Luciano Petech observes, "The traditional dates [in Tibetan sources] for these events vary and are much too early; the most commonly accepted are 1254 and 1260. The first date must be ruled out, as Khubilai [Mong.: Qubilai] in 1254 was simply a prince and had no authority to make such a gift."[87] He further points out that Chinese dynastic histories do not offer any clarifications on these dates. On the issue of territorial control, Petech states that Sakya authority over Ngari in western Tibet was "theoretical, while Amdo and Khams [eastern Tibet] were directly controlled by the imperial authorities."[88] Dungkar Rinpoché historically contextualizes Sakya-Yuan relations by using Mongol reign titles and listing the territorial extent of Sakya authority according to Tibetan texts. He states, "In the Wood-Ox year of the fourth *rab-byung* cycle, in the year 1264, Qubilai Sechen Khan bestowed thirteen myriarchies of Tibet, excluding Ngari and Amdo, to Drogön Pakpa as an offering for receiving tantric empowerments for the first time."[89] Dungkar Rinpoché cites the *Chronicles of the Sakya* (*Sa skya'i gdung rabs rin chen bang mdzod*) on this and then details the census that was conducted after Qubilai's bestowal of the thirteen myriarchies.[90] Although Shakabpa, Petech, and Dungkar all highlight the importance of the donor-preceptor relationship, they do so in very different ways. Dungkar Rinpoché cites Tibetan historical texts to put forth that Pakpa "under the direct orders of the Yuan Central Government, ruled over both religious and secular domains in the Tibetan region and controlled all of Tibet beginning in 1264."[91]

In order to understand how Dungkar's historical analysis relates to disputes over Tibet's historical status, we must first look at the Chinese Communist Party's changing positions on the historical status of Tibet. One of Elliot Sperling's research agendas was to show how the CCP's assertions about Tibet's historical status have changed over time in its attempt to legitimize its rule over Tibetan polities; he stressed how these claims are not equivalent to the entitlements and treaties of earlier Sino-Tibetan relations in the Qing or Ming dynasties, despite the CCP's ahistorical views of geographical borders.[92] To this end, he identified two main CCP interpretations of Tibet's historical status vis-à-vis China: the "since the Yuan Dynasty" thesis and the "since ancient times" thesis.[93] The former claims that Tibet became part of China in the Yuan Dynasty—a flashpoint that Dungkar Rinpoché's history subtly subverts by providing many examples of how the Yuan Dynasty is not equivalent to the People's Republic of China. The latter position states that Tibet has been part of China "forever."

If Dungkar Rinpoché had been aware of the "since ancient times" thesis, his *An Explanation of the Merging of Religious and Secular Rule in Tibet* unambiguously rejected it. This is made clear by the way that he treats the era that stretches from the collapse of the Tibetan empire until the establishment of Sakya rule over Tibet:

> When the Buddhist religion (*sangs rgyas chos lugs*) declined in India, the Buddhist religion revived in the Tibetan region (*bod sa gnas*). This period in the history of Tibet (*bod*) is referred to as "the diffusion of Buddha-Dharma (*sangs rgyas kyi bstan pa*) from India to the north." Later, this further expanded through Gansu and Qinghai [provinces], Mongolia, and Khalkha. This period in the history of Tibet is called "the diffusion of the Dharma from northern lands to the north." For a period of 392 years (846–1238), from Langdarma's suppression of the Buddhist religion and the subsequent fragmentation of Tibet (*bod*) until the unification of one Tibetan region under the Emperor of the Yuan Dynasty, Möngke Khan (*yon rgyal rabs kyi gong ma mong gol han*), the situation was such that the political regimes of the inner Fatherland (*mes rgyal nang khul*) and the Tibetan regions were divided.[94]

In the above passage, Dungkar Rinpoché rejects any notion of a "since ancient times" thesis by stating that Tibet was politically fragmented and not united with the "inner Fatherland," a somewhat ambiguous term that could refer either to the Yuan Dynasty or to China. His clever rhetorical choices neither assert Tibetan historical independence nor claim that Tibet was part of China since ancient times. He treads much more carefully around the "since Yuan dynasty" thesis. When he wrote *An Explanation of the Merging of Religious and Secular Rule in Tibet* in 1977, the official line was that Tibet had been part of China "since the Yuan Dynasty," yet he makes clear that the Yuan Dynasty and the People's Republic of China are not equivalents.

The "since ancient times" thesis was politicized long after Dungkar Rinpoché finished his text. The evolution from the "since Yuan Dynasty" thesis to the "since ancient times" thesis is evident in a 2009 speech by Sun Yong, the vice-director of the Tibetan Academy of Social Sciences. Elliot Sperling translates this from an article in the *People's Daily* (Ch. *Renmin Ribao* 人民日报):

> When we say today that Tibet has been a part of China since ancient times, it is an historical fact. To say "since ancient times" is not the same as saying "since the Yuan Dynasty"; it is rather to say "since human activity began." In this regard saying "Tibet has been a part of China since ancient times" is also not to say "the regime in Tibet since ancient time has always been a part of the area effectively governed by political authority from the Central Plains or the political authority of the Central Government." Rather, it's to say that "the history of this piece of land, Tibet, has, since human activity began, been a part of Chinese history." Whether it's as a part of the history of China's borderlands or as a part of the history of China's minority nationalities, it is nevertheless absolutely not part of the history of any foreign country.[95]

"Since ancient times" became the CCP's position toward the historical status of Tibet in the aftermath of the demonstrations across the Tibetan plateau in 2008.

In making his argument,[96] Sun Yong clarifies why the "since Yuan Dynasty" model became outmoded:

> The formulation "only after Tibet entered into China's territory during the Yuan Dynasty did it become a part of China" has an obvious flaw. The famous Tibetologist Wang Furen pointed out in the 1980s that saying Tibet entered China's territory during the Yuan Dynasty is tantamount to saying Tibet had a period outside the Motherland; that prior to the thirteenth century Tibet was not within China. This does not accord with the historical fact of the evolutionary process of China's historical inseparability.[97]

The statement makes clear how history can be used to serve the Chinese state's position on the Tibet issue. Today, "since ancient times" is the dominant historical narrative on Sino-Tibetan relations. Before that, PRC histories equated the Mongol military excursions into Tibet with its becoming "China's territory."

When we look at Tibetan Buddhist texts and Chinese dynastic histories, as Dungkar Rinpoche did to research his historical writings, facts tell us otherwise, as they do not include Tibet within the carefully delineated geographical boundaries of China.[98] In other words, when it comes to the historical status of Tibet, the CCP ignores the historical record in Chinese and Tibetan sources and treats the Mongol Yuan Dynasty as if it were equal to the nation-state of China.[99] When Dungkar Rinpoché wrote *An Explanation of the Merging of Religious and Secular Rule in Tibet* for the CCP's United Front, he must have been well aware that history served the state and that the historical status of Tibet stood within the "since the Yuan Dynasty" thesis. His narrative, however, contrasts that of this CCP mouthpiece. He uses Tibetan and Mongol titles, refers to the relevant dating systems, and showcases administrative titles, citing the Tibetan historical texts that contain this information. In this way he shows the complexities of Inner Asian history and the role of Tibetans therein.

Dungkar Rinpoché also addresses this historical flashpoint in "An Explanation of Select Major Terminologies in the *Red Annals*," hereafter, "Terminologies in the *Red Annals*."[100] This text is a commentary on the original *Red Annals* (*Deb ther dmar po*), an important early Tibetan history written by Tselpa Künga Dorje (1309–1364).[101] Two years after finishing *An Explanation of the Merging of Religious and Secular Rule in Tibet*, Dungkar Rinpoché's commentary and the *Red Annals* appeared in one volume (1981); it was one of the first efforts to reprint Tibetan historical texts by the Minzu Publishing House.[102] Pema Bhum explains the significance of this text:

> The *Red Annals* itself only has 151 pages [145 pages in the 2004 version], but Dungkar Rinpoché's work has 311 pages, covering 683 terms. Although the terminology he defines is from the *Red Annals*, by way of his detailed explanation, Dungkar Lozang Trinlé covers the breadth of Tibetan history, religion as well as Buddhist texts for a tremendous contribution. The text became, and continues to be, an important tool for young generations to study classical literature.[103]

Dungkar Rinpoché's "Terminologies in the *Red Annals*" offers another view on the Sakya-Yuan time period. In this text, he was not writing under the commission of the CCP's United Front. He writes about the complexities of

Mongol-Tibetan history in ways that subtly and carefully subvert the simplified nation-state version of history. He discursively unites Tibetans, ignores progressive stages of Marxist historical materialism, and showcases the great heroes of Tibetan civilization, thereby dismissing Han pejorative stereotypes of Tibet as backward.

For my research, I consulted "Terminologies in the *Red Annals*" in volume 6 of his *Collected Works* (2004). In this text, Dungkar Rinpoché underscores how Mongol forces entered Tibet and uses the word "Bod mi" for Tibetan people living in Amdo.[104] His choice of terminology does not seem to be arguing for a "greater Tibetan" territory but certainly emphasizes a collective "Tibetan" people.[105] In setting up Sakya Paṇḍita as a great statesman, he details the violent military campaigns under the Mongol leader Köten:

> [In 1240] when Köten dispatched forces into Tibet (Böd) under the command of Dorta Nakpo (Dor rta nag po) [Mongolian: Dorda Darqan], every Tibetan (Böd mi) they saw in the areas of western Amdo (Mdo stod) and eastern Amdo (Mdo smad), they killed, setting houses on fire and plundering livestock until they arrived in Central Tibet (Dbus gtsang). They set the Royal Temple of Phanpo ('Phan-po) alight and killed over five hundred monks, and they also caused great damage at Reting (Rwa sgreng) Monastery. In all these places, they couldn't even surrender; through plundering, killing, and burning nothing remained, not even a name.[106]

When retelling this history, he names the geographic areas of western and eastern Amdo and Central Tibet but doesn't clarify borders. He discursively unites the people of these areas through the use of "Böd mi"[107] for "Tibetans." He does not use terms for regional affiliations, even though he refers to ethnic Tibetans who lived outside of Central Tibet.[108]

His narrative also focuses on the heroes in Tibetan history.[109] For example, he praises Sakya Paṇḍita as a great peacemaker and statesman, explaining that an upshot of Köten's military campaigns was the invitation of the Sakya hierarch to serve as his religious preceptor. Other histories tell us that when Sakya Paṇḍita, a.k.a. Sapan, arrived at the Mongol court with his two nephews, Pakpa ('Phags pa) and Chakna Dorje (Phyag na rdo rje), Köten was away from Jang-ngö (Byang ngos; Ch. Liangzhou) to attend the *quriltai*, the assembly of Mongol lords, in which his brother Güyüg ascended to the position of khan. When Köten returned to court in 1247, Sakya Paṇḍita entered a new diplomatic role. He sent a letter advising heads of monastic estates and lay aristocrats to submit to the Mongols and to allow them to collect taxes and levy troops.[110]

"Terminologies in the *Red Annals*" highlights Sakya Paṇḍita's role in bringing peace to Tibet:

> [As a result of Sapan's letter], the Tibetan masses were able to generate faith in the policies of the Yuan Dynasty and had established the motivations and support for the act of uniting Tibet with the Fatherland. For eight whole years until Sakya Paṇḍita passed away, the Yuan Dynasty ensured peace and stability without needing any military force in Tibetan regions. The venerable Sakya Paṇḍita is a Tibetan religious figure whose great legacy was the act of uniting the Tibetan region with the Fatherland.[111]

Unlike the Beijing English version of *An Explanation of the Merging of Religious and Secular Rule in Tibet*, which stresses that "Tibet" merged into China's territory, here Dungkar Rinpoché highlights Sakya Paṇḍita's role in uniting the Tibetan regions with the "Fatherland," which as above can be read as a reference to "China" or from this context can be read in reference to the Yuan Dynasty. There is no explicit mention of China (*krung go*) or the "central government" (*krung dbyang*) here. Of course we do read Marxist terminology in such phrases as "the Tibetan masses" and the omission of "Mongolia" (still part of the USSR at the time of writing).

Dungkar Rinpoché finds ways to accurately tell history by deploying ambiguous terminology and not parroting the CCP version of Tibet's historical status. His writing these two texts in the aftermath of the Cultural Revolution was significant not only because they were the first of their kind at this time but also because in writing them and teaching about Tibetan history, he pioneered Tibetan studies as a secular, academic pursuit. It is for these reasons that scholars who lived in China's Tibet view Dungkar Rinpoché so highly. As the Tibetan writer and scholar Gedun Rabsal points out:

> When I read *Chos srid zung 'brel* [*Merging of the Religious and Secular in Tibet*], I really don't pay much attention to the parts where propaganda lines are used obviously. I pay attention to actual scholarly findings and narratives; these are great to read. This is to say, as a reader, I have to make a selective approach to understand the text more precisely. This is also true with many other Tibetan writings during the Cultural Revolution or about that period of time.[112]

Dungkar Rinpoché with his capacities as a learned *geshé* and an intellectual versed in Marxist theory discursively unites Tibet to bolster a shared "national" past that once was thwarted by sectarian and regional differences.

Shaping the Modern Construct of Religion in Tibetan Discourse

In a bid to unmoor Tibetan history from its Buddhist roots and bring notions of modernity on Tibetan terms rather than in a Han paternalistic way, Dungkar Rinpoché carves out discursive space for Tibetan history within Marxist ideology and Tibetan ideas on governance, and in that process adopts the construct *chöluk* (*chos lugs*) for "religion." This term peppered throughout *An Explanation of the Merging of Religious and Secular Rule in Tibet* is etymologically related to *chö* of *chö-sī zung-drel*. When *chö* is rendered into English as "religious," this indicates a heuristic move from its origins in Indo-Tibetan Buddhist philosophical discursive networks with a range of meanings and interpretations around the construct of "dharma" from "phenomena" to Buddhist teachings and practices. Dungkar Rinpoché navigates between this genealogy found in historical-philosophical texts and other forces, such as state-led institutionalization of religion and the expansive discursive network on religion in China.

Within the PRC, discourse on religion cast at its widest envelops a wide-range of categories, from state-recognized "religion" (Ch. *zōngjiào* 宗教) to "exotic ethnic customs" (Ch. *mínzú fēngqíng* 民族风情);[113] at its narrowest, it is reduced to the five officially recognized religions of China, one of which is Buddhism. As other scholars, such as Ashiwa and Wank and Goossaert and Palmer, among others, have shown, this discursive network on religion involves a variety of actors (officials, religious leaders, scholars, etc.) who alternately reproduce the discursive regimes of official policy and also vie for their own interests and those of their constituencies.[114] As an incarnate lama, former Religious Affairs Bureau local official, and member of the official Buddhist Association of China, Dungkar Rinpoché plugged *chöluk* into this discursive network in order to legitimize the different Buddhist traditions of Tibet, with associated customs, rituals, texts, and the indigenous Bön tradition in the hope that the government would protect "religion" as it had promised in the 1950s.

Dungkar Rinpoché uses the term *chöluk* as an overarching category for all of Tibet's Buddhist schools as well as Bön (*bon po'i chos lugs*).[115] He identifies the Nyingma *chöluk* (*nying ma'i chos lugs*)[116] as the earliest Buddhist school in Tibet. He also classifies the Sakyapa as a *chöluk* (*sa skya ba'i chos lugs*)[117] along with Karma Kagyu *chöluk* (*karma bka' brgyus kyi chos lugs*),[118] Kagyu *chöluk* (*bka' brgyud chos lugs*),[119] and Gélukpa *chöluk* (*dge lugs pa'i chos lugs*).[120] In these cases, *chöluk* could be rendered into English as "sect" or "tradition;" however, he not only applies the term to each of these individual traditions but also uses it as a larger overarching construct that includes all of them. This is found in his usage of constructs such as "impartial *chöluk*" (*chos lugs ris med*)[121] and "*chöluk* philosophical systems" (*chos lugs grub mtha'*) as inclusive discursive categories for all religious traditions.

Dungkar Rinpoché must have been aware of all the various emic terms found in Buddhist and Bön texts. In Tibetan historical texts, *chöluk* (*chos lugs*) is more often understood as a "Dharma system," in the sense of a general term for an entire way of life according to doctrine, ritual, and laws; examples of this can be found in the fifteenth-century Buddhist history *The Blue Annals*.[122] In Thuken Losang Chökyi Nyima's *The Crystal Mirror of Philosophical Systems* (*grub mtha' shel gyi me long*), a different term is used, "philosophical systems" (*grub mtha'*), as the overarching category for all Buddhist schools, Bön, and the religions of China, such as Daoism. An example of *chöluk* (*chos lugs*) in the *Crystal Mirror* describes Bön texts as the "Bön Dharma system" (*bon po'i chos lugs*).[123] Despite the array of choices in Buddhist and Bön texts, such as "dharma" (*chos*), "philosophical systems" (*grub mtha'*), and "teachings" (*bstan pa*), among others, in this text Dungkar Rinpoché consistently uses the name of the particular tradition, e.g., "Géluk-pa" for adherents of the Géluk, or he refers to the tradition as a *chöluk* (*chos lugs*), as in the examples above.

The following passage exemplifies the way Dungkar Rinpoché writes about *chö* and *chöluk,* as Dharma system, sect or tradition, and overarching category. The year is 1270; in the wake of Pakpa's appointment as imperial preceptor, Dungkar Rinpoché explains that the great Tibetan statesman, like his uncle Sakya Paṇḍita, strove for peace and unity among all Tibetan religious traditions. Dungkar Rinpoché portrays Pakpa as convincing Qubilai Khan to take an ecumenical position:

At that time, Qubilai thought of issuing an edict to ban other *chöluk,* except for Sakya-pa *dharma (sa skya ba'i chos),* in all Tibetan regions. Pakpa pleaded with the emperor, saying that there are various *chöluk* in Tibet, and each had different objects of faith. With the exception of Bönpo *chöluk,* all belonged to Buddhism (*sang rgyas chos lugs*). If they were not permitted to follow their own respective faith and aspirations (*dad mos*), then this would not only harm the policy and reputation of the emperor himself but also would not benefit my Sakya-pa *chöluk (sa skya ba'i chos lugs).* Therefore, it was necessary to let the various *chöluk* philosophical systems (*grub mtha'*) follow their own faith and aspirations. The emperor considered this and agreed.[124]

Through his interpretation of this historical event, Dungkar Rinpoché strategically plays with the historical roots of the Tibetan term *chö* for "Dharma" and *chöluk* (*chos lugs*) as "Dharma system" and as a modern construct for "religion."

He thereby applies *chöluk* as an overarching category and uses this historical precedent to underscore Pakpa's role as an ecumenical statesman unifying all of Tibet's religious schools.

The use of *chöluk* in this way accords with one contemporary interpretation of *chö-sī zung-drel* in exile and also the construct of "religion" in Chinese state discourse. Former prime minister of the Tibetan Central Administration in exile Samdhong Rinpoché explained how he understands the notion of *chö* (*chos*) in *chö-sī zung-drel* in an interview with Trine Brox:

> The *chos* does not refer to *nang pa'i chos*—the Buddhist dharma—or the Bon *chos*—or the Christian *chos*, or the Muslim *chos*. It refers to all of them. It refers to all the religious denominations or all the religious traditions. And whatever you do in your politics, in your state management that should be governed by the teachings of the dharma, teachings of *chos*. If that is possible, then I think that would be the best way of governing a nation or state.[125]

Similarly, in Dungkar Rinpoché's interpretation of "the merging of religious and secular rule," he takes up the related term *chöluk* (*chos lugs*) as an overarching category for all religions. Yet unlike Samdhong Rinpoché, who views *chö* (*chos*) "dharma" as ethical and moral guidance to be used in politics, Dungkar Rinpoché redefines the historically attested variants of *chö* to identify this as a domain that, according to Marxist ideology, must be separated from politics. However, Dungkar Rinpoche's effort to create a domain for "religion" in the Tibetan context is not a matter of simply conforming to Chinese-Marxist ideology.

Dungkar Rinpoché discursively positions *chöluk* in order to legitimize a variety of aspects of Tibet's religious and cultural traditions within the state corporatist system. He drew from Tibetan traditional texts and from ongoing state translation projects to reinvent *chöluk* in state discourse on "religion." Both Dungkar Rinpoché and Mugé Samten, on a team of other Tibetan and Chinese scholars, collated and edited an important reference work, *The Tibetan-Chinese Dictionary* (*Bod rgya tshig mdzod chen mo*; Chi. *Zanghan da cidian* 藏汉大辞典), in the mid to late 1970s. The entry for *chöluk* attests to the fact that it serves as a translation for the Chinese term for "religion" (*zōngjiào* 宗教).[126] Dungkar Rinpoche was not the first scholar to use *chöluk* for that modern construct.

Other sources confirm that the term *chöluk* was employed as "religion" prior to the writing of Dungkar Rinpoché's history. It seems that Tibetan Buddhist monastic scholars began to reinvent religion in Tibetan language discourse through their work on translation projects. For example, Geshé Sherab Gyatso, the head of the Buddhist Association of China from its early days until its disbanding in the Cultural Revolution, was responsible for one of the earliest attested uses of *chöluk* for "religion" in contradistinction to "secular" state formation when he helped translate and edit the Tibetan edition of Sun Yatsen's *Three Principles of the People*.[127] *Chöluk* is also found in the Tibetan version of the Seventeen Point Agreement, which recognized the PRC's sovereignty over Tibet, a document proofread and edited by Mugé Samten. The Tibetan language version of the Chinese Constitution of 1954, a project involving Tséten Zhabdrung, also used *chöluk* for "religion."[128] This move seems to harken back to the more open religious policy before the Cultural Revolution and foreshadows the new policies on religion that would be outlined in "The Basic Viewpoint and Policy on the Religious Question During Our Country's Socialist Period," referred to as Document 19, which was issued on March 31, 1982.

Positioned within state-led efforts to institutionalize religion and plugged into the discursive network on religion in China, Dungkar Rinpoché took up the CCP's commission to write a history of Tibet in a way that used policy as both a code to follow official expectations and as a cover for his own intellectual agenda.[129] Early on in the PRC, Dungkar Rinpoché became part of the state corporatist system of religious management when he was appointed to a position within the Dagpo-Kongpo Division of the Religious Affairs Bureau in 1956.[130] The Religious Affairs Bureau had been set up under the State Council in Beijing in 1954, and soon thereafter, lower branches, such as the Dagpo-Kongpo Division, were established at provincial and local levels to oversee the implementation of religious policy.[131] In 1959, Dungkar Rinpoché was also given a position in the Buddhist Association of China (BAC)'s Tibetan Regional Division.[132] In this capacity, he was clearly aware of the CCP's notion of the "five characteristics" of religion whereby Tibetan Buddhism was classified as both "feudal" and compounded by ethnic minority-nationality issues.[133] Other sources inform us that being labeled as a religion had an advantage over other designations, such as "superstitious" (Chi. *míxìn*) or worse, "heterodox teachings" (Chi. *xiéjiào*, 邪教),[134] both of which could mean persecution or death for members of that group. Despite the state control exercised over organized "religion," the designation nonetheless legitimized the group. By using religion as a category, Dungkar Rinpoché thereby legitimizes a wide array of religious and cultural traditions in Tibet.

When he wrote *An Explanation of the Merging of Religious and Secular Rule in Tibet*, addressing the category of "religion" had numerous challenges because his intended audience were CCP cadres. Up until that point, Marx's comment that "religion was the opiate of the masses" were interpreted by some hardliners as though "religion" were synonymous with "superstition" or "heterodox" and therefore something to be eradicated. In contrast, the new policy outlined in Document 19, which came out two years after the first publication of Dungkar Rinpoché's work in 1980, viewed religion as both a positive and negative force in society and defined religious freedom as the freedom of choice to believe in religion as a private matter.[135] The varying interpretations must have been discussed in 1977–79 at the time of writing, because the latter more liberal Marxist view is underscored in the concluding section of *An Explanation of the Merging of the Religious and the Secular:*

> Now under the leadership of China's Communist Party, the Tibetan masses have been liberated from the feudal system of merging religious and secular rule and are enjoying personal freedom and leading a happy life. All monks who truly have faith in the Dharma are also liberated by dint of the separating religious from secular rule. Those who are patriotic and law-abiding enjoy freedom of religious belief and are well-taken care of by the government.[136]

This passage signals that religious freedom was considered an individual private matter and was available to patriotic citizens, including monks, much in line with Document 19. Moving between divergent networks of Chinese Marxism and state-led institutionalization of religion, Dungkar Rinpoché mined *chöluk* from Tibetan language historical-religious texts to legitimize a vast array of Tibet's religious and cultural life within state discursive networks.

This is significant because it shows how Dungkar Rinpoché uses *chöluk* as a modern construct. Similar to the way the Chinese term *zōngjiào* (宗教) was used to distinguish "modern religion" from "teachings" (*jiao* 教) to boost a nationalistic agenda, based on its relationship with other value-laden ideas associated with modernity, such as separating religion from politics, education, and science, *chöluk* as used by Dungkar Rinpoché certainly carries modern notions of separating church and state and religious practice as private belief.[137] By using the category of *chöluk, An Explanation of the Merging of Religious and Secular Rule in Tibet* discursively unites previous sectarian-regional affiliations that had precluded national unity, further bolstering a shared Tibetan identity. However, in his attempt to legitimize Tibet's various cultural-religious traditions, Dungkar Rinpoché might have gone too far in bringing *chöluk* under the hegemonic discourse of the state.

In contrast, Mugé Samten's *A History of Traditional Fields of Learning* does not use the term *chöluk* for "religion," which indicates that these two scholars took different approaches to promoting Tibetan Buddhist culture in the PRC.

ཇེ་དགུ་དགེ་བཤེས་གནས་བརྟན་རྒྱ་མཚོ་མཆོག་གི་སྐུ་པར།

FIGURE 4.1   Mugé Samten, studio portrait

The Collected Works of Mugé Samten Gyatso [in Tibetan]

RIKNÉ, "FIELDS OF LEARNING," AS AN APPROACH TO TIBETAN HISTORY

In the spring of the Iron-Bird year (1981), Mugé Samten wrote *A Concise Expla-nation of the Traditional Fields of Learning in Tibet* (*Bod du rig gnas dar tshul mdor bsdus bshad pa*), hereafter, *A History of Traditional Fields of Learning.*[138] Like Dungkar Lozang Trinlé's *An Explanation of the Merging of Religious and Secular Rule in Tibet,* Mugé Samten's comprehensive approach to Tibetan his-tory has the literary marker of "an explanation" (*bshad pa*), indicating that it is an academic essay. Mugé Samten's history is included in his *Collected Works* (1997) and was reprinted in a bilingual Tibetan-English edition at the Library of Tibetan Works and Archives (2005).

Mugé Samten's historiographical approach does not enmesh Tibetan history within state discourse on religion because he keeps Buddhism within its discur-sive home as one of the five major *rikné,* alternately translated as "fields of learn-ing," "fields of knowledge," or "cultural sciences." It is unclear why Mugé Samten wrote this work at this time. According to his autobiography, *Luminous Mirror,* he attended a meeting of the Ngaba Prefecture Consultative Committee in which they discussed "policy on religion" (*chos lugs srid jus*) sometime between February and May.[139] The colophon to *A Concise Explanation of the Traditional Fields of Learning in Tibet* tells us that he wrote this in the spring of 1981, but it doesn't clarify if the meeting was the impetus for writing. This work could also have served a didactic purpose, as his autobiography tells us that he opened two schools in that same year and also worked on a Sanskrit-Tibetan dictionary.[140] With the implementation of Deng Xiaoping's economic reforms, the political situation in which he wrote this text was slightly less restrictive than the circumstances in which Dungkar Rinpoche wrote his history immediately following the Cultural Revolution in 1977–78. Nonetheless, the state of Tibetan language texts and education remained dire. This was a motivating force for both Mugé Samten and Dungkar Rinpoché to write histories of "Tibet" (Bod) even though these two polymaths took vastly different historiographical approaches.

The way Mugé Samten expressed his moral agency was by using the category of *rikné* as a fount for cultural pride in order to push back the devaluing rhetoric of Han paternalism. Whereas Dungkar Rinpoché wedged Tibetan culture and history within the limited space afforded by CCP policy, Mugé Samten was unwilling to move the category of "Buddhism" out of its discursive home as one of the five major *rikné* (*rig gnas*). Unlike Dungkar Rinpoché's text, Mugé Samten's *A History of Traditional Fields of Learning* seldom, if ever, mentions "religion" in state discourse. In my reading of the Tibetan text, I could not find the term *chöluk* (*chos lug*) for "religion" at all. Instead, the author employs the term "teachings" (*bstan pa*), as in "Géluk Teachings" (*dge lugs pa'i bstan pa*). He thereby elides state discourse, which defined the parameters of "religion,"[141] and creates his own expanded interpretation of *rikné*.

Mugé Samten's work consists of two main chapters, 1, "Development of *Rikné* During the Early Diffusion of the Dharma in Tibet," and 2, "Development of *Rikné* During the Later Diffusion of the Dharma in Tibet," and two other concise chapters, 3 and 4, on "Diffusion of *Rikné* in China," and "Diffusion of *Rikné* in Mongolia" respectively. His prose tends to be terse and moves forward at a steady tempo, uninterrupted by the frequent poetic embellishments in Tséten Zhabdrung's literary oeuvre or the historical details central to Dungkar Rinpoché's writings.

The first chapter highlights cultural and technological advances during the first diffusion of the Dharma from circa the seventh to ninth centuries. He lists the first eight semimythical kings of Tibet, then comments on the reign of the ninth king, Pudhey Gungyel (spu de gung rgyal), and his minister Rulekye (ru las skyes) as "marked by innovations (*yar rgyas*) in the fields of **science** and **technology**."[142] He covers various technological advancements, including the invention of the plow, metal processing, and construction projects, with such statements as "the king and his minister also began the construction of bridges and roads that greatly facilitated travel and the transportation of goods."[143] As discussed in the introduction, *rikné* is a rich discursive category that was imported from India and underwent various interpretations in Tibet. José Cabezón and Roger Jackson underscore the limitations of adapting the Indian "fields of knowledge" in Tibetan discourse by highlighting the fact that Tibetan texts on Buddhism far outnumber those on the "the science of construction" (*bzo rig pa*), yet both are considered major *rikné*.[144] Mugé Samten does not critically examine the category of *rikné* itself. However, in this chapter, he emphasizes the topics of engineering and construction. It is unclear if this was an attempt to generate pride in Tibet's past scientific advances in line with five major *rikné* or if he was alluding to Deng Xiaoping's Four Modernizations, which were adopted to rejuvenate China's economy in 1977: science and technology, agriculture, industry, and national defense. Mugé Samten highlights technological advances to counter CCP rhetoric on the backwardness of Tibet.

He similarly highlights advances and developments in ethics, medicine, and language during the first diffusion of the Dharma.[145] He emphasizes cultural achievements, such as the invention of the Tibetan script by Thonmi Sambhota and the development of early Bön literature. He states, "During this period, Bön (*Bon*) narratives (*sgrung*), and symbolic languages (*lde'u*), that were considered fields of learning (*rig gnas*), appeared in Tibet."[146] Unlike Dungkar Lozang Trinle's identification of "Bönpo religion," Mugé Samten only uses the emic description "Bön," indicating a choice not to use *chöluk*. Describing the reign of Trisong Detsen (755–797/8), he emphasizes the development of the curriculum for the study of medicine based on the Four Medical Tantras (*rgyud bzhi*).[147] Throughout this first chapter, Mugé Samten discursively constructs *rikné* as an all-inclusive category for many types of knowledge to glorify the advanced state of Tibetan culture at this time.

The second chapter, "Development of *Rikné* During the Later Diffusion of the Dharma in Tibet," presents *rikné* as more synonymous with Buddhist scholasticism. He writes an array of short biographies on many luminaries from all of Tibet's Buddhist traditions, including Dromtönpa (1004–1064), Sakya Paṇḍita (1189–1251), Shongtön Lotsawa Dorje Gyeltsen (dates unknown, disciple of Sakya Paṇḍita), Pang Lotsawa Lodö Tenpa (1276–1342), Butön Rinpoché (1290–1364), Tsongkhapa Lobzang Drakpa (1357–1419), Panchen Lozang Chökyi Gyeltsen (1570–1662), Taranatha (1575–1634), the Great Fifth Dalai Lama (1617–1682), and Künkhyen Jamyang Zhépai Dorje (1648–1721). On Tsongkhapa, the founder of his Géluk tradition, Mugé Samten writes: "With the scholarship of Tsongkhapa, the tradition of explanation and practice of sutra and tantra reached its full flowering, and thus the study of *rikné* spread through Tibet."[148] He discusses Tsongkhapa's legacy in considerable detail and then concludes the chapter with the statement, "Later, many great scholars such as Zogchen Peltrul (1808–1887), Jamyang Khyentse Wangpo (1820–1892), Kongtrul Yönten Gyatso (1813–1899), Ju Mipham (1846–1912), and others appeared in the Land of Snows, and the minds of the fortunate were satiated with the nectar of good explanations on the inner and outer Tibetan traditional knowledge."[149] The chronological narrative ends in 1912, the year that the Republic of China was founded. He avoids any current political issues. His focus is on the ambrosia (*bdud rtsi*) of Tibetan intellectual history, which is centered on *rikné* to induce pride in diverse aspects of Tibetan culture, including Buddhism.

Mugé Samten's concluding remarks both address the dismal state of Tibetan language education and forthrightly reject the rhetoric of Han paternalism by advocating for education in the traditional fields of knowledge:

> Needless to say, Tibet lags behind in modern scientific developments. However, if we discard traditional knowledge because of this deficiency in the scientific field, we shall not be able to establish anything new. In the recent past the Tibetan language has been neglected, and all knowledge transmitted through Chinese.... Therefore I think that if we were to impart education to Tibetan students in Tibetan, it would be much more beneficial for the progress. Let the wise throw light on this matter for further research progress.[150]

He advocates for Tibetan language and a broad education in *rikné*, the traditional fields of learning including Buddhism, because Chinese secularization policies erased so many aspects of Tibetan culture, including the Tibetan language. In the next chapter, we will learn more about Mugé Samten's political efforts in reversing language policy that was detrimental to reading Tibetan.

Mugé Samten's historiographic approach differs markedly from that of Dungkar Lozang Trinlé's *An Explanation of the Merging of Religious and Secular Rule in Tibet*. Mugé Samten draws upon the category of *rikné* to emphasize technological advances in Tibet and the achievements of great savants in Buddhist history. By keeping the narrative focus on *rikné*, Mugé Samten directly counters the rhetoric of backwardness to show Tibet's long history.

In his later writings, Dungkar Rinpoché also focuses on the topic of *rikné*, as seen in a later text written for his students at Minzu University. "Science of Tibetan Catalogues" draws attention to the unimaginable destruction to all aspects of Tibetan culture, including the five major and five minor fields of knowledge or *rikné*:

> In this land of Tibet surrounded by a rosary of Snow Mountains, early transla-
> tors (*lotsawa*) and scholars translated many treatises including Buddhist scrip-
> tures and their commentaries from the languages of Kashmir, Khotan, China,
> and India into Tibetan; many scholars of our nationality also composed their
> own commentaries. In order to do any sort of investigative research on the Five
> Minor Fields of Knowledge and Five Major Fields of Knowledge, it is first of all
> necessary to have precious source documents; of the many, some were printed
> in woodblock and others had not yet been printed or had not been able to be
> printed. Since there were exceptionally many of them, the state of the ten fields
> of knowledge in the Snow Lands of Tibet was like that of a storehouse of gems
> assembled into one precious treasury of knowledge for our nation and the
> world. However, the tragedy of the so-called "Cultural Revolution" happened,
> and we had never experienced anything like that before in all of Tibetan
> history—struck by a loss so great that it was akin to being annihilated by a
> natural disaster, destroying those precious documents of Tibet culture that had
> accumulated for over thirteen hundred years, since the Tibetan script first
> came into use.[151]

This is the foreword for a text that details research methods in Tibetan studies, written for his students. It shows Dungkar Rinpoché's deep appreciation of Tibetan Buddhist history coupled with an urgent concern to preserve Tibetan texts.

Due to the annihilation of Tibetan culture, akin to a natural disaster, Dung-kar Rinpoché took to restoring Tibetan history with the means available to him. In 1977, he accepted the assignment to write about the "merging of reli-gious and secular rule" (*chos srid zung 'brel*). In doing so, he discursively unites Tibetans in a shared political-religious history framed by Marxist ideology with Chinese characteristics. Later when he was reassigned to the Beijing Minzu University, Dungkar Rinpoché became a key figure in organizing, promoting, and teaching Tibetan studies. He stewarded one of the most developed subfields of Tibetan studies in China, the study of ancient Tibet during the seventh to ninth centuries. Matthew Kapstein observed that this field transitioned from traditional modes of knowledge to form a "new Tibetology."[152] Two of Dungkar Rinpoché's students contributed to the development of this subfield: Döndrup Gyel (Don grub rgyal) and Chen Qingying.[153] Döndrup Gyel, who became known as an icon of modern Tibetan literature, was also a historian. Chen

Qingying is one of the foremost experts in Tibetan history in China; his research is based on both Tibetan language and Chinese language historical texts.[154] Dungkar Rinpoché inspired the next generation of scholars who thus continued to build on his efforts to invent a new type of Tibetology.

Even though Dungkar Rinpoché was commissioned by the United Front Department of the CCP to write *An Explanation of the Merging of the Religious and the Secular in Tibet,* his narrative is grounded on Tibetan historical texts. By navigating state discourse and Marxist ideology, he created a discursively unified Tibetan history that included its diverse religious traditions at a time when no such history existed in the PRC. Dungkar Rinpoché's innovate approach not only cleverly wedges his interpretations of Tibetan history within the political openings afforded by Chinese state policy but also creates a secular past for Tibet and thereby establishes a shared national consciousness for Tibetans in the PRC.

While Dungkar Lozang Trinlé's work may not completely agree with CCP policy on key points in Sino-Tibetan relations, as previously observed by readers of the censored English language translation, he applies Marxist theory to emphasize the need for the separation of "religion" and "politics" in the case of Tibet. In contrast, Mugé Samten uses the construct of the fields of knowledge, which includes Buddhism as one of the five major *rikné*, as a symbol of the enduring legacy of Tibetan culture.

When Dungkar Rinpoché spoke with Tenzin Gelek, he emphasized that his philosophy was the knowledge that emerged from reading and analyzing texts and declared, "The most salient point is to understand Tibetan history well!"[155] Similarly, at Indiana University in 2007, His Holiness the Dalai Lama, in a private audience with a few Tibetan studies students, including myself, instructed us to "Study Tibetan history well!" Fortunately, due to the flourishing of Tibetan-language publishing in the People's Republic of China coupled with international digital projects, such as the Buddhist Digital Resource Center, readers of Tibetan have access to not only several versions of Dungkar Rinpoché's and Mugé Samten's histories but also even more primary sources than were available to the authors themselves. This signals that the immediate danger that faced the Three Polymaths in the wake of the Cultural Revolution, the very extinction of Tibetan texts and culture, has been thwarted.

However, the contested ground of Tibetan history is precarious. It remains to be seen if the unprecedented access that we now have to Tibetan historical texts will yield unbiased accounts of Tibet's past because, as my late professor Elliot Sperling pointed out, how we interpret Tibet's history touches on so many social and political issues that people still vie over today. In the *yang-dar* era, the Three Polymaths strove to make Tibetan history accessible under almost unimaginable circumstances. They found ways to express truth to power, showing the force of human ingenuity and the importance of scholarship even in the most difficult circumstances. Tséten Zhabdrung, Dungkar Rinpoché, and Mugé Samten left indelible marks in the academic field of Tibetan studies in China. However, as we will discuss in the next chapter, not all their efforts were successful. The Tibetan institution of reincarnation suffered in the Maoist years and in many ways has never recovered, whereas pride in Tibetan literary culture lives on.

5

Diverging Lineages

Aphoto in *Ethnic Nationalities Pictorial* (*Mi rigs brnyan par*, Ch. *Mínzú huàbào* 民族画报) shows college students packed in a classroom at Minzu University in Beijing.[1] The eager learners have pens in hand. Some gaze forward. Some are writing. All are dressed in Mao-style suits. The classroom is crowded, eight in each row of desks, at least nine rows deep. The students sit behind two professors, Dungkar Rinpoché and Kelsang Gyurmé (Skal bzang 'gyur med);[2] all look attentively toward the speaker. Facing this group, Tséten Zhabdrung sits at a desk on which a tape recorder and microphone are positioned as if also keen to capture his words.[3] This photograph appears in a feature article on Tséten Zhabdrung titled "The Scholar Striving to Develop Tibetan Culture" that was translated into Tibetan from a front-page story that had run in the Chinese *Guangming Daily* (Ch. *Guāngmíng rìbào* 光明日报) three months earlier.[4] This image capturing a teaching moment also exemplifies a kind of secularization, because all aspects of Tséten Zhabdrung's Buddhist identity are absent from the snapshot and article.

Paradoxically, most Tibetans in the photograph must have known that Tséten Zhabdrung was a recognized *tülku* (*sprul sku*), literally "emanation body." However, neither article identifies him as such, i.e., an incarnate lama, nor refers to him as a "lineage holder" (*brgyud 'dzin*), an embodied source of Buddhist knowledge with the authority to transmit teachings. In short, Tséten Zhabdrung's religious identity was omitted from these state-run print media, even though he embodied the tradition, which undoubtedly drew students to him.

In this chapter, I explore some of these paradoxes by looking at how Tséten Zhabdrung, Mugé Samten, and Dungkar Rinpoché exercised their moral agency in parallel efforts to revive Buddhist traditions and to promote Tibetan

FIGURE 5.1 Tséten Zhabdrung and Dungkar Rinpoché with students at Minzu University
in Beijing

Mi rigs brnyan par 9 (1983)

language education. This will show how they crisscrossed between religious and
secular spheres that were being defined by the Chinese state led by Deng Xiaoping from 1978 until 1992. For many years of the socialist era of the People's
Republic, between 1950 and 1959, and then from 1978 until their respective
deaths, each of the Three Polymaths worked at various state institutions (e.g.,
research institutes, government offices, secular universities) and on translation
and dictionary projects, and concurrently transmitted Dharma teachings at
Buddhist temples and monasteries. Each of the Three Polymaths trafficked
between religious and secular institutions to publish, research, and teach on
Tibetan language, culture, and history, and thereby promoted the construction
of Tibetan national identity within the confines of state discourse, despite having experienced the brunt of the state's attempts at forced secularization during
the Cultural Revolution.

The first part of this chapter brings Tséten Zhabdrung's subjective autobiographical reflections on the importance of education in conversation with the
tülku institution as one of the main forms of ecclesiastical succession in Tibet.
As we will read, his subjective viewpoints on the value of transmitting Buddhist
forms of knowledge across generations dovetail with his prescriptions needed to
revive the *tülku* institution in the post-Mao era. His autobiography ends chronologically in 1978. The goal of reviving the *tülku* institution then takes on new
life as Tséten Zhabdrung's prescriptive measures on ethics and education are
marshaled by the Tenth Panchen Lama. These values still influence the recognition of *tülku* in China today even as two state organizations, the State Administration for Religious Affairs (SARA) and the United Front, increase their control over this foundational Tibetan Buddhist tradition.

Parallel to the Three Polymaths' efforts to revive Buddhist institutions, they each advocated for Tibetan language education. In the second section of this chapter, I bring select passages from textual sources (*Acoustic Ambrosia*, *A General Commentary on Poetics*, *Dungkar Encyclopedia*, and *Luminous Mirror*) and information gathered from oral interviews conducted with Tibetan studies scholars educated in the early post-Mao era in conversation with relevant secondary sources in order to examine some of the ways that each scholar contributed to the development of Tibetan studies as an academic discipline. My focus is on the literary arts and Tibetan language because in the aftermath of the Cultural Revolution, the state of Tibetan studies writ large was abysmal—with severe shortages of Tibetan language publications and qualified teachers. All three scholars engaged in various activities to fill this enormous gap. Over time, their efforts to preserve and promote the Tibetan language in the post-Mao era would be continued by the next generation of Tibetan writers, scholars, and intellectuals in their construction of Tibetan national identity around language. The younger cohort, emboldened by their teachers, mined the symbolic title of the "Three Polymaths" from Tibetan annals and bestowed it upon Dungkar Rinpoché, Tséten Zhabdrung, and Mugé Samten for their efforts in rescuing Buddhism and Tibetan language from the ashes of destruction.

THE *TÜLKU* INSTITUTION AND KNOWLEDGE TRANSMISSION

Tséten Zhabdrung's reflections on the *tülku* institution as told in his autobiography underscore the importance of knowledge transmission. His subjective account is descriptive; it opens a door to understanding the pedagogies and discursive practices employed in his training as a Géluk Buddhist monk. At the same time, it also prescribes certain qualities that a *tülku* should embody.

As will become clear from reading translated sections of *Acoustic Ambrosia*, his autobiographical narrative intertwines incarnation lineage with scholasticism and guru-disciple transmission. Two to three years after he finished his autobiography, his recommendations and views on the qualities of an incarnate lama manifested in concrete actions to restore the institution of reincarnate lamas, a process that had not happened for twenty years. The framework for identifying *tülku* laid out in *Acoustic Ambrosia* aligns with later efforts to recognize *tülku* on the basis of intellectual and ethical dispositions. These proposals were enacted in close cooperation with the Tenth Panchen Lama, Chökyi Gyelt-sen. Sadly, neither lama lived to witness the recognition of any new *tülku* in post-Mao China. In 1991, six years after Tséten Zhabdrung's death and two years after the Panchen Lama's death, the government finally permitted the recognition of new *tülku*. Since the early 2000s, efforts to control the process have resulted in a backlash from recognized *tülku*, some of whom follow prescriptions like those laid out by Tséten Zhabdrung in his autobiography.

On Virtue

In *Acoustic Ambrosia,* Tséten Zhabdrung remembers crucial aspects of his own education in terms of "virtues" (*yon tan*), which he assesses to be of far more importance than his status as an incarnate lama or *tülku*. Moral excellence, for him, is acquired and cultivated through edification; it is not necessarily an innate quality. An authentic Buddhist practitioner cultivates virtues through studying authoritative texts with authentic teachers who are capable of transmitting wisdom across generations. Through the interpretative lens of moral and educational virtues, this section of his autobiography offers an entryway into a nuanced Géluk intellectual history of the *tülku* institution. With a combination of erudition and humor, Tséten Zhabdrung points out the fallibilities of this tradition of ecclesiastical succession. He also describes and prescribes the virtues (*yon tan*) that *tülku* should embody. He never doubts the esoteric mastery necessary for transferring one's consciousness at death. Unlike Dungkar Rinpoché in his history of Tibet, Tséten Zhabdrung does treat the *tülku* institution through the lens of Marxist-historical materialism. His ambivalence comes from recognizing human foibles, especially in the form of excessive desire—avarice. To counter these base tendencies, a Buddhist practitioner must cultivate moral excellence.

Virtue, for Tséten Zhabdrung, begins by training with an authentic, learned teacher. Tséten Zhabdrung recalls how at the tender age of nine he was instructed by his root lama, Jigmé Damchö Gyatso, to create a "record" or *top-yik* (*thob yig*) of all the Buddhist teachings that he received. The autobiographer humbly tells his readers about his learning difficulties and how he needed assistance from an older monk to write down "guided instructions," pronounced *trī* (*khrid*), and "transmission" (*lung*). As he got older, he explains, he learned to record the Buddhist teachings he received and mastered different calligraphic scripts, eventually assembling the records in a large book.[5]

Georges Dreyfus's seminal work on Géluk pedagogy, *The Sound of Two Hands Clapping*, clarifies the difference between these modes of instruction in the Tibetan context. There are several types of *trī* or "guided instructions." Among the most important in regard to scholastic learning is "textual instruction" (*dpe khrid*), whereby a teacher offers a close analysis, sometimes a line-by-line interpretation, of the text being studied at the time.[6] A transmission (*lung*) frequently precedes textual instruction. This involves a ritual whereby an authoritative teacher reads the text aloud and the listeners receive transmission by hearing it. The guru is authorized to recite the scripture because she received specific training from her teachers before her.[7] As Dreyfus points out, the role of "transmission" varies according to different Buddhist traditions. Some place more emphasis on it than others, especially in the diaspora communities today. Both transmission and instruction connect the expertise of the guru with textual authority, but again, as Dreyfus emphasizes, there are varying interpretations of how closely the authoritative words of the guru should be followed.[8]

Tséten Zhabdrung's *Acoustic Ambrosia* does not draw attention to such nuances. His autobiography edifies his readers on the close connections between transmission, instructions, and authority (of text and guru). The author links these through his autobiographical memories, with a story from his life as an example showing how he interprets a *lung* textual transmission in terms of what he calls "virtue" (*yon tan*).

Acoustic Ambrosia recounts that in 1920, the ten-year-old Tséten Zhabdrung received a transmission from his root guru, Jigmé Damchö Gyatso. The text was a poem written by Kelden Gyatso (Skal ldan rgya mtsho, 1607–1677), a Géluk polymath from Repgong's Rongbo Monastery in Amdo.[9] Emphasizing the importance of scholastic learning and the continuity of lineage, Kelden Gyatso penned a didactic poem inspired by Sakya Paṇḍita's *Gateway to Learning*, which instructed on the threefold system of scholastic education: exposition (*'chad*), debate (*rtsod*), and composition (*rtsom*). In his poem, Kelden Gyatso offers words of advice to inspire young monks in their studies. Tséten Zhabdrung remembers this transmission of Jigmé Damchö Gyatso's reading of Kelden Gyatso's poem:

> Most students from India and Tibet, during their youth,
> by persevering at the scriptures of Sūtra and Tantra,
> like a mighty river coursing, they master
> all they wish in exposition, debate, and composition;
> and transform into accomplished polymaths.
> May this bring liberation to self and others![10]

Tséten Zhabdrung tells his readers how he logged this in his record (*thob yig*) of all Buddhist teachings.

Through this chorus of past lineage masters, Tséten Zhabdrung then switches to a didactic tone to admonish his potential monastic readers: "By citing the above transmission, it means that if you are born as an incarnate lama, but do not cultivate *virtue* (*yon tan*) and only become entangled in wealth, then it is inappropriate. In order to cultivate *virtue*, it is absolutely necessary to train in Sūtra, Tantra and the ten fields of learning altogether, with a teacher, who possesses the characteristics of being a teacher."[11] Tséten Zhabdrung interprets the transmission he received from his teacher in a moralistic and ethical way connected with virtue, which for him involves scholastic education.

Tséten Zhabdrung's autobiographical telling of what happened serves a didactic purpose—to address the ethical and educational requirements of an incarnate lama in particular. Virtue for Tséten Zhabdrung was about self-cultivation and education in Buddhist canonical texts with a teacher who embodied the necessary traditional knowledge and ethical comportment that qualified him to transmit them. In his retelling of this transmission, Tséten Zhabdrung adds his voice to a lineage of earlier lamas (from Sakya Paṇḍita via many other lamas to Kelden Gyatso and eventually to Jigmé Damchö Gyatso), as if creating a choir praising traditional Buddhist discursive practices and pedagogy. In some ways, Tséten Zhabdrung's rhetorical technique is similar to the notion of autobiographical ventriloquy as developed by Sarah Jacoby in her study on the twentieth-century treasure revealer Sera Khandro Kunzang Dekyong Wangmo, whereby the authoritative voice of the guru speaks truth on behalf of the protagonist.[12] In chapter 2, I drew attention to how Mugé Samten uses a similar technique by deflecting praise from himself through the voice of his guru. However, that is slightly dissimilar from the recording of the singular voice of the guru through the autobiographer's pen.

In Tséten Zhabdrung's life writing, the power of speech and truth emerge from a chorale, a lineage of past masters. These voices lend authority and authenticity to the autobiographer, offering him the opportunity to make connections between these teachings and his didactic admonitions, which are the beginning of a central argument for the reinstatement of the *tülku* tradition in the early 1980s. In an interesting parallel, Annabella Pitkin shows in her study of the twentieth-century Kagyu master Khunu Lama that the ideal of transmission not only establishes the lama's own authority but also opens up "the possibility of a re-appropriation of tradition, which can enable a high level of individual agency, intellectual independence, and freedom from institutionalized authority."[13] Like

Khunu Lama, Tséten Zhabdrung not only establishes his own authority but also adapts tradition for new purposes.

Tséten Zhabdrung adds his voice to an authoritative lineage of past masters and creatively draws upon traditional modes of knowledge transmission in order to reassess the *tülku* institution within the sociopolitical context of post-Mao China. This heuristic move is grounded within the historical and cultural context in which he was writing.

An Ensemble of Texts to Assess the Tülku Institution

Tséten Zhabdrung wrote *Acoustic Ambrosia* fifteen years before the state government of the People's Republic of China authorized the recognition of new reincarnate lamas. This fact is important to consider in relation to one of the most interesting sections in his autobiography, a history of the *tülku* institution in the Tibetan context. Similar to how Tséten Zhabdrung makes a didactic point of how incarnate lamas need to possess the virtue of a Buddhist scholastic education, his historical analysis of the *tülku* institution serves a clear purpose. Tséten Zhabdrung assesses the *tülku* institution and sketches the qualities that reincarnate lamas should possess, which became central concerns for Géluk lamas after 1980.

Tséten Zhabdrung brings a metaphorical chorus of authoritative Buddhist texts to bear on his analysis. He gathers his ensemble, including the Second Dalai Lama, Gendün Gyatso (1475–1542), the Fifth Dalai Lama, Ngawang Gyatso (1617–1682), Sumpa Paṇḍita Yeshé Paljor (1704–1788), Changkya Rolpai Dorjé (1717–1786), and Arik Geshé Chenmo Jampa Öser (d. 1803) for two intertwined purposes.[14] First, he addresses several inherent institutional faults. This critique is not from a Marxist historical materialistic perspective. Rather, he explains how this institution can be easily manipulated by people who are consumed with bias, greed, and corruption. In a somber tone, he illustrates how these negative traits came into play during his own recognition process. Second, he gathers historical texts as proof of virtues. He builds his case based on past scholarly voices who simultaneously recognize human weakness and maintain that authentic *tülku* possess esoteric mastery. At the end of the day, however, whether an individual is a recognized *tülku* or not, Tséten Zhabdrung claims, if he is a Buddhist practitioner, he must cultivate virtue.

Through the writings of the Fifth Dalai Lama, Tséten Zhabdrung addresses the political weakness of the institution and its tendency to foster avarice. He ties together the anxiety caused by the long interregnum period before a new reincarnate lama is recognized and how some people attempt to use this uncertainty for their own gains. Tséten Zhabdrung paraphrases the Fifth Dalai Lama's autobiography, *A Fine Silken Dress*,[15] to explain the historical traditions of succession in Tibet:

> *A Fine Silken Dress* states that in Tibet, there are two ways of recognizing a lama, which are different from that in India: 1) through patrilineage, and 2) through rebirth. As for the first way, an example of which is the Sakya family's successive Dakchen, the qualities of the Two Systems (*lugs gnyis*) [the temporal and spiritual] through patrilineal inheritance ensure no gap. So disciples and supporters are at ease. It is the opposite case for the [second method,] recognition through rebirth. There is a great deal of worry when a lama passes away. Then all over the country, due to the deception created by a child's mother and father, people act like frightened rabbits, placing any child among the row of seats to take as his own without hesitation. This certainly seems like a fox posing as a lion.[16]

The Fifth Dalai Lama's use of animal metaphors underscores humans' carnal instincts. He scathingly accuses parents of lying about their children in order to gain access to the lion throne of power and prestige. Tséten Zhabdrung cites this passage from the *Fine Silken Dress* to illustrate how politically unstable the *tülku* system is as a form of ecclesiastical succession because it is easily corrupted.

The tone in *Acoustic Ambrosia* becomes more humorous as Tséten Zhabdrung shares a caustic tale and a joke, both dealing with the theme of exploitation of the *tülku* office. He quotes another Amdo lama, Arik Geshé, who on his deathbed reportedly said, "Given the choice, I would transmigrate to Tuṣita Heaven and not reincarnate. If I must be reborn, then find a child who cannot only recite flawlessly from memory *The Great Treatise on the Stages of the Path* and *The Great Treatise on the Stages of Mantra*, but who also does not stop uttering this even when being chased by a wild dog; for this is my reincarnation."[17] Another witty anecdote blatantly mocks the greedy behavior of an incarnate lama from western Bāyan (Ch. Hualong 化隆) County: A villager holding his toddler son addresses this *tülku* as *alak tsang*, an honorific title in Amdo dialect, asking, "Alak tsang, is my son an incarnate lama? He keeps asking me for this and that!"[18] Tséten Zhabdrung retells these stories to articulate the most blatant tension in the *tülku* institution.

Incarnate lamas are supposed to renounce worldly attachments, yet they inherit enormous wealth, generating a system that creates the causes and conditions for attachment and avarice. As Tséten Zhabdrung explains:

When an old monk passes away, then a search is made for a so-called *"tülku"* (*sprul sku*) or *"zhabdrung"* (*zhabs drung*). When an "old *ngak-pa"* (*sngags rgan*) dies, then a search is conducted for a so-called *"ku-lo"* (*sku lo*) or *"kuba"* (*sku 'ba'*). After this, people use them in whatever way they can as a base for business, to amass material things by merely chanting and without studying anything meaningful; in every way possible they deceive ignorant people. For someone who cherishes the Teachings, this is certainly horrifying.[19]

Tséten Zhabdrung's admonishment echoes the views of the eighteenth-century Amdo scholar Sumpa Paṇḍita Yeshé Paljor (1704–1788), who like the Fifth Dalai Lama places blame on greedy parents for taking advantage of this system. Sumpa Paṇḍita writes, "A few parents falsely proclaim their son, who had been born before the death of a lama, as his incarnation. Other people will replace an incarnate lama who dies young with a youth of the same age. They are doing this only as a means to attract wealth and property."[20] Tséten Zhabdrung cites a few other historical texts that provide examples of corruption in the system; however, he does not launch into a full-scale critique of the *tülku* institution.

Rather, Tséten Zhabdrung turns to texts that for him demonstrate the virtue of esoteric mastery. Such evidence is found, for example, in the biography of the Second Dalai Lama, Gendün Gyatso (Dge 'dun rgya mtsho, 1475–1542). He was recognized as the reincarnation of Gendün Drup (Dge 'dun grub, 1391–1474) at a point in historical time when the *tülku* process was not common within the nascent Géluk tradition.[21] Other sources tell us that Gendün Gyatso was older, age twelve, when he was awarded the title of the First Lower Residence (*gzim khang 'og ma*) Incarnation of Drepung Monastery in 1487.[22] Later in his life he expanded Drepung, making it one of the most significant Géluk institutions in all of Tibet, no doubt in part because it was founded by Tsongkhapa Lozang Drakpa (1357–1419) and his immediate disciples. Gendün Gyatso and his previous incarnation, Gendün Drup, were posthumously recognized as the second and first Dalai Lamas after this title was given to Sönam Gyatso (Bsod nams rgya mtsho, 1543–1588) by the Tümed Mongol ruler Altan Khan (1507–1582).[23] The fact that Gendün Gyatso was recognized as a *tülku* while still a preteen rather than as a young boy is significant to Tséten Zhabdrung's later argument for the reestablishment of the *tülku* institution in the post-Mao era.

Tséten Zhabdrung explains that when Gendün Gyatso was still a toddler sitting on his father's lap, he heard the sound of thunder in the sky and said to his father, "That must be similar to the sound of Master [Tsongkhapa] Lozang Drakpa giving Dharma teachings." The father asked, "How is it similar to Master Lozang Drakpa giving Dharma teachings?" The child then responded with a passage from the *Ornament for the Mahāyāna Sūtra*:

> Rely on a Mahāyāna teacher who is disciplined, calm, thoroughly
>   pacified;
> Who has superior knowledge, diligence, and a wealth of transmissions,
> Who has realized emptiness, has skill in instructing students,
> Has great compassion, and has abandoned all regrets.[24]

This is a Dharma teaching that Tsongkhapa had given to his previous incarnation, Gendün Drup. Tséten Zhabdrung does not question the authenticity of a boy reciting Dharma teachings given to him in a previous life. From his perspective, an authentic incarnate lama must exhibit such behaviors, especially knowledge of Buddhist teachings.[25]

Tséten Zhabdrung further warns that a lack of knowledge of basic Buddhist concepts, such as the three poisons (desire, ignorance, and hatred), karma, and the *trikāya* (the Three Bodies of the Buddha), could have a negative impact on the level of realization a Buddhist practitioner achieved. The tone of his autobiography switches here. He no longer draws upon historical narratives and strongly criticizes *tülku* who claim to be incarnate lamas but lack knowledge of Buddhist concepts:

> Bodies of the Buddha are three: Truth, Enjoyment, and Emanation;
> Only a Buddha manifests an emanation body.
> I admit that those lamas, who can't even count the three Buddha
>   bodies,
> Are really deluded to claim themselves as authentic emanation bodies![26]

In this section of *Acoustic Ambrosia*, Tséten Zhabdrung then weighs the relative significance of *tülku* status vis-à-vis the importance of receiving a Buddhist education. For him, the latter—knowledge of Buddhist texts, practices, and pedagogies—takes precedence over the former. Tséten Zhabdrung's short verse didactically underscores this by emphasizing the qualities of a learned and ethical lama:

It is appropriate for ordinary people to venerate a Buddhist teacher,
when the lama possesses knowledge, follows vows purely,
has pure intentions and few desires; but then the methods of gazing into
butter lamps and rolling tsampa balls are unnecessary.[27]

The butter lamps and tsampa balls symbolize the rites involved in the *tülku* recognition process. When Tséten Zhabdrung describes these as unnecessary, he puts forth the notion that the virtues of knowledge and ethical morality constitute a true Buddhist teacher. The status of *tülku* is in and of itself relatively unimportant. These various themes on the importance of education, the fallibility of the institution due to human greed, and the vital role of authentic lamas are intertwined in his remembrances of his own recognition and come to bear on the qualities of *tülku* in the post-Mao era.

Subjectivity and Virtue (yon tan)

Acoustic Ambrosia details the author's subjective viewpoints on his own recognition and coming of age as a *tülku*. He starts this section by recalling a Buddhist idea on the favorable conditions of rebirth in the human realm: "It is truly beyond my knowledge from which of the Six Realms of Beings I transferred. However, I must have had a fortunate rebirth from a previous lifetime because I met teachers of the Mahāyāna tradition and became a Buddhist monk. There is no doubt that there is a connection between a fortunate rebirth and strong dedication prayers."[28] Interestingly, the appendix in the *Dungkar Encyclopedia* called "The Clear Mirror: A Chronology" shares the same view on the preciousness of human life from a Buddhist perspective: "In 1927, the author [i.e., Dungkar Rinpoché] of this historical chart first obtained a favored and fortunate human birth."[29] "A favored and fortunate human birth" (*dal 'byor gyi mi lus*) refers to the precious rarity of human birth and its unique advantages, in particular the eight favorable circumstances and ten fortunate qualities, such as being born in a Buddhist country. As might be expected from a Buddhist polymath, Tséten Zhabdrung describes his birth as an incarnate lama as resulting from karma. However, his self-narrative also deals with more worldly, controversial topics, such as the dispute surrounding his recognition as a *tülku*.

Again in this section, the autobiographer stresses the importance of virtue. *Acoustic Ambrosia* remembers how a group of local Tibetan leaders refused to include him on the list of candidates for recognition. Tséten Zhabdrung as a toddler was called "nameless grandson of Tsering Döndrup from Yadzi." The local leaders of the mountainous region to the north, the Garwa Kadruk or "Six Encampments" along the Tsongkha range (between Hualong and Minhe Counties of Qinghai Province today) at first rejected his nomination.

The boy's candidacy was dismissed because he was of mixed Chinese and Tibetan ancestry. Instead, the son of a prominent Nyingma lama called Gurong Jikdrel Chöying (Dgu rong 'Jigs bral chos dbyings) had been placed at the top of the list. The Six Encampments leaders and monastic search committee went to the head of Dītsa (Lde tsha) Monastery, Amdo Zhamar Paṇḍita (1852–1912),[30] to seek his blessing for the recognition of their preferred candidate. Amdo Zhamar Paṇḍita reportedly scolded the group and ordered the "nameless grandson of Tsering Döndrup from Yadzi" to be included among the five candidates. A few days later, Amdo Zhamar Paṇḍita examined butter lamps and recognized "the nameless grandson" as the reincarnation of Tséten Zhabdrung, who was also called Tak Lama. As Tséten Zhabdrung remembers, "Zhamar Paṇḍita then gave me a protective amulet, a ceremonial cloth, and a letter that contained the instructions for an important White Tara long-life ritual. My grandfather took care of these things until I reached adulthood."[31] In reflecting on his ascension to the Tak Throne, the name of Tséten Zhabdrung's sole monastic seat, the author recapitulates some of the themes on virtue from his historical analysis of the *tülku* institution.

Tséten Zhabdrung articulates his doubts about the *tülku* institution in terms of the factionalism caused by prejudices toward his ethnically diverse heritage. Simultaneously, he shows respect and gratitude toward the authority of Zhamar Paṇḍita. A belletristic poem pauses the narrative flow of *Acoustic Ambrosia*, to bring these intertwining factors together:

> Whether or not I am the rebirth of Tak Lama,
> I effortlessly passed the raised threshold
> to the gates of ordination vows; the bell tolled
> and Tak Lama's name was bestowed on me.
>
> What foolishness to impose good and bad on lamas
> who are Tibetan or Chinese; during the Tang Dynasty
> wasn't Xuan Zang a learned master of Nalendra?
> To be a lama, one must cultivate *virtue* (*yon tan*)!

With immeasurable kindness Zhamar Paṇḍita
in brilliant wisdom of past, present, and future,
took the burden of recognizing me, using butter lamps,
carrying me out of the prison of a layperson's life.[32]

Tséten Zhabdrung's literary flourishes include strict meter; each line is nine syllables long. The verse is also replete with cultural references that may be difficult to understand without further explanation. The first stanza uses his alternative title of Tak Lama to lay bare the author's simultaneous awe and ambivalence at being recognized. It also stresses that more important, he is honored to have the distinct privilege of becoming a monk. This sense of gratitude for the opportunity is echoed in the third stanza, which also pays homage to Zhamar Paṇḍita as an authoritative source of Buddhist knowledge.

The middle stanza resolves the prejudices toward him regarding his mixed ethnic heritage by emphasizing virtue (*yon tan*). "Virtue" stresses again the idea of education or knowledge of Buddhist doctrine and history, echoing themes in his historical analysis of the *tülku* institution. This stanza refers to the well-known historical example of Xuan Zang (602–664) to protest ethnic prejudice. Xuan Zang was one of the most famous monks in Chinese Buddhist history. After twenty years of traveling to Buddhist centers dotted across Central Asia and India, including the great monastic university of Nālanda, he returned to the Chinese capital of Chang'an with hundreds of Buddhist texts and was welcomed by still-reigning Emperor Taizong of the Tang Dynasty, but he rejected official posts, preferring a quiet monastic life instead.[33] In this context, Tséten Zhabdrung seems to rebuke the local Six Encampments leaders for their ethnic prejudice against him as being part Chinese, a bias that affected his recognition process. The verse hinges on the middle stanza, which didactically claims, "to be a lama, one must cultivate *virtue*!"

This voice adds to the chorus of past Buddhist masters whom the author called upon to celebrate the virtue of Buddhist knowledge and its transmission. The section of *Acoustic Ambrosia* on the *tülku* institution and his recognition as a *tülku* concludes, "Due to these reasons, I came to understand that what is called virtue (*yon tan*) is more than just the mere recitation of liturgical texts. In this way, surely it was that karmic predispositions were awakened in me."[34] Tséten Zhabdrung's account ties together knowledge transmission, scholarly learning, and ethical comportment as qualities that authentic *tülku* must cultivate. These same characteristics would be brought to bear in his efforts to restore the institution. His autobiographical writings on virtue presage the role that he would play in that restoration, even though he did not live long enough to witness it.

BUDDHIST INSTITUTIONS IN THE *YANG-DAR* ERA

When Tséten Zhabdrung put pen to paper to write *Acoustic Ambrosia*, he had no institutional affiliation whatsoever. He had been let out of prison on medical parole in 1976 and recovered some personal freedoms in 1978. However, he was only exonerated and "rehabilitated" (Ch. *píngfǎn* 平反) in 1983,[35] the same year that the two articles on his achievements appeared in nationwide Chinese news outlets, as documented at the beginning of this chapter. Between 1976 and 1978, Tséten Zhabdrung was at a relative's home recuperating from nearly a dozen years of imprisonment. During this period, he was not allowed the freedom of movement to visit his monasteries.[36] The reputation and recognition that he had enjoyed in the 1950s as a Géluk polymath, evident in the request from His Holiness the Dalai Lama's office for a copy of his teacher's *Collected Works,* were temporarily overlooked. His published works on diverse topics, such as poetics, local Buddhist history, and grammar, all lay dormant, almost forgotten. He had not yet been given employment, even though he had worked as a professor in the late 1950s and had translated important state documents, such as the 1954 Constitution and Mao's *Collected Works.* This began to change in mid-1978 when he received the invitation to work at the Northwest Minzu University (formerly nationalities institute) in Lanzhou. Tséten Zhabdrung's autobiography ends at this point.

How his autobiographical reflections on the *tülku* institution manifested in efforts to reestablish this important institution in the last seven years of his life becomes evident in other sources, including the Chinese Buddhist Association's journal, a biography by a close monastic disciple, and interviews with his former students from Northwest Minzu University and a few monastic disciples. No new *tülku* had been officially identified since 1959, and none would be officially recognized until 1991.[37] The first steps toward the reestablishment of the institution did not come from the state but in a reunion of two spiritual friends, two Géluk Buddhist hierarchs, in 1980.

Panchen Lama Chökyi Gyeltsen and Tséten Zhabdrung

The Tenth Panchen Lama, Chökyi Gyeltsen, and Tséten Zhabdrung had ties of affinity long before their reunion in the summer of 1980. The two lamas shared the same birthplace in the area now known as Xunhua Salar Autonomous

FIGURE 5.2 Tséten Zhabdrung and the Tenth Panchen Lama

Mi rigs brnyan par 9 (1983)

County. Their life paths crossed frequently. In the post-Mao era, they would become allies in their efforts to restore monasteries and the *tülku* institution.

Although it is unclear when exactly the two lamas first met, it is clear that Tséten Zhabdrung knew the future Panchen Lama as a youth. Three years after the death of the Ninth Panchen Lama in 1937, different search parties found three possible candidates for his reincarnation. One boy with the given name Gonpo Tséten was born (in 1938) in the small village of Bīdo (Bis mdo; Ch. Wendu 文都), about fifteen miles from Tséten Zhabdrung's hometown of Yadzi. In 1941, there were complications surrounding the recognition of the Panchen Lama.[38] *Acoustic Ambrosia* records that at this time, Ngulchu Lozang Chöphel (Dngul chu blo bzang chos 'phel), a member of the search committee that found Gonpo Tséten, stopped at the nearby hermitage of Ewam, where he met with Tséten Zhabdrung to discuss this.[39] It seems unlikely that the three-year-old was present at this meeting, but it is unclear.

Other sources tell us that in the meantime, Gonpo Tséten was ordained into monkhood and given the ordination name Lozang Trinlé Lhundrup Chökyi Gyeltsen. This same publication explains that he was not recognized as the

Tenth Panchen Lama for another decade due to a number of factors: disputes between the search parties, the civil war between the Chinese Communists and Nationalists, the warlord Ma Bufang's rule over Qinghai, and political stagnation during the interregnum period in Central Tibet. The Tibetan government and the Dalai Lama officially recognized the boy from Bīdo, the monk Chökyi Gyeltsen, as the Tenth Panchen Lama in 1951.[40] Shortly before, he had traveled to Beijing. The timing of the visit coincided with the arrival of the delegation for the signing of the Seventeen Point Agreement in May of that year.[41] By autumn, the young Panchen Lama was able to leave the nation's capital to ascend the throne at his monastic seat at Tashilhunpo Monastery in Shigatsé. On his return journey, he stopped in Qinghai, where he met Tséten Zhabdrung. The two developed a spiritual friendship that would last for over thirty years.

Acoustic Ambrosia details how in early autumn of 1951, Tséten Zhabdrung and the Panchen Lama met during a Kalachakra ceremony at Kumbum Monastery.[42] They were united again in Beijing with His Holiness the Dalai Lama at Yonghegong Temple when Tséten Zhabdrung was given honors for translating the 1954 Constitution.[43] The Panchen Lama returned to his hometown of Bīdo in early 1962, where he again met with Tséten Zhabdrung.[44] By piecing together evidence from *Acoustic Ambrosia*, personal interviews, a local Chinese history, and the provenance of the 70,000 Character Petition, it seems that they discussed the horrific famines throughout this area in the late 1950s.[45] Soon after this visit, the Panchen Lama wrote his famous 70,000 Character Petition to Mao Zedong, which candidly addressed the hardships Tibetans had endured as result of Chinese policies.[46] Before the official launch of the Cultural Revolution, both the Panchen Lama and Tséten Zhabdrung were criticized and arrested.

In 1968, the Panchen Lama was incarcerated at Qincheng Prison in Beijing. No one knew whether he was dead or alive until 1978, when a news agency reported his appearance at the Chinese Political Consultative Conference meeting in Beijing.[47] In March 1979, during the course of Wei Jingsheng's trial for his involvement in the Democracy Wall Movement, it was learned how much the Panchen Lama had suffered. Wei's protest of the human rights abuses at Qincheng Prison recorded in one of his essays reports, "The Panchen Lama once refused food. He declared that he did not wish to live any longer and that his remains should be 'delivered to the Central Committee of the Party.'"[48] Miraculously, both the Panchen Lama and Tséten Zhabdrung survived their prison sentences. In 1980, the Panchen Lama was reinstated as a vice-chairman of the National People's Congress.[49] He was then free to travel. He returned to his hometown and toured the surrounding region. During this visit, he was reunited with his friend Tséten Zhabdrung.

The two became allies in their attempts to advocate for the reestablishment of the system for recognizing reincarnate lamas in China. According to one informant who was with the Panchen Lama and Tséten Zhabdrung on this tour, they discussed finding the reincarnation of Marnang Dorjé Chang, Jigmé Damchö Gyatso (Tséten Zhabdrung's former root guru), at this time.[50] Evidence that they visited Jigmé Damchö Gyatso's monastery is found in "*Avadāna* of Silver Flowers*," a twenty-page poem written in January 1981 to commemorate the Panchen Lama's tour of the region the previous summer.[51]

Replete with hope that Buddhist teachings will once again flourish, "*Avadāna* of Silver Flowers" does not directly state that the Panchen Lama and Tséten Zhabdrung talked about recognizing *tülku* during this time. Tséten Zhabdrung remembers the monstrous destructiveness of the Cultural Revolution during their visit to Karing Monastery and laments that they saw the Eight Stupas containing Jigmé Damchö Gyatso's relics reduced to rubble.[52] While the poet grieves past losses, the overall tone of the poem conveys affectionate warmth.

FIGURE 5.3   Eight stupas at Karing Monastery, June 2015

Photograph by Nicole Willock

FIGURE 5.4 Tséten Zhabdrung and the Tenth Panchen Lama

Courtesy of Jigmé Chöpak

With an insatiable eagerness, Tséten Zhabdrung recalls meeting with the Panchen Lama in a way that evokes hope for reuniting in the future:

> Not satiated by seeing Buddha marks;
> not contented by the lute's timbre;
> O Treasure of Compassion, please, come, again and again!
> Only you can provide such a feast![53]

Tséten Zhabdrung poetically articulates that seeing the Buddha marks belonging to the Panchen Lama, the Treasure of Compassion, brings him utmost joy. The excitement that he expresses through this poem on the reunion with the Panchen Lama serves as a reminder of the relief and hope that he and certainly many others must have shared when the state permitted religious activities, such as visiting newly reopened Buddhist monasteries after nearly twenty years of prohibition.

The Three Great Virtues of Tülku

Information gathered from disparate sources—interviews, a biography on Tséten Zhabdrung, and the Panchen Lama's speeches—sheds light on how both Tséten Zhabdrung and the Panchen Lama advocated for the reinstatement of the *tülku* institution in the early 1980s. When I interviewed Jigmé Samdrup, a Tibetologist and former student of Tséten Zhabdrung, in Beijing in 2015, he succinctly summed up Tséten Zhabdrung's stance: "It was well known that Tséten Zhabdrung thought that *tülku* needed to have 'three great virtues' (*yon tan chen po gsum*). The first is education. They should enjoy studying and want to read about Buddhism. The second virtue concerns their willingness to maintain monastic vows. The third virtue is the correct temperament. They must be kind and compassionate."[54] As I reflected on this interview, it became apparent how these "three great virtues" crystallized what I had read in *Acoustic Ambrosia*. The "three great virtues" are further corroborated, although not quite as succinctly, in two other textual sources—a biography of Tséten Zhabdrung and a reprint of the Tenth Panchen Lama's final speech before his death.

The last seven years of Tséten Zhabdrung's life are chronicled by Jigmé Tekchok ('Jigs med theg mchog) in an "addendum" (*kha skong*) to *Acoustic Ambrosia*.[55] It states that Géluk hierarchs including Tséten Zhabdrung; the Sixth Jamyang Zhépa (b. 1948), who was enthroned at Labrang Tashikyil Monastery in 1952;[56] and Alak Sertri (A lags gser khri, dates unknown)[57] all met in Beijing in 1983 alongside the events surrounding the thirtieth anniversary of the founding of the Buddhist Association of China to discuss the reinstatement of the *tülku* institution and to debate the parameters for the recognition of reincarnate lamas.

A photo in *Voice of the Dharma* (Ch. *fǎyīn* 法音), the official journal of the Chinese Buddhist Association, commemorates this event and documents that Tséten Zhabdrung, Dungkar Rinpoché, and the Panchen Lama, among many others, were in attendance in a joint meeting of the CCP and the Chinese Buddhist Association in early December 1983.[58] It is important to consider the state's policies toward religion at this point in time. Géluk hierarchs could gather on the sidelines of this large meeting in Beijing to discuss such an important topic as reincarnation because one year earlier the Chinese Communist Party had issued "Document 19, the Basic Viewpoint and Policy on the Religious Question During Our Country's Socialist Period," which permitted the revival of religious activities within certain parameters.[59] *Voice of the Dharma* published a speech given by the Panchen Lama celebrating the commemorative events and underscoring the government's policy on religion and the constitutional guarantees on religious freedom.[60] The published speech does not mention the topic of recognizing *tülku*.

Jigmé Tekchok's addendum reports that on the second day of the eleventh month,[61] the important issue of finding new reincarnate lamas was raised by the Sixth Jamyang Zhépa during a meeting.[62] Tséten Zhabdrung and Alak Sertri joined in support of this discussion. Everyone present "rejoiced like strewn flowers because this was on everyone's minds, but no one could talk about it."[63] Then Tséten Zhabdrung reportedly stated that *tülku* should be recognized based on

党 和 国 家 领 导 人 同 参 加 中 国 佛 教 协 会

Panchen Lama

会 第 四 届 理 事 会 第 二 次 会 议 全 体 人 员 合 影　一九八三年十二月七日

Dungkar Rinpoché　　Tséten Zhabdrung

FIGURE 5.5　Two frames of a photo in *Voices of the Dharma* depict Buddhist Association of China members with party and national leadership. Beijing, 1983.

Fayin no. 5

the follow qualities: "Based on the whole situation, [factors such as]: current circumstances, early history, and standard textual references, rather than finding a three- or four-year-old and placing him on a silk-covered throne as before, it would be more appropriate and a better fit to find a candidate in a range older than twelve years old but younger than fifteen who shows sign of intelligence and moral conduct." [64] The addendum continues:

> The Panchen Lama heard this and praised Tséten Zhabdrung, saying, "I myself have supported this idea for a while now." Then he continued, "Everyone, it will be good for the two systems, if a few *tülku* with these virtues are found in each area." There was a lot of discussion about this. Then the Panchen Lama authored a regulation (*'grig yig*) on Buddhist management and made a decree saying that it was important to have high-quality lamas and monks and not too many of either.[65]

According to Jigmé Tekchok's account, the three main factors crucial for finding reincarnations were age, intelligence, and moral character.[66] These three qualities are similar to the "three great virtues" (education, willingness to observe monastic vows, and temperament) mentioned by Jigmé Samdrup. Further, this proposal is interesting to consider in relation to Tséten Zhabdrung's reference to the recognition of Gendün Gyatso at age twelve in *Acoustic Ambrosia*.

Despite this lively discussion and the Panchen Lama's support, no new *tülku* had been officially recognized at the time of Tséten Zhabdrung's death two years after this meeting, in 1985. However, his suggestions on the parameters for recognition are restated, in slightly different terms, in one of the Panchen Lama's final speeches. The Panchen Lama candidly addresses the dire situation of the *tülku* institution in a speech recorded at Tashilhunpo Monastery in Central Tibet, three days before his own death on January 28, 1989.

This speech stresses the wish for the reinstatement of the *tülku* institution and emphasizes the role that local monasteries should play in the recognition process. The Panchen Lama states, "Historically, the system of recognizing *tülku* and looking after them by their respective monasteries have been very effective in preserving and promoting the Buddhist teachings, taking care of the monasteries, filling the spiritual needs of the local faithful and preserving the culture of nationalities."[67] Before offering his thoughts on how the institution should be restored, he candidly calls out extreme leftists who "hijacked the Party's religious policy and did not implement it with fairness," so that "the destruction of Buddhism was carried out."[68] He talks about his attempts to notify the government of the needs of the Tibetan people, and how he was criticized for writing the 70,000 Character Petition that called attention to those needs. After praising the policy changes launched at the Third Plenary Session of the 11th Central Committee of the Communist Party of China in 1978, he dives into the issue of recognizing *tülku*.

The Panchen Lama's remarks reiterate many of Tséten Zhabdrung's statements on the three virtues of *tülku* and also emphasize limiting the number of reincarnate lamas. He states, "We do not need too many *tülku*. The quality of *tülku*, however, should be good." He then argues, "*Tülku* should be recognized when they are about ten years old. . . . That is the age when it is possible to gauge the child's character, intelligence, and religious propensity."[69] Echoing Tséten Zhabdrung's assessment of the overall importance of Buddhist education in *Acoustic Ambrosia*, the Panchen Lama reasons: "If the recognition of *tülku* is aimed at preserving and promoting Buddhism and administering the monasteries, it is not necessary to look for someone who is merely an authentic reincarnation. Everyone should keep this in mind. I think that someone with the knowledge of Buddhism, gentle character, and ability to serve the cause of Buddhism is better than a mere authentic reincarnation."[70] In similar ways, the Panchen Lama and Tséten Zhabdrung construct the parameters of authority around education and the moral character of the individual. In 1987, the Panchen Lama founded the Beijing Buddhist College, also known as the Tibetan Buddhist Institute of China, to foster the education of monastics. It has since become a center for officially recognized *tülku* to receive political education as well.[71] The Tenth Panchen Lama's and Tséten Zhabdrung's recommendations for the recognition process were not heeded by the state, but they seem to have influenced local Buddhist communities.

In 1991, a State Council directive permitted reincarnations, limiting the number of recognitions according to the size and influence of monasteries.[72] When this was first implemented, it seemed as if each local Buddhist community would manage the recognition of *tülku*, as the Panchen Lama had recommended in 1983. One of the first to be recognized officially was the Sixteenth Karmapa, on June 25, 1992. Later that same summer, Dungkar Rinpoché returned to the throne of his monastery in the Kongpo region of southern Central Tibet to bestow Buddhist teachings for the first time since the Cultural Revolution. In the summer of 1993, the reincarnations of Tséten Zhabdrung and Tséten Khenpo were both recognized and enthroned within a few months of each other.[73] According to sources who wished to remain anonymous, Jigmé Damchö Gyatso's reincarnation was also found around this time.

The opportunity for Tibetan Buddhist hierarchs to take the lead in the recognition process was short-lived. The state began to exercise its control over the *tülku* institution in 1995 and continues to do so today, with some unintended

FIGURE 5.6 Dungkar Rinpoché at monastic seat ca. 1993

Courtesy of Latse Library

consequences. Controversy erupted over the recognition of the Eleventh Panchen Lama when the Dalai Lama's candidate, Gendün Chökyi Nyima, disappeared from public view. For many years he was considered the world's youngest
political prisoner. Recent reports suggest he is living a normal life under a pseudonym. Many analysts believe that the Communist Party's chosen candidate for
the Panchen Lama could aid in securing CCP control over the institution of the
Dalai Lama after the death of His Holiness the Fourteenth Dalai Lama, Tenzin
Gyatso.[74] His Holiness has publicly stated that he will not be reborn in an
authoritarian state.

By late 1996, the launching of the "Strike Hard" campaign sparked CCP
denouncements of the Dalai Lama, such as "whilst promoting splittist activities
aloft the banner of religion, the Dalai Lama clique resorts to any and every available means to further their aims."[75] This campaign took place alongside state
attempts at "patriotic education" and forced monastics to comply with denounc-
ing the Dalai Lama.[76] The increased political pressure prompted the high-
ranking incarnate lama of Kumbum Monastery, Arjia Rinpoché, to go into
exile.[77] In 2005, the State Administration for Religious Affairs issued Order

No. 5, "Measures on the Management of Tibetan Buddhist Reincarnations," which required all reincarnate lamas to register their status with this arm of the CCP.[78] The measure effectively placed control over the future recognition of *tülku* in the hands of the state.[79] It does not seem a coincidence that there has been backlash against these policies as local Buddhists subvert them in a variety of ways, some of which echo the ideas put forth by Tséten Zhabdrung.

While efforts by Tséten Zhabdrung and the Tenth Panchen Lama to reinstate the primary mode of ecclesiastical succession in Tibet did little to influence state policy, they certainly influenced local practices. Charlene Makley notes that in the mid-1990s, Jamyang Zhépa and Gungtang Rinpoché, two important lamas at Labrang Monastery, publicly advocated "quality" of monks over "quantity."[80] There have been reports of "self-appointed *tülku*, who are living in their monasteries and recognized by the local communities" but are not officially recognized.[81] Both reports are not surprising, considering that Jamyang Zhépa and other Géluk leaders were present when the Tenth Panchen Lama issued directives to find a few virtuous *tülku* in 1983. Another strategy taken up by local Buddhists is to rescind the status of *tülku*. Two informants who asked to remain anonymous told me that Dungkar Rinpoché expressly wished his incarnation lineage to end with his death.[82] Although I heard a recent report that his reincarnation has been found, I have not received confirmation of this. During a research trip in 2015, anonymous sources said that the current incarnations of Tséten Zhabdrung and Jigmé Damchö Gyatso no longer wish to claim their status as *tülku*. I was told that although people still believe them to be authentic lamas, they do not want to live a monastic's life or take up the responsibilities of their position officially. This is particularly interesting considering that both the Panchen Lama and the Sixth Tséten Zhabdrung emphasized intellect and moral conduct over official status. The future of this mode of ecclesiastical succession in China remains precarious, especially as the Chinese state seems intent on exercising its control over this institution for political reasons.

Continuing Dharma Traditions—Mugé Samten and Tséten Zhabdrung

Alongside the restoration of the *tülku* institution, a main priority for the few well-educated remaining Tibetan Buddhist hierarchs in post-Mao China was the reinstatement of Buddhist education, the transmission of textual knowledge, and the performance of ritual practices at newly opened monasteries. All Three Polymaths actively engaged in these activities at their local monasteries and occasionally taught in other Tibetan regions.

When *"Avadāna* of Silver Flowers" poetically tells of the Tenth Panchen Lama's tour of Bīdo Monastery, Karing Monastery, and Dentik Monastery in the summer of 1980,[83] it records the reopening of these small monasteries after almost twenty years of forced closure. From our historical vantage point today, we can say that such moments represent aspects of the "revival" of Tibetan Buddhist institutions in the post-Mao era. Ethnographic studies at Tibetan Buddhist monasteries, such as Drepung in the Tibetan Autonomous Region; Larung Gar in Serta; Rongbo Monastery in Repgong, Qinghai Province; and Labrang Tashikyil in Gansu Province detail that this revival was complex, involving local communities, the state apparatus, and the monastic population. It entailed not only the rebuilding of monastic structures (buildings, stupa, statues, etc.), but also their repopulation with monks and nuns, who required training from learned Buddhist teachers.[84] The situation was dire in the early 1980s because so few teachers had survived the political purges of the Maoist years, yet the transmission of knowledge in the Tibetan Buddhist context requires instruction about Buddhist texts and rituals from an authentic lama. Interviews with a few eyewitnesses, the addendum to Tséten Zhabdrung's life narrative, and Mugé Samten's autobiography tell us about the types of teachings they gave at their monastic communities from 1980 until their respective deaths.

As mentioned above, Jigmé Tekchok's addendum chronicles the last seven years of his teacher's life.[85] This documents how people came to pay their respects to Tséten Zhabdrung at his residence and how he corresponded with other lamas, such as Kirti Rinpoché, from 1979 onward.[86] It also records amounts of money donated for the rebuilding of sites such as Dentik. It provides a few more details on the reunion between Tséten Zhabdrung Tenth Panchen Lama in Bīdo after the Cultural Revolution, which was in the fifth month of 1980.[87] A few months later they toured Karing Monastery and then Dentik Monastery, as recorded in *"Avadāna* of Silver Flowers."[88] Before the two lamas were reunited, Tséten Zhabdrung taught his *General Commentary on Poetics* to monastics and also traveled to Kumbum Monastery. These facts indicate that the policy changes enacted in Beijing in 1978 began to result in some religious freedom in this area of Qinghai Province. Other studies remind us that 1980 was the same year that Khenpo Jigmé Phuntsok founded Larung Gar, which has since become one of the largest Buddhist centers in the world, "for the express purpose of reviving Buddhist scholarship and meditation."[89] David

Germano's pioneering study of Larung Gar and other ethnographies by Charlene Makley at Labrang Monastery and Rongbo Monastery show that the revival of monastic life was a complex process.[90] Mugé Samten's autobiography states that his main monastery opened the following year and gives some insight into the state mechanisms at work there.

Luminous Mirror relates that when Mugé Samten attended a joint meeting of the provincial politburo, United Front, and local Religious Affairs Bureau in Chengdu in 1981, he learned that these bodies had approved the reopening of Mugé's Tashi Khorlo Monastery. After that, efforts were made for its cultural preservation.[91] According to my interviews with eyewitnesses, the rebuilding of Tséten Zhabdrung's other monasteries also began in 1981 and included Tséten Monastery, Tuwa Monastery, Gongkya Monastery, and Kathung Monastery. Tséten Zhabdrung traveled for the first time to Central Tibet that summer with his four graduate students, visiting Ganden Monastery and lecturing at the Medical College.[92] The surviving photos documenting him, his students, and the monks reveal the devastation of Ganden Monastery (see fig. I.4). Meanwhile in Qinghai Province, other monasteries, such as Gartsé Monastery in Repgong, opened their doors in 1981.[93] The year of Hu Yaobang's speech in Lhasa allowing for the exercise of ethnic-nationality identity, it became possible for lamas such as Tséten Zhabdrung, the Panchen Lama, and Mugé Samten to travel to visit monasteries, but it seems to have been around 1981 when Buddhist practices and rituals were allowed to resume.

Tséten Zhabdrung went to monasteries throughout Amdo during his summer breaks from teaching at Northwest Minzu University in Lanzhou, visiting them at first and then giving teachings. Professor Lugyel Bhum (Glu rgyal 'bum)

FIGURE 5.7   Tséten Zhabdrung with Ngapö Ngawang Jigmé at the Norbulingka in Lhasa, 1981

Courtesy of Jigmé Chöpak

of Qinghai Nationalities University was a student of one of Tséten Zhabdrung's main monastic disciples, Shardong Rinpoché (Shar dong rin po che, d. 1922–2001). Similar to Tséten Zhabdrung, Shardong Rinpoché was both a professor (at Qinghai Nationalities University) and an incarnate lama, at Jakyung Monastery. Professor Lugyel Bhum remembered that in the early 1980s

> Alak Shardong Rinpoché invited Tséten Zhabdrung to Jakyung. At that time, many Rinpoché came. He [Tséten Zhabdrung] gave Dharma teachings for forty-five days, such as the reading transmission of the Tibetan canon, especially from the Kanjur and the *vinaya*. . . . On top of that, he gave several empowerments, e.g., the Vajrabhairava initiation. It lasted for forty-five days. I stayed there the whole time.[94]

Tséten Zhabdrung also traveled to Rongbo Monastery in Repgong to give teachings and ordinations in the summer of 1984,[95] four years after its assembly hall was consecrated and its doors reopened.[96] From these eyewitness reports and the addendum in his autobiography, it becomes clear that empowerments (*dbang*) and reading transmissions (*lung*) formed the core of his activities in these two instances.

Likewise, by 1984, Mugé Samten reports being permitted to travel to give Dharma teachings throughout northern Sichuan. His autobiography mentions that he taught at Ngaba's Gomang Gar Monastery, a branch of Labrang Tashikyil Monastery. He gave monks instructions on the Refuge Prayer; Guru Puja; the Hundred Deities in Tuṣita; the White Mañjuśrī Prayer; the Three Lineage Accomplishment; White and Green Tara Prayers; the Outer, Inner, and Secret Ritual Prayers of Dharmaraja; the Permission Rituals of White Mañjuśrī;, White Akshobhya; and the Sixteen-Arhat Prayer. He gave a reading transmission of *A Guide to the Bodhisattva's Way of Life*, *Chanting the Names of Mañjuśrī*, and the *Amitayus Sutra*, and gave a commentary on Seven-Point Mind Training. Later that year at the request of Kirti Rinpoché, he also traveled to Kirti Monastery, where he gave two hundred monks White Mañjuśrī empowerments and other teachings.[97]

In his MA thesis on Mugé Samten as a "vernacular intellectual," Dhondup Tashi identifies instructions, empowerments, transmissions, and ordination as central to the "the continuation of tradition, which depends in a large part on a scholar-monk who can lead in instructions and rituals."[98] When Mugé Samten visited monasteries throughout Amdo in the remaining years of his life, he revived these rituals, passing on instructions on texts and practices to the next generation.

Dungkar Rinpoché gave Dharma teachings at his monastery in Kongpo in southeastern Tibet in 1992, a year after the law allowing for the recognition of incarnate lamas passed. It remains to be investigated if he traveled to other monasteries to give teachings. Learned scholars, such as Mugé Samten, Tséten Zhabdrung, Shardong Rinpoché, and many others not only initiated efforts to reopen local monasteries but also transmitted numerous Dharma teachings to make sure that monasteries were not hollow shells.[99]

Other anthropological studies on both the revival of Tibetan Buddhism and the indigenous Tibetan religion of Bön in post-Mao China indicate that religious resurgence was extraordinarily fast and widespread, but not without problems, such as commodification.[100] For example, in her ethnography on the ethics of Géluk monastic revival in Qinghai Province, Jane Caple points out that there were no working Tibetan Buddhist monasteries in the late 1970s and within two decades, thousands of monasteries were reconstructed and repopulated, yet the ethical parameters of maintaining the mundane bases of monastic Buddhism leave many moral aspects of this revival open for debate.[101]

In the early 1980s, Géluk hierarchs never received political support from the state to restore the *tülku* institution, yet efforts by Tibetan lamas, including all Three Polymaths, laid the groundwork for an extraordinary religious revival in Tibetan areas of China. While now in the twenty-first century, Tibetan Buddhism has become a globalized religious movement,[102] in the early 1980s, the efforts by all Three Polymaths to rebuild monasteries, give empowerments, and/ or ordain monastics occurred as local initiatives. Parallel to their endeavors to revitalize local Géluk Buddhist practices, rituals, and institutions, their secular academic contributions transcended traditional regional and sectarian affiliations to forge Tibetan national identity around language.

ACADEMIC LINEAGES

At the onset of this chapter, I introduced a photo from *Ethnic Nationalities Pictorial* that depicted two of the Three Polymaths in a Beijing classroom. The snapshot disregards the religious identities of both Buddhist scholars and symbolically represents some of the dynamic processes occurring more generally at this time, including the secularization of Tibetan Buddhist knowledge transmission and the survival and continuance of Tibetan culture to the next generation. In order to draw attention to how Tséten Zhabdrung, Mugé Samten, and Dungkar Lozang Trinlé were involved, I weave some of their contributions to secular Tibetan language education into this chapter on restoring Buddhist institutions in the post-Mao era.

Up until their respective deaths, they each expressed their moral agency not only through the revival of Buddhist traditions, such as the reinstatement of the *tülku* institution, giving Dharma teachings, or advocating for the rebuilding of monasteries in their respective localities, but also by harnessing the political openings afforded by the state policy on ethnic nationalities to promote Tibetan language education through their publications and teaching at state-run universities; each project had diffuse consequences. They revived Tibetan language education, which had been nonexistent during the Cultural Revolution, and over time, language became a focal point of Tibetan identity. For some, this signified a kind of national consciousness.

In the secular classroom, the Three Polymaths had to meet the unprecedented challenges and opportunities of the post-Mao era. A new generation of students, Tibetans who spoke a range of local dialects and non-Tibetans, were permitted to engage in Tibetan studies in an academic setting, but many were illiterate in the written language or unaware of the vast literary corpus of the Tibetan textual tradition.

Memories of Tibetan Language Education in the Late 1970s and Early 1980s

A verse from Tséten Zhabdrung's *"Avadāna* of Silver Flowers" metaphorically describes the Maoist period as a giant monster that opened its fearsome mouth as wide as the space between earth and sky. Its fangs gnashed ferociously at monastic institutions and devoured Tibetan texts, so-called "poisonous weeds."[103] Tséten Zhabdrung's metaphor, which I embellish here, is a reminder of how the author wrote about the leftist extremism of the Maoist years. The pervasive destruction of Tibetan society and culture was incomprehensible, a monstrosity. When the author wrote *"Avadāna of* Silver Flowers," he had been a professor for two years at Northwest Minzu University. As a teacher on the frontlines of Tibetan language education, he must have been horrified by the lack of Tibetan language publications and skilled educators for Tibetan language instruction at this time.

Memories of those who lived through this era add perspective on the state of Tibetan language publications and education in the aftermath of the Cultural Revolution. Pema Bhum, founder of the Latse Project, and former director of

FIGURE 5.8 Tséten Zhabdrung, 1983

Mi rigs brnyan par 9

the Latse Library in New York City (until it closed in June 2020), recalls that when he started studying with Tséten Zhabdrung at the Northwest Minzu University in 1979, among 130 incoming students, he was one of only seven undergraduates who had learned to read and write Tibetan before entering college.[104] Pema Bhum had gained these language skills by surreptitiously copying Tibetan texts during the Cultural Revolution, which he details in his memoirs, *Six Stars with a Crooked Neck*.[105] Professor Lugyel Bhum of Qinghai Nationalities University recalled that even though he graduated from Malho's Teacher's College in Tibetan language instruction and became a teacher in Malho County (Rma lho dzong; Ch. Henan xian) in 1970, "it was impossible to get Tibetan language books and that many *pecha* were burnt during that time."[106] *Pecha* are rectangular-shaped traditional Tibetan woodblock prints of Buddhist texts.

   A revered Nyingma lama shared a similar memory. His story exemplifies the loss and disappointment that many must have felt at not being able to learn the Tibetan language, the foundation for understanding a vast textual tradition, founts of cultural pride and wisdom. I requested an interview with one of the most important contemporary Nyingma Buddhist teachers in China today, Khenchen Tsultrim Lodrö (b. 1962), to inquire if his teacher, Khenpo Jigmé Phuntsok, had connections with any of the Three Polymaths. There don't seem to have been any direct links between these great lamas. Nonetheless, I retell this short memory, with Khenchen's permission, because it gave me new insights on how the activities of the Three Polymaths, especially Mugé Samten's writings in this case, touched many lives in ways that I had not anticipated learning about.

Khenchen Tsultrim Lodrö was only four years old in 1966, the year that the Cultural Revolution was launched. When I had the opportunity to speak to him about this project, he poignantly told me about the momentous occasion of holding a Tibetan language book replete with meaningful content for the first time in the late 1970s.[107] According to his official biography, Khenchen Tsultrim Lodrö became a monk after pursuing a secular education. During his studies, he had profound insight that academic pursuits could not alleviate the suffering of the world, so he sought counsel with the late Jigmé Phuntsok, the founder of Larung Gar, and became his disciple. Since his master's passing, Khenchen Tsultrim Lodrö has been a vice principal at Larung Gar, one of the largest Buddhist communities and institutes in the world with over 40,000 residents at its peak.[108] He travels abroad and has a large following of disciples among Chinese, Tibetans, Europeans, Australians, and North Americans.[109] When he described how significant it was for him to see a Tibetan text in his youth, I gained a new perspective on the direness of the situation for Tibetan language publishing at that time and how rare and meaningful it was to read Tibetan language in print.

In a solemn voice, Khenchen Tsultrim Lodrö told me about a time when he was a teenager and he was living at home in Drango (Brag 'go; Ch. Luhuo 炉霍) in Ganze Prefecture of Sichuan Province. It was the end of the Cultural Revolution, around 1979. One afternoon after school, a friend gave him an extremely rare object—a book. Its title was *Entryway to a Clear Mind: On Tibetan Writing* (*Bod kyi yi ge'i spyi rnam blo gsal 'jug ngogs*), by the Buddhist scholar Mugé Samten. When Khenpo returned to his family's home, he promptly handed this book to his father, who took it and skimmed through it. His father paused, took a deep breath, opened the book again, and read a section aloud as tears filled his eyes. The teenager, in awe of his father's grief, humbly asked why he was crying. His father responded that it was because he hadn't seen Tibetan script in such a long time, much less a book that expounded the value of Tibetan language and culture.[110]

Pema Bhum and Professor Lugyel Bhum went on to become scholars in Tibetan studies, and Khenchen Tsultrim Lodrö is one of the great living Buddhist scholar-practitioners today. Their memories serve to remind us of the fact that in 1979–1980, the time span in which Mugé Samten's *Entryway to a Clear Mind: On Tibetan Writing* and Dungkar Rinpoché's *The Merging of Religious and Secular Rule in Tibet* had their first print runs, the state of Tibetan language publications in China writ large was abysmal. These were not the only challenges facing teachers and students of Tibetan.

In the late 1970s and early 1980s, students were not only confronted with a shortage of available Tibetan-language books and teachers,[111] they also were indoctrinated with Han paternalistic propaganda, so that the younger generation had little pride in learning their own language. The Tenth Panchen Lama bluntly addressed this problem in a speech: "Not only the Chinese people, quite a number of Tibetans also oppose the use of Tibetan language in Tibet."[112] He also called attention to the inadequate state of Tibetan language publishing and education while bolstering pride in the long history of Tibetan language:

> We have so far treated Tibetan culture and religion with disdain, not with respect. . . . The Tibetan language was developed about 1,300 years ago. From then to 1959—whether we remained backward or made mistakes—we managed our life on the world's highest plateau by using only Tibetan. Whether the Tibetan written language is adequate or not, we had everything written in our own language, be it Buddhism, crafts, astronomy, astrology, poems, logic. All administrative works were also done in Tibetan.[113]

The Panchen Lama's speech dismisses Han chauvinistic propaganda on "backwardness" by highlighting the historical functionality of Tibetan language. Such testimonies speak to the gravity of the situation in the post-Mao era on many levels—from a shortage of teachers to a lack of books to the state-supported indoctrination on the backwardness of Tibetan culture and language.

To meet these challenges, Mugé Samten, Dungkar Lozang Trinlé, and Tséten Zhabdrung wrote prolifically and taught widely to promote Tibetan medium publications and education. This occurred parallel to their efforts in revitalizing Buddhist institutions. To find out what it was like to study Tibetan at universities in the post-Mao era, I interviewed a few former undergraduate and graduate students of Tséten Zhabdrung who now have careers in Tibetan studies.

Similar to how the articles in *Ethnic Nationalities Pictorial* and *Guangming Daily* cloaked Tséten Zhabdrung's status as a lineage holder and *tülku*, former graduate students remember that it was forbidden to show any indication of his identity as a Buddhist lama in the classroom, even though students, professors, and writers recognized him as a great polymath, a *khépa*.

One of Tséten Zhabdrung's former graduate students, Dawa Lodrö, put it this way: "Alak-tsang was a great Buddhist master (*blo dpon chen po*)—this is commonly recognized and all agree upon this, but at college, I didn't learn anything about Buddhism."[114] Similarly, Dawa Lodrö's classmate, the eminent historian Pu Wencheng, stated that he didn't study any Buddhist teachings with his teacher. In my interview with him in 2015, he lamented that he had not studied Buddhist texts with Tséten Zhabdrung, such as his commentary on Tsongkhapa's *The Great Treatise on the Stages of the Path to Enlightenment*.[115] Some other former university students, such as Jigmé Samdrup, Pema Bhum, and Lugyel Bhum, received private instruction in Buddhist practices and texts, only after asking multiple times.

Pema Bhum explained to me that as a student in 1981 he was unsure how to approach Tséten Zhabdrung to take lessons with him. Then a monk friend encouraged him to ask Tséten Zhabdrung for lessons on *The Great Treatise on the Stages of the Path to Enlightenment*. This monk explained to Tséten Zhabdrung that Pema Bhum had memorized much of Jigmé Damchö Gyatso's commentary on the topic. After that, Pema Bhum would go to ask Tséten Zhabdrung questions about this text. Pema Bhum also received instruction in Tibetan calligraphy starting at around this time. Tséten Zhabdrung was an incredibly talented calligrapher.[116]

Tséten Zhabdrung taught Tibetan poetics at Northwest Minzu University based on his textbook-commentary written in 1957. When I interviewed Dawa Lodrö, he explained how Tséten Zhabdrung's course grew in popularity:

> At that time [ca. 1978], when Alak-tsang [Tséten Zhabdrung] taught us *General Commentary on Poetics* (*Snyan ngag spyi don*) from cover to cover, it was only for the four of us [graduate students], but many people listened in on his class. The room was bigger than this one. There were 15–20 students, sometimes even 30 students. Cadres from various departments whose job was related to Tibetan language, such as the Minzu Publishing Houses, other teachers in the school, and students from other classes came to lessons.[117]

Dawa Lodrö described studying Tséten Zhabdrung's *General Commentary on Poetics* with the master himself: "It was like suddenly being awoken from a deep sleep. These *śloka* [couplets] were like keys. Once you had this key in your hands, then you could open any lock. That was the feeling I had."[118] Within a few years, the classroom would be filled beyond capacity.

Pema Bhum studied poetics with Tséten Zhabdrung a few years after Dawa Lodrö. Pema Bhum recalled that there were between eighty and one hundred people who attended Tséten Zhabdrung's class on the art of poetics in 1984. On a given day, they would learn several types of "adornments" or "ornamentations" (*rgyan*, Skt. *alaṃkāra*) according to the definition and examples in *A General Commentary on Poetics*. As he explained in an interview:

> Then the students would read through several different examples of this ornamentation. Some ornamentations have different subtypes. For example, there are four different subtypes of the ornamentation that "expresses the natural disposition of the subject" (*rang bzhin brjod pa'i rgyan*). After studying these various types of ornamentations by looking at their definitions, examples, and explanations, the students in Tséten Zhabdrung's class would be required to compose their own examples of the specific ornamentation under discussion. The five undergraduates and four graduate students would have to hand this in as homework. The following day in class, these would be recited aloud in class. Tséten Zhabdrung would comment on each and every composition.[119]

When Dawa Lodrö was asked to teach at Northwest Minzu University in the 1990s, he chose to use Tséten Zhabdrung's textbook for his classes on Tibetan literature because "it was so clearly written and easy to learn from."[120]

Dawa Lodrö went on to become a founding editor of one of the most important literary magazines for modern Tibetan literature, "*Drang char*" (*Sbrang char*), alternately translated as "Spring Rain" or "Light Rain." He began at *Spring Rain* shortly after graduating from Northwest Minzu University, when the journal started in the mid-1980s. According to the eminent Tibetan historian Tsering Shakya, this premier literary journal in Tibet has "more than any other publication, shaped and established the foundation of modern Tibetan literature."[121] Due to his position at *Spring Rain*, Dawa Lodrö was at the epicenter of intellectual debates on what constitutes "modern Tibetan literature." He personally knew many of the key figures from the old guard as well as young literary savants.

In one of my interviews with Dawa Lodrö, I asked how he assessed the roles of the Three Polymaths—Mugé Samten, Dungkar Lozang Trinlé, and Tséten Zhabdrung—in the history of Tibetan literature. He eloquently evaluated their influence as follows:

Their contributions were more important than calling something "literature." Mugé Samten, Dungkar Lozang Trinlé, and Tséten Zhabdrung were of the "previous generation," but they lived in a "new generation." Their guiding ideas were old-fashioned and traditional, even though they lived into a new age. Their writings and thoughts still belong to the old school because they learned those thoughts from the past generation and accepted those thoughts from the previous generation. They read books in the traditional manner. Even though they went into the new generation, the guiding thoughts of their writings and their thoughts on education were still old time and traditional. Of course they have some new aspects in respect to literature; but from the literary perspective, all their writings are traditional literature.[122]

I would add that because of their capacities as polymathic scholars, they had profound and diffuse influences on the next generation.

Over time, as Mugé Samten, Dungkar Lozang Trinlé, and Tséten Zhabdrung published writings, such as their treatises on poetics, works on Tibetan history, and academic essays, and embraced their roles as secular professors inside classrooms, they gained the title of the "Three Polymaths" who promoted the survival and continuance of Tibetan culture in the aftermath of the darkest hour of her history.

The Three Polymaths' Promotion of Tibetan Language and Their Legacies

Each of the Three Polymaths' various efforts in publishing and teaching planted seeds for further growth in various subfields of Tibetan studies, including linguistics, literature, history, and Buddhist studies. I focus here on the import of promoting Tibetan language usage and Tibetan medium education because it lies at the heart of all these various subfields. I link specific projects that each scholar worked on with other secondary sources to highlight the diffuse consequences of their endeavors. Mugé Samten's political work is seen as part of a larger project on advocating for a common Tibetan language. Dungkar Rinpoché's encyclopedia has become an important Tibetological resource and fount of pride in Tibetan language. Tséten Zhabdrung's innovative approach to Tibetan poetics paved the way for new developments in modern Tibetan literature. All of these projects centered on Tibetan language, which over time would become a focal point for Tibetan identity construction.

One of Mugé Samten's political wins for Tibetan language is also viewed as a step in a much longer, more arduous journey toward the development of a common Tibetan language.[123] Linguists point out that Tibetan is not a singular language but polynomic, which means its unity is abstract and several coexistent forms are recognizable.[124] The three "canonical dialects"—Amdo, Kham, and Central Tibetan—are related to the written standard language, which can serve as lingua franca between Tibetan speakers whose dialect differences are mutually unintelligible. Despite the many contemporary difficulties facing Tibetan language usage and education, the Chinese state has at times both supported and thwarted the development of a common language.[125] Mugé Samten's autobiography reminds readers that early efforts toward that goal were stopped in the late 1950s.

Luminous Mirror discusses state-driven language policies created for state-sponsored, that is, "official," Tibetan language publications in 1959. In early 1980, Mugé Samten railed against these rules to streamline the language along the lines of the dictates for the simplification of Chinese language. In his autobiography, Mugé Samten remembers that they "wreaked havoc on Tibetan grammar."[126] He was infuriated in particular by the replacement of five genitives in literary Tibetan (that have variant spellings determined by the final letter of the modified word) with only one, *gi*. Other sources inform us that he used his oratory skills to rally support to reverse these state-implemented grammar rules by lecturing for a day at Northwest Minzu University. His essay "An Analytical Critique of 'Essential Points'" (Gnad bsdus kyi dgag yig mtha' dpyad) on this issue was mimeographed and distributed by various publishing houses from Lhasa to Ngaba.[127] Eventually, it sparked political change. In January 1980 after twelve days of debate at a minority languages conference in Beijing, the grammar reforms were revoked and then were returned to classical Tibetan conventions.[128]

Mugé Samten's political win is viewed by Marielle Prins, a linguist developing phonology and grammar of Gyelrong dialects,[129] as part of a larger debate on the development of a common Tibetan language. She observes that an awareness of a common Tibetan identity has "replaced regional chauvinism" and that "Tibetan Common Language has become a focal point around which to express Tibetan identity and pride in Tibetan culture among a growing number of students, scholars, and intellectuals."[130] Prins's work highlights the importance of language as a key factor in Tibetan identity construction in the PRC. This also relates to one of Tséten Zhabdrung's goals and an upshot of modern Tibetan literature, which I will detail shortly. The ongoing debates on the development of a common language have ramifications beyond the realm of this project on the Three Polymaths. Mugé Samten received accolades from the community of Tibetan scholars for his efforts.

Mugé Samten writes in his autobiography that he received a letter from Dungkar Lozang Trinlé in Beijing recognizing this success.[131] His autobiographical memories in *Luminous Mirror* remind readers that alongside his advocacy work for standardized Tibetan, he was also on the ground teaching in the classrooms of newly opened schools in largely nomadic areas of Hongyuan (Hong yon) and Dzögé (mdzod dge) in 1981.[132] He continued to teach at local schools and at *minzu* universities, to give Buddhist teachings and ordinations, and to support the rebuilding of local monasteries for the remainder of his days. Dungkar Rinpoché's biographical entry on Mugé Samten in his encyclopedia extols his bravery and intellectual acumen for championing classical literary conventions.

Mugé Samten died in 1993 and is still remembered for his polymathic activities, especially for the way he supported Tibetan language education. In August 2016, a three-day academic conference in honor of Mugé Samten's work was organized by the Songpan (Ch. Zungchu) County Party Committee and the County People's Government. There was representation from the Buddhist Association of China. Li Weiguo of the Standing Committee of the autonomous prefecture and the United Front Work Department gave a speech. The vice-chairman of Ngaba Prefecture's Political Consultative Conference, Tatsa Tülku, represented Mugé Samten's students and gave a talk. According to this news report, which appeared on the web in English, "About one hundred people including leaders from the central authorities, the province, the prefecture, professors and scholars, specialists from universities and academic institutions, lamas and tülkus from Buddhist academies and so on attended the seminar."[133] The article also states that a new documentary film on the life of Mugé Samten was shown. Representation from academic circles included a professor from Qinghai Nationalities University and Dawa Lodrö, Tséten Zhabdrung's former graduate student and editor at *Spring Rain*. He presented on Mugé Samten's poems. Such meetings, similar to the one honoring Dungkar Rinpoché's contributions to Tibetan studies in India in 2017, discussed in chapter 4, have become locations for secular academics and Buddhist scholars to come together.

One of Dungkar Rinpoché's enduring legacies is his pioneering reference work, *Dungkar Encyclopedia*, which has become a source for not only research in Tibetan studies[134] but also cultural pride among Tibetan studies students at Minzu University in Beijing. As I detailed in the introduction to this book, this project began in the early 1960s when Dungkar Rinpoché first taught at Minzu University. Toward the end of the Cultural Revolution, while Dungkar Rinpoché was working at the Cultural Relics Office in Lhasa, he started his research again by collecting more terms. After he resumed his professorial position at Minzu University in 1978 and then became vice general director of the China Tibetology Research Center, he was able to gain the institutional support needed for such a massive project. However, by the time Dungkar Rinpoché passed away in 1997, it had not yet been published. His former students at Minzu University and colleagues at the China Tibetology Research Center published this work posthumously in 2002.

This same reference work became a source of cultural pride for Tibetan studies students at Minzu University fifteen years after Dungkar Rinpoché's death. From 2011 to 2013, ethnically Tibetan undergraduates enrolled in the Tibetan studies program at Minzu University recruited other students, including their Chinese classmates, to volunteer on the "DungGar project," which involved digitizing the contents of the *Dungkar Encyclopedia*. One of the main student organizers, Sheep Brother, explained their motivations. Their goal was "to protect our mother tongue," because "if we stop using our mother language, our language would ultimately disappear."[135] The DungGar project was published online in 2013.[136] In her sociological study on Tibetan identity at Minzu University, Miaoyan Yang views the DungGar project as exemplifying how Tibetan students in China use technology to promote usage of their native language, which for many became important to internal ethnic identity construction.

While Mugé Samten advocated for a common Tibetan language by getting rid of detrimental state policies and Dungkar Rinpoché worked tirelessly on his encyclopedia, Tséten Zhabdrung drew upon the discursive space afforded by the state policy on ethnic nationalities to advocate for Tibetan language education. As detailed in chapter 4, the Tenth Panchen Lama interpreted identity construction around "four commonalities," which were "nationality language, costume, customs, and territory," as evident in his 70,000 Character Petition from 1962. Tséten Zhabdrung self-identifies as Tibetan based on four similar criteria in his autobiography, even though he was of mixed Chinese-Tibetan heritage. As he states in *Acoustic Ambrosia*, "My early paternal ancestors were Chinese and not mixed with the seed of other ethnicities. Since my father's generation, my family is a mix of Chinese and Tibetan, but if I base my own ethnicity on language both written and spoken, customs and territory, then I am Tibetan."[137] This is important because it shows how Tibetan intellectuals used the discursive political space of state policy to construct their own identity.

In some of Tséten Zhabdrung's other writings, he marshals literary Tibetan to promote a common language between speakers of various dialects. While in the PRC it grew increasingly difficult to unite Tibetan territories politically, in works on literature and language it was possible to discursively unite Tibetans, in part because *minzu* policy permitted "language" as one of the main factors of identity construction. The connections between the 1950s and the post-Mao era come to the fore again in Tséten Zhabdrung's *A General Commentary on Poetics*. The original print in 1957 and subsequent prints after 1981 underscore written literary Tibetan as a unifying force. Tséten Zhabdrung wrote:

> Similar to countless blazing stars strewn upon
> a dark and boundless sky, I delight in
> teaching diligently on the hundred ornaments,
> glorious poetics praised by Indian scholars.
>
> With words common among Tibetans in
> Amdo, Kham, and Central Tibet, nomads and farmers,
> compose mellifluous words,
> write with a flash of the pen![138]

He proudly charges literary Tibetan with the discursive ability to unite speakers of all three main dialects of Tibetan language.

Tséten Zhabdrung not only makes the case that the literary language is common across dialectical differences, but also delights in phonetic "wordplay" (*sgra rgyan*). When he muses with "difficult" (*bya dka' ba*) phonetic figures in the above poem, he defies a historical claim that the Tibetan language wasn't as sophisticated as Sanskrit in handling this particular type of literary adornment. This argument was picked up on by later Tibetan writers and became integral to assertions of Tibetan identity around language, as I detail later in this chapter. When Tséten Zhabdrung pens the first quatrain of the original Tibetan using only one vowel, *a,* for each of the nine syllables in all four lines, he delights in the capaciousness of the Tibetan language. Similarly, in the second stanza, each line (also nine syllables long) is written using only one vowel per line. The first line solely uses the vowel *o*; the second, *i*; the third, *e*; and the fourth, *u*. These literary acrobatics, a skill in Tibetan phonetics, was but one type of wordplay. A great showman of Tibetan poetics, Tséten Zhabdrung discursively unites the different vernacular dialects to deliver a striking poem.

In Tséten Zhabdrung's autobiography, *Acoustic Ambrosia*, he recalls that he wrote this work for students at Qinghai Nationalities University in 1957, "in order to accord to modern times."[139] Twenty years later, in the aftermath of the Maoist years, his commentary once again became a textbook for teaching poetics. In reprint after reprint the above verse delighting in mellifluous words common among all Tibetans begins chapter 2 on literary figures. Both Dungkar Lozang Trinlé and Mugé Samten also wrote influential commentaries on poetics, which they taught at Minzu University in Beijing and Southwest Minzu University respectively.

The Three Polymaths' efforts to rescue Tibetan language to benefit the "new generation" paved the way for thriving intellectual and societal debates that continue to this day, not only among Tibetans in China and in exile but also among other interested parties, such as academics and those interested in Tibetan culture more broadly.

Intellectual Debates and Pride Centered on Tibetan Language

Tséten Zhabdrung's *A General Commentary on Poetics,* like Dungkar Rinpoché's later treatise, introduced classical Tibetan literary theory to students enrolled at a Chinese state-run university for the first time. For Tséten Zhabdrung and Dungkar Rinpoché "mellifluous words" (*snyan ngag*) had a wide range of discursive applications. When Tséten Zhabdrung prescribes that mellifluous words be used for lecturing, teaching, debating, critiquing, and praising others,[140] it becomes clear that the discursive parameters of this literary theory stretch far beyond writing verse. Poetic techniques lay at the foundation of learning how to write in rhetorically effective and aesthetically pleasing ways. Debates on what constitutes modern Tibetan literature in the post-Mao era often involved heated discussions on this Tibetan literary aesthetic.

Tséten Zhabdrung's interpretation of "mellifluous words" planted intellectual seeds to foster the growth of modern Tibetan literature as the next generation of scholars debated what constitutes "modernity" and "Tibetanness" (especially vis-à-vis *kāvya*'s Sanskrit roots and as one of the minor fields of learning or *rikné*). This discursive opening was supported by the emergence of new venues for Tibetan literary writing, such as *Spring Rain*, and sheltered from political turbulence due to state policies that supported ethnic nationality identity as constructed around language. In this way, intellectual debates on what constitutes modern Tibetan culture and literature are historically intertwined with the legacy of the Three Polymaths' informal academic teaching lineages that emerged in the early 1980s.

Foremost in this informal academic lineage was the literary sensation Döndrup Gyel (Don grub rgyal, 1953–1985), who is often memorialized as the father of modern Tibetan literature. Döndrup Gyel shot to fame for his poem "Waterfall of Youth" (Lang tsho'i rbab chu); with its cascading free verse and its refreshing cries for new freedoms, it became the source of new lifeblood in Tibetan literature. Nancy Lin points out, however, that the popular notion of Döndrup Gyel as a trailblazing cultural icon who rejected Tibet's Indic influence is somewhat misleading. Building on Matthew Kapstein's observation that Döndrup Gyel did not so much "reject" Tibet's Indic literary past as "immerse himself within and reevaluate it,"[141] Nancy Lin shows how Döndrup Gyel vernacularized Indic models to make poetry easier to understand for contemporary readers.[142] He became a literary sensation by innovating with this classical literary form and adding free verse forms.

Techniques on how to adapt poetic forms for modern times were encouraged by his teacher, Dungkar Lozang Trinlé. Döndrup Gyel also received some instruction from Tséten Zhabdrung. As Dawa Lodrö explained to me in an interview in 2015:

Döndrup Gyel was not Tséten Zhabdrung's student, but if Döndrup Gyel didn't understand something he would go to visit him. Döndrup Gyel went to visit Tséten Zhabdrung twice in Qinghai and he went to see him in Lanzhou. I brought Döndrup Gyel to Tséten Zhabdrung's room in Lanzhou and they talked for one and a half hours. . . . In the traditional way, if someone doesn't understand something, he will go to consult someone else; then that person becomes the teacher. So in the traditional way, they had a teacher-student relationship, but he did not formally study with him.

"The monastic vanguard," to use Lauran Hartley's terminology for the generation of scholars that included the Three Polymaths, laid the foundation for the next generation of writers and scholars to adapt and/or reject certain aspects of this literary-aesthetic theory in their writings. Lama Jabb in his pathbreaking work, *Oral and Literary Continuities in Modern Tibetan Literature,* foregrounds the endurance of styles, genres, and literary techniques such as *kāvya,* i.e., "mellifluous words," and folk-style *gur* on the emergence of modern Tibetan literature, even as some of the contemporary generation of writers reject them.[143] One of the concerns in the early post-Mao era was how to make mellifluous words accessible to students who didn't understand the Indic references replete with abstruse kennings and wordplay.

One way Tséten Zhabdrung's *A General Commentary on Poetics* (1957) paved the way for the development of modern Tibetan literature was by rejecting outmoded topics and replacing them with new modern subject matter. For example, when Tséten Zhabdrung explains how to "expresses the natural disposition of the subject" (*rang bzhin brjod pa'i rgyan*; Sanskrit: *svabhāvokti alaṃkāra*),[144] he modifies one of its four subtypes, "expressing the inherent nature of an object through its functions,"[145] with a contemporary topic. In the following poetic example, he doesn't use any of the canonical themes for belletristic verse;[146] instead he adapts this form to express the function of a contemporary topic—a watch:

> Displaying numbers, twenty-four hours—day and night,
> indicating correctly evening, morning; midnight and noon,
> following time, not stopping for a minute,
> the shape of a bracelet—a marvelous wristwatch![147]

Another case of this type of adaptation can be found in *Entryway to a Clear Mind* by Mugé Samten. Drawing upon the theme of technology, one aspect of Deng Xiaoping's Four Modernizations, Mugé Samten uses a similar literary form[148] to proudly boast of the technological innovations of a land-line phone:

Ode to a Telephone

> Crossing a hundred thousand *li*,
> whether or not the line is made of steel,
> conversations are carried,
> the miracle of technology—a telephone![149]

Tséten Zhabdrung started to adopt modern content to classical poetic forms in the mid-1950s, and as we read in Mugé Samten's example, this approach was revived again in the late 1970s. A similar move to expand traditional topics is evident in Dungkar Rinpoché's "Offerings to the Communist Party," written in a genre usually reserved for Buddhist religious purposes, a text translated by Pema Bhum elsewhere.[150] More significantly than using old forms for new content, Tséten Zhabdrung claims that it was such innovations and adaptations by Tibetan savants over hundreds of years that made this art form so beautiful in Tibetan despite its Indic roots.

Tséten Zhabdrung and Dungkar Lozang Trinlé claim "mellifluous words" as Tibetan by way of refuting an analogy crafted by earlier Tibetan scholars, who had asserted that the coarse wooly language of Tibetan could not be used to craft beautiful poetry in the same way as silky Sanskrit literary figures, such as puns, and phonetic wordplay (*sgra rgyan*; Skt. *śabdālaṃkāra*). With access to a wider range of texts, Gedun Rabsal has shown that this analogy, which Tséten Zhabdrung and Dungkar Lozang Trinlé incorrectly attributed to Sakya Paṇḍita, originated with Khamtrül Tenzin Chökyi Nyima (Khams sprul bstan 'dzin chos kyi nyi ma, 1730–1779).[151] Regardless of their incorrect attribution, Tséten Zhabdrung and Dungkar Rinpoché both refute the analogy. They aver that through a series of literary innovations, Tibetan savants crafted mellifluous words as their own art form, equally as beautiful as her Sanskrit mother. As Tséten Zhabdrung explains in *A General Commentary on Poetics*:

> This [i.e., the impossibility of using difficult wordplay in Tibetan] certainly must have been the case during the time when [Daṇḍin's] *Mirror of Poetics* had not yet been translated. However, later, due to the graciousness of the translators Shongtön (Shong [ston]) and Pang Lodrö Tenpa (Dpang [blo gros brtan pa]), gradually a great development took place in the art of poetics. Due to these efforts, difficult phonetic wordplay based on Tibetan words, although dissimilar to those of India, is evident today in marvelous works written by scholars of each of the various schools of Buddhism since Jé Tsongkhapa and his disciples, who were masters of speech. As these works testify, the art of brocade was accomplished however one desired, with the weaving of fine silk and also with that of coarse wool.[152]

Tséten Zhabdrung's move to view the development of Tibetan language through a historical lens reclaims the magnificence of the coarse wool, the Tibetan language, to be as beautiful as the silk Sanskrit in making the brocade art of fine poetry. He celebrated the masterful literary works of Tibetan savants in order to introduce them to his students for the first time at Qinghai Nationalities University in the mid-to-late 1950s. Dawa Lodrö used the same text as a key to open the door to his own understanding of Tibetan literature and drew upon it to teach his own students in the 1990s.

In a letter exchange between Döndrup Gyel and his colleague Sanggyé, the influence of Dungkar Lozang Trinlé and Tséten Zhabdrung on Döndrup Gyel and his cohort becomes apparent as they discuss how to further develop Tibetan literary theory. Döndrup Gyel draws upon his teachers' analogy to Sakya

Paṇḍita to construct the parameters of "selectivity," i.e., what is appropriate to accept (*blang*) and to reject (*dor*) for modern Tibetan literature.[153] Döndrup Gyel's epistle to Sanggyé on his MA thesis reveals their mutual concern about the development of modern Tibetan poetics:

> You wrote, "Although Sakya Paṇḍita translated here and there and also explained through commentary . . . the difficult poetic figures based on phonetics, etc. can't be applied to Tibetan language, like [applying] a design for silk brocade onto a homespun woolen cloth." Sapan's work of selectivity (*blang dor*) wasn't complete. Although there are a lot of things to understand and think about in your writing, the essence of your thinking is that Tibet needs a treatise on the science of poetic figures that accords with its own characteristics.[154]

Döndrup Gyel views Sapan's (Sakya Paṇḍita) contribution as the first step in a long process of selectivity, of deciding what to accept or reject, in order to modernize and develop the Tibetan language. Whereas Dungkar Rinpoché and Tséten Zhabdrung allowed for new topics to be added to the canon, they never left the parameters set in *kāvya* theory. Döndrup Gyel and his colleagues went further than their teachers to propose the creation of a new indigenous Tibetan poetic theory and took on free verse forms.[155] As they draw upon this analogy of Tibetan language as coarse homespun wool, their excitement and pride in Tibetan literary language comes through.

Pema Bhum's essay, "Heartbeat of a New Generation," underscores the disparities between traditional monastic writers and the next generation of poets in two main areas: poetic metrics and the relative democratization of the Tibetan literary world. He wrote, "Certain senior monastic scholars, such as Tséten Zhabdrung, Mugé Samten, and Jikme Tekchok, wrote poems during this period, but their works were all in metered verse—and monastic circles never evinced the great surge of would-be writers that occurred among lay students at secular middle schools and colleges."[156] In a similar interplay between literary innovation and traditional authority, Matthew Kapstein suggests, Döndrup Gyel's short story "Tülku" caused such a stir in the early 1980s because its author was a bright, young, skeptical man who upset traditional modes of authority, whereas in the past, critiques of traditional institutions came from within the domain of the religious elite.[157] Indeed, as we read early on in this chapter, Tséten Zhabdrung also critiqued greedy *tülku*, but his autobiography did not cause an uproar.

Pema Bhum further explains that since he wrote "Heartbeat of a New Generation," for a conference on Tibetan language and literature organized by the late Chögyel Namkhai Norbu in Italy in 1991, there has been a notable increase of young monks and women publishing free verse and traditional forms in literary journals. Female poets had been underrepresented. Since then, women Tibetan poets, such as Pelhamo and Tsering Kyi, have emerged on the literary scene. Lama Jabb identifies Tsering Kyi (Tshe ring skyid) as one of the few contemporary female poets to tackle taboo themes of sexuality, including lesbian relationships, unrequited love, and sexual assault.[158] Pema Bhum points out that the monastic circles to which Tséten Zhabdrung and Mugé Samten belonged never imagined that Tibetan literature and especially poetry would evolve to become so democratized. Yet they certainly planted the seeds for Tibetan literature to become a source of cultural pride and a focal point for Tibetan identity construction. The notion of "ethnic nationality pride" (*mi rigs kyi la rgyal*) dominated Tibetan poetry and literature between 1980 and 1987.[159]

This trend of connecting Tibetan language and literature with Tibetan identity seems to continue, and for some scholars, it represents a kind of national identity. Findings from a recent sociological study connect the study of modern Tibetan language with Tibetan identity construction. Research conducted at the Minzu University of China in Beijing suggests that Tibetan students are constructing their identity around language usage. Miaoyan Yang, who researched the "DungGar Project," also found that "Tibetan language has been used as the determining factor in internal ethnic boundary making."[160] Ethnically Tibetan students who received instruction in Chinese were considered to be "Hanified." On the other hand, her findings show that Tibetan students who were majors in Tibetan studies and received instruction in Tibetan understood that "being a Tibetan means assuming an ethnic mission of promoting Tibetan language and culture. These students come from a diversity of Tibetan regions. The educational trajectory of these students reflects a strong link with Tibetan language and culture."[161] This study links language with Tibetan identity construction in the PRC alongside what Yang calls an "ethnic mission" for the survival of Tibetan culture.

Although Lama Jabb's research is on modern Tibetan literature, his thesis on Tibetan identity in many ways dovetails with Yang's findings. He views Tibetan identity construction around language and literature as national identity:

> The modern Tibetan literary text is itself national. It powerfully articulates Tibetan cultural identity, not only by cherishing the memories and practices of the past or remembering recent tragedies and current plights, but also through reviving, reusing and sustaining older forms of narrative and poetry in

innovative ways. It contributes to the re-forging of the Tibetan nation by turning to these nationally cohesive forces, acting as a unifying mode of communication and a fertile locus where all things Tibetan are voiced, discussed, negotiated, debated, and proclaimed.[162]

This assertion has met with some pushback by other scholars of modern
Tibet. Xaver Erhard, a research fellow at Leipzig University, has critiqued Lama
Jabb's thesis for his ahistorical treatment of Tibetan national identity. As Erhard
explains:

> More problematic is [Lama] Jabb's second argument, which presents modern
> Tibetan literature as preoccupied with the Tibetan nation. Jabb seems to fol-
> low Dreyfus' advice and seeks out cultural trends and motifs crucial for Tibetan
> identity formation. Or, in Jabb's words, how "a fusion of oral and written lan-
> guages is employed in the reconstruction of Tibetan national identity" (p. 30).
> However, his dehistoricizing conception of Tibet and a Tibetan nation seems
> problematic in as much as it does not take into account that concepts such
> as the "*chol kha gsum*, three key provinces" (p. 20) of Tibet, on which Jabb bases
> his concept of Tibet, over the course of history designated different and fluctu-
> ating geographical and territorial entities.[163]

Erhard raises an important point on the contested ground of Tibet's national
history. As I detailed in chapter 4, there is widespread scholarly consensus that
the historical development of a Tibetan national identity had been thwarted by
strong sectarian and regional affiliations; if we relate this to Lama Jabb's thesis,
this was despite the historical existence of a common literary language. This line
of inquiry is further confounded by the fact that identity and culture shift as
moral agents construct, deconstruct, and reconstruct these categories under
changing historical and social circumstances. A clear example of this is Tséten
Zhabdrung's autobiographical construction of his own Tibetanness based
on the *minzu* paradigm. In my reading of Lama Jabb's thesis that "the modern
Tibetan literary text is itself national," I view this claim as situated in the current sociohistorical context.

In other words, by bringing these different sources together, we can see how
Tibetan language *has become* a central part of Tibetan identity construction
since the late 1970s for many Tibetans, especially those educated in Tibetan language in the PRC. The roots for this development were established in the early
post-Mao era. In part, this can be traced back to the Three Polymaths' various

FIGURE 5.9 Prince's cave and Tséten Zhabdrung's residence on the thirtieth anniversary of Tséten Zhabdrung's death, June 2015, Dentik Monastery

Photograph by Nicole Willock

efforts in promoting Tibetan language as a fount of cultural pride in the aftermath of the Cultural Revolution.

In the early summer of 2015, I returned to Dentik Monastery for a special occasion, the thirtieth anniversary commemorating Tséten Zhabdrung's death. After I went home to Virginia, the symbolic connection between the historical Three Polymaths' heroic efforts to save Buddhism in the first millennium and the survival of Tibetan Buddhist culture in twentieth-century China crystallized for me and eventually manifested in a central theme of this book.

My journal entry for that June day evokes a kaleidoscope of memories. As I mentally revisit it, I am reminded of life's impermanence and its contradictions. On June 28, I sat as a passenger in the back of a sedan driven by Tséten

Zhabdrung's nephew, Jigmé Chöpak. My friend and colleague Padma'tsho joined me. We stopped to visit a teacher who works at a newly constructed elementary school with over two hundred students a few miles outside the entrance gates to Dentik. As I reflect on that, I am comforted by the fact that young girls are educated there because, as I found out later that day, girls are still discouraged from attending the community youth classes offered at Dentik. As we drove farther up the mountain, I noted that the path that I had traversed on foot eight years prior had been paved over. The new road and gate showed that the plans for the travel industry to reach the Cave of Buddhist Adepts were coming to fruition. In another conversation, I heard that thieves had attempted to steal the sixteen precious objects that go on display at the Anyé Lugyel festival. I was told that the burglars had been caught and now the artifacts were under lock and key. I observed the damage to Tséten Khenpo's complex caused by mudslides and listened to ongoing environmental concerns. The journal entry sparks an ebb and flow of reflection, remembrances, and emotions. When this mental wandering ceases and I find myself back at my desk, a profound stillness and sense of gratitude awaken in me. I am aware that all of the events on that day in Dentik, those ongoing contradictions of human life, could have not happened. History could have taken a different turn.

Remembering that day made me realize how fortunate I was to have experienced such moments as the ceremony honoring the thirtieth anniversary of Tséten Zhabdrung's passing. I sat in front of his reliquary stupa, among monastics, relatives, friends, admirers, laypeople, boys and girls, men and women of all ages, so many people that we flowed out into the courtyard, all gathered together to honor the enduring legacies of Tséten Zhabdrung's precious life. He contributed to the flourishing of human activity at Dentik and at academic centers in Xining, Beijing, and Lhasa—with all of its wisdom, beauty, and contradictions. I am grateful to this person whose writings I have spent years translating and contemplating.

As a result of that visit, I began interviewing non-Géluk Buddhist practitioners and women scholars to have a more balanced view of Tséten Zhabdrung's contributions. A couple of those conversations influenced the course of my research. An interview with Professor Tsering Thar later that same summer, facilitated by Eveline Washul, brought home the importance of Dungkar Rinpoché's legacy in Tibetan studies. Many subfields remain to be studied, such as his contributions to ancient Tibetan history, Bön history, and the great Tibetan epic of Gesar, which is immensely popular in China. In 2016, thanks to Professor David Germano at the University of Virginia, I had the opportunity to converse with Khenchen Tsultrim Lodrö. His story about the importance of

FIGURE 5.10 Tséten Zhabdrung's reliquary stupa, Dentik Monastery, September 2008

Photograph by Nicole Willock

reading Mugé Samten's *Entryway to a Clear Mind: On Tibetan Writing* in the late 1970s made me realize how profound and diffuse the impact of the writings and teachings of all three scholars were on the next generation. Both interviews became like beacons pointing to the "Three Polymaths" after the Cultural Revolution. I had heard this title so often in interviews and had read it over and over again. Its multilayered significance all of sudden became clear. It was, above all, a symbol of hope.

Yet I also see a kind of irony in using this symbolic epithet. The historical tenth-century Three Polymaths lived in a world that supported their choices to live as Buddhist monks. In twentieth-century China, in order to promote Tibetan language in secular settings, the two monks of this trio—Mugé Samten and Tséten Zhabdrung—had to obey state policies that required abandoning their religious identities in public spaces. As their autobiographies testify, both Mugé Samten and Tséten Zhabdrung lived as Géluk Buddhist monastics following the strict rules of conduct outlined in the *vinaya*, yet they were not allowed to wear their monastic robes when teaching at a minzu university or participating in other public forums, such as the political consultative conference meetings. In religious venues, such as a meeting of the Buddhist Association of China, Tséten Zhabdrung donned his robes (see figure 5.5). This is another indication of how the state defines the parameters of religion and the secular and how this affects the lives of individuals.

Anthropologist Toni Huber brings attention to the important role of Chinese institutions and policies in the construction of Tibetan identity. He also reminds us that the discursive construction of what Tibetan culture is, who sets the boundaries for what it is, and what it should be are constantly coming into public discourse. Tibetologists in the West have underestimated the role of Chinese state institutions and policy regimes "in facilitating the construction of Tibetan identities that transcend the frequently invoked parochial referents of local communities."[164] In alignment with Huber's observations, this study further shows that the parameters of what constitutes Tibet are constantly being negotiated and vied over in dynamic processes among intellectuals, scholars, lamas, and the Chinese state, even as members of these various groups hold different agendas and approaches.

Three members of the Tibetan elite—Tséten Zhabdrung, Dungkar Rinpoché, and Mugé Samten—alternatively resisted, drew upon, complied with, and subverted state policies to advocate for Tibetan language, religion, and history in the post-Mao era. In doing so, they set in motion different ways of constructing Tibetan identity and culture in the aftermath of monstrous destruction. Through their contributions in publishing and teaching, they transmitted their polymathic knowledge to the next generation, nurturing younger intellectuals, writers, and scholars in Tibetan studies, who regardless of their ethnic identity were well educated in Tibetan language. Their combined legacy is interwoven in a global network of Tibetologists, continuing Buddhist lineages and establishing informal academic ones.

Each of the Three Polymaths acted as a moral agent, based on their respective capacities as learned Buddhist scholars to contribute to the survival and continuance of Tibetan culture at a crucial historical juncture. Their various efforts were part of ongoing processes and cannot be reduced to a simplistic paradigm of either resisting or conforming to the state. Tibetan Buddhist leaders of the 1950s had hope that Tibetan culture could and would thrive within the People's Republic of China. This hope was rekindled in the aftermath of twenty years of devastating destruction and great personal losses to each of these three men. When the opportunity arose, Tséten Zhabdrung and Mugé Samten wrote their autobiographies to remember a past in which Buddhist values prevailed, and Dungkar Rinpoché created a secular past for Tibet centered on the notion of Buddhist governance viewed through a Marxist lens. From 1976, for the remainder of their respective lives, they crisscrossed between religious and secular institutions to publish, research, and teach on Tibetan language, culture, and history. Due to these efforts, the next generation of Tibetan scholars, such as Pema Bhum and Dawa Lodrö, among others, began to refer to them by the title of the "Three Polymaths"—which symbolically represented the survival and continuance of Tibetan studies and Buddhism in a new era of the Dharma's re-diffusion.

Notes

INTRODUCTION

1. This is a pseudonym.
2. Bu ston Rin chen grub, *Bu ston chos 'byung* (Xining: Krung go bod kyi shes rig dpe skrun khang, 1988), 193–195; E. Obermiller, trans, *The History of Buddhism in India and Tibet by Bu-ston*, originally published as *Bu ston chos 'byung* [in Tibetan] (Delhi: Classics India Publications, 1999 [reprint]), 203–205; 'Gos lo tsā ba gzhon nu dpal, *Deb ther sngon po* [The blue annals] (Chengdu: Si khron mi rigs dpe skrun khang, 1984 [reprint]), 89–94; Georges Roerich, trans., *The Blue Annals (Deb ther sngon po)* by 'Gos lo-tsā-ba Gzhon nu dpal (Delhi: Motilal Banarsidass, 1996 [reprint]), 63–67; Christopher Beckwith, *The Tibetan Empire in Central Asia* (Princeton, N.J.: Princeton University Press 1987), 168–169; see also Sam van Schaik, "The Decline of Buddhism I: Was Lang Darma a Buddhist?," February 28, 2008, https://earlytibet.com/2008/02/28/lang-darma/. The Dunhuang Manuscript IOL J 76 records the name of "Dan tig" in the tenth century in a variant of the sutra; see Sam van Schaik, "Amdo Notes II," July 13, 2010, https://earlytibet.com/2010/07/15/amdo-notes-ii/.
3. Ronald Davidson, *Tibetan Renaissance: Tantric Buddhism in the Rebirth of Tibetan Culture* (New York: Columbia University Press, 2005), 84–90.
4. For detailed accounts on the complexities of the periodization and relevant sources, see: Davidson, *Tibetan Tantric Buddhism in the Renaissance*, 84–91; Heather Stoddard, "Rekindling the Flame: A Note on Royal Patronage in Tenth Century Tibet," in *The Relationship between Religion and State (chos srid zung 'brel) in Traditional Tibet,* ed. Christoph Cüppers (Lumbini: Lumbini International Research Institute, 2004), 49–105.
5. This source is available for download at https://odu.academia.edu/NicoleWillock. *Dan tig dgon pa'i dkar chag/dan dou si jianshi* 丹斗寺简史 [A guidebook to Dentik monastery], trans. Nicole Willock (Rig pa'i chos 'dzin/Ch. ni ke 妮科) ([n.p.], 2008), 5–6.
6. Tshe tan zhabs drung, "Mdo smad grub pa'i gnas chen dan tig shel gyi ri bo le lag dang bcas pa'i dkar chag don ldan ngag gi rgyud mngas" (*Zither of meaningful words: a catalogue of Domé's sacred place: Dentik, the crystal mountain and its branch monasteries*), in *Tshe tan zhabs drung rje btsun 'Jigs med rigs pa'i blo gros mchog gi gsung 'bum* [The collected works of the venerable Tshe tan zhabs drung 'Jigs med rigs pa'i blo gros], ed. 'Jigs med chos 'phags (Beijing: Minzu chubanshe,

2007), 3: 279–401. This text is referred to throughout this book as *A Catalogue of Dentik Monastery*.

7. It is hard to pin down exactly when this title began to be applied to Tséten Zhabdrung, Dungkar Rinpoché, and Mugé Samten. Pema Bhum remembers this was soon after the publication of Dungkar Rinpoche's grammar book (*mtsho sngon zhing chen gyi slob grwa chung 'bring gi bod kyi brda sprod sum rtags slob khrid kyi zur lta'i dpyad gzhi*) in 1978; Pema Bhum, "An Overview of the Life of Professor Dungkar Lozang Trinlé Rinpoché, *Trace Foundation's Latse Library Newsletter* 5 (2007–2008), 24–25. Gyalmo Drukpa (Rgyal mo 'grug pa, Ch. Zhou Hua), a research fellow at China Tibetology Research Center, confirmed that this terminology was widespread. When he gives talks on the current state of Tibetan studies in China, he frequently refers to these scholars together as the "Three Polymaths after the Cultural Revolution" (*mkhas pa mi gsum rig gnas gsar brje gyi rjes la*). Interview via social media facilitated by Gedun Rabsal, October 5, 2019. This title has also appeared in Tibetan-language online journals, such as *Tibet News* in an article titled, "Three Scholars of the 'Yang-dar' Era" (*Bstan pa yang dar skabs kyi bod kyi mkhas pa mi gsum*), March 3, 2018, http://tb.tibet.cn/tb/people/201803/t20180328_5591229.html; and on social media outlets, such as Weixin, which I detail in the next chapter. The title first appeared in English in an obituary for Dungkar Rinpoché, "Leading Scholar Dies, Cultural Criticism Stepped Up," *Tibet Information Network*, London, August 4, 1997.

8. Robert Barnett, "Beyond the Collaborator–Martyr Model: Strategies of Compliance, Opportunism, and Opposition with Tibet," in *Contemporary Tibet: Politics, Development and Society in a Disputed Region*, ed. Barry Sautman and June Dreyer (Armonk, N.Y.: M. E. Sharpe, 2006), 25.

9. Holmes Welch, *The Buddhist Revival* (Cambridge, Mass.: Harvard University Press, 1968), 2–3.

10. Melvyn C. Goldstein, "Introduction," in *Buddhism in Contemporary Tibet: Religious Revival and Cultural Identity,* ed. Melvyn C. Goldstein and Matthew Kapstein (Berkeley: University of California Press, 1998), 10–14.

11. Goldstein, "Introduction," 11.

12. Charlene Makley translates this term as "Buddhist restoration"; see *The Battle for Fortune: State-led Development, Personhood, and Power Among Tibetans in China* (Ithaca, N.Y.: Cornell University Press, 2018), 60–62.

13. Cf. Paul Nietupski, *Labrang Monastery: A Tibetan Buddhsit Community on the Inner Asian Borderlands, 1709–1958* (Lanham, Boulder, and New York: Rowman & Littlefield, 2011).

14. Melvyn Goldstein, *A History of Modern Tibet, 1913–1951: The Demise of the Lamaist State* (Berkeley: University of California Press, 1991), 37.

15. Irmgard Mengele, *dGe-'dun-chos-'phel: A Biography of the 20th-Century Tibetan Scholar* (Dharamsala: Library of Tibetan Works and Archives, 1999); Gendun Chopel, *Grains of Gold: Tales of a Cosmopolitan Traveler*, trans. Thupten Jinpa and Donald S. Lopez Jr. (Chicago: University of Chicago Press, 2014); Gendun Chopel, *In the Faded Forest*, ed. and trans. Donald S. Lopez Jr. (Chicago: University of Chicago Press, 2009); Heather Stoddard, *Le mendiant de l'Amdo* (Paris: Société d'ethnographie, 1986) and "Progressives and Exiles," in *The Tibetan History Reader,* ed. Gray Tuttle and Kurtis Schaeffer (New York: Columbia University Press, 2013), 597.

16. Donald S. Lopez Jr., "Introduction," in Gendun Chopel, *In the Faded Forest*, 11.

17. The Tibetan-language colophon at the end of the Tibetan section of this work stated that the text was prepared by Yang Zhifu (Yang khi hphu, Byams pa rnam rgyal) and was edited and corrected by his teacher Shes rab rgya mtsho 'Jam dpal dgyes pa'i blo gros. See Meng Zang weiyuanhui [Tibet-Mongolian association], *Sanmin zhuyi yaoyi* [The three principles of the people] (Taipei: Taiwan, 1971), 120.

18. Gray Tuttle, *Tibetan Buddhists in the Making of Modern China* (New York: Columbia University Press, 2005), 202.

19. "Mi rigs don gcod U yon lhan khang; Ch. mínzú shìwù wěiyuánhuì 民族事务委员会."

20. "'Thab phyogs gcig sgyur bu'u; Ch. tǒngyī zhànxiàn gōngzuò bù 统一战线工作部."

21. "Chos don U yon lhan khang; Ch. zōngjiào shìwù jú 宗教事务局."

22. The State Administration for Religious Affairs (SARA), the former Religious Affairs Bureau (RAB), was renamed as such in 1998. See Vincent Goossaert and David Palmer, *The Religious Question in Modern China* (Chicago: University of Chicago Press, 2012), 346. For the equivalent Tibetan terms for these three key institutions, I consulted Melvyn Goldstein, *The New Tibetan-English Dictionary of Modern Tibetan* (Berkeley: University of California Press, 2001). On the state corporatist system of religious management, see Goossaert and Palmer, *The Religious Question*, 152–155. See also The State Ethnic Affairs Commission of the People's Republic of China website: http://www.seac.gov.cn/.

23. On the history of *minzu* discourse, see Thomas Mullaney, *Coming to Terms with the Nation: Ethnic Classification in Modern China* (Berkeley: University of California Press, 2011), 1–4; and James Liebold, *Reconfiguring Chinese Nationalism: How the Qing Frontier and Its Indigenes Became Chinese* (New York: Palgrave MacMillan, 2007), 8.

24. Miaoyan Yang, *Learning to Be Tibetan: The Construction of Ethnic Identity in China* (Lanham, Boulder, New York, London: Lexington Books, 2017), 5–10.

25. Yang, *Learning to Be Tibetan*, 5.

26. "Qinghai Nationalities University," accessed April 12, 2020, http://www.qhmu.edu.cn/.

27. See Gerald Roche's work on how linguistic diversity among ethnic Tibetans has been erased. Roche, "Articulating Language Oppression: Colonialism, Coloniality and the Erasure of Tibet's Minority Languages," *Patterns of Prejudice* 53, no. 5 (2019): 487–514, https://doi.org/10.1080/0031322X.2019.1662074. Stevan Harrell, "Introduction: Civilizing Projects and Reactions to Them," in *Cultural Encounters on China's Ethnic Frontiers* (Seattle: University of Washington Press, 1995).

28. Stoddard, "Tibetan Publications and National Identity in Tibet," 135–149.

29. "Minzu chubanshe," *State Ethnic Affairs Commission*, March 3, 2009, https://web.archive.org/web/20150924095905; http://www.seac.gov.cn/gjmw/mwjs/2009-03-05/1165370091213573.htm.

30. Dmu dge bsam gtan, "Rtsom pa po rang gi byung ba brjod pa rang gsal A dar sha" [Luminous mirror: the author's own telling of what happened]; hereafter "Rang gsal A dar sha" [Luminous mirror], in *Rje dmu dge bsam gtan rgya mtsho mi 'jigs dbyangs can dga' ba'i blo gros dpal bzang po'i gsung 'bum* [Collected works of Dmu dge bsam gtan, ocean of marvelous wisdom of the fearless Sarasvatī] (Xining: Mtsho sngon mi rigs dpe skrun khang, 1997), 1: 575.

31. Tsering Shakya, *The Dragon in the Land of Snows: A History of Modern Tibet Since 1947* (New York: Columbia University Press, 1999), 37.

32. See Goldstein, *A History of Modern Tibet, 1913–1951*, 690–694.

33. See Goldstein, *A History of Modern Tibet, 1913–1951*, 698–736; Tsering Shakya, *The Dragon in the Land of Snows*, 49.

34. Dalai Lama, "Biography and Daily Life," accessed April 10, 2020; https://www.dalailama.com/the-dalai-lama/biography-and-daily-life/birth-to-exile.

35. Dmu dge bsam gtan, "Rang gsal A dar sha" [Luminous mirror], 1: 576.

36. Goldstein, *A History of Modern Tibet, 1913–1951*, 812–813.

37. Goossaert and Palmer, *The Religious Question*, 153.

38. Goossaert and Palmer, *The Religious Question*, 153.

39. "Krung go nang bstan mthun tshogs, Ch. zhōngguó fójiào xiéhuì, 中国佛教协会."

40. Goossaert and Palmer, *The Religious Question*, 153.

41. Holmes Welch explains the Buddhist Association of China's constitution goals as, "To unite all the country's Buddhists so that they will participate, under the leadership of the People's Government, in movements for the welfare of the motherland and the defense of world peace; to help the People's Government fully carry out its policy of freedom of religious belief; to link up Buddhists

from different parts of the country; and to exemplify the best traditions of Buddhism." *Buddhism Under Mao* (Cambridge, Mass: Harvard University Press, 1972), 20.

42. Welch, *Buddhism Under Mao*, 10; see also Tuttle, *Tibetan Buddhists in the Making of Modern China*.

43. Xue Yu, "Buddhist Efforts at Reconciliation of Buddhism and Marxism in the Early Years of the People's Republic of China," in *Recovering Buddhism in Modern China*, ed. Jan Kiely and J. Brooks Jessup (New York: Columbia University Press, 2016), 177–215.

44. Dung dkar blo bzang 'phrin las, *Dung dkar tshig mdzod chen mo* [Dungkar encyclopedia] (Beijing: China Tibetology Publishing House, 2002), 1706.

45. *Dung dkar tshig mdzod chen mo*, ed. [n.a.], "Rtsom pa po ngo sprod mdor bsdus" [The author's brief biography], in *Dung dkar tshig mdzod chen mo* [Dungkar encyclopedia] (Beijing: Zhonguo zangxue chuban she [China Tibetology publishing house], 2002), 13.

46. Tsering Shakya, *The Dragon in the Land of Snows*, 205–208.

47. Interview with a former monk from Tséten Monastery, May 2008. According to Tséten Zhab-drung, the eighth Tséten Khenpo, Jigmé Rigpé Nyingpo (Tshe tan mkhan po 'Jigs med rigs pa'i snying po) "remained forever" (*brtan par bzhugs pa*) in his forty-seventh year, which would be 1958. Tshe tan zhabs drung, "Dan tig kgi dkar chag" [A catalogue of Dentik monastery], 2007, 3: 379.

48. Dmu dge bsam gtan, "Rang gsal A dar sha" [Luminous mirror], 1: 587.

49. "The Chinese People's Political Consultative Conference," Embassy of the People's Republic of China, accessed April 10, 2020; http://lr.china-embassy.org/eng/gyzg/jgiejgi/tfgajg/t372885.htm.

50. "Zi khron zhing chen srid gros skabs bzhi pa'i rgyun las U yon." Dmu dge bsam gtan, "Rang gsal A dar sha" [Luminous mirror], 1: 596.

51. "Zhōngguó rénmín zhèngzhì xiéshāng huìyì quánguó wěiyuánhuì 中国人民政治协商会议全国委员会." According to his son's biography, Dungkar Rinpoché was one of the Tibetan regional representatives from the fourth to sixth CPPCC sessions (1975–1988), but the fourth session had only one meeting in 1975, so it seems more likely that this occurred in 1978, when the Chinese People's Political Consultative Conference met alongside the National Congress. Dung dkar 'jigs med, "Sprul sku nas slob dpon chen mo—nga'i A pha lags phyir dran byas ba" [From tulku to professor: in remembrance of my father], *Krung go'i bod ljongs* [Chinese: Zhongguo Xizang; English: *China's Tibet*] 4, no. 27 (July 2014): 48. On Samding Dorje Phagmo, see Hildegard Diemberger, *When a Woman Becomes a Religious Dynasty* (New York: Columbia University Press, 2007), 308.

52. Pema Bhum, "An Overview of the Life of Professor Dungkar Lozang Trinlé Rinpoché," 25.

53. Pema Bhum, "An Overview of the Life of Professor Dungkar Lozang Trinlé Rinpoché," 25.

54. Tsering Shakya brought attention to the polarized state of modern Tibetan studies when he wrote, "Developments within Tibet since 1950 were not examined by western scholars. While this was partly because those areas remained inaccessible to foreigners, there was also a residual sense that there was nothing worthy of study in post-1950 Tibet; as if the apparent demise of traditional society rendered further studies valueless and uninteresting. This attitude appears to have been widespread among scholars in the Tibetan field, so that for example, contemporary language and literature have received little or no analysis. This absence of scholarly interest in contemporary developments in Tibet has tended to allow the field to be dominated by polemical writings from both sides." Tsering Shakya, "The Development of Modern Tibetan Studies," in *Resistance and Reform in Tibet*, ed. Robert Barnett and Shirin Akiner (New Delhi: Motilal Banarsiddass, 1994), 9. Since Tsering Shakya's pioneering dissertation work, *The Emergence of Modern Tibetan Literature: Gsar rtsom* (Dissertation School of Oriental and African Studies, University of London, 2004), subsequent research has made this a thriving field that is not as

politically polarized as historical studies. See Lauran Hartley, "Heterodox Views and the New Orthodox Poems: Tibetan Writers in the Early and Mid-Twentieth Century," in *Modern Tibetan Literature and Social Change*, ed. Lauran Hartley and Patricia Schiaffini-Vedani (Durham, N.C.: Duke University Press, 2008), 3–31; see 10–13 on how the contemporary writer Ju Kelzang drew from Giteng Rinpoché's poem "Young Döndrup." Lama Jabb similarly emphasizes a continuity between pre-1950 and post-1976 Tibetan literature; see *Oral and Literary Continuities in Modern Tibetan Literature: The Inescapable Nation* (Lanham and Boulder: Lexington Books, 2015).

55. Scholarly attention has been given to aspects of Tibetan religious life in the post-1978 era including: Tibetan monastic institutional rebuilding, recommencement of Tibetan pilgrimage, the emergence of the Ter-treasure movement in eastern Tibet and China, and the gendered process of incorporating Labrang Monastery into the PRC. On the rebuilding of monasteries and restoration of monastic sites, see Åshild Kolås and Monika Thowsen, *On the Margins of Tibet: Cultural Survival on the Sino-Tibetan Frontier* (Seattle: University of Washington Press, 2005). On pilgrimage, see Matthew T. Kapstein, "A Pilgrimage of Rebirth Reborn: The 1992 Celebration of the Drigung Powa Chenmo," in *Buddhism in Contemporary Tibet*, 95–119; the collected essays in Alex McKay, ed., *Pilgrimage in Tibet* (Richmond, Surrey: Curzon Press, 1998); Toni Huber, *The Cult of Pure Crystal Mountain: Popular Pilgrimage and Visionary Landscape in Southeast Tibet* (Oxford: Oxford University Press, 1999). On the "Ter Movement" see David Germano, "Re-membering the Dismembered Body of Tibet: Contemporary Visionary Movements in the People's Republic of China," in *Buddhism in Contemporary Tibet*, 53–94. On gender and Labrang Monastery, see Charlene Makley, *The Violence of Liberation: Gender and Tibetan Buddhist Revival in Post-Mao China* (Berkeley: University of California Press, 2007).

56. Gray Tuttle's pathbreaking work, *Tibetan Buddhists in the Making of Modern China*, paved the way for this study by showing the prominent role of Tibetan Buddhists in modern Chinese state formation during the Republican era. On relations between religion and the state in the PRC, I am also influenced by the reworking of Asad's theories in the case of China. On the modern construct of religion as integral to modern state formation, I am indebted to the scholarship within two collected volumes, one edited by Mayfair Yang, *Chinese Religiosities: Afflictions of Modernity and State Formation* (Berkeley: University of California Press, 2008) and the other edited by Yoshiko Ashiwa and David L. Wank, *Making Religion, Making the State* (Stanford, Calif.: Stanford University Press, 2009). See also Goossaert and Palmer, *The Religious Question in Modern China*, and Peter van der Veer, *The Modern Spirit of Asia: The Spiritual and the Secular in China and India* (Princeton, N.J.: Princeton University Press, 2013).

57. See Talal Asad, *Genealogies of Religion: Discipline and Reasons of Power in Christianity and Islam* (Baltimore, Md.: John Hopkins University Press, 1993) and *Formations of the Secular: Christianity, Islam and Modernity* (Stanford, Calif.: Stanford University Press, 2003).

58. Ashiwa and Wank, "Introduction," in *Making Religion, Making the State*, 5.

59. Ashiwa and Wank, "Introduction," in *Making Religion, Making the State*, 8.

60. Saba Mahmood, *Politics of Piety: The Islamic Revival and the Feminist Subject* (Princeton, N.J.: Princeton University Press, 2005), 34. See also Saba Mahmood, "Feminist Theory, Embodiment, and the Docile Agent: Some Reflections on the Egyptian Islamic Revival." *Cultural Anthropology* 16, no. 2 (May 2001): 202–236; Judith Butler, *Gender Trouble: Feminism and the Subversion of Identity* (New York and London: Routledge Classics, 1990); and Michel Foucault, "The Subject and Power," in *Michel Foucault: Beyond Structuralism and Hermeneutics*, ed. H. Dreyfus and P. Rabinow (Chicago: University of Chicago Press, 1983).

61. Mahmood, *Politics of Piety*, 34.

62. Mahmood, *Politics of Piety*, 29.

63. Orit Avishai, "'Doing Religion' in a Secular World: Women in Conservative Religions and the Question of Agency," *Gender and Society* 22, no. 4 (August 2008): 409–433.

64. Robert Ford Campany, "On the Very Idea of Religions (in the Modern West and in Early Medieval China)," *History of Religions* 42 (2003): 318, cf. Anne Swidler, *Talk of Love: How Culture Matters* (Chicago: Chicago University Press, 2001), 24–25.

65. Holly Gayley and Nicole Willock, "Theorizing the Secular in Tibetan Cultural Worlds," *Himalaya, the Journal of the Association of Nepal and Himalayan Studies* 36, no. 1 (2016): 12–21.

66. See Nils Ole Bubandt and Martijn van Beek, *Varieties of Secularism in Asia: Anthropological Explorations of Religion, Politics and the Spiritual* (New York: Routledge, 2012), 12.

67. Holly Gayley, *Love Letters from Golok: A Tantric Couple in Modern Tibet* (New York: Columbia University Press, 2017), 86.

68. José Cabezón adapted this analytical category from Western medieval studies to identify features that are useful for cross-cultural analysis. See Cabezón, *Buddhism and Language: A Study of Indo-Tibetan Scholasticism* (Albany: State University of New York Press, 1994) and *Scholasticism: Cross Cultural Perspectives* (Albany: State University of New York Press, 1998).

69. Jonathan Gold, *The Dharma's Gatekeepers: Sakya Paṇḍita on Buddhist Scholarship in Tibet* (Albany: State University of New York Press, 2007), ix.

70. Gold, *The Dharma's Gatekeepers*, x.

71. See David Jackson, *The Entrance Gate for the Wise Section III* (Wien: Arbeitskreis für Tibetische und Buddhistische Studien, Universität Wien, 1987); Gold, *The Dharma's Gatekeepers*; and Dge 'dun rab gsal, *Rig pa'i khye'u: dus rabs bcu bsum par tha snyad rig gnas bod la ji ltar slebs pa las 'phros pa'i dbyad rtsom dang gzhan* [Papers on the arrival of the literary field of knowledge in Tibet during the thirteenth century and beyond] (Dharamshala: Library of Tibetan Works and Archives, 2017).

72. Gold, *The Dharma's Gatekeepers*, 19.

73. Georges Dreyfus, *The Sound of Two Hands Clapping: The Education of a Tibetan Buddhist Monk* (Berkeley: University of California Press, 2003), 119.

74. Georges Dreyfus argued that there were two basic models of curriculum: that of the debating institution (*rtsod grwa*), found at the Three Seats of Learning, the Densa-sum, and the commentarial institution (*bshad grwa*), found in the three non-Geluk traditions. See Dreyfus, *The Sound of Two Hands Clapping*, 111.

75. Dreyfus, *The Sound of Two Hands Clapping*, 119.

76. Dreyfus, *The Sound of Two Hands Clapping*, 119.

77. Gold, *The Dharma's Gatekeepers*, 24.

78. See José Cabezón and David Jackson, eds., *Tibetan Literature: Studies in Genre* (Ithaca, N.Y.: Snow Lion, 1996).

79. With a few exceptions, the Tibetan-language sources used in this study are accessible from collections at large research libraries in the United States, such as the C. V. Starr East Asian Library at Columbia University in New York City and the Herman Wells Library at Indiana University in Bloomington, Indiana, as well as the Buddhist Digital Resource Center (BDRC).

80. Dungkar Lozang Trinlé, "Tibetan Wood Block Printing, Ancient Art and Craft," trans. Tsering Gonkatsang, *Himalaya* 36, no. 1 (Spring 2016): 163–171.

81. Nicole Willock, "Rekindling Ashes of the Dharma and the Formation of Modern Tibetan Studies: The Busy Life of Alak Tséten Zhabdrung," *Trace Foundation's Latse Library Newsletter* 6 (2009–2010): 2–25.

82. Ulrike Roesler, "Classifying Literature or Organizing Knowledge? Some Considerations on Genre Classifications in Tibetan Literature," in *Tibetan Literary Genres, Texts, and Text Types: From Genre Classification to Transformation*, ed. Jim Rheinigans (Leiden, Boston: Brill, 2015), 31–53.

83. Although sometimes literary titles are added by later editors, in these cases, based on internal textual evidence and biographic knowledge, the titles are self-penned.

84. The notes by Matthew Akester in his translator's introduction detail extensively autobiographies and biographies written in Tibetan and in English or translated; see Tubten Khétsun, *Memories of Life in Lhasa Under Chinese Rule*, trans. Matthew Akester (New York: Columbia University Press, 2008), xv–xvii.

85. Kurtis Schaeffer, "Tibetan Biography: Growth and Criticism," in *Edition, éditions, l'écrit au Tibet, évolution et devenir*, ed. Anne Chayet, Cristina Scherrer-Schaub, Françoise Robin, and Jean-Luc Achard (München: Indus Verlag, 2010), 263–306.

86. Andrew Quintman, *The Yogin and the Madman: Reading the Biographical Corpus of Tibet's Great Saint Milarepa* (New York: Columbia University Press, 2014), 7.

87. Tubten Khétsun, *Memories of Life in Lhasa*, xiv.

88. This is based on textual evidence within the autobiography as well as my interviews with Jigmé Chöpak ('Jigs med chos 'phags), Tséten Zhabdrung's nephew, who was a driving force behind the publication of the thirteen-volume *Collected Works* (2007). Tséten Zhabdrung's autobiography details when he wrote his life story:

> rang lo re brgyad pa'i lha babs dus chen nyin rang gyi byung ba brjod pa bden gtam rna ba'i bdud rtsis 'di 'bri ba'i mgo tshugs shing sgra dbyangs nyid kyis yi ger 'bebs pa'i ram btegs te phyi lo'i brgyad pa'i tshes mgor mtshams 'di la thug gi bar brtsams zin.

> On the Day of Divine Descent [the 22nd day of the eighth month] of my sixty-eighth year I began writing this piece titled, "Acoustic Ambrosia: A Truthful Telling of What Happened," with Drayang's (Sgra dbyangs) help in putting the words down. In the following year, in the first ten days of the eighth month, I was able to finish it.

> Tshe tan zhabs drung 'Jigs med rigs pa'i blo gros, "Mnyam med shākya'i dbang bo'i rjes zhugs pa 'jigs med rigs pa'i blo gros rang gi byung ba brjod pa bden gtam rna ba'i bdud rtsi" [Acoustic ambrosia: a truthful telling of what happened by Jigmé Rikpé Lodro, a disciple of the powerful, matchless Shākya], hereafter "Rna ba'i bdud rtsi" [Acoustic ambrosia], in *Mkhas dbang Tshe tan Zhabs drung 'Jigs med rigs pa'i blo gros kyi gsung rtsom* [The collected works of the scholar Tshe tan zhabs drung 'Jigs med rigs pa'i blo gros] ed. 'Phrin las (Xining: Qinghai minzu chubanshe, 1987), 1: 796.

89. Tshe tan zhabs drung, "Rna ba'i bdud rtsi" [Acoustic ambrosia], 1987, 1: 783–784.

> In my fifty-third year in the Water Tiger Year (1962) on the auspicious day of the winter solstice, led by Shardong Lozang Shedrup Gyatso (Shar gdong mchog sprul Blo bzang bshad sgrub rgya mtsho); my relative Mani Tülku Jigmé Legshé Drayang (rang dbon Ma ni'i sprul sku 'Jigs med legs bshad sgra dbyangs); Riku Tülku Gendün Ngawang Tendar (Ri khud sprul sku Dge 'dun ngag dbang bstan dar) accompanied by my students, Tsering Dorje (Tshe ring rdo rje) and Tséten, a lama from Tuwa Monastery (mthu ba bla ma Tshe brtan), presented me with a long silk *khatag* and various high-quality articles, and then urged me to write my autobiography using clear words and an intelligible style mixing both poetry and prose.

90. Interview with Jigmé Chöpak, July 2015.

91. Dmu dge bsam gtan, "Rang gsal A dar sha" [Luminous mirror], 1: 525–693.

92. Clifford Geertz, *The Interpretation of Cultures* (New York: Basic Books, 1973), 93–95.

93. Quintman, *The Yogin and the Madman*, 6–7.

94. E. Gene Smith, *Among Tibetan Texts* (Boston: Wisdom, 2001), 13–14.

95.   dad dang dam tshig gtsang ba'i slob tshogs kyis|
      don nyer dbyu gus rna ba'i rnga bo cher|

yang yang bsnun pa ma sron mgrin pa'i mkhar|
byung ba brjod pa'i sgra brgya dbang med ldir|

Tshe tan zhabs drung, "Rna ba'i bdud rtsi" [Acoustic ambrosia], 1987, 1: 500.

96. On the many variations and adaptations of this literary art, see the collected essays in Yigal Bronner, David Shulmann, and Gary Tubb, eds., *Innovations and Turning Points: Toward a History of Kāvya Literature* (Oxford: Oxford University Press, 2014).

97. These texts are: Dung dkar rin po che, "Snyan ngag la 'jug tshul tshig rgyan rig pa'i sgo 'byed" [Gateway to the art of literary figures for writing poetry]; in *Mkhas dbang dung dkar blo bzang 'phrin las kyi gsung 'bum* [Collected works of the great scholar Dungkar Lozang Trinle], ed. Rnam rgyal ra 'Phrin las rgya mtsho, 8 vols. (Beijing: Mi rigs dpe krun khang minzu chubanshe, 2004), vol. 1; Tshe tan zhabs drung, *Snyan ngag spyi don* [A general commentary on poetics] (Lanzhou: Gan su'u mi rigs dpe skrun khang, 2005, reprint); and Mugé Samten, "Bstan bcos la 'jug pa'i sgo mchod par brjod pa dang rtsom dam bca' ba bshad pa" [Reverence for the door that opens (poetic) commentaries and explanations of precious writings], in *Rje dmu dge bsam gtan rgya mtsho mi 'jigs dbyangs can dga' ba'i blo gros dpal bzang po'i gsung 'bum* [= Collected works of Dmu dge bsam gtan, ocean of marvelous wisdom of the fearless *Sarasvatī*], 6 vols. (Xining: Mtsho sngon mi rigs dpe skrun khang, 1997), vol. 4. Note that Mugé Samten's commentary is not studied in this book.

98. Tshe tan zhabs drung, *Snyan ngag spyi don* [A general commentary on poetics], 11.

99. Tséten Zhabdrung's Chinese name is Caidan Xiarong (才俱夏蓉).

100. Tshe tan zhabs drung, "Pan chen thams cad mkhyen cing gzigs pa chen po mdo smad 'khrungs gzhis phyogs su phebs pa'i legs mdzad cha shas tsam gyi ngo mtshar ba'i gtam gyi rtogs pa brjod pa dngul gyi me tog" [Avadana of silver flowers], in *Tshe tan zhabs drung rje btsun 'jigs med rigs pa'i blo gros mchog gi gsung 'bum* [Tséten Zhabdrung's collected works], ed. 'Jigs med chos 'phags (Beijing: Minzu chubanshe, 2007) 3: 263–278.

101. On *avadāna*, see J. N. Bhattacharya and Nilanjana Sarkar, eds., *Encyclopedic Dictionary of Sanskrit Literature* (Delhi: Global Vision Publishing House, 2004), 120.

102. Tshe tan zhabs drung, "Rtogs pa brjod pa dngul gyi me tog" [Avadāna of silver flowers], in *Collected Works*, 2007, 3: 278.

103. Tshe tan zhabs drung, "Rtogs brjod dngul gyi me tog" [Avadāna of silver flower (excerpt)], *Sbrang char* 16, no. 1 (1985): 29–30.

104. Dmu dge bsam gtan, "Bod kyi yi ge spyi rnam blo gsal 'jug ngogs" [Entryway to a clear mind: on Tibetan writing], in *Rje dmu dge bsam gtan rgya mtsho'i gsung 'bum* (Zi ling: Mtsho sngon mi rigs dpe skrun khang, 1997), 5: 1–304.

105. See note 97.

106. See "Sgrigs stangs," in Dung dkar blo bzang 'phrin las, *Dung dkar tshig mdzod chen mo* [Dungkar encyclopedia], 17.

107. According to the Buddhist Digital Resource Center (T220), *tshig mdzod* is a general term for "lexical material." It can include terms between primary and target languages or be specialized subject material; https://www.tbrc.org/#!rid=T220. This term is frequently translated as "dictionary," but in the case of the "Dung dkar tshig mdzod chen mo," "encyclopedia" is more apt because the entries hold detailed information. These terms, along with "Tha snyad gsar bsgrigs deb" [= The dictionary of new terms], were twentieth-century publication formats in the Tibetan context that accompanied Chinese colonization efforts. See Pema Bhum, "The Dictionary of New Terms and the Chinese-Tibetan Dictionary," *Trace Foundation's Latse Library Newsletter* (Fall 2005): 13–18.

108. See "mjug byung" [epilogue], *Dung dkar tshig mdzod chen mo* [Dungkar encyclopedia], 2386–2387.

109. Dge 'dun rab gsal, "bstan rtsis kun las btus pa dang lo tshigs dwangs shel me long gnyis bsur ba'i dpyad zhib thor bu zhig" [Notes comparing "A clear mirror: a chronology" and "A

comprehensive chronology"]; see https://www.tsanpo.com/forum/21992.html, accessed March 9, 2019.

110. Mugé Samten, *A History of Traditional Fields of Learning: A Concise History of Dissemination of Traditional Fields of Learning in Tibet (Bod du rig gnas dar tshul mdo bsdus bshad pa)*, tran. Sangye Tendar [bilingual edition, in English and Tibetan], (Dharamshala: Library of Tibetan Works and Archives, 2005).

I. THREE POLYMATHS

1. For this line of inquiry, I am indebted to Robert Ford Campany's analysis that draws upon Ann Swidler's research. See "On the Very Idea of Religions (in the Modern West and in Early Medieval China)," *History of Religions* 42 (2003): 287–319.

2. "Bstan pa yang dar skabs kyi bod kyi mkhas pa mi gsum" (Tibet's three polymaths of the *yang-dar* era), accessed April 9, 2018, http://mp.weixin.qq.com/s/cEmQi_DnlMdBKoFtriwCJg. The article was found under the category of "Zangzu lishi" (藏族历史), Chinese for "Tibetan history." I am indebted to Gedun Rabsal, who first shared the link with me on November 18, 2017. I accessed it again on January 12 and April 9, 2018. When I looked on June 11, 2018, the content had been removed. The same content (slightly reordered) appeared in an online journal, *Krung go'i bod ljongs dra ba (Tibet.CN)* attributed to the editor, Rin chen, "*Bstan pa yang dar skabs kyi bod kyi mkhas pa mi gsum*" (Three polymaths of the "*yang-dar*" era), March 3, 2018, last accessed October 28, 2019, https://web.archive.org/web/20190702181514/http://tb.tibet.cn/tb/people/201803 /t20180328_5591229.html.

    The banner of the Tibetan language article states that the editor originally published this on the web (*yong khongs nged dra ba*). This signals that Rinchen, the editor, is perhaps also the author of the article on Weixin, but no authorial attribution was provided. See also note 7 in the previous chapter.

3. It literally means "again" (*yang*) "to spread" (*dar*), referring to "The Teachings" (*bstan pa*), i.e, Buddhadharma.

4. Personal communication with Zla ba blo gros, *Sbrang char* (Spring rain) editorial office, Xining, May 2008.

5. Tshe tan zhabs drung, "Rna ba'i bdud rtsi" [Acoustic ambrosia], 1987, 1: 513–514.

6. For western equivalents of Tibetan dates, I referred to Dieter Schuh, *Untersuchungen zur Geschichte der tibetische Kalenderrechnung* (Wiesbaden: Franz Steiner Verlag Gmbh, 1973), 223.

7. Tshe tan zhabs drung, "Rna ba'i bdud rtsi" [Acoustic ambrosia], 1987, 1: 511.

8. bdag gi mes po gong ma rnams ni rigs gzhan gyi rtsi dang ma 'dres pa'i rgya nag gi rigs yin zhing| bdag gi pha nas bzung rgya bod kyi rigs 'dres ma can du gyur par ma zad| nga rang ni skad yig goms srol gnas yul bzhi'i sgo nas rigs 'byed pa'i dbang du btang na bod kyi rigs su gtongs te| Tshe tan zhabs drung, "Rna ba'i bdud rtsi" [Acoustic ambrosia], 1987, 1: 505. On the Chinese adaptation of ethnic classification categories developed by Stalin, cf. Thomas Mullaney, *Coming to Terms with the Nation: Ethnic Classification in Modern China* (Berkeley: University of California Press, 2011), 80–85.

9. Cf. Gray Tuttle, "Local History in A mdo: The Tsong kha Range (ri rgyud)," *Asian Highlands Perspectives* 6 (2010): 23–97.

10. The Tibetan spelling of this monastery varies. See Tuttle, "Local History in A mdo," 33.

11. The entry under "'Jigs med rigs pa'i blo gros" in the *Mdo smad lo rgyus chen mo* mistakenly identifies Tshe tan Zhabs drung as an incarnation of Tshe tan mkhan po, but these were two different

incarnation lineages. See Hor tshang 'Jigs med, *Mdo smad lo rgyus chen mo* [Extensive history of Amdo] (Dharamsala: Library of Tibetan Works and Archives, 2009), 6: 414.

12.   Luciano Petech, *Aristocracy and Government in Tibet 1728–1959* (Roma: Istituto Italiano per il medio ed estremo Oriente), 238.

13.   The Chinese characters are based on my fieldwork in 2008 and not represented in the Tibetan narrative.

14.   Tshe tan zhabs drung, "Rna ba'i bdud rtsi" [Acoustic ambrosia], 1987, 1: 529–531; 554–557; Tshe tan zhabs drung, "Mdo smad grub pa'i gnas chen dan tig shel gyi ri bo le lag dang bcas pa'i dkar chag don ldan ngag gi rgyud mangs," abbreviated as "Dan tig gi dkar chag" [A catalogue of Dentik Monastery], in *Tshe tan zhabs drung rje btsun 'Jigs med rigs pa'i blo gros mchog gi gsung 'bum* [The collected works of the venerable Tshe tan zhabs drung 'Jigs med rigs pa'i blo gros] (Beijing: Mi rigs dpe skrun khang, 2007), 3: 279–402.

15.   A short biography on his life is found in Tshe tan zhabs drung, "Rna ba'i bdud rtsi" [Acoustic ambrosia], 1987, 1: 747.

16.   The Collected Topics form the basis for teaching students the techniques and fundamental concepts in debate. For a description of the monastic curriculum and the role of the Collected Topics, see Georges Dreyfus, *The Sound of Two Hands Clapping: The Education of a Tibetan Buddhist Monk* (Berkeley: University of California Press, 2003), 79–149, especially p. 110.

17.   As Lauran Hartley noted, Marnang Dorjé chang Jigmé Damchö Gyatso was considered to be the incarnation of Giteng Rinpoché's deceased teacher Jigmé Samten ('Jigs med bsam gtan, 1814–1897); therefore, Giteng Rinpoché was especially vested in his pupil's education. See Lauran Hartley, "Heterodox Views and the New Orthodox Poems: Tibetan WritersWriters in the Early and Mid-Twentieth Century," in *Modern Tibetan Literature and Social Change*, ed. Lauran Hartley and Patricia Schiaffini-Vedani (Durham and London: Duke University Press, 2008), 11.

18.   Tshe tan zhabs drung, "Rna ba'i bdud rtsi" [Acoustic ambrosia], 1987, 1: 653–654.

19.   According to two local informants who wish to remain anonymous, this occurred in 1965, before the Cultural Revolution started. This was not confirmed by other sources.

20.   Tshe tan zhabs drung, "Rna ba'i bdud rtsi" [Acoustic ambrosia], 1987, 1: 583.

21.   Tséten Zhabdrung wrote, "According to the wishes of tantric masters of Mthu ba grong, 'Od dkar brag rdzong or Ra ma 'dan ma, Cha rgya, Ka thung, and Tshe tan, I implemented the monastic constitutions (*bca' yig*), appointed the official positions for the year, and then I took the lead in a few Dharma sessions, taking on the appearance of a tantric master by holding the vajra and drum, and saying [the Nyingma Guru Rinpoché prayer, which begins with] 'In the first of earlier eons . . . (*sngon gyi bskal ba dang bo la*)' as the words of the rites rolled off my tongue," Tshe tan zhabs drung, "Rna ba'i bdud rtsi" [Acoustic ambrosia], 1987, 1: 583. See also Tshe tan zhabs drung, "Rna ba'i bdud rtsi" [Acoustic ambrosia], 1987, 1: 567–568, 587, 599, 615, 653–657.

22.   Tséten Zhabdrung wittily relayed that he adhered to his monastic vows throughout his life, despite crying when his head was first shaved at age six. Because the Sixth Dalai Lama had cried when his head was shaved the first time, this was construed as a sign that a monk would renounce his vows. Tshe tan zhabs drung, "Rna ba'i bdud rtsi" [Acoustic ambrosia], 1987, 1: 537.

23.   Tshe tan zhabs drung, "Rna ba'i bdud rtsi" [Acoustic ambrosia], 1987, 1: 538–539, 569–570, 798.

24.   These include among others: "An Analysis of a Few Mistakes in Golo's Historical Dates" ('Gos los [Gzhon nu dpal] lo tshigs bkod pa'i skor las 'ga' zhig nor ba'i dpyad pa); "An Analysis of Historical Dates in the *New Red Annals* by Panchen Sonam Drakpa" (Paṇ chen bSod [nams] grags [pa] kyi rgyal rabs 'phrul gyi lde mig deb dmar gsar ba'i lo tshigs kyi dpyad pa); "An Analysis of the Historical Dates in Pawo Tsuklak Trengwa's *History of Buddhism*" (Dpa' bo gtsug lag 'phreng ba chos 'byung gi lo tshigs kyi dpyad pa); "An Analysis of the Historical Dates in the Fifth Dalai Lama's *Feast of the Early Years of the Buddhist Era*" (Rgyal dbang lnga ba rin po che'i deb ther rdzogs ldan gzhon nu'i dga' ston gyi lo tshigs la dpyad pa; "An Analysis of Historical Dates in Regent Sangye

Gyatso's Works; Including the *White Beryl* and *Corrections to the White Beryl*, etc." (Sde srid Sangs rgyas rgya mtsho'i bai [DUrya] dkar dang [bai DUrya] g.ya' sel sogs kyi lo tshigs la dpyad pa); "An Analysis of Historical Dates in Compositions by Sumpa Yeshe Paljor (Sum pa Ye shes dpal 'byor gyis bsgrigs pa'i lo tshigs la dpyad pa)," all in *Mkhas dbang Tshe tan zhabs drung gi dpyad rtsom mkho bsdus* [A useful collection of essays by the great scholar Tshe tan zhabs drung] (Lanzhou: Gansu minzu chuban she, 1991).

25. Tshe tan zhabs drung, "Rna ba'i bdud rtsi" [Acoustic ambrosia], 1987, 1:590.

26. Tshe tan zhabs drung, "Rna ba'i bdud rtsi" [Acoustic ambrosia], 1987, 1:753.

27. This is similar to other Tibetan authors at the time. As Lauran Hartley stated, "The projects of the 1950s maintained a critical thread of continuity from the pre-Communist era, laying the foundation for later literary negotiation." See "Heterodox Views and the New Orthodox Poems," 24.

28. Held in the rare books collection of the East Asian Library at Columbia University. I would like to express my gratitude to Lauran Hartley for this information.

29. I am deeply indebted to Pema Bhum for this information.

30. "*dengs rabs dang mthun pa,*" see Tshe tan zhabs drung, "Rna ba'i bdud rtsi" [Acoustic ambrosia], 1987, 1:778.

31. Tshe tan zhabs drung, "Rna ba'i bdud rtsi" [Acoustic ambrosia], 1987, 1: 778.

32. This history of Tibetan grammar (*Thon mi'i zhal lung*) is an extremely influential work. It is now in its tenth print run at 40,030 copies.

33. Tshe tan zhabs drung, "Rna ba'i bdud rtsi" [Acoustic ambrosia], 1987, 1:787. Tséten Zhabdrung did not specify the name of the prison he was incarcerated in for twelve years. He only mentions being confined in "*khri mon,*" a poetic name for prison. I am grateful to Gedun Rabsal for his assistance in translation of this term. Dungkar Rinpoché's brief biography on Tséten Zhabdrung states that he was incarcerated in Nantan (南滩) prison. See Dung dkar Blo bzang 'phrin las, *Dung dkar tshig mdzod chen mo* [Dungkar encyclopedia] (Beijing: Zhongguo Zangxue chubanshe, 2002), 1706. This was further affirmed by personal communication in March 2008.

34. Tshe tan zhabs drung, "Rna ba'i bdud rtsi" [Acoustic ambrosia], 1987, 1: 789.

35. Tshe tan zhabs drung, "Rna ba'i bdud rtsi" [Acoustic ambrosia], 1987, 1: 799.

36. Personal communication with Pema Bhum, October 2, 2009, Latse Library, New York City.

37. Personal communication with Gao Rui (Gna' gong dkon mchog tshe brtan), September 19, 2008, Lanzhou, China.

38. "Caidan xiarong jiangxuejin zhongxue xiangmu shewei" (才旦夏茸奖学金中学项目设立) [Setting up the Tséten Zhabdrung scholarship fund project], *Qinghai News*, www.qhnews.com/index /system/2006/10/11/000009177.shtml as of February 16, 2017.

39. Name withheld. Personal communication, September 2008.

40. Personal communication with Gao Rui (Gna' gong dkon mchog tshe brtan), September 19, 2008, Lanzhou, China.

41. Dmu dge bsam gtan, "Rang gsal A dar sha" [Luminous mirror], 1: 529.

42. Dmu dge bsam gtan, "Rang gsal A dar sha" [Luminous mirror], 1: 531. For Western calendrical equivalents, see Schuh, *Untersuchungen zur Geschichte der tibetische Kalenderrechnung*, 224.

43. See Dhondup Tashi, "A Monastic Scholar Under China's Occupation of Tibet: Mugé Samten's Autobiography and His Role as a Vernacular Intellectual" (MA thesis, University of British Columbia, January 2019).

44. Dmu dge bsam gtan, "Rang gsal A dar sha" [Luminous mirror], 1: 531.

45. Dmu dge bsam gtan, "Rang gsal A dar sha" [Luminous mirror], 1: 531.

46. Dmu dge bsam gtan, "Rang gsal A dar sha" [Luminous mirror], 1: 531.

47. Dmu dge bsam gtan, "Rang gsal A dar sha" [Luminous mirror], 1: 531.

48. Dmu dge bsam gtan, "Rang gsal A dar sha" [Luminous mirror], 1: 533.

49. Dmu dge bsam gtan, "Rang gsal A dar sha" [Luminous mirror], 1: 534.

50.   Dmu dge bsam gtan, "Rang gsal A dar sha" [Luminous mirror], 1: 534–535.

51.   Dmu dge bsam gtan, "Rang gsal A dar sha" [Luminous mirror], 1: 560.

52.   Dmu dge bsam gtan, "Rang gsal A dar sha" [Luminous mirror], 1: 561.

53.   Dmu dge bsam gtan, "Rang gsal A dar sha" [Luminous mirror], 1: 562.

54.   Paul Kocot Nietupski, *Labrang Monastery: A Tibetan Buddhist Community on the Inner Asian Borderlands, 1709–1959* (Lanham, Md.: Rowman & Littlefield, 2011), 188.

55.   Dmu dge bsam gtan, "Rang gsal A dar sha" [Luminous mirror], 1: 570.

56.   Dmu dge bsam gtan, "Rang gsal A dar sha" [Luminous mirror], 1: 571.

57.   Dmu dge bsam gtan, "Rang gsal A dar sha" [Luminous mirror], 1: 571–573.

58.   Dmu dge bsam gtan, "Rang gsal A dar sha" [Luminous mirror], 1: 564, "bdag chab srid kyi phyog la rgyus med."

59.   Xue Yu, "Buddhist Efforts at Reconciliation of Buddhism and Marxism in the Early Years of the People's Republic of China," in *Recovering Buddhism in Modern China*, ed. Jan Kiely and J. Brooks Jessup (New York: Columbia University Press, 2016), 177–215.

60.   Dmu dge bsam gtan, "Rang gsal A dar sha" [Luminous mirror], 1: 574–576.

61.   Dmu dge bsam gtan, "Rang gsal A dar sha" [Luminous mirror], 1: 576.

62.   Dmu dge bsam gtan, "Rang gsal A dar sha" [Luminous mirror], 1: 577.

63.   Dmu dge bsam gtan, "Rang gsal A dar sha" [Luminous mirror], 1: 578–579.

64.   Wylie: lha rgyal gling srid gzhung rig gnas kho'i kho krang zhon pa.

65.   Dmu dge bsam gtan, "Rang gsal A dar sha" [Luminous mirror], 1:583.

66.   Wylie: Krung dbyang mi rigs dpe skrun khang. The Chinese is not given in the text, but this is the Tibetan transcription of the Chinese: Zhongyang Minzu chubanshe (中央民族出版社), more commonly referred to as "Minzu chubanshe" or "Minzu Press." Dmu dge bsam gtan, "Rang gsal A dar sha" [Luminous mirror], 1: 597.

67.   Dmu dge bsam gtan, "Rang gsal A dar sha" [Luminous mirror], 1: 597. See also Mao Zedong, *Mao' tse tung gi gsung rtsom gces bsdus* [Mao Zedong's collected works] [in Tibetan] (Beijing: Beijing minzu chubanshe, 1992 [reprint]).

68.   Dmu dge bsam gtan, "Rang gsal A dar sha" [Luminous mirror], 1: 597.

69.   Lauran Hartley, "Con**text**ually Speaking: Tibetan Literary Discourse and Social Change in the People's Republic of China" (PhD diss., Indiana University, 2003), 168; Tsering Shakya, "Politicisation and the Tibetan Language," in *Resistance and Reform in Tibet*, ed. Robert Barnett and Shirin Akin (London: C. Hurt & Co.; Delhi: Motilal Banarsidass, 1994). 159; Dmu dge bsam gtan, "Rang gsal A dar sha" [Luminous mirror], 1: 600.

70.   Dmu dge bsam gtan, "Rang gsal A dar sha" [Luminous mirror], 1: 590–594.

71.   Dmu dge bsam gtan, "Rang gsal A dar sha" [Luminous mirror], 1: 596.

72.   Dmu dge bsam gtan, "Rang gsal A dar sha" [Luminous mirror], 1: 599.

73.   Personal communication.

74.   Dmu dge bsam gtan, "Bod kyi yi ge spyi rnam blo gsal 'jug ngogs" [Entryway to a clear mind: on Tibetan writing], in *Rje dmu dge bsam gtan rgya mtsho'i gsung 'bum* [Mugé Samten's collected works] (Xining: Mtsho sngon mi rigs dpe skrun khang, 1997), 5: 25.

75.   Dmu dge bsam gtan, "Rang gsal A dar sha" [Luminous mirror], 1: 600.

76.   Dmu dge bsam gtan, "Rang gsal A dar sha" [Luminous mirror], 1: 603.

77.   Lama Jabb points out that this work avoids erotic poetry; see *Oral and Literary Continuities in Modern Tibetan Literature: The Inescapable Nation* (Lanham, Md. and Boulder, Colo.: Lexington Books, 2015), 224 n. 6.

78.   Dmu dge bsam gtan, "Rang gsal A dar sha" [Luminous mirror], 1: 606–607.

79.   Dmu dge bsam gtan, "Rang gsal A dar sha" [Luminous mirror], 1: 694.

80.   Dmu dge bsam gtan, "Rang gsal A dar sha" [Luminous mirror], 1: 609–694.

81. Wylie: 'Bar khams khul srid gros.

82. Dmu dge bsam gtan, "Rang gsal A dar sha" [Luminous mirror], 1: 707.

83. One biography is by Lhag pa phun tshogs, "Dung dkar rin po che'i dgongs pa shul 'dzin byas nas bod rig pa dar rgyas gong 'phel gtong dgos—mkhas pa'i dbang po dung dkar rin po che mchog la snying thag pa nas dran gso zhu" [Heartfelt commemoration of the Venerable Dungkar Rinpoché: The need to set in motion the prosperity of Tibetan Studies having inherited the legacy of Dungkar Rinpoché], in *Mkhas dbang Dung dkar blo bzang 'phrin las kyi gsung 'bum* [Collected works of the scholar Dungkar Lozang Trinle], vol. 1 (Beijing: Nationalities Publishing House, 2004), 1–20; see also "Rtsom pa po ngo spro mdor bdus" [A brief biography on the author], in *Dung dkar tshig mdzod chen mo* [Dungkar encyclopedia] (Beijing: Zhongguo Zangxue chubanshe, 2002), 13–16.

84. Pema Bhum, "An Overview of the Life of Professor Dungkar Lozang Trinle," *Trace Foundation's Latse Library Newsletter* 5 (2007–2008): 18–35.

85. Dung dkar 'jigs med, "Sprul sku nas slob dpon chen mo—nga'i A pha lags phyir dran byas ba" [From tulku to professor: in remembrance of my father], *Krung go'i bod ljongs*, Zhongguo Xizang 中国西藏 [China's Tibet] 4, no. 27 (July 2014): 46–51.

86. Bstan 'dzin dge legs, "Chos dung karpo'i rang mdangs/ slob dpon chen mo dung dkar blo bzang 'phrin las mchog nub phyogs yul du snga phyir mjal ba'i bag chags rab rim" [In memory of meeting Dungkar Rinpoché in the west—the Resplendent White Conch], *gTam Tshogs* [Collection of sayings] 1, no. 37 (July 2017): 11–43.

87. Dung dkar 'jigs med, "Sprul sku nas slob dpon chen mo" [From tulku to professor], 46.

88. Lhag pa phun tshogs, "mkhas pa'i dbang po dung dkar rin po che mchog la snying thag pa nas dran gso zhu" [Heartfelt commemoration of the Venerable Dungkar Rinpoché], 3.

89. There is no entry in the chronological tables at the end of his encyclopedia on this event. According to Dungkar Jigmé this occurred in 1932, but Lhakpa Phuntsok's biography, "Rtsom pa po ngo spro mdor bdus" [A brief biography on the author] in *Dung dkar tshig mdzod chen mo*, and the appendix at the end of volume 2 of the author's *Collected Works* all give 1931.

90. See "Rtsom pa po ngo spro mdor bdus" [A brief biography on the author] in *Dung dkar tshig mdzod chen mo*, 13. On the monastic curriculum in general, see also Dreyfus, *The Sound of Two Hands Clapping*, 79–149.

91. See "Rtsom pa po ngo spro mdor bdus" [A brief biography on the author] in *Dung dkar tshig mdzod chen mo*, 13.

92. Pema Bhum, "An Overview of the Life of Professor Dungkar Lozang Trinle," 20; Dung dkar 'jigs med, "Sprul sku nas slob dpon chen mo" [From tulku to professor], 50.

93. "Rtsom pa po ngo spro mdor bdus" [A brief biography on the author], in *Dung dkar tshig mdzod chen mo*, 14.

94. Dung dkar blo bzang 'phrin las, "*lo tshigs dwangs shel me long*" [The clear mirror: a chronology] in *Dung dkar tshig mdzod chen mo*, 2379.

95. Thanks to Eveline Yang for deciphering the Chinese characters.

96. Dung dkar 'jigs med, "Sprul sku nas slob dpon chen mo" [From tulku to professor], 49.

97. Personal communication with Heather Stoddard via Skype, October 8, 2017.

98. Dung dkar 'jigs med, "Sprul sku nas slob dpon chen mo" [From tulku to professor], 47; Pema Bhum, "An Overview of the Life of Professor Dungkar Lozang Trinle," 22.

99. Pema Bhum, "An Overview of the Life of Professor Dungkar Lozang Trinle," 30–31.

100. Dung dkar 'jigs med, "Sprul sku nas slob dpon chen mo" [From tulku to professor], 49.

101. Photo courtesy of Thupden Trinley. See Pema Bhum, "An Oveview of the Life of Professor Dungkar Lozang Trinle," 31.

102. Matthew Akester, "Obituary: Dungkar Losang Trinley," *Independent,* August 25, 1997, https://www.independent.co.uk/news/people/obituary-dungkar-losang-trinley-1247293.html.

103. Tibet Information Network, "Leading Scholar Dies, Cultural Criticism," August 4, 1997, https://www.columbia.edu/itc/ealac/barnett/pdfs/link2-dlt-obit.pdf.

104. Tenzin Monlam, "Tibetan Scholar Dungkar Rinpoche's 20th Death Anniversary," *Phayul*, July 24, 2017, http://www.phayul.com/news/article.aspx?id=39319&t=1.

105. Gerald Vizenor, *Manifest Manners: Narratives on Postindian Survivance* (Lincoln and London: University of Nebraska Press, 1999), vii, 3–5, 66–68.

106. Ann Swidler, *Talk of Love and How Culture Matters* (Chicago and London: University of Chicago Press, 2001), 19.

107. Swidler, *Talk of Love*, 22.

108. Ronald Davidson, *Tibetan Renaissance: Tantric Buddhism in the Rebirth of Tibetan Culture* (New York: Columbia University Press, 2005), 88–92; Heather Stoddard, "Rekindling the Flame: A Note on Royal Patronage in Tenth Century Tibet," in *The Relationship between Religion and State* (chos srid zung 'brel) *in Traditional Tibet*, ed. Christoph Cüppers (Lumbini: Lumbini International Research Institute, 2004), 49–104.

109. Bu ston Rin chen grub, *Bu ston chos 'byung* (Pe cin [Beijing]: Krung go bod kyi shes rig dpe skrun khang, 1988), 193–195; E. Obermiller, trans, *The History of Buddhism in India and Tibet by Buston*, originally published as *Bu ston chos 'byung* [in Tibetan] (Delhi: Classics India Publications, 1999 [reprint]), 203–205; 'Gos Lo tsā ba Gzhon nu dpal, *Deb ther sngon po* [*The blue annals*] (Chengdu: Si khron mi rigs dpe skrun khang, 1984 [reprint]), 89–94.

110. 'Gos lo tsā ba gzhon nu dpal, *Deb ther sngon po* [*Blue annals*], 89–94; Georges Roerich, trans., *The Blue Annals* (*Deb ther sngon po*) (Delhi: Motilal Banarsidass, 1996 [reprint]), 63–67.

111. Tséten Zhabdrung drew upon many sources before coming to a conclusion on Gongpa Rabsel's dates. His comparison of a range of historical sources and calculations deserves further attention, which lies beyond the scope of this study. One of his main points concerned Gongpa Rabsel's young age at the time of ordination. He also claimed that Gongpa Rabsel's ordination of the men from Tibet, especially Lumé, is historically attested. He based most of his claims on a text called *Tshul she'i chos 'byung* (Tshul she's religious history), which dates Klu mes' ordination at 976 C.E. See "Mnyams med sha'kya'i rgyal bo 'das 'phrungs kyi lo tshigs gtsor gyur pa'i bstan rtsis lo sum stong tsam re'u mig gi rnam gzhag mthong tshad kun las btus pa," and "Bla chen dgongs pa rab gsal gyi rnam par thar ba mdo tsam brjod pa thub bstan khang bzang mdzes pa'i tog," both in *Tshe tan zhabs drung rje btsun 'jigs med rigs pa'i blo gros mchog gi gsung 'bum* (Beijing: Mi rigs dpe skrun khang, 2007), 7: 145 and vol. 3: 187–190. Cf. Davidson, *Tibetan Renaissance*, 92–99.

112. Luciano Petech, "Tibetan Relations with Sung China and with the Mongols," in *China Among Equals: The Middle Kingdom and Its Neighbors, 10th–14th Centuries*, ed. Morris Rossabi (Berkeley: University of California, Press, 1983), 173–174. On Tibetan rulership and the Tsongkha kingdom, see Tsutomu Iwasaki, "The Tibetan Tribes of Ho-hsi and Buddhism During the Northern Sung Period," *Acta Asiatica* 64 (1993): 20–239; see also Rolf Stein, *Recherches sur l'épopée et la barde au Tibet*, Bibliothèque de l'Institute des hautes études chinoises, vol. 13 (Paris: Presses universitaires de France, 1959), 145.

113. Tshe tan zhabs drung, "Rna ba'i bdud rtsi" [Acoustic ambrosia], 1: 558–559.

> lo de'i dpyid phyogs dan tig gi dge ba'i bshes gnyen lha rams pa ngag dbang tshul khrims kyis dbus gtsang nas byin rten du ma gdan drangs nas rang dgon du phebs dus rten rnams la zhib mjal zhus| lha rams pa tshang la gsol ja drangs thog bdag gis mkhas pa mi gsum zhes pa gang dang gang red ces zhus par| khong bas gtsang ba rab gsal| g.yo dge 'byung| dmar śākyamuni gsum red gsungs pa dga' bzhin du sems la bzung|

114. *Dan dou si jian shi* (*Dan tig dkar chag*) [*A brief history of Dentik monastery*]. Sections translated into English by Nicole Willock (rigs pa'i chos 'dzin; Ni ke) ([n.p.]. Retrieved at monastery, 2008), 6.

115.   Interview with anonymous informant at Tséten Monastery, May 2008. In her fieldwork in Amdo, Jane Caple noted stories of locals protecting and hiding sacred objects. See Jane E. Caple, *Morality and Monastic Revival in Post-Mao Tibet* (Honolulu: University of Hawai'i Press, 2019), 31. Tsering Shakya documents how later campaigns during the Cultural Revolution, such as smashing "The Four Olds" (old thoughts, old culture, old customs, and old habits), caused widespread destruction in Tibetan cultural areas and the Autonomous Region; see Tsering Shakya, *The Dragon in the Land of Snows*, 315–324. On how the Cultural Revolution affected minorities, see June Teufel Dreyer, *China's Forty Millions* (Cambridge and London: Harvard University Press, 1976), 205–235.

116.   Tshe tan zhabs drung, "Rna ba'i bdud rtsi" [Acoustic ambrosia], 1: 779.

117.   Toni Huber, "Putting the *gnas* back into *gnas-skor*," in *Sacred Spaces and Powerful Places in Tibetan Culture,* ed. Toni Huber (Dharamsala: Library of Tibetan Works and Archives, 1999), 88.

118.   Mkhas shing grub pa'i skyes chen rim byon du mas zhabs kyi bcags shing byin gyis brlabs pa'i brag rdzong. Tshe tan zhabs drung, "Dan tig dkar chag" [A catalogue of Dentik monastery], 3:280.

119.   "'Phags pa rgyal bu don grub kyi mdo," in *Bka' 'gyur* (sde dge par phud), mdo sde, volume aH (76). TBRC W22084.

120.   The first section of *A Catalogue of Dentik* is on the reasons it is a natural place for meditation. It details the lives of these three important Buddhist figures. Tshe tan zhabs drung, "Dan tig dkar chag" [A catalogue of Dentik monastery], 3: 281–339. Tséten Zhabdrung also wrote a biography of Gongpa Rabsel, a section of which is devoted to the Three Polymaths; see "Bla chen dgongs pa rab gsal gyi rnam par thar pa mdo tsam brjod pa thub bstan khan bzang mdzes pa'i tog," 3: 199.

121.   Mugé Samten, *A History of Traditional Fields of Learning: A Concise History of Dissemination of Traditional Fields of Learning in Tibet (Bod du rig gnas dar tshul mdo bsdus bshad pa)*, trans. Sangye Tandar Naga [bilingual edition, in English and Tibetan] (Dharamshala: Library of Tibetan Works and Archives, 2005), 29–30. "Then having loaded the books of Tripitaka onto a mule's back, the three scholars Tsang Rabsel, Yo Gejung and Mar Shakyamuni hiding by day and traveling by night, fled . . . They went to the Amdo region and stayed near the Machu River. Their residence of monastery was formed at Dentik where they spent their time in meditation. The fame of these three scholars spread far and wide. Their relics were preserved in Xining. Lachen Gongpa Rabsel (953–1035) was their disciple who is credited with the reviving the fire of the Teaching from the lower regions, and therefore his fame spread like the sound of thunder."

122.   Mugé Samten, *A History of Traditional Fields of Learning*, 34.

123.   *"mkhas pa mi gsum," Dung dkar tshig mdzod chen mo*, 443.

124.   Dung-dkar blo-bzang 'phrim-las, *The Merging of Religious and Secular Rule in Tibet*, trans. Chen Guansheng (Beijing: Foreign Languages Press, 1991), 31–33.

125.   Pema Bhum, "An Overview of the Life of Professor Dungkar Lozang Trinlé Rinpoché," 25.

126.   Information Office of the State Council of the People's Republic of China, China's White Papers on Tibet (September 1992), Beijing, accessed November 12, 2017; http://www.china.org.cn/e-white/tibet/index.htm.

127.   Personal communication with Zla ba Blo gros and Sangs rgyas rgyal in interviews in April 2008 and July 2008 respectively.

128.   Charlene Makley, *The Battle for Fortune: State-led Development, Personhood, and Power Among Tibetans in China* (Ithaca, N.Y.: Cornell University Press, 2018), 17.

129.   Makley, *The Battle for Fortune*, 60–61.

130.   In the speech cited by Makley, the term *yang-dar* is not used. It remains to be researched at what point this term began to be used in reference to the post-Mao era. It was used by many of my Tibetan interlocutors during my fieldwork in Qinghai in 2008 and 2015.

2. "TELLING WHAT HAPPENED"

1. Martsang (Dmar Gtsang) is formed by combining the first syllables of the names of Dmar Shakyamuni and Gtsang rab gsal. It is known in Chinese by the name Baimasi. On how the Third Thu'u bkwan, Blo bzang chos kyi nyi ma (1727–1802), embellished the *Blue Annals* in order to connect the three historical polymaths with the lives of his teachers, see Nicole Willock, "Thu'u bkwan's Literary Adaptations of the Life of Dgongs pa rab gsal," in *Trails of Tibetan Tradition: Papers for Elliot Sperling*, ed. Roberto Vitali (Dharamsala: Amnye Machen Institute, 2014), 586–590.

2. The Tibetan term *chu* translates as "river" in this context.

3. This type of poetic sparring is common in Tibetan literary culture. See Gedun Rabsal and Nicole Willock, "Dictums for Developing Virtue," in *A Gathering of Brilliant Moons: Practice Advice from the Rimé Masters of Tibet,* ed. Holly Gayley and Joshua Schapiro (Somerville, Mass.: Wisdom, 2017).

4. Tshe tan zhabs drung, "Mnyam med shākya'i dbang bo'i rjes zhugs pa 'jigs med rigs pa'i blo gros rang gi byung ba brjod pa bden gtam rna ba'i bdud rtsi" [Acoustic ambrosia: a truthful telling of what happened by Jigmé Rikpé Lodro, a disciple of the powerful, matchless Shākya], in *Mkhas dbang Tshe tan Zhabs drung 'Jigs med rigs pa'i blo gros kyi gsung rtsom* [The collected works of the scholar Tshe tan zhabs drung 'Jigs med rigs pa'i blo gros], ed. 'Phrin las (Xining: Qinghai minzu chubanshe, 1987), 1: 503.

5. Wylie: "Dza landha ra." It is considered a sacred place in India in Tibetan tantric texts. See David Snellgrove, *The Hevajra Tantra: A Critical Study: Part I: Introduction and Translation, Part II: Sanskrit and Tibetan Text* (London: School of Oriental and African Studies, 1959) 1: 70; cf. Samuel Beal, *Chinese Accounts of India. Translation of Si yu ki: Buddhist Records of the Western World* (Calcutta: Susil Gupta, 1958), 2: 209.

6. Tshe tan zhabs drung, "Rna ba'i bdud rtsi" [Acoustic ambrosia], 1987, 1: 503.

7. Lama Jabb identified certain literary features characterizing continuance—historical endurance, style, language, metrics—to counter the notion of historical rupture triggered by China's colonial rule of Tibet. Lama Jabb, *Oral and Literary Continuities in Modern Tibetan Literature: The Inescapable Nation* (Lanham, Md. and Boulder, Colo.: Lexington Books, 2015), 1–20.

8. Lauran Hartley, "Heterodox Views and the New Orthodox Poems: Tibetan Writers in the Early and Mid-Twentieth Century," in *Modern Tibetan Literature and Social Change*, ed. Lauran Hartley and Patricia Schiaffini-Vedani (Durham, N.C. and London: Duke University Press, 2008), 24.

9. Perry Link, *The Uses of Literature: Life in the Socialist Chinese Literary System* (Princeton, N.J.: Princeton University Press, 2000), 3–11, 104–116.

10. Matthew Akester, "Translator's Introduction," in Tubten Khétsun, *Memories of Life in Lhasa Under Chinese Rule* (New York: Columbia University Press, 2008), ix.

11. Andrew Quintman, *The Yogin and the Madman: Reading the Biographical Corpus of Tibet's Great Saint Milarepa* (New York: Columbia University Press, 2014), 23–24 and "Life Writing as a Literary Relic: Image, Inscription, and Consecration in Tibetan Biography," *Material Religion* 9, no. 4 (December 2013): 470–479.

12. Paul John Eakin, *How Our Lives Become Stories* (Ithaca, N.Y. and London: Cornell University Press, 1999), 4.

13. On Tibetan genres of literature, see José Cabezón and Roger Jackson, eds., *Tibetan Literature: Studies in Genre* (Ithaca, N.Y.: Snow Lion, 1996). For important studies on Tibetan life writing, see Janet Gyatso, *Apparitions of Self: The Secret Autobiographies of a Tibetan Visionary* (Princeton, N.J.: Princeton University Press, 1999); Kurtis Schaeffer, *Himalayan Hermitess: The Life of a Tibetan Buddhist Nun* (Oxford and New York: Oxford University Press, 2004); Kurtis Schaeffer, "Tibetan Biography: Growth and Criticism," in *Edition, éditions, l'écrit au Tibet, évolution et*

devenir, ed. Anne Chayet, Cristina Scherrer-Schaub, Françoise Robin, and Jean-Luc Achard (München: Indus Verlag, 2010), 263–306; Linda Covill, Ulrike Roesler, and Sarah Shaw, eds., *Lives Lived, Lives Imagined: Biography in the Buddhist Traditions* (Boston: Wisdom, 2010); Isabelle Henrion-Dourcy, "A Look at the Margins: Autobiographical Writing in Tibetan in the People's Republic of China," in *Writing Lives in China, 1600–2010: Histories of the Elusive Self,* ed. Marjorie Dryburgh and Sarah Dauncey (New York: Palgrave Macmillan, 2013), 206–235; Quintman, *The Yogin and the Madman*; Amy Holmes-Tagchungdarpa, *The Social Life of Tibetan Biography: Textuality, Community, and Authority in the Lineage of Tokden Shakya Shri* (Lanham, Md.: Lexington Books, 2014); Sarah Jacoby, *Love and Liberation: Autobiographical Writings of the Tibetan Buddhist Visionary Sera Khandro* (New York: Columbia University Press, 2014); Jim Rheinigans, ed., *Tibetan Literary Genres, Texts, and Text Types: From Genre Classification to Transformation* (Leiden, Boston: Brill, 2015); and Holly Gayley, *Love Letters from Golok: A Tantric Couple in Modern Tibet* (New York: Columbia University Press, 2017). For excellent case studies in both China and Tibet see Benjamin Penny, ed., *Religion and Biography in China and Tibet* (Richmond, Surrey: Curzon Press, 2002).

14. J. N. Bhattacharya and Nilanjana Sarkar, eds., *Encyclopaedic Dictionary of Sanskrit Literature* (Delhi: Global Vision Publishing House, 2004), 120; *Bod rgya tshig mdzod chen mo* (Chi. 藏汉大词典) [=*Tibetan-Chinese dictionary*], 3 vols., ed. Zhang Yisun (Beijing: Mi rigs dpe skrun khang, 1985), 2: 566. Here *rnam-thar* is cognate with "biography" (*zhuànjì* 传记) and "tales of eminent monks" (*gāocéng zhuàn* 高僧传) in Chinese, followed by the definition "books that record the activities of religious figures" (记载宗教徒事亦的著作). The Tibetan definition provided here is slightly different: "writings on the historical achievements of holy people" (*skyes bu dam pa'i mdzad spyod lo rgyus kyi gzhung*) or "treatises of realization" (*rtogs pa brjod pa'i bstan bcos*).

15. Hagiography began with the Bollandists in the *Acta Sanctorum* project to categorize medieval Christian saints. See, Hippolyte Delehaye, *The Work of the Bollandists Through Three Centuries 1615–1915* (Princeton, N.J.: Princeton University Press, 1922), 37. Studies by medievalists, such as Patrick Geary, *Living with the Dead in the Middle Ages* (Ithaca, N.Y.: Cornell University Press, 1994), and Caroline Walker Bynum, *Fragmentation and Redemption: Essays on Gender and the Human Body in Medieval Religion* (New York: Zone Books, 1991) have inspired the study of hagiographies in Tibetan studies. See Schaeffer, *Himalayan Hermitess*, 46–49; Quintman, *The Yogin and the Madman,* 20–25.

16. Bhattacharya and Sarkar, eds., *Encyclopaedic Dictionary of Sanskrit Literature,* 120.

17. Gedun Rabsal, unpublished conference paper, presented at a meeting of the Tibet and the Literary five-year Seminar of the American Academy of Religion; University of California, Berkeley, September 2015.

18. Gyatso, *Apparitions of Self,* 6.

19. Eakin, *How Our Lives Become Stories,* 98.

20. My understanding of how autobiography as a genre in the Euro-American context resonates with Tibetan life writing and therefore justifies the use of the term relies on viewing the narrative as an expression of the life of a real—culturally and historically situated—individual. Smith and Watson point out that biography and autobiography share common threads, and although the authorial signatures have distinguishing features, they can be melded to create hybrid forms, and this is done all the time; see Sidonie Smith and Julia Watson, *Reading Autobiography: A Guide for Interpreting Life Narratives* (Minneapolis: University of Minnesota Press, 2001), 4–7; 137–163. Another key feature that Tibetan autobiography shares with its Western counterparts has to do with relationality in life writing; cf. Eakin, *How Our Lives Become Stories,* 71–88, and Jacoby, *Love and Liberation,* 76–130.

21. Philippe Lejeune, *On Autobiography* (Minneapolis: University of Minnesota Press, 1989), 19–21; cf. Smith and Watson, *Reading Autobiography,* 8–9.

22. *Spong bdun*: the vow to abandon the three unvirtuous actions of body and four of speech. Tsepak Rigzin, *Tibetan-English Dictionary of Buddhist Terminology* (Dharamsala: Library of Tibetan Works and Archives, 1997), 198.

23. Tshe tan zhabs drung, "Rna ba'i bdud rtsi" [Acoustic ambrosia], 1987, 1: 500–501. I am grateful to Benjamin Garceau, who helped with the poetic flourishes of my translation.

24. Samten G. Karmay, "Introduction," in *'Khrul ba'i rol rtsed. The Illusive Play: The Autobiography of the Fifth Dalai Lama* (Chicago: Serindia, 2014), 1.

25. As detailed below, a clear model for both authors studied here is the Fifth Dalai Lama's autobiography, *A Fine Silken Dress*, alternatively translated as *Illusive Play*. The first chapter of this work is "Request to Write an Autobiography." See Karmay, *The Illusive Play*, 17.

26. Gyatso, *Apparitions of Self*, 105.

27.   des na yod la med ces khengs mi skyung|
        med la yod ces rdzun lab mi byed pa'i |
        rang gi de nyid ma bcos lhug pa ru|
        rtsom la byung ba brjod pa zhes su gdags|

    Tshe tan zhabs drung, "Rna ba'i bdud rtsi" [Acoustic ambrosia], 1987, 1: 500; Nicole Willock, "A Buddhist Polymath in Modern China" (PhD diss., Indiana University, 2011), 234.

28. Pema Bhum (Pad ma 'bum), "The Heart-Beat of a New Generation: A Discussion of New Poetry," trans. Ronald Schwartz, *Lungta: Contemporary Tibetan Literature* 12 (Summer 1999): 4.

29. Jampa Samten Shastri, ed., *Catalogue of the Library of Tibetan Works and Archives, Historical Works* (Dharamsala: Library of Tibetan Works and Archives, 1983). Kurtis Schaeffer searched for the terms *rnam thar*, several variants of *rnam thar*, and *rtogs brjod* using the TBRC database; see "Tibetan Biography," 267. He didn't search for *byung ba brjod pa* as a category of biography. In my search using the TBRC public domain, *byung ba brjod pa* came up in sixty-nine book titles.

30. 'Jam dgon Kong sprul Blo gros mtha' yas (1813–99) produced an astonishing literary output of more than ninety volumes in the Dpal spungs edition of his *Collected Works* (*gsung 'bum*). The *Thun mong ma yin pa'i mdzod* (ten volumes) is his collected writings. The tenth volume contains three biographical texts on the life of Kong sprul, the first of which is entitled a *byung ba brjod pa*. The complete title is: *Phyogs med ris med kyi bstan pa la 'dung shing dge sbyong gi gzugs brnyan 'chang ba blo gros mtha' yas kyi sde'i **byung ba brjod pa** nor bu sna tshogs mdog can*, which is an autobiography, edited and completed by Gnas gsar Bkra 'phel. See also E. Gene. Smith, *Among Tibetan Texts* (Boston: Wisdom, 2001).

31. The full title of this autobiography is "Dīrghā yur indra dzi na'i **byung ba brjod pa** zol med ngag gi rol mo." The Tibetan section of the title translates as "Genuine song: the telling of what happened." Cf. *Catalogue of the Library of Tibetan Works and Archives, Historical Works,* ed. Jampa Samten (Dharamsala: Library of Tibetan Works and Archives, 1983), 3: 271; *Rare Tibetan Historical and Literary Texts from the Library of Tsepon W.D. Shakabpa Series 1*, compiled by T. Tsepal Taikhang (New Delhi: Tsepal Taikhang, 1974), folio 228–361. Lauran Hartley noted that the common title for Mdo mkhar ba Tshe ring dbang rgyal's text, *Bka' blon rtogs brjod* [Autobiography of a cabinet minister], is not found in the text. The first part of the title, *Dīrghā yur indra dzi na*, renders the author's name in Sanskrit: Dīrghāyur-indrajina. See Lauran Hartley, "Self as a Faithful Public Servant: The Autobiography of Mdo mkhar ba tshe ring dbang rgyal (1697–1763)," in *Mapping the Modern in Tibet, PIATS: Proceedings of the Eleventh Seminar of the International Association of Tibetan Studies Königswinter 2006*, ed. Gray Tuttle (Bonn, Germany: International Institute for Buddhist Studies, 2011), 45–72. On the first Tibetan novel, see Beth Newman's translation of *Tales of the Incomparable Prince* (New York: HarperCollins, 1996).

32. Gyatso, *Apparitions of Self*, 105.

33. The Tibetan term *rtogs brjod* can be literally translated as a "realization account" or "telling of realizations." It is one of the so-called Twelve Branches of Excellent Speech (*gsung rab yan lag bcu gnyis*). John Strong describes *avadāna* literature (in his explanation of the Pali and Sanskrit recensions of the *Aśokāvadāna*) as follows: "an *avadāna* is a narrative of the religious deeds of an individual and is primarily intended to illustrate the workings of karma and the values of faith and devotion. It can often be moralistic in tone but at the same time there is no denying that it has certain entertainment value.... Unlike jātakas, however, the main protagonist of the *avadāna* is usually not the Buddha himself, but a more ordinary individual, often a layman." *The Legend of King Aśoka: A Study and Translation of the Aśokāvadāna* (Princeton, N.J.: Princeton University Press, 1983), 22; see also Quintman, *The Yogin and the Madman*, 6–7.

34. rang gi bya byed rang la lkog tu ma gyur mngon sum tu snang ba rnams la **med la yod** dang yod la med ces pa'i g.yo sgyu'i tshig dang bral ba'i sgo gsum | bde sdug bar ma'i zlos gar 'di ltar bsgyur zhes; Ngag dbang blo bzang rgya mtsho, "Za hor gyi ban de Ngag dbang blo bzang rgya mtsho'i 'di snang 'khrul ba'i rol rtsed rtogs brjod kyi tshul du bkod pa du kū la'i gos bzang," in *Rgyal dbang lnga pa chen po'i gsung 'bum* [Collected works of the fifth Dalai Lama], vol. 1 (Dharamsala: Nam gsal sgron ma, 2007) folio 18–19; accessed via BDRC: WMDL03. Samten Karmay translated this passage as follows: "So what one does is not hidden, but transparent in oneself. There is no need to prevaricate about it. No flaw is committed in talking honestly about how the dance of one's life—with pleasure or pain through the Three Doors—took place,. Karmay, *The Illusive Play*, 19.

35. des na yod la med ces khengs mi skyung|
    med la yod ces rdzun lab mi byed pa'i |
    rang gi de nyid ma bcos lhug pa ru|
    rtsom la byung ba brjod pa zhes su gdags|

    Tshe tan zhabs drung, "Rna ba'i bdud rtsi" [Acoustic ambrosia], 1987, 1: 500; Willock, "A Buddhist Polymath,"234.

36. Personal communication, 'Jigs meds chos 'phag, June 2015.

37. Dmu dge bsam gtan, "Rang gsal A dar sha" [Luminous mirror], 1: 527.

38. Karmay, *The Illusive Play*, 1.

39. kun gzigs lnga ba chen pos

    sgro btags gleng mo'i mi gtsang phung bo'i lus|
    sgra don snyan 'gyur rin chen rgyuan sprad nas|
    rdzun gyi gar bsgyur lce bde'i brjod pa la|
    snying bor rlom yang E ratna yi 'bras| zhes dang

    Dmu dge bsam gtan, "Rang gsal A dar sha" [Luminous mirror], 1: 527. This is verbatim in Ngag dbang blo bzang rgya mtsho, "kū la'i gos bzang" [Fine silken dress], folio 8; accessed via BDRC: WMDL03.

40. Dmu dge bsam gtan, "Rang gsal A dar sha" [Luminous mirror], 1: 575. Unlike the Great Fifth's long descriptive title to his autobiography, Muge Samten's only uses the Sanskrit word *ādarśa* ("luminous mirror") as an attribute.

41. Rang gyis **byung ba** dang de'i skabs kyi 'jigs rten gyi 'gyur ba bcas **brjod** na| phyis su lo rgyus brtag dpyad byed pa l'ang mkho ba'i skabs srid pas cung zad **brjod pa** la zhugs so|
    Dmu dge bsam gtan, "Rang gsal A dar sha" [Luminous mirror], 1: 528.

42. Zla ba blo gros, personal communication, May 2008.

43. Andrew Quintman, "Life Writing as Literary Relic: Image, Inscription, and Consecration in Tibetan Biography," *Material Religion* 9, no. 4 (December 2013): 476.

44. On the devastating famines starting in 1958 and escalating from 1959 to 1962, see Jonathan Spence, *The Search for Modern China* (London and Sydney: Hutchison, 1990), 582–583.

45.   On the secularizing campaigns in Tibet, see Tsering Shakya, *The Dragon in the Land of Snows: A History of Modern Tibet Since 1947* (New York: Columbia University Press, 1999), 314–347; On how secularization has been integral to the CCP's Marxist agenda in China, cf. Spence, *Modern China*, 439, 601–609, 633.

46.   Thanissaro Bhikkhu (Ajaan Geoff), trans., "Upaddha Sutta: Half of the Holy Life," Buddhasutra .com, accessed April 12, 2019, http://buddhasutra.com/files/upaddha_sutta.htm.

47.   The Tibetan term for spiritual friend (*dge bshes*) often translates the Sanskrit term *kalyāṇamitratā*. See *Sam bod rgya gsum gshan sbyar gyi tshig mdzod* [Sanskrit, Tibetan, Chinese, trilingual dictionary], ed. Rnam rgyal tshe ring (Chi. An Shiying), (Beijing: Mi rigs dpe skrun khang, 2005), 26.

48.   Dmu dge bsam gtan, "Rang gsal A dar sha" [Luminous mirror], 1: 531; Tshe tan zhabs drung, "Rna ba'i bdud rtsi" [Acoustic ambrosia], 1987, 1: 513–514. See notes 87–89 in the introduction.

49.   Padmakara Translation Group, *Nagarjuna's Letter to a Friend* (Ithaca, N.Y. and Boulder, Colo.: Snow Lion, 2005), 51.

50.   Here I add to Bikkhu Bodhi's interpretation of "Spiritual Friendship," *Buddhist Publication Society Newsletter* 5 (2007), accessed April 12, 2019, http://www.bps.lk/olib/nl/nl057.pdf #nameddest=a.

51.   Patrul Rinpoché, *Words of My Perfect Teacher*, trans. the Padmakara Translation Group (New Delhi: Vistaar Publications, 1994), 137.

52.   Georges Dreyfus, *The Sound of Two Hands Clapping: The Education of a Tibetan Buddhist Monk* (Berkeley: University of California Press, 2003), 254.

53.   David Germano details the importance of ethical purification in the aftermath of the Cultural Revolution in his pathbreaking study on Khenpo Jikphun. See Germano, "Re-membering the Dismembered Body of Tibet: Contemporary Tibetan Visionary Movements in the People's Republic of China," in *Buddhism in Contemporary Tibet: Religious Revival and Cultural Identity*, ed. Melvyn Goldstein and Matthew Kapstein (Berkeley: University of California Press, 1998), 70.

54.   Dmu dge bsam gtan, "Rang gsal A dar sha" [Luminous mirror], 1: 562.

55.   Dreyfus, *Sound of Two Hands Clapping*, 254.

56.   Dreyfus, *Sound of Two Hands Clapping*, 257.

57.   Dreyfus, *Sound of Two Hands Clapping*, 254–260.

58.   Yon tan rgya mtsho, *Chos sde chen po bla brang bkra shis 'khyil* [History of Labrang Tashikyil Monastery] (Paris: N.P., 1987) [scanned photocopy of dbu chen manuscript, held at TBRC], 283; Blo bzang lhun grub rdo rje, *Krung go'i bod brgyud dgon pa'i dkar chag las kan su'u glegs bam* [China's Tibet: a catalogue of Buddhist monasteries, their antiquities and liturgical objects, volume on Gansu province] (Lanzhou: kan su'u mi rigs dpe skrun khang, 2009).

59.   Dmu dge bsam gtan, "Rang gsal A dar sha" [Luminous mirror], 1: 539–569. It is somewhat unclear from Mugé Samten's autobiography exactly when he received the degree. It is implied that this occurred in the summer ceremony. See Dmu dge bsam gtan, "Rang gsal A dar sha" [Luminous mirror], 1: 562–563. It seems that there were two ceremonies annually, awarding the *geshe doram* once in summer and once in winter; see Blo bzang lhun grub rdo rje, *Krung go'i bod brgyud dgon pa'i dkar chag las kan su'u glegs bam*, 8. Dungkar Rinpoché's short biography of Mugé Samten doesn't provide the exact date. It states, "two years and eight months after [Mugé Samten] became a 'dorampa' (*rdo rams pa*) Labrang was liberated"; *Dung dkar tshig mdzod chen mo* [Dungkar encyclopedia] (Beijing: Zhongguo Zangxue chubanshe, 2002), 1633. "Liberation" occurred in late August/early September 1949; see Paul Kocot Nietupski, *Labrang Monastery: A Tibetan Buddhist Community on the Inner Asian Borderlands, 1709–1959* (Lanham, Md.: Rowman & Littlefield, 2011), 188–189. See also, "Author's Biography" in the English translation of Muge Samten's *A History of Traditional Fields of Learning: A Concise History of Dissemination of Traditional Fields of Learning in Tibet* (*Bod du rig gnas dar tshul mdo bsdus bshad pa*), trans. Sangye Tandar Naga

[bilingual edition, in English and Tibetan] (Dharamshala: Library of Tibetan Works and Archives, 2005), vii.

60. Nietupski, *Labrang Monastery*, 183.

61. skyabs mgon thams cad mkhyen pa khong gyi zhal nas| tshogs 'du'i thog gsung gnang ste [...] khong A khu bsam gtan yang | chos 'jig rten gnyis kar rnam dpyod che ba yin gshis dge rgan du bsko bzhag byas pa yin| khyed rnams kyis kyang brtsi bkur dang gsung brtsi dgos| zhes sogs gsungs|

   Dmu dge bsam gtan, "Rang gsal A dar sha" [Luminous mirror], 1: 563.

62. Jacoby, *Love and Liberation*, 132.

63. Jacoby, *Love and Liberation*, 20–21.

64. Tsering Shakya, *The Dragon in the Land of Snows*, 245, 251, 300–305.

65. Dung dkar blo bzang 'phrin las, *Dung dkar tshig mdzod chen mo* [Dungkar encyclopedia], 1633.

66. Tsongkhapa, *The Great Treatise on the Stages of the Path to Enlightenment*, trans. Lamrim Chenmo Translation Committee (LCTC), 3 vols. (Ithaca, N.Y.: Snow Lion, 2000), especially vol. 2.

67. Holmes Welch, *The Buddhist Revival in China* (Cambridge, Mass.: Harvard University Press, 1968), 51–71.

68. This is alternatively translated as "Nationalities Affairs Commission" (Mi rigs don byed U yon lhan khang; Ch. mínzú shìwù wěiyuánhuì 民族事务委员会). See Dmu dge bsam gtan, "Rang gsal A dar sha" [Luminous mirror], 1: 575.

69. See June Teufel Dreyer, *China's Forty Millions* (Cambridge and London: Harvard University Press, 1976), 104; Thomas Mullaney, *Coming to Terms with the Nation: Ethnic Classification in Modern China* (Berkeley: University of California Press, 2011).

70. The State Nationalities [Ethnic] Affairs Commission, for example, played a crucial role in facilitating the Dalai Lama and Panchen Lama's visit to Beijing in 1954; see Melvyn Goldstein, *A History of Modern Tibet: The Calm Before the Storm, 1951–1955* (Berkeley: University of California Press, 2007), 2: 487–490.

71. Dmu dge bsam gtan, "Rang gsal A dar sha" [Luminous mirror], 1: 570–571.

72. "The Sixth Gungtang, Jigmé Tenpai Wangchuk," *Treasury of Lives*, accessed April 13, 2018, https://treasuryoflives.org/biographies/view/Jigmé-Tenpai-Wangchuk/8128.

73. de'i skabs gung thang rin po ches bdag 'bod pa gnag ste| gsol ras gnang| spyi sger gyi don dang | rig gnas dang lo rgyus sogs gyi gsung 'phros mang bo gnang | bdag rgya yul du 'gro rgyu byed bzhin pa'i skabs shig tu yang gung thang rin po ches sku mdun du bos nas sngar bzhin gsol ras dang | gsung 'phros gnang| zhals nas khyod nged cag gi lho rgyu zhabs dras kyi khongs su gtogs pa gyis| khyod la drung chen mkhan po'i go sa ster| khyod 'dir 'dug mi 'dod na stod phyogs su song na chog gsungs| bdag gis stod phyogs su 'gro mi 'dod| rgya yul du 'gro 'dod tshul sogs zhus| khong gis rgya yul du 'gro na pe cin du song na bzang| nga'i tshab byas nas ma'o kru'u zhi dang kru'u tsung zi lin la 'tshams zhu ba byas nas song na| dmigs bsal gyi blta rtogs yod| 'gro sgo tshang ma ngas gtong gsungs| 'gro rgyu bla ma la zhu dgos mod| khong A lags yongs 'dzin rdo rje 'chang A mchog dgon grong gis gdan 'dren zhus nas der phebs te|

   Dmu dge bsam gtan, "Rang gsal A dar sha" [Luminous mirror], 1: 571.

74. Holmes Welch, *Buddhism Under Mao* (Cambridge, Mass: Harvard University Press, 1972), 19; Gray Tuttle, *Tibetan Buddhists in the Making of Modern China* (New York: Columbia University Press, 2005), 219; Heather Stoddard, "Progressives and Exiles," in *The Tibetan History Reader*, ed. Gray Tuttle and Kurtis Schaeffer (New York: Columbia University Press, 2013), 596–598, and Stoddard, "Tibetan Publications and National Identity," in *Resistance and Reform in Tibet*, ed. Robert Barnett and Shirin Akiner (Delhi: Motilal Banarsidass, 1994), 129, 143.

75. To my knowledge, Li Weihan was the head of the Ethnic Affairs Commission at this time. I am unable to identify this person with certainty. I transcribed the name based on the Tibetan spelling (Dbyang cin ren) according to the pronunciation guide in Ma Xueren, ed., *Hànzàng duìzhào*

fóxué cídiǎn 汉藏对照佛学词典 (Rgya bod shan sbyar sangs rgyas chos gzhung gi tshig mdzod) [Chinese-Tibetan bilingual Buddhist dictionary] (Gansu: Gansu'u mi rigs dpe skrun khang, 2007), 887–894.

76. Mugé Samten refers to Tibet as "Bod ljongs."

77. It is unclear if Mugé Samten is referring to the head of the provincial level or the state level of the ethnic affairs commission. Dmu dge bsam gtan, "Rang gsal A dar sha" [Luminous mirror], 1: 575.

78. Dmu dge bsam gtan, "Rang gsal A dar sha" [Luminous mirror], 1: 575.

79. Dmu dge bsam gtan, "Rang gsal A dar sha" [Luminous mirror], 1: 576.

80. Tsering Shakya, *Dragon in the Land of Snows*, 143.

81. Willock, "A Buddhist Polymath," 64–74.

82. Tshe tan zhabs drung, "Rna ba'i bdud rtsi" [Acoustic ambrosia], 1987, 1: 769; Willock, "A Buddhist Polymath," 114–115.

83. Tshe tan zhabs drung, "Rna ba'i bdud rtsi" [Acoustic ambrosia], 1987, 1: 529–530.

84. Tshe tan zhabs drung, "Rna ba'i bdud rtsi" [Acoustic ambrosia], 1987, 1: 530–531; Willock, "A Buddhist Polymath," 123–125.

85. Dreyer, *China's Forty Millions*, 98.

86. Tshe tan zhabs drung, *Dan dou si jian shi* (Dan tig dkar chag) [A brief history of Dentik monastery] [n.p.]. Retrieved at monastery, 2008, 3: 379.

87. On the implementation of the Constitution at this time, see Yu-Nan Chang, "The Chinese Communist State System Under the Constitution of 1954," *The Journal of Politics* 18, no. 3 (August 1956): 520–546. *The China Daily* English online archiver dated March 10, 2011 (2011-03-10), accessed November 30, 2017, published a black-and-white photo of many people euphorically waving flags and marching through the streets.

88. Tsering Shakya, *Dragon in the Land of Snows*, 122.

89. See for example, the front cover of *Mi rigs brnyan par* 4 (August 1956).

90. See Patricia Berger, *Empire of Emptiness: Buddhist Art and Political Authority in Qing China* (Honolulu: University of Hawai'i Press, 2003); Wen-shing Chou, *Mount Wutai: Visions of a Sacred Buddhist Mountain* (Princeton, N.J.: Princeton University Press, 2018), 183 n. 11.

91. Tséten Zhabdrung called this room the *rje sku* or "Venerable Image" chapel. Several examples in his autobiography refer to *rje sku* as Tsongkhapa; therefore I believe it is a reference to Tsongkhapa. I am grateful to Nancy Lin, who pointed out to me that there is a Tsongkhapa Chapel in the Yonghegong.

92. Dga' ldan lha brgya ma.

93. The three main aspects of which are: bodhicitta (*byang chub sems*), emptiness (*stong pa nyid*), and renunciation (*nges 'byung*).

94. Wylie: yon tan gyi gzhi gyur ma or Yon tan kun gyi gzhir gyur drin can rjed. This and Lam gtso are both texts by Tsong kha pa.

95. Wylie: "Rgyal ba ma lus ma" is the name of a prayer.

96. Tshe tan zhabs drung, "Rna ba'i bdud rtsi" [Acoustic ambrosia], 1987, 1: 770.

97. Tshe tan zhabs drung, "Rna ba'i bdud rtsi" [Acoustic ambrosia], 1987, 1: 769–770.

98. See Dieter Schuh, *Untersuchungen zur Geschichte der tibetische Kalenderrechnung* (Wiesbaden: Franz Steiner Verlag Gmbh, 1973), 234.

99. Tshe tan zhabs drung, "Rna ba'i bdud rtsi" [Acoustic ambrosia], 1987, 1: 772–773.

100. Tshe tan zhabs drung, "Rna ba'i bdud rtsi" [Acoustic ambrosia], 1987, 1: 771.

101. Tshe tan zhabs drung, "Rna ba'i bdud rtsi" [Acoustic ambrosia], 1987, 1: 772.

102. Bstan 'dzin rgya mtsho, "Bka' 'bum rin po che par byang smon tshig," in *'Jigs med dam chos rgya mtsho bka' 'bum*, volume pa, folio 1 [Collected works of Jigmé Damcho Gyatso]. Printed form woodblocks at Reb gong Monastery, retrieved 2008.

103. Tshe tan zhabs drung, "Rna ba'i bdud rtsi" [Acoustic ambrosia], 1987, 1: 776.

104. The building of Baodi Monastery at Xiangshan, "The Fragrant Hills," was under the direction of Cangkya Rolpé Dorjé and sponsored by the Qianlong Emperor. See Chou, *Mount Wutai*, 19–21. Chou also details Cangkya Rolpé Dorjé's biography (*namtar*) by another great Géluk polymath, Rolpé Dorjé's disciple, Tuken (Thu'u kwan blo bzang chos kyi nyi ma, 1737–1802); see *Mount Wutai*, 87–88.

105. Tshe tan zhabs drung, "Rna ba'i bdud rtsi" [Acoustic ambrosia], 1987, 1: 782–783.

106. 同年在北京参加宪法和毛泽东著作哲学部分的翻译和审定，受到毛泽东，周恩来的接见，并参加庆祝中华人民共和国成立5周年的国庆盛典。

    In that same year [1954], Caidan Xiarong [=Tshe tan zhabs drung] took part in translating and editing the National Constitution and the Works of Mao Zedong. He had an audience with Mao Zedong and Zhou Enlai and at the same time attended the celebration of the fifth anniversary of the establishment of the People's Republic of China.

    Hualong xianzhi 化隆县志 [Hualong county gazetteer] (Xi'an: Shanxi renmin chubanshe, 1994), 749.

107. Chou, *Mount Wutai*, 57–58.

108. Dmu dge bsam gtan, "Rang gsal A dar sha" [Luminous mirror], 1: 587.

109. "Tradition, viewed in this way, is not a set of symbols and idioms that justify present practices, neither is it an unchanging set of cultural prescriptions that stand in contrast to what is changing, contemporary, or modern. Nor is it a historically fixed social structure. Rather the past is the very ground through which subjectivity and self-understanding of a tradition's adherents are constituted. An Islamic discursive tradition, in this view, is therefore a mode of discursive engagement with sacred texts, one effect of which is the creation of sensibilities and embodied capacities (of reason, affect, and volition) that in turn are the conditions reproduction." Saba Mahmood, *Politics of Piety: The Islamic Revival and the Feminist Subject* (Princeton, N.J.: Princeton University Press, 2005), 115.

110. In other words, this piece follows the criteria of the "autobiographical pact." See Lejeune, *On Autobiography*, 19–21.

111. A photographic reproduction of the original Tibetan artifact was published as "An Ode to Mao" [Chi. Maozhuxi song, 毛主席颂] in *A Collection of Historical Archives of Tibet*, accompanied by typed Chinese and English translations. Composed in neat *U-chen* calligraphy, the verses were written on four separate pieces of looseleaf Tibetan paper (*pecha*), which were then pasted onto, or perhaps sewn into, an ornate brocade frame. The preface included the measurements of the entire object: 77 cm x 34.9 cm (29.8 inches x 20.9 inches). Archives of the Tibetan Autonomous Region (Xizang zizhiqu dang'an guanbian, 西藏自治区档案馆编), *A Collection of Historical Archives of Tibet* (Beijing: Cultural Relics Publishing House, 1995), identified as object: 107-1, 107-2, 107-3, 107-4, 107-5, 107-6, 107-7, [no page number]. Buddhist Association of China (Zhongguo fojiao xiehui, 中国佛教协会), "Maozhuxi song (毛主席颂)" [An ode to Mao], *Xiandai foxue* (现代佛学) [Modern Buddhist studies] 9 (1954): 1–4. See Lauran Hartley's pioneering work on this material in "Con**text**ually Speaking: Tibetan Literary Discourse and Social Change in the People's Republic of China (1980–2000)" (PhD diss., Indiana University, 2003), 139.

112. Archives of the Tibetan Autonomous Region, *A Collection of Historical Archives of Tibet*, 107-1, 107-2, 107-3, 107-4, 107-5, 107-6, 107-7, [no page number]; cf. note 111.

113. Although the editors do not recognize *monlam* as a genre per se, Manfred Taube recognized prayer as a subgenre in the category of Esoteric Buddhism; see José Cabezón and Roger Jackson, eds., *Tibetan Literature: Studies in Genre* (Ithaca, N.Y.: Snow Lion, 1996), 20–32.

114. The final two stanzas here are my own translation based on the Tibetan in Archives of the Tibetan Autonomous Region, *A Collection of Historical Archives of Tibet*, 107-2, second folio. See also Buddhist Association of China, "Ode to Mao," 1–2.

115. Translation of the first four stanzas are by Lauran Hartley with a few minor edits by myself; see Hartley, "Contextually Speaking," 137–138.

116. The first chapter of the seminal Tibetan history titled the *Blue Annals* recounts the story of Mang pos bkur pa (Sanskrit: Mahāsammata), abbreviated as Mang bkur in this poem, as a sagely king. He is descended from "gods of light" (Wylie: *'od gsal*; Sanskrit: *ābhāsvara*) to become the first king who lived at a time with other sentient beings. The Śākya clan to which Siddhārtha Gautama belonged is perceived to be of his progeny. See Georges Roerich, trans., *The Blue Annals (Deb ther sngon po)* (Delhi: Motilal Banarsidass, 1996 [reprint]), 3, 12–18. I am grateful to Nancy Lin, who also directed me to the entry on the Pali Canon website, http://www.palikanon.com/english/pali_names/maha/mahasammata.htm, accessed on January 28, 2018. See also Stanley Jeyaraja Tambiah, *The Buddhist Saints of the Forest and the Cult of Amulets: A Study in Charisma, Hagiography, Sectarianism, and Millennial Buddhism* (Cambridge: Cambridge University Press, 1984), 120.

117. See Toni Huber, *The Holy Land Reborn: Pilgrimage and the Tibetan Reinvention of Buddhist India* (Chicago: University of Chicago Press, 2008).

118. For example, a verse in the Nartang Kanjur (Snar thang Bstan 'gyur) catalogue (*dkar chag*) celebrates a history of Buddhism in Tibet that culminates with the rule of Miwang Polhané as a righteous *cakravartin* king. Polhané as a lay ruler was celebrated as an ethical and just king who supported Buddhist projects, such as the printing of the catalogue, completed on November 21, 1742, that praised him. See Nancy Grace Lin, "Adapting the Buddha's Biographies: A Cultural History of the Wish-Fulfilling Vine in Tibet, Seventeenth to Eighteenth Centuries" (PhD diss., University of California, Berkeley, 2011), 80–81.

119. Hartley, "Heterodox Views and the New Orthodox Poems," 17.

120. Archives of the Tibetan Autonomous Region, *Collection of Historical Archives of Tibet*, 107-2. See also Buddhist Association of China, "Ode to Mao," 1–2.

121. The Chinese and English translation of the Tibetan *btsan por g.yo pa* is "imperialism." The Tibetan term for imperialism found in Melvyn Goldstein's *The New Tibetan-English Dictionary of Modern Tibetan* (Berkeley: University of California Press, 2001) is *tsen-po ring-lug* (Wylie: btsan po'i ring lugs). Since only *tsen-po* is mentioned, I read the Tibetan as "imperialists."

122. Lauran Hartley noted the differences between the Tibetan text and the Chinese and English translations, including the omission of information found in the Tibetan colophon and that silver was offered along with the poem to Mao. Hartley, "Contextually Speaking," 139.

123. gser ldan khor yug yangs pa'i sdug bsngal gyi| mon pa'i bcing ba ma lus yongs bkrol nas| dge legs snang ba gsar pa'i 'od 'bum gyis| dbugs 'byin bkra shis dga' ston sbyin gyur cig| Archives of the Tibetan Autonomous Region, *A Collection of Historical Archives of Tibet*, 107-2.

124. Archives of the Tibetan Autonomous Region, *A Collection of Historical Archives of Tibet*, 107-2, second folio.

125. This wordplay begins in the second verse (folio 1) and continues through each line of the first folio with the exception of one couplet that hails Chairman Mao (ma'o kru zhi mchog) directly, marked by ellipses here. The bolded text is in red ink in the original: tshangs chen 'jig rten **mes** po'i byed pa dang| mang bkur **rgyal** po'i dpal dang mnyam nyid du| leg byas bye pas bkod pa'i mi yi **gtso**| 'dzam gling **'dzin** ma gsal ba'i nyi ma bzhin| gtsug lag nor bu'i chu gter g.yo ba'i **rlabs**| rgya **chen** nam mkha'i pha mthar 'grim pa can| . . .'di ni bdag cag skyong ba'i **ma'o** zhes| 'gro kun kun dga'i ri mo 'god pas bral| nye 'khon **kru** rda: bral pa'i mdza' gcugs gyis| **zhi** ba'i lam bzang ston mdzad rtag brtan shog| Archives of the Tibetan Autonomous Region, *A Collection of Historical Archives of Tibet*, 107-2, first folio.

126. See the next chapter on "mellifluous words" and how each of the Three Polymaths wrote about poetics.

127. According to Holmes Welch, the BAC's constitution goals were "To unite all the country's Buddhists so that they will participate, under the leadership of the People's Government, in movements for the welfare of the motherland and the defense of world peace; to help the People's Government fully carry out its policy of freedom of religious belief; to link up Buddhists from different parts of the country; and to exemplify the best traditions of Buddhism." *Buddhism Under Mao*, 20.

128. Holmes Welch translated this as *Modern Buddhism*. He points out that the journal "Modern Buddhism" (Xiandai foxue) [Modern Buddhist studies] was launched on June 18, 1950, in order to transmit policy to Buddhists throughout the country, to handle complaints about local cadres, to reform Buddhist doctrine and the monastic system, and to cultivate contacts with overseas Buddhists; see Welch, *Buddhism Under Mao*, 11.

129. Buddhist Association of China, "Ode to Mao," 1.

130. It seems that the artifact in Archives of the Tibetan Autonomous Region, *A Collection of Historical Archives*, is written in the Dalai Lama's own hand, whereas the one in *Modern Buddhist Studies* is a copy.

131. Buddhist Association of China, "Ode to Mao," 1–3.

132. I am grateful to Clemens Büttner for the reference in the *Hanyu dacidian* (漢語大詞典). "語體文" means to write a text on the basis of vernacular Chinese, "以通行的口語寫成的文章."

133. Buddhist Association of China, "Ode to Mao," 28.

134. Welch, *Buddhism Under Mao*, 129–130, 144.

135. This is the title of the first chapter of Tsering Shakya's history, *The Dragon in the Land of Snows*. The second volume of Melvyn Goldstein's *A History of Modern Tibet* is similarly subtitled, "A Calm Before the Storm."

136. Stoddard, "Tibetan Publications and National Identity," 127.

137. Elliot Sperling, *The Tibet-China Conflict: History and Polemics* (Washington, D.C.: East-West Center, 2004), 31–35.

138. Tuttle, *Tibetan Buddhists in the Making of Modern China*.

139. Fabienne Jagou, *The Ninth Panchen Lama (1883–1937): A Life at the Crossroads of Sino-Tibetan Relations*, trans. Rebecca Bissett Buechel (Paris: École Française d'extrême-Orient, 2011), 94–97.

140. Xue Yu, "Buddhist Efforts at Reconciliation of Buddhism and Marxism in the Early Years of the People's Republic of China," in *Recovering Buddhism in Modern China*, ed. Jan Kiely and J. Brooks Jessup (New York: Columbia University Press, 2016), 179–181.

3. MELLIFLUOUS WORDS ON THE HUMAN CONDITION

1. de lta na yang brtse med dus kyi srin| khros pa'i za byed gnam sa gdangs pai'i khyon| mche ba'i mtshon cha gtsigs pa'i gcong rong du| bzlog med rngams za'i tshul de ya re nga| 'jigs rung gi nyams kyi rgyan|

Tshe tan zhabs drung, "Pan chen thams cad mkhen cing gzigs pa chen po mdo smad 'khrungs gzhis phyogs su phebs pa'i legs mdzad cha shas tsam gyi ngo mtshar ba'i gtam gyi rtogs pa brjod pa dngul gyi me tog" [Avādana of silver flowers: a wonderous account of the Panchen Lama's visit to Amdo, his birthplace], in *Tshe tan zhabs drung rje btsun 'jigs med rigs pa'i blo gros mchog gi gsung 'bum*, ed. 'Jigs med chos 'phags (Beijing: Minzu chubanshe, 2007), 3:271.

2. See for example, Warren Smith, *Tibetan Nation: A History of Tibetan Nationalism and Sino-Tibetan Relations* (Boulder: Westview Press, 1996).

3. These numbers are general figures and perhaps on the lower side. The census data from the Central Tibetan Administration in 2010 reported that there were over 127,000 Tibetans living in exile. See Press Trust of India, "127935 Tibetans Living Outside of Tibet," *Hindustan Times*, December 4, 2010; https://web.archive.org/web/20110927215516/, http://www.hindustantimes.com/127935-Tibetans-living-outside-Tibet-Tibetan-survey/Article1-634405.aspx; See also Julia Meredith Hess, *Immigrant Ambassadors: Citizenship and Belonging in the Tibetan Diaspora* (Stanford, Calif.: Stanford University Press, 2009); Shushum Bhatia, Tsegyal Dranyi, and Derrick Rowling, "A Social and Demographic Study of Tibetan Refugees in India," *Social Science and Medicine* 54 (2002): 411–422; International Campaign for Tibet, "Tibetan Refugees," https://savetibet.org/why-tibet/tibetan-refugees/, accessed January 15, 2020.

4. Tsering Shakya, *The Dragon in the Land of Snows: A History of Modern Tibet Since 1947* (New York: Columbia University Press, 1999), 163–184, 237–275, 287–346.

5. Tshe tan zhabs drung, "Mnyam med shAkya'i dbang bo'i rjes zhugs pa 'jigs med rigs pa'i blo gros rang gi byung ba brjod pa bden gtam rna ba'i bdud rtsi" [Acoustic ambrosia: a truthful telling of what happened by 'Jigs med rigs pa'i blo gros, a disciple of the powerful, matchless shākya]," in *Mkhas dbang tshe tan zhabs drung 'jigs med rigs pa'i blo gros kyi gsung rtsom*, ed. 'Phrin las (Xining: Qinghai minzu chubanshe, 1987), 1: 79.

6. In Buddhism, the water deity Varuṇa (*chu lha*) resides in the west. See Zhang Yisun, ed. *Bod rgya tshig mdzod chen mo* (Ch. 藏汉大词典) [=*Tibetan-Chinese Encyclopedia*] (Beijing: Mi rigs dpe skrun khang, 1985), 1: 813.

7. A Buddhist epoch during which the teachings are reduced to merely outward symbols (*rtag tsam 'dzin pa*).

8. The "lamp of existence / saṃsāra" (*srid pa'i sgron me*) is a kenning or poetic synonym (*mngon brjod*) for the sun.

9. kye ma skye dgu'i bsod nams skud pa'i rkya| blo ldan spu rtse'i lang tsho rnyed pa na| phan bde'i gter chen thub bstan nyin mor byed| chu lha'i ngang bar gzhol ba su yis 'gog| kye ma dge sbyong cha byad 'dzin bzhin du| rgyal ba'i bka' dang dbyen spyo'i nyes spyod kyis| lung rtogs dar chen skyod pa'i grub bo che| rgya mtsho'i gting du bying ba su yis skyob| kye ma bstan 'dzin gral du 'gying bag gis| bslab khrims rtswa ltar dor ba'i bag med kyis| ngur smrig 'dzin pa'i chos sde dbang med du| zhig ral nyams chag gyur pa su yis bshol| kye ma phyag dang mchod pas bkur ba'i zhing| mchog gsum rten la sdang bzhin mtshon cha yis| bshig pa'i dkar min las kyi 'bras bu la| bsams na da dung bde bar mnal phod dam| kye ma rmongs sel dam chos glegs bu'i tshog| rkang ba'i mchil lham mthil la gtsags pa gang| dar ma yis kyang mtshan dgung ma rmis pa| lag tu blangs pa de dag skyi re g.ya'| kye ma bka' dang bstan bcos bye ba'i mdzod| rin chen sa le sbram gyis bzhengs pa dag| byin zar byin nas gser la rngam pa dag| phyi ma'i 'phrang las bde bar thar 'gyur ram| kye ma 'jigs snang gzhan ngor mi 'dod bzhin| stod smad sbu gu can gyi gos g.yogs nas| rtags tsam 'dzin pa la yang dbang med par| gces srog yal ba'i pha mtha' su yis lon| zhes bya ba ni rgyal bstan srid pa'i sgron me re zhig chu 'dzin stug po'i dbyings su thim pa la bzod dka'i mya ngan gyi non pa'i tshul zur tsam gleng ba'i bar skabs kyi tshigs bcad do||

    Tshe tan zhabs drung, "Rna ba'i bdud rtsi" [Acoustic ambrosia], 1987, 1: 779–780.

10. This trauma can be either personal or political; see Sidonie Smith and Julia Watson, *Reading Autobiography: A Guide for Interpreting Life Narratives* (Minneapolis: University of Minnesota Press, 2001), 21.

11. Mugé Samten's and Tséten Zhabdrung's accounts of these events are included within their autobiographies.

12. Gu Hua [=Hua Ku], *A Small Town Called Hibiscus,* trans. Gladys Yang (Beijing: China Publications Centre, 1983). See also Lucien Pye, "Reassessing the Cultural Revolution," *The China Quarterly* 108 (December 1986): 597–612; and Lu Xinhua, Liu Xinwu, et al., *The Wounded: Stories of*

the Cultural Revolution, trans. Geremie Barmé and Bennett Lee (Hong Kong: Joint Publishing Company, 1979).

13. Melvyn Goldstein, Ben Jiao, and Tanzen Lhundrup, *On the Cultural Revolution in Tibet: The Nyemo Incident of 1969* (Berkeley: University of California Press, 2009).

14. Tsering Shakya, *The Dragon in the Land of Snows: A History of Modern Tibet Since 1947* (New York: Columbia University Press, 1999), 320–321.

15. Destroying the "Four Olds" hit all aspects of society; it even meant changing "feudal" personal and street names to revolutionary ones. At times, opposing factions of the Red Guard groups fought, leading to chaos and violence. See also Roderick Macfarquhar and Michael Schoenhals, *Mao's Last Revolution* (Cambridge, Mass.: The Belknap Press of Harvard University Press, 2006); Tsering Shakya, *The Dragon in the Land of Snows,* 113–115; Goldstein et al., *On the Cultural Revolution in Tibet.*

16. Tsering Shakya, *The Dragon in the Land of Snows,* 314–347.

17. Jonathan Spence, *The Search for Modern China* (London: Hutchinson, 1991), 603–617.

18. Joy Blakeslee, *Ama Adhe: The Voice That Remembers: The Heroic Story of a Woman's Fight to Free Tibet* (Somerville, Mass.: Wisdom, 1997); Palden Gyatso, *Autobiography of a Tibetan Monk,* trans. Tsering Shakya (New York: Grove Press, 1997).

19. Melvyn Goldstein, William Siebenschuh, and Tashi Tsering, *The Struggle for Modern Tibet: The Autobiography of Tashi Tsering* (Armonk, N.Y.: M. E. Sharpe, 1997), 119–120.

20. Palden Gyatso, *Autobiography of a Tibetan Monk,* 130.

21. Rinzang, "My Conversation with Akhu Yarphel," trans. Gedun Rabsal and Nicole Willock, in *Conflicting Memories: Retellings of Tibetan History Under Mao,* ed. Robbie Barnett, Francoise Robin, and Benno Weiner (Leiden: Brill Inner Asian Book Series, 2020).

22. On disorientation and trauma in life writing, see Smith and Watson, *Reading Autobiography,* 24; Paul John Eakin, *How Our Lives Become Stories: Making Selves* (Ithaca, N.Y.: Cornell University Press, 1999), 106–110.

23. Melvyn Goldstein, Dawei Sherap, and William R. Siebenschuh, *A Tibetan Revolutionary: The Political Life and Times of Bapa Phüntso Wangyal* (Berkeley: University of California Press, 2004), 241–256.

24. Goldstein et al., *A Tibetan Revolutionary,* 246.

25. Pema Bhum (Pad ma 'bhum), *Dran tho smin drug ske 'khyog,* trans. Lauran Hartley, in *Six Stars with a Crooked Neck: Tibetan Memoirs of the Cultural Revolution* [bilingual edition] (Dharamsala: Bod-kyi-dus-bab, Tibet Times, 2001), 87.

26. Pema Bhum, *Dran tho smin drug ske 'khyog,* 140–141.

27. Tubten Khetsun, *Memories of Life in Lhasa Under Chinese Rule,* trans. and introduction by Matthew Akester (New York: Columbia University Press, 2008).

28. Dmu dge bsam gtan, "Rtsom pa po rang gi byung ba brjod pa rang gsal A' dar sha," [Luminous mirror: the author's own telling what happened], in *Rje dmu dge bsam gtan rgya mtsho mi 'jigs dbyangs can dga' ba'i blo gros dpal bzang po'i gsung 'bum* (Zi ling: Mtsho sngon mi rigs dpe skrun khang, 1997), 1: 591–592.

29. Victoria Sujata, "Translator's Preface," in *Songs of Shabkar: The Path of a Tibetan Yogis Inspired by Nature* (Cazedero, Calif.: Dharma Publishing, 2011), xi.

30. Tshe tan zhabs drung, "Rna ba'i bdud rtsi" [Acoustic ambrosia], 1987, 1: 786.

31. khyad par du bdag dang bdag gi skye ba snga rol gyi nan ta' zhin gnyis rgyud gcig yin pa'i dbang du btang na| khong bas gong ma'i bkas dmag dpon gyi srid bskyangs pa'i skabs su hos 'khrug gi mgo gnon phyir gte bo brgya phrag du ma khrims la sbyar ba kho na'i rnam smin yang tshe de la bshags pas ma dag pa 'dra yod tshe bdag gi steng du cis kyang 'bab nges pa ni las 'bras kyi chos skor la thos bsam re byas myong ba|

     Tshe tan zhabs drung, "Rna ba'i bdud rtsi" [Acoustic ambrosia], 1987, 1: 786–787.

32. Nicole Willock, "A Tibetan Buddhist Polymath of Modern China" (PhD diss., Indiana University, 2011), 74–75.

33. For an account of this siege, see Jonathan Lipman, *Familiar Strangers: A History of Northwest China* (Seattle: University of Washington Press, 1997), 142–162.

34. de'i phyir rang lo nga drug pa shing sbrul lo'i bcu ba'i lnga mchod nyin nas bzung rang lo re bdun pa me 'brug lo'i drug pa'i bcu gsum par lo ngo bcu gnyis kyi ring la rgyal bo'i chad pa'i las kyi 'jigs pa thog tu babs nas| phyis mtshams dang nang mtshams rim gyis bsdams pa'i tshul ltar mthar khri smon du gnas 'cha' dgos byung|

    Tshe tan zhabs drung, "Rna ba'i bdud rtsi" [Acoustic ambrosia], 1987, 1: 787.

35. Smith and Watson, *Reading Autobiography*, 10.

36. Eakin, *How Lives Become Stories*, 74.

37. Eakin, *How Lives Become Stories*, 72–76.

38. Orit Avishai, "'Doing Religion' in a Secular World: Women in Conservative Religions and the Question of Agency," *Gender and Society* 22, no. 4 (August 2008): 413.

39. Tshe tan zhabs drung, *Snyan ngag spyi don* [A general commentary on poetics] (Lanzhou: Gan su'u mi rigs dpe skrun khang, 1957, 1982, 2005), 3.

40. It may seem odd that math is included in the language arts, however, geometry was needed for large compositions of a difficult poem, called "Auspicious Wheel" (*kun bzang 'khor lo*).

41. Jonathan Gold, *The Dharma's Gatekeepers: Sakya Paṇḍita on Buddhist Scholarship in Tibet* (Albany: State University of New York Press, 2007), 14–20.

42. José Ignacio Cabezón, *A Dose of Emptiness: An Annotated Translation of sTong thun chen mo of Mkhas grub dGe legs dpal bzang* (Albany: State University of New York Press, 1992), 405 n. 3.

43. Dmu dge bsam gtan, "Rang gsal A dar sha" [Luminous mirror], 1: 591.

44. Dmu dge bsam gtan, "Rang gsal A dar sha" [Luminous mirror], 1: 591.

45. Tsongkhapa, *The Great Treatise on the Stages of the Path to Enlightenm*ent. Trans. Lamrim Chenmo Translation Committee (LCTC) (Ithaca, N.Y.: Snow Lion, 2000), 268–313.

46. Thupten Jinpa, *Mind Training: The Great Collection* (Boston: Wisdom, 2006), 2.

47. The seven points are as follows: 1) presentation of the preliminaries, 2) training in the two awakening minds, 3) taking adversaries onto the path of enlightenment, 4) presentation of a lifetime's practice in summary, 5) the measure of having trained the mind, 6) the commitments of mind training, and 7) the precepts of mind training. See Thupten Jinpa, *Mind Training*, 1–10.

48. Thupten Jinpa, *Mind Training*, 83.

49. Tshe tan zhabs drung, "Rna ba'i bdud rtsi" [Acoustic ambrosia], 1987, 1: 787.

50. Eakin, *How Lives Become Stories*, 181.

51. Dmu dge bsam gtan, "Rang gsal A dar sha" [Luminous mirror], 1: 591.

52. This is a practice to increase the merit of one's visualizations. See Lama Zopa Rinpoché, *Extensive Offering Practice: A Practice to Accumulate the Most Extensive Merit with Lights and Other Offerings* (N.p.: Foundation for the Preservation of the Mahayana Tradition Education Services, 2003), 4–5.

53. Tshe tan zhabs drung, "Rna ba'i bdud rtsi" [Acoustic ambrosia], 1987, 1: 787.

54. Dung dkar blo bzang 'phrin las, *Dung dkar tshig mdzod chen mo* [Dungkar encyclopedia] (Beijing: Zhongguo Zangxue chubanshe, 2002), 1707. On the history of this massive prison complex in the middle of Xining, the capital of Qinghai Province, see James D. Seymour and Michael Anderson, *New Ghosts and Old Ghosts: Prison and Labor Reform Camps in China* (London and New York: Routledge East Gate Books, 1998), 133–135.

55. Tshe tan zhabs drung, "Rna ba'i bdud rtsi" [Acoustic ambrosia], 1987, 1: 787.

56. Dmu dge bsam gtan, "Rang gsal A dar sha" [Luminous mirror], 1: 593–594.

57. See Dieter Schuh, *Untersuchungen zur Geschichte der tibetische Kalenderrechnung* (Wiesbaden: Franz Steiner Verlag Gmbh, 1973), 239.

58. zla shel kha ba'i ri tshom phreng bsgrigs pa'i| bho ta'i ljongs chen snang byed yi ge'i brnyan| wa ler gsal mdzad thon mi A nu'i drin| bskal ba'i mthar yang cha tsam ji ltar gzhal| rang lo zla tshes la'o| 'chad pa skal bzang thos pa'i skal bzang thos pa'i bang mdzod gtams| rtsod pa phra zhib rigs pa'i rgya mtsho yangs| rtsom pa dbyangs can pi wang 'jebs shing snyan| mkhas pa'i bya ba rnam gsum A ho rmad|| rang lo zla tshes la'o| 'phags chen thub pa'i gzhung lugs rab 'byams mkhas| thos don nyams bzhes bdag 'dzin smad pas btsun| ngan rtogs wa skyes kun 'joms bka' srol bzang| A tis ha yi chos tshul ci yang lhag| rang lo zla tshes la'o| lta ba E wam mnyam sbyor rgya yis btab| sgom pa lhag mthong shes rab mchog gis mdzes| spyod pa phyin drug bsdu bzhi'i bcud kyis brgyan| 'jam mgon tsong kha'i ring lugs mtshungs zlas dben| rang lo zla tshes la'o|

    Tshe tan zhabs drung, "Rna ba'i bdud rtsi" [Acoustic ambrosia], 1987, 1: 788–789.

59. Tshe tan zhabs drung, *Snyan ngag spyi don* [A general commentary on poetics], 108–114.

60. The dotted syllables are, in order: 'chad rtsod rtsom mkhas mkhas btsun bzang lta sgom mdzes sbyod.

61. rang lo re gcig gi lo mjug tu sems kyi nyam snang skyid de bar yod pa'i mtshan dgung 'gar gnyid mi khugs pa'i go skabs la brten kha kha sum cu tshang ba'i tshigs bcad 'ga' sngas la mgo bzhag nas blot hog tu bsgrigs pa|

    Tshe tan zhabs drung, "Rna ba'i bdud rtsi" [Acoustic ambrosia], 1987, 1: 788.

62. Janet Gyatso shows how complex and potentially dangerous "experience" can be in her analysis of three Tibetan meditation traditions. "Healing Burns with Fire: The Facilitations of Experience in Tibetan Buddhism," *Journal of the American Academy of Religion* 67, no. 1 (1999): 113–147, especially 117–121.

63. Gyatso, "Healing Burns with Fire," 119.

64. Sheldon Pollock, trans. and ed., *A Rasa Reader: Classical Indian Aesthetics* (New York: Columbia University Press, 2016), 59.

65. Dan Martin, "Indian Kāvya Poetry on the Far Side of the Himālayas: Translation, Transmission, Adaptation, Originality," in *Innovations and Turning Points: Toward a History of Kāvya Literature*, ed. Yigal Bronner, David Shulman, and Gary Tubb (Oxford: Oxford University Press, 2014), 580 n. 31. 1) *ro*, meaning "taste" or "flavor"; 2) *dngul-chu*, "quicksilver"; 3) *bcud*, "nutritive essence;" 4) *ngang*, "continuing state"; and 5) *nyams*, "experience."

66. Tshe tan zhabs drung, *Snyan ngag spyi don* [A general commentary on poetics], 3–4.

67. Dung dkar blo bzang 'phrin las, "Snyan ngag la 'jug tshul tshig rgyan rig pa'i sgo 'byed" [Gateway to the art of literary figures for writing poetry], in *Mkhas dbang dung dkar blo bzang 'phrin las kyi gsung 'bum,* ed. Rnam rgyal ra 'phrin las rgya mtsho (Beijing: minzu chubanshe, 2004), 1: 44.

68. Tshe tan zhabs drung, *Snyan ngag spyi don* [A general commentary on poetics], 4.

69. This quote is from Tshe tan zhabs drung, *Snyan ngag spyi don* [A general commentary on poetics], 15. The same idea is found in Dung dkar blo bzang 'phrin las, "Snyan ngag la 'jug tshul tshig rgyan rig pa'i sgo 'byed" [Gateway to the art of literary figures for writing poetry], 1: 54.

70. Dung dkar blo bzang 'phrin las, "Snyan ngag la 'jug tshul tshig rgyan rig pa'i sgo 'byed" [Gateway to the art of literary figures for writing poetry], 1: 54.

71. snyan ngag gi nyams ches khyad par du 'phags par 'gyur| Tshe tan zhabs drung, *Snyan ngag spyi don* [A general commentary on poetics], 22.

72. Georges Dreyfus, "Is Compassion an Emotion? A Cross-cultural Exploration of Mental Typologies," in *Visions of Compassion: Western Scientists and Tibetan Buddhists Examine Human Nature,* ed. Anne Harrington and Richard J. Davidson (Oxford: Oxford University Press, 2002), 36.

73. Dreyfus, "Is Compassion an Emotion?," 41.

74. Georges Dreyfus explains "that there is, or I should say there was, no Tibetan word for our word emotion. I said 'there was' because by now Tibetan teachers [in the West] have been exposed to

this question so many times that they have created a new word (*tshor myong*) to translate our emotion. It appears, however, that this neologism, which means literally 'experience of feeling,' is not
very meaningful yet. It is only slowly gathering meaning and is not able to mediate between the
traditional Tibetan Buddhist and the modern English contexts." Dreyfus, "Is Compassion an
Emotion?," 31.

75.   Catherine Lutz, "Opening and Retrospectives: What Matters," *Cultural Anthropology* 32, no. 2
(June 2017): 182.

76.   Pollock, *A Rasa Reader*, 6.

77.   Tshe tan zhabs drung, *Snyan ngag spyi don* [A general commentary on poetics], 15. This chart is
inspired by the one provided in Lauran Hartley, "Con**text**ually Speaking: Tibetan Literary Discourse and Social Change in the People's Republic of China (1980–2000)" (PhD diss., Indiana
University, 2003), 20. While providing an overview of affective states and their psycho-physical
responses, this chart also simplifies a far more complex aesthetic theory, which needs further
research in Tibetan studies. See also Dragomir Dimitrov, *Mārgavibhāga: Die Unterscheidung
der Stilarten, Kritische Ausgabe des ersten Kapitels von Daṇḍins Poetik Kāvyādarśa und der tibetischen Übertragung Sñan ṅag me loṅ nebst einer deutschen Übersetzung des Sanskrittexts* (Marburg: Indica et Tibetica Verlag, 2002). Pollock explains that in the Indian context, four factors
are integral to the notion of "aesthetic elements" and that the choice to translate "aesthetic elements" and "stable emotions" (*sthāyibhāvā*) as such is one of the great difficulties in rendering
these materials into English; see Pollock, *Rasa Reader*, xiv–xv. Jonathan Gold notes that Sakya
Pandita's *Gateway to Learning* had nine *rasas*; see *The Dharma's Gatekeepers*, 173–181.

78.   Tshe tan zhabs drung, "Rtogs pa brjod pa dngul gyi me tog" [*Avadāna* of silver flowers], 3:271. See
note 1 in this chapter.

79.   Ottone M. Riccio, *The Intimate Art of Writing Poetry* (Englewood Cliffs, N.J.: Prentice-Hall,
1980 [reprint 2000]), 28. Emphasis is in the original text.

80.   Eakin, *How Our Lives Become Stories*, 47–52.

81.   Holly Gayley, *Love Letters from Golok: A Tantric Couple in Modern Tibet* (New York: Columbia
University Press, 2017), 86.

82.   Prasenjit Duara, *Rescuing History from the Nation: Questioning Narratives of Modern China* (Chicago: University of Chicago Press, 1995), 5.

4. DUNGKAR RINPOCHÉ ON THE CONTESTED GROUND OF TIBETAN HISTORY

1.   Elliot Sperling, "Tibet and China: The Interpretation of History Since 1950," *China Perspectives* 3
(2009): 25, http://journals.openedition.org/chinaperspectives/4839; see also Elliot Sperling, *The
Tibet-China Conflict: History and Polemics* (Washington, D.C.: East-West Center Washington,
2004).

2.   Vincent Goossaert and David Palmer, *The Religious Question in Modern China* (Chicago: University of Chicago Press, 2012), 317.

3.   José Casanova, *Public Religions in the Modern World* (Chicago: University of Chicago Press,
1994), 19–39; José Casanova, "The Secular, Secularizations and Secularisms," in *Rethinking Secularism*, ed. Craig Calhoun, Mark Juergensmeyer, and Jonathan VanAntwerpen (New York:
Oxford University Press, 2011), 60.

4.   Goossaert and Palmer, *The Religious Question*; Mayfair Yang, *Chinese Religiosities*; Yoshiko
Ashiwa and David L. Wank, eds., *Making Religion, Making the State: The Politics of Religion in*

Modern China (Stanford, Calif.: Stanford University Press, 2009); Rebecca Nedostup, *Superstitious Regimes: Religion and the Politics of Chinese Modernity* (Cambridge, Mass. and London: Harvard University Press, 2009).

5. As used here, "secularization" does not refer to the progressive decline of religious beliefs. What I present is *not* a cross-cultural theory of secularization. On "religion" as a historical project, see Tasal Asad, *Genealogies of Religion: Discipline and Reasons of Power in Christianity and Islam* (Baltimore, Md.: John Hopkins University Press, 1993), 29. For Talal Asad's comments on José Casanova's three aspects of "secularization" and theory on the genealogy of secularism as an ideology, see Asad, *Formations of the Secular: Christianity, Islam and Modernity* (Stanford: Stanford University Press, 2003), 181–182; 192–194.

6. Goossaert and Palmer, *The Religious Question*, 6.

7. David Germano, "Re-membering the Dismembered Body of Tibet: Contemporary Tibetan Visionary Movements in the People's Republic of China," in *Buddhism in Contemporary Tibet: Religious Revival and Cultural Identity,* ed. Melvyn Goldstein and Matthew Kapstein (Berkeley: University of California Press, 1998), 53–94; Holly Gayley, *Love Letters from Golok: A Tantric Couple in Modern Tibet* (New York: Columbia University Press, 2017).

8. Wang Yao, "Hu Yaobang's Visit to Tibet, May 22–31, 1980: An Important Development in the Chinese Government's Tibet Policy," in *Resistance and Reform in Tibet,* ed. Robert Barnett and Shirin Akiner (Delhi: Motilal Banarsidass, 1994), 287.

9. The press associated with the Cultural Relics Office published the Dalai Lama's "Ode to Mao Zedong," studied in chapter 2, after Dungkar Rinpoché left this office.

10. The evidence for the dates he was employed at the Cultural Relics Office (Bod ljongs rig rdzas do dam U yon lhan khang) leans toward 1976, but not all sources are in agreement. According to "Gangs can mkhas pa'i khyu mchog dung dkar blo bzang 'phrin las kyi mdzad rim," an appendix at the end Dungkar Rinpoché's *Collected Works* (volumes 4 and 7) that has separate pagination from the rest of the volume, Dungkar Lozang Trinlé worked there in 1976. There is no mention of this in his own "Lo tshigs dwangs shel me long" [The clear mirror: a chronology]. According to his son's biography, he took the position in the Cultural Relics Office in 1975. See Dung dkar 'jigs med, "Sprul sku nas slob dpon chen mo—nga'i A pha lags phyir dran byas ba" [From tulku to professor: in remembrance of my father], *Krung go'i bod ljongs,* Zhongguo Xizang 中国西藏 [China's Tibet] 4, no. 27 (July 2014): 50. Pema Bhum states that he worked there in 1976 as "part of his reform through labor" work assignment; see "An Overview of the Life of the Professor Dungkar Lozang Trinle Rinpoché," *Trace Foundation's Latse Library Newsletter* 5 (2007–2008): 22.

11. Pema Bhum, *Six Stars and a Crooked Neck: Tibetan Memoirs of the Cultural Revolution* (dran tho smin drug ske 'khyog). Trans. Lauran R. Hartley [bilingual Tibetan and English] (Dharamsala: Tibet Times, 2001).

12. Pema Bhum, "An Overview of the Life of the Professor Dungkar Lozang Trinle Rinpoché," 22–23.

13. Melvyn Goldstein and Matthew Kapstein, "Introduction," *Buddhism in Contemporary Tibet: Religious Revival and Cultural Identity* (Berkeley: University of California Press, 1998), 11.

14. Elliot Sperling, "Tibet and China: The Interpretation of History Since 1950," *China Perspectives* 3 (2009): 30.

15. Samten G. Karmay, "Mountain Cults and National Identity in Tibet," in *Resistance and Reform in Tibet,* ed. Robert Barnett and Shirin Skinner (Delhi: Motilal Banarsidass, 1994), 114.

16. Samten G. Karmay, "Mountain Cults and National Identity in Tibet," 115.

17. John Avedon, *In Exile from the Land of Snows* (New York: HarperCollins, 1997), 14.

18. Elliot Sperling, "'Orientalism' and Aspects of Violence in the Tibetan Tradition," in *Imagining Tibet: Perceptions, Projections and Fantasies*, ed. Thierry Dodin and Heinz Räther (Boston: Wisdom, 2001), 320.

19. Donald S. Lopez Jr., *Prisoners of Shangri-la* (Chicago: University of Chicago Press, 1998), 11.

20. Heather Stoddard, "Tibetan Publications and National Identity," in *Resistance and Reform in Tibet*, ed. Robert Barnett and Shirin Akiner (Delhi: Motilal Banarsidass, 1994), 125.

21. Dung-dkar blo-bzang 'phrim-las, *The Merging of Religious and Secular Rule in Tibet*, trans. Chen Guansheng (Beijing: Foreign Languages Press, 1991), 51–52.

22. Tsering Shakya, "Whither the Tsampa Eaters?," *Himal* 6, no. 5 (1993).

23. See Melvyn Goldstein, "The Dragon and the Snow Lion: The Tibet Question in the 20th Century," *Tibetan Review* (April 1991).

24. For example, Melvyn Goldstein states: "I use 'Tibet' to mean the political entity that was equivalent to Tibet in the 1930s and 1940s, that is to today's Tibet Autonomous Region, and not the artificially conceptualized 'greater Tibet' that Tibetans in exile would like to see created." Goldstein, "The Tibet Question in the 20th Century," 9. For a comparison of the contested views of Tibet's territory, see Carole McGranahan, *Arrested Histories: Tibet, the CIA, and Memories of a Forgotten War* (Durham, N.C. and London: Duke University Press, 2010), 37–52, especially 49.

25. See Stevan Harrell, *Cultural Encounters on China's Ethnic Frontiers* (Seattle: University of Washington Press, 1995); Thomas Mullaney, *Coming to Terms with the Nation: Ethnic Classification in Modern China* (Berkeley: University of California Press, 2011); Miaoyan Yang, *Learning to Be Tibetan: The Construction of Ethnic Identity in China* (Lanham, Md.; Boulder, Colo.; New York; London: Lexington Books, 2017).

26. Mullaney, *Coming to Terms with the Nation*, 90; Stevan Harrell, "Introduction: Civilizing Projects and the Reaction to Them," in *Cultural Encounters on China's Ethnic Frontiers*, 23.

27. Tibet Information Network/Robert Barnett, *A Poisoned Arrow: The Secret Report of the 10th Panchen Lama* (London: Tibet Information Network, 1997), 69–70.

28. Tibet Information Network/Robert Barnett, *A Poisoned Arrow*, xii–xiii.

29. Department of Information and International Relations (DIIR), *From the Heart of the Panchen Lama: Major Speeches and a Petition: 1962–1989* (Dharamsala: DIIR Central Tibetan Administration, 2003), 7.

30. Tsering Shakya, *The Dragon in the Land of Snows: A History of Modern Tibet Since 1947* (New York: Columbia University Press, 1999), 391.

31. Harrell explains, "A civilizing project is thus not a unified thing, either in its purposes and methods or in the reaction of the people civilized. Only one thing remains constant: the assumption of cultural superiority by the economically powerful center and the use of the superiority, and the supposed benefits it can confer on the peripheral peoples, as an aspect of hegemonic rule." Harrell, "Introduction," 36.

32. Yang, *Learning to Be Tibetan*, 69, 86; Harrell, "Introduction," 36.

33. Information Office of the State Council of The People's Republic of China, *White Papers on Tibet* (Beijing, 1992), accessed March 10, 2016, http://www.china.org.cn/e-white/tibet/9-9.htm.

34. John Powers notes that in 1958 Wang Feng argued that China's minorities needed the leadership of the Chinese Communist Party because they considered Tibetans not as advanced. See Powers, *The Buddha Party* (Oxford: Oxford University Press, 2017), 196.

35. Harrell, "Introduction," 25–26.

36. Goossaert and Palmer, *The Religious Question*, 154.

37. Goossaert and Palmer, *The Religious Question*, 155.

38. Goossaert and Palmer, *The Religious Question*, 155.

39. This information is omitted from the author's *Collected Works* (2004) and the Beijing-sanctioned English translation (1991). See Dung dkar blo bzang 'phrin las, "Bod kyi chos srid zung 'brel skor bshad pa"

[An explanation of the merging of religious and secular rule in Tibet], in *Mkhas dbang dung dkar blo bzang 'phrin las kyi gsung 'bum: Bod kyi chos srid zung 'brel lam lugs skor bshad pa* [Dungkar Lozang Trinle's collected works: an explanation of the merging of religious and secular rule in Tibet], ed. Rnam rgyal ra 'phrin las rgya mtsho (Beijing: Minzu chubanshe, 2004), vol. 4; Dung-dkar blo-bzang 'phrim-las, *The Merging of Religious and Secular Rule in Tibet,* trans. Chen Guansheng.

40. de sngon 1977 lor| krung gung bod rang skyong ljongs tang U dang| rang skyong ljongs 'thab phyogs cgic gyur pu'u nas| gus rang la bod kyi chos srid zung 'brel gyi lam lugs de gang 'dra byas nas byung ba'i skor gyi lo rgyus zhig 'bri dgos pa'i las 'gan gnang byung zhing|

    Dung dkar blo bzang 'phrin las, "Bod kyi chos srid zung 'brel skor bshad pa" [An explanation of the merging of religious and secular rule in Tibet], in *Dung dkar blo bzang 'phrin las kyi gsung rtsom 'phyogs bsgrigs* [A collection of Dungkar Lozang Trinlé's essays] (Beijing: Zhongguo zangxue chubanshe, 1997), 481.

41. Pema Bhum, "An Overview of the Life of Professor Dungkar Lozang Trinle Rinpoche," 27–29.

42. Tsering Shakya, "The Development of Modern Tibetan Studies," in *Resistance and Reform in Tibet,* ed. Robert Barnett and Shirin Akiner (New Delhi: Motilal Banarsiddass, 1994), 10.

43. Dung dkar blo bzang 'phrin las, "Bod kyi chos srid zung 'brel," 2004, 4: 106–107; Dung-dkar blo-bzang 'phrim-las, *The Merging of Religious and Secular Rule in Tibet,* trans. Chen Guansheng, 76; Melvyn Goldstein, *A History of Modern Tibet: Demise of a Lamaist State* (Berkeley: University of California Press, 1989), 21; see note 31.

44. One obituary stated, " 'He was well disposed towards the Chinese, so none of us who are from the same class would trust him,' recalled one Tibetan, another former dignitary, who worked for nine years in the same forced labour gang based in Toelung, near Lhasa, where they dug drains and constructed small power plants. 'During class struggle sessions he would say that he had done good deeds for the Party and would blame others, even though he was the same class as us, the landlord class,' said the Tibetan, who now lives in India." Tibet Information Network News Updates, "Leading Scholar Dies, Cultural Criticism," (August 4, 1997), accessed March 18, 2019, http://www.columbia.edu/itc/ealac/barnett/pdfs/link2-dlt-obit.pdf.

45. Tsering D. Gonkatsang, "Dungkar Lobzang Trinlé," *Himalaya* 36, no. 1 (Spring 2016): 176.

46. Pema Bhum, "An Overview of the Life of Professor Dungkar Lozang Trinlé Rinpoché," 26–27.

47. Dung-dkar blo-bzang 'phrim-las, *The Merging of Religious and Secular Rule in Tibet,* trans. Chen Guansheng, 76, 98.

48. Dung dkar blo bzang 'phrin las, "Bod kyi chos srid zung 'brel" [Merging of religious and secular rule in Tibet], 2004, 4:140. Both sections in Tibetan: bod kyi chos srid zung 'brel lam lugs nang rgyun ring 'tsho ba bskyal te sangs rgyas chos lugs dang bshu gzhog gral rim gyi bag chags gting zab yod pa'i sprul sku'i ming can nga rang 'dra ba yang| krung go gung khran tang gi byams brtse'i thugs khur 'og gsar brje'i las don nang zhugs nas| mar le'i gsung rtsom dang| ma'o tse tung gi gsung rtsom slob sbyong byas pa dang chabs cig zhar dang zhor la spyi tshogs tshan rig dang| rang byung tshan rig snga rabs bod kyi lo rgyus yig cha mang po bltas pa brgyud| rtsod sgrub dngos gtso smra ba'i lo rgyus lta tshul la go ba cung zad gting zab tsam lon thub pa dang mthong rgya che ru song ba 'di la blta dus| de sngon rang nyid dgon pa'i nang bla ma byas te 'dzam gling spyi tshogs kyi 'gyur ldog dang| spyi tshogs 'phel rgyas kyi gnas tshul gang yang shes rtogs ma byung ba de dang bsdur na dga' tshor skyes 'os pa'i grub 'bras red bsam gyi 'dug sngar song lo rgyus kyi yig cha rnying pa dang| lo rgyus kyi bya ba rnying pa| lo rgyus kyi dngos po rnying pa bcas la zhib 'jug dang brtag| dbyad byas pa'i go rim brgyud deng rabs kyi bya dngos gsar par ngos 'dzin dang bslab bya len rgyur rang nyid la blo sgo chen po phye thub pa byung bar brten| bod kyi chos srid zung 'brel gyi lam lugs gang 'dra byas nas byung ba'i lo rgyus skor la rang gi lta tshul dngos gnas gang yod sbas gsang med par bris pa yin pas gzigs pa po rnams kyis rtsom yig 'di la legs bcos dang skyon cha gang yod dgongs 'char dang| rin thang bral ba'i bka' slob yod pa zhu rgyu bcas|

49. Dung-dkar blo-bzang 'phrim-las, *The Merging of Religious and Secular Rule in Tibet,* trans. Chen Guansheng, 98.

50. For the Tibetan text, see note 48 above. The Beijing English translation reads: "I realize that one's level of understanding can be raised by studying and analyzing historical events, annals, and relics and by learning lessons from the past. This book attempts to present my point of view on the history of the Tibetan polity based on the merging of religion and secular rule. Readers are welcome to give their comments and opinions on it." Dung-dkar blo-bzang 'phrim-las, *The Merging of Religious and Secular Rule in Tibet,* trans. Chen Guansheng, 98.

51. Bstan 'dzin dge legs [Tenzin Gelek], "Chos dung kar po'i rang mdangs/ slob dpon chen mo dung dkar blo bzang 'phrin las mchog nub phyogs yul du snga phyir mjal ba'i bag chags rab rim," *Gtam tshogs* 37, no. 1 (July): 9.

52. See David L. McMahan, *The Making of Buddhist Modernism* (Oxford: Oxford University Press, 2008), 63–67; 89–115.

53. Examples of these different translations can be found in the essays in a volume dedicated to the topic. See Christoph Cüppers, ed., *The Relationship Between Religion and State (chos srid zung 'brel) in Traditional Tibet* (Lumbini: Lumbini International Research Institute, 2004).

54. Casanova, "The Secular, Secularizations and Secularisms," 59–60.

55. I was able to find only one other work on Tibetan history published in the PRC prior to Dungkar Rinpoche's *Merging of Religious and Secular Rule,* and it was written in Chinese: Ya Hanzhang (牙含章), *Xizang lishi de xin pianzhang* 西藏历史的新篇章 [New essays in Tibetan history] (Chengdu: Sichuan minzu chubanshe, 1979).

56. For an overview of this research, see Holly Gayley and Nicole Willock, "Theorizing the Secular in Tibetan Cultural Worlds," *Himalaya* 36, no. 1 (Spring 2016): 12–19.

57. Dieter Schuh, "Srid ohne Chos? Reflektionen zum Verhältnis von Buddhismus und säkularer Herrschaft im tibetischen Kulturraum," in *The Relationship Between Religion and State (chos srid zung 'brel) in Traditional Tibet*, ed. Christoph Cüppers (Lumbini: Lumbini International Research Institute, 2004), 291.

58. Yumiko Ishihama, "The Notion of 'Buddhist Government' (chos srid) Shared by Tibet, Mongol and Manchu in the Early 17th Century," in *The Relationship Between Religion and State (chos srid zung 'brel) in Traditional Tibet*, ed. Christoph Cüppers (Lumbini: Lumbini International Research Institute, 2004), 30.

59. David Seyfort Ruegg, "Introductory Remarks on the Spiritual and Temporal Orders," in *The Relationship Between Religion and State (chos srid zung 'brel) in Traditional Tibet,* ed. Christoph Cüppers (Lumbini: Lumbini International Research Institute, 2004), 9.

60. Goldstein, *A History of Modern Tibet*, 542. According to Goldstein, the translation by Lobsang Lhalungpa was from a Tibetan copy of the original letter; see 543 n. 33.

61. Trine Brox, "Changing the Tibetan Way: Contested Secularisms in the Tibetan Diaspora," in *Tibetan Studies: An Anthology, PIATS 6: Proceedings for the International Association of Tibetan Studies,* ed. Saadet Arslen and Peter Schwieger (Andiast: International Institute for Tibetan and Buddhist Studies, 2010).

62. Pema Bhum, "An Overview of the Life of Professor Dungkar Lozang Trinlé Rinpoché," 20. According to a table of major life events included in the appendix of volumes 4 and 7 of his *Collected Works*, Dungkar Rinpoche was His Holiness's debate partner in Abhidharma (*mngon pa mdzod kyi bgro gleng 'bul mkhan*). See Rnam rgyal ra 'phrin las rgya mtsho, ed., "Gangs can mkhas pa'i khyu mchog dung dkar blo bzang 'phrin las kyi mdzad rim" [A biographical timeline of Tibet's top scholar Dungkar Lozang Trinle], *Mkhas dbang dung dkar blo bzang 'phrin las kyi gsung 'bum* (Beijing: Minzu chubanshe 2004), 4 and 7 (appendix): 2. This fact is not mentioned in Dungkar Lozang Trinle, *Dung dkar tshig mdzod chen mo* [Dungkar encyclopedia] (Beijing: Zhongguo Zangxue chubanshe, 2002), 2377. spyi lo 1959 'gor smon lam skabs ta' la'i bla mas lha rams pa'i mtshan rtags bzhes| zla'i 3 tshes 12 nyin ta la'i bla ma bstan 'dzin rgya mtsho rgya gar du bros byol phebs| In the Gregorian year 1959, during the Monlam Festival, the Dalai Lama was

awarded the Geshe Lharampa. On the 12th day of the 3rd month (March 12), the Dalai Lama went into exile in India.

63. This volume also has a significant addendum: his encyclopedic notes accompanying this work, which are approximately the same length as the text itself.

64. Tibetan: "En ke si'i hphu lu hri rgyal po hphu li di li zhi wa'i len skye phreng bzhi." Dorje Rabtan (Rdo rje rab brtan) translated it from the Chinese and Dungkar Rinpoché transcribed it and commented on it; Dung dkar blo bzang 'phrin las, "Bod kyi chos srid zung 'brel" [Merging of religious and secular rule in Tibet], 2004, 4: 2; for the Tibetan translation of Engels's essay, see 2004, 4: 4–6. An online English translation of Engel's essay is available: https://marxists.catbull .com/archive/marx/works/1842/10/king-prussia.htm, accessed January 25, 2019.

65. "chos srid zung 'brel zer ba yul gyi rgyal po dang chos bdag gnyis ka mi gcig gis byas pa," in Dung dkar blo bzang 'phrin las, "Bod kyi chos srid zung 'brel gyi lam lugs la thog ma'i zhib 'jug byas pa'i shes tshor gnad bsdus" [Essential points reflecting on the initial research on the system of merging the religious and secular in Tibet], in Dung dkar blo bzang 'phrin las kyi gsung 'bum, 2004, 4: 7–8.

66. "dang po| chos srid zung 'brel gyi lam lugs ma byung gong chos srid tha dad du gnas pa'i dus skabs kyi gnas tshul dang chos lugs phan tshun bar gyi 'thab rtsod skor|" "Part 1: Interreligious Struggles and the Status of the Conditions Separating Religion and Politics Prior to the Establishment of Buddhist Governance," in Dung dkar blo bzang 'phrin las, "Bod kyi chos srid zung 'brel skor bshad pa" [An explanation of the merging of religious and secular rule in Tibet], 1997, 483.

67. "gnyis pa| chos srid zung 'brel gyi lam lugs dngos su 'go tshugs pa dang| chos lugs grub mtha' khag gi mtho rim mi snas chos lugs byed spyad nas phan tshun dang 'phrog res byas pa'i 'thab rtsod skor|." "Part 2: The Struggles to Seize Political Power Using Religion by the Elites of Various Religious Sects and the Establishment of Buddhist Governance," in Dung dkar blo bzang 'phrin las, "Bod kyi chos srid zung 'brel skor bshad pa" [An explanation of the merging of religious and secular rule in Tibet], 1997, 548.

68. Dung dkar blo bzang 'phrin las, "Bod kyi chos srid zung 'brel skor bshad pa" [An explanation of the merging of religious and secular rule in Tibet], 1997, 483–547; Dung-dkar blo-bzang 'phrim-las, The Merging of Religious and Secular Rule in Tibet, trans. Chen Guansheng, 1–41.

69. "Imperialists" refers to the foreign powers. Here in particular it refers to the Younghusband Expedition, a British military incursion into Tibet in 1904. "A reactionary" is anyone who wishes to go back to the previous political status quo. One of Mao's goals to ensure the success of the Chinese revolution was to get rid of any "reactionary elements."

70. Dung dkar blo bzang 'phrin las, "Bod kyi chos srid zung 'brel skor bshad pa" [An explanation of the merging of religious and secular rule in Tibet], 1997, 548–613; Dung-dkar blo-bzang 'phrim-las, The Merging of Religious and Secular Rule in Tibet, trans. Chen Guansheng, 42–94.

71. For an example of this, the Beijing-sanctioned English language publication reads: "A handful of Tibetan reactionary high-ranking officials even took the fourteenth Dalai Lama under duress to the border town of Yadong, where they were ready to set up a so-called 'independent state' with the support of the imperialists." Dung-dkar blo-bzang 'phrim-las, The Merging of Religious and Secular Rule in Tibet, trans. Chen Guansheng, 91. Cf. Dung dkar blo bzang 'phrin las, "Bod kyi chos srid zung 'brel," 1997, 614.

72. See Powers, The Buddha Party.

73. Sperling, "Tibet and China: The Interpretation of History Since 1950," and The Tibet-China Conflict.

74. According to Dungkar Rinpoché, Pakpa was awarded the title of "Imperial Preceptor" (di'i shri) in 1270. Dung dkar blo bzang 'phrin las, "Bod kyi chos srid zung 'brel skor bshad pa" [An explanation of the merging of religious and secular rule in Tibet], 1997, 553.

75. Dung dkar blo bzang 'phrin las, "Bod kyi chos srid zung 'brel skor bshad pa" [An explanation of the merging of religious and secular rule in Tibet], 1997, 554.

76. 'Gro mgon 'phags pa ni dus skabs de'i bod kyi mnga' bdag chen po gsum gyi spyi'i gtso bdag yin pa| Dung dkar blo bzang 'phrin las, "Bod kyi chos srid zung 'brel skor bshad pa" [An explanation of the merging of religious and secular rule in Tibet], 1997, 555.

77. "Map of Yuan Dynasty, 1330" in Christopher Atwood, *Encyclopedia of Mongolia and the Mongol Empire* (New York: Facts On File, 2004), 604.

78. Dung-dkar blo-bzang 'phrim-las, *The Merging of Religious and Secular Rule in Tibet*, trans. Chen Guansheng, 44.
    Cf.: lo de'i phyi lo bod kyi rab byung bzhi pa'i lcags spyi lo 1240 lo go dan rgyal po blon po dor rta nag pos sne khrid pa'i dpag dpung bod du btang| bod du chos lugs thog mkhas shos su yin zhib 'jug byas te| rab byung bzhi'i shing 'brug spyi lo 1244 lor yon rgyal rabs kyi gong ma go dan rgyal pos sa skya pan chen mes rgyal nang khul du gdan drangs| bod kyi rab byung bzhi pa'i chu byi spyi lo 1251 lor yon shan tsung [Ch. xianzong] mong gol han gyis srid dbang bzung rjes kyi phyi lo chu glang spyi lo 1253 lor bod du dmag dpung btang nas bod yongs rdzogs gong bu bcig gyur byas pa dang| dus mtshungs mnga' khongs su dud tshang zhib bsher byas|
    Dung dkar blo bzang 'phrin las, "Bod kyi chos srid zung 'brel skor bshad pa" [An explanation of the merging of religious and secular rule in Tibet], 1997, 551–552.

79. See note 78.

80. Atwood, *Encyclopedia of Mongolia*, 302; 362–365; 604–606; 625.

81. 'gro mgon 'phags pas bod kyi rang byung ba bzhi pa'i shing glang (hu pi li se chen khan gyi kri yon lo dang po) spyi lo 1264 lo nas lo gsum ring srid dbang bzung| Dung dkar blo bzang 'phrin las, "Bod kyi chos srid zung 'brel skor bshad pa" [An explanation of the merging of religious and secular rule in Tibet], 1997, 556.

82. Atwood, *Encyclopedia of Mongolia,* 75.

83. Atwood, *Encyclopedia of Mongolia*, 321. See also Luciano Petech, "Tibetan Relations with Sung China and with the Mongols," in *China Among Equals: The Middle Kingdon and its Neighbors, 10th–14th Centuries*, ed. Morris Rossabi (Berkeley: University of California Press, 1983), 180–183.

84. Atwood, *Encyclopedia of Mongolia*, 321.

85. Derek F. Maher, "Translator's Introduction," in *Tsepon Wangchuk Deden Shakabpa, One Hundred Thousand Moons: An Advanced Political History of Tibet*, trans. Derek F. Maher (Leiden and Boston: Brill, 2010), xvii.

86. Shakabpa, *One Hundred Thousand Moons,* trans. Maher, 249.

87. Petech, "Tibetan Relations with Sung China," 190.

88. Petech, "Tibetan Relations with Sung China," 190.

89. rab byung bzhi pa'i shing glang| spyi lo 1264 lor hu bi li se chen khan gyis 'gro mgon 'phags pa la gsang sngags kyi dbang thengs dang po zhus pa'i dbang yon du| mgna' ris dang mdo smad gnyis phud pa'i bod khri sko bcu gsum phul| Dung dkar blo bzang 'phrin las, "Bod kyi chos srid zung 'brel skor bshad pa" [An explanation of the merging of religious and secular rule in Tibet], 1997, 552.

90. Dung dkar blo bzang 'phrin las, "Bod kyi chos srid zung 'brel skor bshad pa" [An explanation of the merging of religious and secular rule in Tibet], 1997, 552–554.

91. See note 75 above.

92. See Sperling, "Tibet and China: The Interpretation of History Since 1950," and *The Tibet-China Conflict.*

93. Sperling, "Tibet and China: The Interpretation of History Since 1950," 25–26.

94. Dung dkar blo bzang 'phrin las, "Bod kyi chos srid zung 'brel skor bshad pa" [An explanation of the merging of religious and secular rule in Tibet], 1997, 544–545; 2004, 4: 63.

95. Translated by Elliot Sperling, "Tibet and China: The Interpretation of History Since 1950," 34–35. Unfortunately the link to the original Chinese article is no longer active; see note 44 in Sperling.

96. Elliot Sperling notes that the Chinese government presented its interpretation of Tibet's historical status in *Concerning the Question of Tibet,* which states that Tibet became part of the territory of China in 1253 when the Yuan dynasty emperor Möngke sent an armed force there. See Sperling, *The Tibet-China Conflict,* 10–11.

97. Translated by Sperling, "Tibet and China: The Interpretation of History Since 1950," 34–35; see note 94 above.

98. Sperling, *The Tibet-China Conflict,* 10–11, 24–25.

99. Sperling, *The Tibet-China Conflict,* 39 n. 24 includes a number of recent PRC histories on Tibet.

100. Pema Bhum, "An Overview of the Life of Dungkar Lozang Trinlé Rinpoché," 27.

101. On the importance of this text, see also Dan Martin, *Tibetan Histories: A Bibliography of Tibetan-language Historical Works* (London: Serindia, 1997), 52–53; David Seyfort Ruegg, "Preceptor-Donor Relations in Thirteenth-Century Tibetan Society and Polity: Its Inner Asian Precursors and Indian Models," in *The Tibetan History Reader,* ed. Gray Tuttle and Kurtis Schaeffer (New York: Columbia University Press, 2013), 215.

102. Heather Stoddard lists a number of historical classics reprinted in new book formats in the 1980s and also includes new social scientific research on Tibet, such as Dungkar Lozang Trinle's *Merging of Religious and Secular Rule in Tibet.* See Stoddard, "Tibetan Publications and National Identity," 138–139.

103. Pema Bhum, "An Overview of the Life of Dungkar Lozang Trinlé Rinpoché," 27.

104. Christopher Atwood shows that after Chinggis Khan conquered the Tangut capital in 1226, ethnic Tibetans were recruited into Mongol armies from the 1230s. "Long before Köten had ever met Sa-skya Paṇḍita, Tibetans had joined Öng'üts, Han, and Tanguts in key positions among the *keshigten* or hostage bodyguard of Prince Köten. From this perspective, Dor-da Darqan's expeditions to Central Tibet to summon Tibetan clerics and their young relatives as hostages into his entourage was simply a continuation of a trend." Christopher Atwood, "The First Mongol Contact with the Tibetans," in *Trails of Tibetan Tradition: Papers for Elliot Sperling,* ed. Roberto Vitali (Dharamsala: Amnye Machen Institute, 2014), 41.

105. Dungkar Rinpoché does not seem to be using the term "Böd mi" in a nationalistic sense as it had been employed in eastern Tibet in the 1940s. He uses the parameters of nationality policy, especially the characteristics of language, culture, and territory, to talk about what constitutes Böd. He does not use this to assert an independent national identity, for example, as the first Tibetan communists did when they marched to join Mao Zedong. At that time, Sangyé Yeshé (Sangs rgyas ye shes, a.ka. Tian Bao) formed the first Böd-pa "Tibetan" Communist area in Gandze (dkar mdzes) in Kham in 1935. The "Independent Böd-pa" division marched to Mao Zedong at Yan'an. Stoddard, "Tibetan Publications and National Identity," 126.

106. lo de'i phyi lo rgyal po go dan gyis blon po dor rta nag pos gtso bor byas pa'i dmag dpung bod du btang nas| mdo stod| mdo smad| sog chu kha rnams su yod pa'i bod mi mthong tshad gsod pa dang| khang pa mer bsreg pa| rgyu nor phrogs pa bcas byed bzhin du dbus gtsang du yong| 'phan po rgyal gyi lha khang mer bsregs nas grwa pa rab tu byung ba lnga brgya tsam dmar gsod byas| rwa sgreng dgon pa la yang gnod 'tshe chen po byas pas mtshon mgo btag ma zhus pa'i sa gnas tshang mar bsregs gsod phrogs gsum gyi mgo nas ming med du gtong ba sogs byas|

　　Dung dkar blo bzang 'phrin las, "Deb ther dmar po'i nang gi gal che'i tshig 'grel gnad bsdus" [An explanation of select major terminologies in the *Red Annals*], in *Mkhas dbang dung dkar blo bzang 'phrin las kyi gsung 'bum: deb ther dmar po'i gal che'i tshig 'grel gnas bsdus* [Dungkar Lozang

Trinle's collected works: an explanation of select major terminologies in the *Red Annals*], ed. Rnam rgyal ra 'phrin las rgya mtsho (Namgyel Ratrinle) (Beijing: Minzu chubanshe, 2004), 6: 200.

107.   Historically, Chinese and Mongol histories did not use the term "Böd mi," but rather referred to the Tibetan people near the Mongol court as "Böri," which Christopher Atwood identified as "Bi-ri," an ethnonym appearing occasionally in Tibetan sources that he suggests referred to nomadic Amdo Tibetans living near the former Tangut capital. See Atwood, "First Mongol Contact with the Tibetans," 22–26.

108.   Tsering Shakya wrote, "There is no indigenous term which encompasses the population denoted by the Western usage. A local term such as Bodpa can be used only restrictively, even today. The nomads of Changthang use it for the people of the Lhasa valley, while for the people of Kham and A mdo it means exclusively the inhabitants of Central Tibet. Significantly, the person using the term Bodpa never identifies himself as part of the group. Among the Tibetan refugee community, Bodpa is now generally accepted to mean the people from Kham, Amdo and U-Tsang. Even here, the term is used specifically to denote the people under Chinese rule and not the refugees themselves, who might have their origins in those regions." "Whither the Tsampa Eaters," 8.

109.   Dung dkar blo bzang 'phrin las, "Deb ther dmar po'i nang gi gal che'i tshig 'grel gnad bsdus" [Terminologies in the *Red Annals*], 6: 202.

110.   Petech, "Tibetan Relations with Sung China," 190.

111.   bod kyi mi dmangs rnams yon rgyal rabs kyi srid jus la yid ches chen po skye thub pa byung ba dang| yon rgyal rabs kyis bod dang mes rgyal gcig gyur byed pa'i bya gzhag la rgyab skor dang skul ma chen po thebs nas sa skya pan chen sku ma 'das bar gyi lo ngo brgyad tsam ring yon rgyal rabs kyis bod sa gnas su dmag dpung btang mi dgos pa'i bde 'jags chen po byung ba bcas| sa skya pan chen ni bod sa gnas dang mes rgyal gong bu gcig gyur bas pa'i bya gzhag nang byas rjes chen po bzhag pa'i bod rigs chos lugs mi sna zhig yin|

   Dung dkar blo bzang 'phrin las, "Deb ther dmar po'i nang gi gal che'i tshig 'grel gnad bsdus" [Terminologies in the *Red Annals*], 6: 202.

112.   Personal communication, February 20, 2020.

113.   Goossaert and Palmer, *The Religious Question*, 320.

114.   See Ashiwa and Wank, "Introduction"; Goossaert and Palmer, *The Religious Question*, 320.

115.   Dung dkar blo bzang 'phrin las, "Bod kyi chos srid zung 'brel skor bshad pa" [An explanation of the merging of religious and secular rule in Tibet], 1997, 483–485; 557. For more explanation on the history of Bön, see Tsering Thar, *Nangshig: A Tibetan Bonpo Monastery and Its Family in Amdo* (Kathmandu, Nepal: Vajra Books, 2016), 17. Tsering Thar explains that Drigung Jigten Gonpo laid out three historical stages of Bön: the primal Bön (*rdol bon*); diffused Bön (*'khyar bon*); and "Bön of transformation" (*bsgyur bon*), not Thuken.

116.   Dung dkar blo bzang 'phrin las, "Bod kyi chos srid zung 'brel skor bshad pa" [An explanation of the merging of religious and secular rule in Tibet], 1997, 509.

117.   Dung dkar blo bzang 'phrin las, "Bod kyi chos srid zung 'brel skor bshad pa" [An explanation of the merging of religious and secular rule in Tibet], 1997, 557.

118.   Dung dkar blo bzang 'phrin las, "Bod kyi chos srid zung 'brel skor bshad pa" [An explanation of the merging of religious and secular rule in Tibet], 1997, 566.

119.   Dung dkar blo bzang 'phrin las, "Bod kyi chos srid zung 'brel skor bshad pa" [An explanation of the merging of religious and secular rule in Tibet], 1997, 568.

120.   Dung dkar blo bzang 'phrin las, "Bod kyi chos srid zung 'brel skor bshad pa" [An explanation of the merging of religious and secular rule in Tibet], 1997, 566–568, 588.

121.   Dung dkar blo bzang 'phrin las, "Bod kyi chos srid zung 'brel skor bshad pa" [An explanation of the merging of religious and secular rule in Tibet], 1997, 588.

122.   Georges Roerich, trans., *The Blue Annals* [*Deb ther sngon po* by 'Gos lo-tsā-ba Gzhon nu dpal], (Delhi: Motilal Banarsidass, 1996 [reprint]), 42. Tibetan: khyed kyi chos lugs ci yin zhes dris pas|

mkhan po'i zhal nas| kho bo'i chos lugs ni rigs pas legs par brtags te gang 'thad pa de byed| mi 'thad pa de mi byed pa yin zer| See also 'Gos lo gzhon nu dpal, *Deb ther sngon po* [The blue annals] Chengdu: Si khron mi rigs dpe skrun khang, 1984 [reprint], 68.

123. Thu'u bkwan blo bzang chos kyi nyi ma, *Grub mtha' she gyi me long* (Lanzhou: Gansu minzu chubanshe, reprint 1984), 385. TBRC W2124; Thuken Losang Chökyi Nyima, *The Crystal Mirror of Philosophical Systems: A Tibetan Study of Asian Religious Thought,* trans. Geshé Lhundub Sopa, ed. Roger R. Jackson (Boston: Wisdom, 2009), 324–325.

124. Dung dkar blo bzang 'phrin las, "Bod kyi chos srid zung 'brel skor bshad pa" [An explanation of the merging of religious and secular rule in Tibet], 1997, 557.

125. Brox, "Changing the Tibetan Way," 130.

126. The entry on *chöluk* defines this term as "religious sects or customs" (*chos kyi grub mtha' 'am| lugs srol*), which is then glossed with the Chinese term for "religion" (Ch. *zōngjiào* 宗教) alongside the Chinese term for "sect" (Ch. *jiàopài* 教派). The same entry also gives several examples of modern usage in both Tibetan and Chinese, such as in the terms for "religious activities" (*chos lugs byed sgo*; Ch. *zōngjiào huódòng* 宗教活动) and "Buddhism," which is literally "the religion of the insider," according to the Tibetan text (*nang pa'i chos lugs*) and "Buddhist teachings" from the Chinese (Ch. *fójiào* 佛教). See Zhang Yisun, ed., *Bod rgya tshig mdzod chen mo* (Ch. 藏汉大词典) [=*Tibetan-Chinese Encyclopedia*] (Beijing: Mi rigs dpe skrun khang, 1985), 1: 844.

127. I am grateful to my late professor Elliot Sperling for his generosity in sharing this source with me. The Chinese-Tibetan bilingual edition of this work was republished by the Mongol-Tibetan Affairs Office of the Republic of China in 1971. The Tibetan language preface stated that this is a reprint of a translation undertaken in 1943 by the Frontier Languages Translation Committee (mtha' mtshams skad yig rtsom sgyur lhan khang) of the Guomindang's Central Organization Department (krung go go ming twang dbyang rtsa 'dzugs las khung). The Tibetan language colophon at the end of the Tibetan section of this work stated that the text was prepared by Yang Zhifu (Yang khi hphu, Byams pa rnam rgyal) and was edited and corrected by his teacher Sherab Gyatso (Shes rab rgya mtsho 'Jam dpal dgyes pa'i blo gros) (N.p.: Meng Zang weiyuanhui 1971), 111–112.

128. Krung hwa mi dmangs spyi mthun rgyal khab kyi rtsa khrims [=The Constitution of the People's Republic of China in Tibetan; Chinese: Zhonghua renmin gongheguo xianfa], 1954. Article 88 states that "Citizens of the People's Republic of China have the freedom of religious belief." The Tibetan term *chöluk* (Wylie: chos-lugs) is used for "religious" here. "Chos lugs" can also be found as the Tibetan translation for "religion" in Mao Zedong's *Collected Works*; see Mao Zedong, *Mao' tse tung gi gsung rtsom gces bsdus* [= Mao Zedong's collected works] (Beijing: Beijing minzu chubanshe, 1992 [reprint]).

129. Ryan Dunch, "Christianity and 'Adaptation to Socialism,'" in *Chinese Religiosities: Afflictions of Modernity and State Formation,* ed. Mayfair Yang (Berkeley: University of California Press, 2008), 172–175; Goossaert and Palmer, *The Religious Question,* 320–322.

130. "Dwags kong yan lag chos tshogs kyi gru'u ren gzhon pa," cf. Dung dkar blo bzang 'phrin las, "Rtsom pa po ngo sprod mdor bsdus" [Author's introduction], in *Dung dkar tshig mdzod chen mo* [Dungkar encyclopedia], 2002, 13.

131. Mayfair Yang, "Introduction," 26–27.

132. "Bod ljong yan lag mthun tshogs," cf. Dung dkar blo bzang 'phrin las, "Rtsom pa po ngo sprod mdor bsdus" [Author's introduction], 2002, 13.

133. The CCP's view of religion in the mid-1950s was encapsulated in the notion of "five characteristics of religion," which were "its long term nature, its mass nature, its ethnic nature, its international nature, and its complex nature." See Goossaert and Palmer, *The Religious Question,* 155.

134. David A. Palmer, "Heretical Doctrines, Reactionary Secret Societies, Evil Cults: Labeling Heterodoxy in Twentieth-Century China," in *Chinese Religiosities: Afflictions of Modernity and State Formation,* ed. Mayfair Yang (Berkeley: University of California Press, 2008), 126–130.

135. "Document 19," in Donald MacInnis, *Religion in China Today: Policy and Practice*, trans. Janice Wickeri (Maryknoll, N.Y.: Orbis Books, 1989) 10; Goossaert and Palmer, *The Religious Question*, 323.

136. Dung dkar blo bzang 'phrin las, "Bod du chos srid zung 'brel kyi skor bshad pa," 2004, 4: 139; Dung-dkar blo-bzang 'phrim-las, *The Merging of Religious and Secular Rule in Tibet,* trans. Chen Guansheng, 99.

137. For examples of this process in other areas of China, see Nedostup, *Superstitious Regimes*, 8–10.

138. Dmu dge bsam gtan, "Bod du rig gnas dar tshul mdor bsdus bshad pa," in *Rje dmu dge bsam gtan rgya mtsho mi 'jigs dbyangs can dga' ba'i blo gros dpal bzang po'i gsung 'bum* [Collected works of Dmu dge bsam gtan, ocean of marvelous wisdom of the fearless *Sarasvatī*] (Zi ling: Mtsho sngon mi rigs dpe skrun khang, 1997), 3: 463; Muge Samten, *Fields of Learning: A Concise History of Dissemination of Traditional Fields of Learning in Tibet (Bod du rig gnas dar tshul mdor bsdus bshad pa)*, trans. Sangye Tandar Naga [bilingual edition, in English and Tibetan] (Dharamshala: Library of Tibetan Works and Archives, 2005), 4.

139. Dmu dge bsam gtan, "Rtsom pa po rang gi byung ba brjod pa rang gsal A' dar sha" [Luminous mirror: the author's own telling what happened], in *Rje dmu dge bsam gtan rgya mtsho mi 'jigs dbyangs can dga' ba'i blo gros dpal bzang po'i gsung 'bum* (Zi ling: Mtsho sngon mi rigs dpe skrun khang, 1997), 1: 601.

140. Dmu dge bsam gtan, "Rang gsal A dar sha" [Luminous mirror], 1: 602.

141. Cf. Goossaert and Palmer, *The Religious Question*, 112.

142. Emphasis mine. Mugé Samten, *Fields of Learning*, trans. Sangye Tandar Naga, 3. Text critical sources on this early history of Tibet do not indicate any use of language that emphasizes technology at this time period. See Per Sørenson, *Tibetan Buddhist Historiography, The Mirror Illuminating Royal Genealogies: An Annotated Translation of the rGyal-rabs gsal-ba'i me long by Bsod rnams rgyal mtshan* (Wiesbaden: Otto Harrasowitz Verlag, 1994), 144–145.

143. Muge Samten, *Fields of Learning*, trans. Sangye Tandar Naga, 4.

144. José Cabezón and Roger Jackson, eds., "Editors' Introduction," *Tibetan Literature: Studies in Genre* (Ithaca, N.Y.: Snow Lion, 1996), 19.

145. Muge Samten, *Fields of Learning*, trans. Sangye Tandar Naga, 71.

146. Dmu dge bsam gtan, "Bod du rig gnas dar tshul mdor bsdus bshad pa," 385–386; Muge Samten, *Fields of Learning*, trans. Sangye Tandar Naga, 4.

147. Muge Samten, *Fields of Learning*, trans. Sangye Tandar Naga, 9.

148. Muge Samten, *Fields of Learning*, trans. Sangye Tandar Naga, 49–50.

149. Muge Samten, *Fields of Learning*, trans. Sangye Tandar Naga, 49–50.

150. Dmu dge bsam gtan, "Bod du rig gnas dar tshul mdor bsdus bshad pa," 455; Muge Samten, *Fields of Learning*, trans. Sangye Tandar Naga, 60, 116.

151. Dung dkar blo bzang 'phrin las, "Bod kyi dkar chag rig pa" [The science of Tibetan catalogues], in *Mkhas dbang dung dkar blo bzang 'phrin las kyi gsung 'bum: Bod kyi dkar chag rig pa*, ed. Rnam rgyal ra 'phrin las rgya mtsho (Beijing: Minzu chubanshe, 2004), 2: 1.

152. Matthew Kapstein, "Tibetan Tibetology? Sketches of an Emerging Discipline," in *Images of Tibet in the 19th and 20th Centuries*, ed. Monica Esposito (Paris: École française d'Extrême-Orient, 2008), 2: 804.

153. Cf. Don grup rgyal and Khrin Chin dbyin [Chen Qingying], *Btsan po khri sde srong btsan gyi lo rgyus mdo tsam brjod pa* (Beijng: Mi rigs dpe skrun khang, 1984).

154. Chen Qingying (陈庆英), *Chen Qingying zangxue lunwenji* (陈庆英藏学论文集) [Chen Qingying's collected essays in Tibetology], 2 vols. (Beijing: Zhongguo zangxue chuban she, 2006).

155. Bstan 'dzin dge legs, "Chos dung karpo'i rang mdangs," 9.

5. DIVERGING LINEAGES

1. Ma Na'i hu'i [?Ma Naihui 马鼐辉], "Bod kyi rig gnas 'phel rgyas gtong bar 'bad brtson gnang mkhan," *Mi rigs brnyan par* (Ch. Minzu huabao) 9 (1983): 8.

2. Thanks to Gedun Rabsal for his help in identifying this professor.

3. As noted above, the article is dated to September 1983. One caption explains that Tséten Zhabdrung was invited to lecture at Minzu University. No further details are given on the topic or exact date. Other photos in this article show Tséten Zhabdrung engaged in various activities while at the nation's capital: conversing with the Panchen Lama, examining old Tibetan *pecha* texts at the Cultural Palace of Nationalities, and sitting with the rank and file at the sixth session of the Chinese People's Political Consultative Conference (CPPCC).

4. Ma Naihui (吗 鼐辉), "Zaoyi gaoshen de zangxue jia" (造诣高深的藏学家) [An erudite Tibetologist], *Guangming ribao* (光明日报), June 21, 1983. This seems to be the same author as for the *Ethnic Nationalities Pictorial (Mi rigs brnyan par)* article (note 1 above). This was likely the original article that was translated into Tibetan for *Ethnic Nationalities Pictorial*.

5. The Tibetan text from Tséten Zhabdrung's autobiography is as follows: 'di dus bla ma rin po ches chos bka' gang thob la thob yig 'bri ba gal che zhes gsungs nas do ru mkhan sprul 'phrin las kyis nged la 'bri ba'i rogs mdzad nas byin| 'di'i rjes nas bzung chos bka' nam thob la brgyud yig dang bcas pa'i thob yig rang gis bris pas phyis su po ti chen po gcig long pa yod| skabs snga phyi 'dir dbu can dbu med| rgyugs bris| lenza wartu dcas kyi phyi mo phyag bris la bstar ba skur gnang mdzad pa bzhin nyin gung rnams su saṁ ṭar sbyong ba chag med kyis brtson pa bsten|

   Bla ma rin po che then told me, "It is important that you keep a record of all teachings that you receive." With that said, I began writing down all the teachings I heard; at first Do ru Mkhan sprul 'phrin las helped me with writing. Since that time, I have continued to keep a record of teachings and list of transmissions, every time I received Dharma teachings, which later went into a large book. At around this time, based on writing samples that had been given to me, including those of different scripts, e.g., *lenza*, *wartu*, *dbu can*, *dbud med*, and *rgyugs bris*, I diligently practiced writing on a wooden board (saM ta), day and night without stopping.

   Tshe tan zhabs drung, "Mnyam med shAkya'i dbang bo'i rjes zhugs pa 'jigs med rigs pa'i blo gros rang gi byung ba brjod pa bden gtam rna ba'i bdud rtsi" [Acoustic ambrosia: a truthful telling of what happened by 'Jigs med rigs pa'i blo gros, a disciple of the powerful, matchless shākya]," in *Mkhas dbang tshe tan zhabs drung 'jigs med rigs pa'i blo gros kyi gsung rtsom*, ed. 'Phrin las (Xining: Qinghai minzu chubanshe, 1987), 1: 547.

6. Georges Dreyfus, *The Sound of Two Hands Clapping: The Education of a Tibetan Buddhist Monk* (Berkeley: University of California Press, 2003), 151.

7. Cf. Dreyfus, *Sound of Two Hands Clapping*, 155.

8. Dreyfus, *Sound of Two Hands Clapping*, 156–157.

9. Cf. Victoria Sujata, *Tibetan Songs of Realization: Echoes from a Seventeenth-Century Scholar and Siddha in Amdo* (Leiden: Brill, 2005).

10. Tshe tan zhabs drung, "Rna ba'i bdud rtsi" [Acoustic ambrosia], 1987, 1: 547.

11. Tshe tan zhabs drung, "Rna ba'i bdud rtsi" [Acoustic ambrosia], 1987, 1: 547.

12. Sarah H. Jacoby, *Love and Liberation: Autobiographical Writings of the Tibetan Buddhist Visionary Sera Khandro* (New York: Columbia University Press, 2014), 132.

13. Annabella Pitkin, "Lineage, Authority and Innovation: The Biography of Khu nu bla ma Bstan 'dzin rgyal mtshan," in *Mapping the Modern: Proceedings from the International Association of Tibetan Studies Conference 2006 Konigswinter, Germany,* ed. Gray Tuttle (Konigswinter: IITBS, International Institute for Tibetan and Buddhist Studies GmbH, 2011), 173–203.

14. Nicole Willock, "The Revival of the Tulku Institution in Modern China: Narratives and Practices," *Revue d'Etudes Tibétaines,* special volume, "The Tulku (sprul sku) Institution in Tibetan
Buddhism," ed. Daniel Hirschberg, Derek Maher, and Tsering Wangchuk, 38 (February 2017):
183–201; http://www.digitalhimalaya.com/collections/journals/ret/index.php?selection=6.

15. See chapter 2, notes 34, 35 above. The title of the Fifth Dalai Lama's autobiography, *Za hor gyi
bande ngag dbang blo bzang rgya mtsho'i 'di snang 'khrul pa'i rol rtsed rtogs brjod kyi tshul du
bkod pa du kū la'i gos bzang,* has been alternatively translated into English as *Illusive Play* or *A
Fine Silken Dress*; see Nancy Lin, "Recounting the Fifth Dalai Lama's Birth Lineages," *Revue
d'Etudes Tibétaines,* special issue on reincarnation in Tibetan Buddhism, ed. Daniel Hirschberg,
Derek Maher, and Tsering Wangchuk, 38 (Février 2017): 125–126; and Samten G. Karmay, trans.,
'Khrul ba'i rol rtsed, Illusive Play: The Autobiography of the Fifth Dalai Lama (Chicago: Serindia,
2014), 17.

16. rgyal dbang lnga ba'i rang rnam du kū la'i gos bzang du| bod yul 'dir rgya gar dang mi 'dra ba'i bla
ma la gdung brgyud kyis 'dzin pa dang skye bas 'dzin pa gnyis yod pa las| dang po ni sa skya gi bdag
chen rim byon ltar lugs gnyis kyi yon tan rnams pha shul bu 'jags lta bus bar gseng med cing bu slob
'khor 'bangs rnams bag phebs pa dang| skye bas 'dzin pa ni de las ldog ste bla ma grongs pa la sems
ngal che zhing yul gru che ge mo na byis pa la pha ma sogs kyis g.yo sgyus bzos pa 'dra la tsham
tshom med par bdag tu bzung ba'i bzhugs gral la chud nges dang skye bo du ma'i ri bong gi cal
'drog la brten wa skyes seng ger brdzu ba'i snang tshul kho na'o| Tshe tan zhabs drung, "Rna ba'i
bdud rtsi" [Acoustic ambrosia], 1987, 1: 521.

17. Tshe tan zhabs drung, "Rna ba'i bdud rtsi" [Acoustic ambrosia], 1987, 1: 525. See also Matthew
Kapstein on how Düjom Dorje in the late nineteenth century felt that his *tülku* status positioned
him as a servant to his sponsors due to all the rituals that he had to perform; *The Tibetans* (Malden, Mass. and Oxford: Blackwell, 2006), 230.

18. Tshe tan zhabs drung, "Rna ba'i bdud rtsi" [Acoustic ambrosia], 1987, 1: 524.

19. bla rgan re grongs na sprul sku'am zhabs drung dang| sngags rgan re grongs na sku lo'am sku 'ba'
zhes gces ming btags pa zhig btsal nas 'don chog tsam las yon tan ci yang mi slob par zang zing
sdud pa'i tshong rten byed ci thub dang| blang dor la rmongs pa'i skye bo rnams bslu gang thub
byed pa ni nges par bstan pa la gces par 'dzin pa zhig gis bltas na shin tu ya nga ba'i gnas so| Tshe
tan zhabs drung, "Rna ba'i bdud rtsi" [Acoustic ambrosia], 1987, 1: 524.

20. Cited in Tshe tan zhabs drung, "Rna ba'i bdud rtsi" [Acoustic ambrosia], 1987, 1: 522.

21. Namdrol Miranda Adams, "The Second Dalai Lama, Gendun Gyatso," *Treasury of Lives,* accessed
February 3, 2020, http://treasuryoflives.org/biographies/view/Second-Dalai-Lama-Gendun
-Gyatso/11114.

22. Leonard W.J. van der Kuijp, "The Dalai Lamas and the Origins of the Reincarnate Lamas," in *The
Tibetan History Reader,* ed. Gray Tuttle and Kurtis R. Schaeffer (New York: Columbia University
Press, 2013), 337.

23. Van der Kuijp, "The Dalai Lamas and the Origins of the Reincarnate Lamas," 336–337.

24. Cited in Tshe tan zhabs drung, "Rna ba'i bdud rtsi" [Acoustic ambrosia], 1987, 1: 519; 2007, 1: 54;
Tsongkhapa, *The Great Treatise on the Stages of the Path to Enlightenment,* trans. Lamrim
Chenmo Translation Committee (Ithaca, N.Y.: Snow Lion, 2000), 71.

25. Tsongkhapa devoted a chapter to the qualities of a buddha expressed in the term *yon tan.* Perhaps
Tséten Zhabdrung is expanding upon this argument. See Tsongkhapa, *Stages of the Path to
Enlightenment,* trans. Lamrim Chenmo Translation Committee, 181–187.

26. Tshe tan zhabs drung, "Rna ba'i bdud rtsi" [Acoustic ambrosia], 1987, 1: 526; in *Tshe tan zhabs
drung rje btsun 'jigs med rigs pa blo gros mchog gi gsung 'bum,* ed. 'Jigs med chos 'phags (Beijing:
Minzu chubanshe, 2007), 1: 60.

27. Tshe tan zhabs drung, "Rna ba'i bdud rtsi" [Acoustic ambrosia], 1987, 1: 526.

28. Tshe tan zhabs drung, "Rna ba'i bdud rtsi" [Acoustic ambrosia], 1987, 1: 513–514.

29. Dung dkar blo bzang 'phrin las, *Dung dkar tshig mdzod chen mo* [Dungkar encyclopedia] (Beijing: Zhongguo Zangxue chubanshe, 2002), 2370.

30. Zhamar was an erudite scholar and effective administrator who had studied in Lhasa in his younger years. See Gray Tuttle, "Local History in A mdo: The Tsong kha Range (*ri rgyud*)," *Asian Highlands Perspectives* (2010): 10–11.

31. Tshe tan zhabs drung, "Rna ba'i bdud rtsi" [Acoustic ambrosia], 1987, 1: 517.

32. Tshe tan zhabs drung, "Rna ba'i bdud rtsi" [Acoustic ambrosia], 1987, 1: 518.

33. Cf. Rene Grousset, *In the Footsteps of the Buddha* (New York: Orion Press, 1971).

34. Tshe tan zhabs drung, "Rna ba'i bdud rtsi" [Acoustic ambrosia], 1987, 1: 546.

35. There is some uncertainty as to when this happened. Due to the press coverage given to Tséten Zhabdrung in 1983, I think this is the most accurate year. Two informants stated that he was rehabilitated a year later, in 1984.

36. Based on my notes from an interview with Tséten Zhabdrung's nephew, June 2015.

37. Vincent Goossaert and David Palmer, *The Religious Question in Modern China* (Chicago: University of Chicago Press, 2012), 366.

38. Department of Information and International Relations, *From the Heart of the Panchen Lama: Major Speeches and a Petition 1962–1989* (Dharamsala: Central Tibetan Administration, 2003), 1.

39. Tshe tan zhabs drung, "Rna ba'i sdud rtsi" [Acoustic ambrosia], 1987, 1: 696. Ngulchu Lobzang Chöphel Rinpoché became the Panchen Lama's main spiritual teacher at Tashilhunpo Monastery in the mid-1950s.

40. Department of Information and International Relations, *From the Heart of the Panchen Lama*, 1.

41. Department of Information and International Relations, *From the Heart of the Panchen Lama*, 1–3.

42. Tshe tan zhabs drung, "Rna ba'i sdud rtsi" [Acoustic ambrosia], 1987, 1: 757.

43. Tshe tan zhabs drung, "Rna ba'i sdud rtsi" [Acoustic ambrosia], 1987, 1: 769–770.

44. Pu Wencheng, *Qinghai Fojiao Shi* (青海佛教史) [History of Buddhism in Qinghai Province] (Xining: Qinghai minzu chubanshe, 2001), 113.

45. Nicole Willock, "A Tibetan Buddhist Polymath of Modern China" (PhD diss., Indiana University, 2011), 43–46.

46. Tibet Information Network/Robert Barnett, *A Poisoned Arrow: The Secret Report of the 10th Panchen Lama* (London: Tibet Information Network, 1997), xvii.

47. Department of Information and International Relations, *From the Heart of the Panchen Lama*, 7.

48. Wei Jingsheng, "Excerpts from Qincheng: A Twentieth Century Bastille published in Exploration, March 1979," accessed February 16, 2019, http://www.weijingsheng.org/doc/en/Excerpts%20from%20Qincheng.htm.

49. Department of Information and International Relations, *From the Heart of the Panchen Lama*, 7.

50. Jigmé Samdrup, personal communication, Beijing, June 23, 2015.

51. The colophon to "*Avadāna* of Silver Flowers" states that this poem was inspired by the "*Avadāna* of Golden Flowers" written by Tséten Zhabdrung's former teacher Giteng Lozang Peldan (1981–1944) to commemorate the occasion of the Ninth Panchen Lama's (1883–1937) visit to Rongbo Monastery at the behest of Shar Kelden Gyatso in that same year (1936). Tshe tan zhabs drung, "Pan chen thams cad mkhen cing gzigs pa chen po mdo smad 'khrungs gzhis phyogs su phebs pa'i legs mdzad cha shas tsam gyi ngo mtshar ba'i gtam gyi rtogs pa brjod pa dngul gyi me tog" [Avadāna of silver flowers: a wondrous account of the Panchen Lama's visit to Amdo, his birthplace], in *Tshe tan zhabs drung rje btsun 'jigs med rigs pa'i blo gros mchog gi gsung 'bum*, ed. 'Jigs med chos 'phags (Beijing: Minzu chubanshe, 2007), 3: 277–278.

52. Tshe tan zhabs drung, "Rtogs pa brjod pa dngul gyi me tog" [*Avadāna* of silver flowers], 3: 271.

53. sku yi mtshan dpe mjal bas mi ngoms shing| gsung gi rgyud mangs nyam pas mi tshim pa| 'di 'dra'i dga' ston khyod min su yis sbyin| da dung yang yang sbyon dang thugs rje'i gter|

Tshe tan zhabs drung, "Rtogs pa brjod pa dngul gyi me tog" [*Avadāna* of silver flowers], 3: 272.

54. Personal communication, June 24, 2015.

55. This biography is considered authentic by the fact that it is included within 'Jigs med chos 'phags, ed., *Tshe tan zhabs drung rje btsun 'jigs med rigs pa'i blo gros mchog gi gsung 'bum* [Collected works of the great Tshe tan zhabs drung 'Jigs med rigs pa blo gros], 13 vols. (Beijing: Mi rigs dpe skrun khang [minzu chuban she], 2007).

56. Charlene Makley, *The Violence of Liberation: Gender and Tibetan Buddhist Revival in Post-Mao China* (Berkeley: University of California Press, 2007), 96, 234.

57. Tsewang Dorje, a scholar at Qinghai Minzu University, informed me that Alak Sertri (A lags Gser khri) was one of the Dzongkar incarnate lamas (Rdzong dkar sku zhabs); personal communication, September 2008, Xining. According to *Acoustic Ambrosia*, the Rdzong dkar sku zhabs were both entrusted to carry out Jigme Damchö Gyatso's last will and testament, along with Tséten Zhabdrung. Tshe tan zhabs drung, "Rna ba'i bdud rtsi" [Acoustic ambrosia], 1987, 1: 722.

58. *Fayin* (法音 (Dharmagosa) [Voice of the Dharma] 5 (Sept. 30, 1983): centerfold.

59. "Document 19," Selected Documents of the Third Plenum of the Eleventh Party Congress, 1982, trans. Janice Wickeri, in Donald MacInnis, *Religion in China Today: Policy and Practice* (Maryknoll, N.Y.: Orbis Books, 1989), 8–26. On the importance of this document for outlining the official policy toward religion, see Goossaert and Palmer, *The Religious Question in Modern China*, 323–324.

60. "Banchan dashi zai qingzhu zhongguo fojiao xiehui chengli sanshi zhou nian cha hui shang de jianghua" (班禅 大师在庆祝中国佛教协会成立三十周年茶会上的讲话 February 7, 1983), Qingzhu zhongguo fojiao xiehui chengli sanshi zhou nian 1953–1983, *Fayin* 法音 [Voice of the Dharma] 6 (December 30, 1983): 10–11.

61. This seems to be according to the Tibetan calendar, but it is unclear from the context.

62. 'Jigs meds theg mchog, "'Jam dbyangs bla ma rdo rje sems dpa'i ngo bo bka' drin mtshungs med rje btsun 'jigs med rigs pa'i blo gros dpal bzang bo'i rnam par thar ba bden gtam rna ba'i bdud rtsi zhes bya ba'i kha skong skal bzang me tog bzhad pa'i 'khri shing," hereafter, "Kha skong skal bzang me tog bzhad pa'i 'khri shing," in *Tshe tan zhabs drung rje btsun 'jigs med rigs pa'i blo gros mchog gi gsung 'bum*, 2007, 1: 356.

63. 'Jigs meds theg mchog, "Kha skong skal bzang me tog bzhad pa'i 'khri shing," 1: 357.

64. 'Jigs meds theg mchog, "Kha skong skal bzang me tog bzhad pa'i 'khri shing," 1: 357.

65. 'Jigs meds theg mchog, "Kha skong skal bzang me tog bzhad pa'i 'khri shing," 1: 357.

66. 'Jigs meds theg mchog's addendum (*kha skong*) was written at the behest of Shardong Rinpoché. Cf. 'Jigs meds theg mchog, "Kha skong skal bzang me tog bzhad pa'i 'khri shing," 1: 402.

67. Department of Information and International Relations, *From the Heart of the Panchen Lama*, 79.

68. Department of Information and International Relations, *From the Heart of the Panchen Lama*, 80.

69. Department of Information and International Relations, *From the Heart of the Panchen Lama*, 87–88.

70. Department of Information and International Relations, *From the Heart of the Panchen Lama*, 87–88.

71. Åshild Kolås and Monika Thowsen, *On the Margins of Tibet: Cultural Survival on the Sino-Tibetan Frontier* (Seattle: University of Washington Press. 2005), 77.

72. Goossaert and Palmer, *The Religious Question in Modern China*, 365–366.

73. Nicole Willock, "The Revival of the Tulku Institution in Modern China: Narratives and Practices," *Revue d'Etudes Tibétaines*, special issue on reincarnation in Tibetan Buddhism, ed. Daniel Hirschberg, Derek Maher, and Tsering Wangchuk, 38 (Février 2017): 196–198.

74. See Elliot Sperling, "The Dalai Lama as Dupe," *Los Angeles Times*, April 3, 2008, accessed March 29, 2019, https://www.latimes.com/archives/la-xpm-2008-apr-03-oe-sperling3-story.html.

75. Tibet Information Network, *Background Briefing Papers: Documents and Statements from Tibet 1996–1997* (London: Tibet Information Network, 1998), 12.

76. Tibet Information Network, *Background Briefing Papers*, 1.

77. Arjia Rinpoché, *Surviving the Dragon: A Tibetan Lama's Account of Forty Years Under Chinese Rule* (New York: Rodale, 2010); cf. Jose Cabezón, "State Control of Tibetan Buddhist Monasticism in the People's Republic of China," in *Chinese Religiosities: Afflictions of Modernity and State Formation,* ed. Mayfair Yang (Berkeley: University of California Press, 2008), 261–291; and John Powers, *The Buddha Party: How the People's Republic of China Works to Define and Control Tibetan Buddhism* (Oxford: Oxford University Press, 2017).

78. "Zangchuan fojiao huofo zhuanshi guanli banfa, 藏传佛教活佛转世管理办法" [Measures on the management of Tibetan Buddhist reincarnations], accessed March 29, 2019, http://www.gov.cn/gongbao/content/2008/content_923053.htm.

79. Xinhua News Agency, "Rule on Living Buddhas aids religious freedom," updated December 27, 2007, accessed March 29, 2019, http://www.chinadaily.com.cn/china/2007-12/27/content_6351750.htm. The state's justification for this policy can be found here: "Fourthly, there are still problems with the reincarnation of living Buddhas although it has been generally well observed to date. Some reincarnated soul boys were appointed against religious ritual and historical convention, and without the government's approval. This violated the normal order of Tibetan Buddhism and undermined the internal integrity of Tibetan Buddhism."

80. Makley, *Violence of Liberation*, 312 n. 28; see also Kolås and Thowsen, *On the Margins of Tibet*, 76; Jane E. Caple, *Morality and Monastic Revival in Post-Mao Tibet* (Honolulu: University of Hawai'i Press, 2019), 149–154.

81. Kolås and Thowsen, *On the Margins of Tibet*, 77.

82. Personal communication, July 2015 and August 2017.

83. "*Avadāna* of Silver Flowers" is clearly divided into eight subsections: 1) Wondrous Words Setting the Stage for a Perfect Topic: Offering Verses to Fields of Holy Persons (pp. 263–264); 2) The Mountains and Forests of the Panchen Lama's Birthplace (pp. 264–266); 3) Marvelous Achievements of Early Buddhists in This Area (266–267); 4) Praise for the Environment and Inhabitants South of the Machu River (267–268); 5) The All-Seeing One, the Panchen Lama, at Bīdo (Bis mdo) Monastery (268–270); 6) Soft Rain Falling from the Sky: The Benefit of The Panchen Lama's Visit to Karing Monastery (270–272); 7) Travels to Gyazhu (Rgya zhu) at the Invitation of Dentik (Dan tig) Monastery, the First Sacred Place in Amdo (272–275); 8) Invitation to the Family Residence of Jikmé Rigpai Lödro (275–277). Tshe tan zhabs drung, "Rtogs pa brjod pa dngul gyi me tog" [*Avadāna* of silver flowers], 3: 263–278.

84. See essays by Melvyn Goldstein, "Revival of Monastic Life at Drepung Monastery," Matthew Kapstein, "A Pilgrimage of Rebirth Reborn: The 1992 Celebration of the Drigung Powa Chenmo," and David Germano, "Re-membering the Dismembered Body of Tibet," in *Buddhism in Contemporary Tibet: Religious Revival and Cultural Identity,* ed. Melvyn Goldstein and Matthew Kapstein (Berkeley: University of California Press, 1998); Makley, *Violence of Liberation*; Kolås and Thowsen, *On the Margins of Tibet*; Charlene Makley, *The Battle for Fortune: State-led Development, Personhood, and Power Among Tibetans in China* (Ithaca, N.Y.: Cornell University Press, 2018); and Caple, *Morality and Monastic Revival in Post-Mao Tibet*.

85. This biography is considered authentic by the fact that it is included within Tséten Zhabdrung's *Collected Works,* edited by his nephew.

86. 'Jigs meds theg mchog, "Kha skong skal bzang me tog bzhad pa'i 'khri shing," 1: 295. In an interview with Kirti Rinpoché in Dharmasala in November 2008, he told me that he corresponded with Tséten Zhabdrung and still had his letters, but I have not seen them.

87.   The dates seem to follow the Tibetan calendar.

88.   'Jigs meds theg mchog, "Kha skong skal bzang me tog bzhad pa'i 'khri shing," 1: 300–301; 303.

89.   Germano, "Re-membering the Dismembered Body of Tibet," 62.

90.   Germano, "Re-membering the Dismembered Body of Tibet;" Makley, *Violence of Liberation*; Makley, *The Battle for Fortune*.

91.   Dmu dge bsam gtan, "Rtsom pa po rang gi byung ba brjod pa rang gsal A' dar sha" [Luminous mirror: the author's own telling what happened], in *Rje dmu dge bsam gtan rgya mtsho mi 'jigs dbyangs can dga' ba'i blo gros dpal bzang po'i gsung 'bum* (Zi ling: Mtsho sngon mi rigs dpe skrun khang, 1997), 1: 602; Dhondup Tashi, "A Monastic Scholar Under China's Occupation of Tibet: Muge Samten's Autobiography and His Role as a Vernacular Intellectual" (MA thesis, University of British Columbia, 2019), 52.

92.   Dawa Lodro, interview, Xining, June 2015; Pu Wencheng, interview, Xining, June 2015.

93.   Caple, *Morality and Monastic Revival in Post-Mao Tibet*, 47.

94.   Personal communication, Qinghai Nationalities University, February 2008.

95.   'Jigs meds theg mchog, "Kha skong skal bzang me tog bzhad pa'i 'khri shing," 1: 357. I am grateful to Gedun Rabsal for his help on the translation of this passage.

96.   Caple, *Morality and Monastic Revival in Post-Mao Tibet*, 25–26.

97.   Dmu dge bsam gtan, "Rang gsal A dar sha" [Luminous mirror], 1: 608–609; Dhondup Tashi, "A Monastic Scholar Under China's Occupation of Tibet," 70–71.

98.   Dhondup Tashi, "A Monastic Scholar Under China's Occupation of Tibet," 54.

99.   Kumbum Monastery is frequently viewed as an exemplar of monastic decline whereby the rebuilding of monastic structures takes precedence over the teachings. See Caple, *Morality and Monastic Revival in Post-Mao Tibet*, 61; 81–93.

100. On the resurgence of Bön traditions and Bön Studies in China, see Samten Karmay and Yasuhiko Nagano, eds., *New Horizons in Bon Studies* (Osaka, Japan: National Museum of Ethnology, 2000); Mona Schrempf and Jack Patrick Haynes, "From Temple to Commodity? Tourism in Songpan and the Bon Monasteries of A'mdo Shar Khog," *Bon: The Everlasting Religion of Tibet, Tibetan studies in Honor of David Snellgrove, East and West* 59, no. 1 (December 2009): 285–312; and Mara Arizago, "An Introduction to the Study of Bon in Modern China," *Bon: The Everlasting Religion of Tibet, Tibetan Studies in Honor of David Snellgrove, East and West* 59, no. 1 (December 2009): 327–335. See also note 84 above.

101. Caple, *Morality and Monastic Revival in Post-Mao China*, 2–9.

102. Goossaert and Palmer, *The Religious Question in Modern China*, 360–372; Dan Smyer Yu, *The Spread of Tibetan Buddhism in China: Charisma, Money, Enlightenment* (London: Routledge, 2011).

103. Tshe tan zhabs drung, "Rtogs pa brjod pa dngul gyi me tog" [*Avadāna* of silver flowers], 3: 271. Pema Bhum's memoirs document how traditional Tibetan teachers were called "cow's demons" or "snake spirits," and their writings and other traditional texts were "poisonous weeds." *Six Stars with a Crooked Neck: Tibetan Memoirs of the Cultural Revolution* (dran tho smin drug ske 'khyog), trans. Lauran R. Hartley [bilingual Tibetan and English] (Dharamsala: Tibet Times, 2001), 124.

104. Pema Bhum, *Six Stars with a Crooked Neck*, trans. Lauran R. Hartley, 147.

105. Pema Bhum, *Six Stars with a Crooked Neck*, trans. Lauran R. Hartley, 147.

106. Personal communication, Qinghai Nationalities Institute, March 15, 2008.

107. Personal communication, Khenpo Tsultrim Lodrö, Charlottesville, Virginia, April 2015; New York City, August 2017. When I interviewed him, he was still going by the title of "Khenpo"; soon thereafter he was elevated to the position of "Khenchen."

108. Reports indicate that restrictions have been placed on the number of permissible residents since this time, and that the transnational network initiated by another one of Larung Gar's leading

lamas has been since shut down; see Richard Finney, "Tibetan Buddhist Centers Linked to Larung Gar Shut Down Under Suspected Chinese Pressure," January 2, 2020, https://www.rfa .org/english/news/tibet/centers-01022020164534.html.

109. Two online biographies in English are easily accessible: on the website for Katog Choling, a transnational organization with multiple centers worldwide, https://katogcholing.com/khenchen; and on *Luminous Wisdom*, his official website, http://www.luminouswisdom.org/; both accessed March 12, 2020.

110. Personal communication, Khenpo Tsultrim Lodrö, Charlottesville, Virginia, April 2015, and New York City, August 2017. Thanks to Dr. Hardie for interpreting.

111. Kolås and Thowsen, *On the Margins of Tibet*, 93–96.

112. The Department of Information and International Relations, *From the Heart of the Panchen Lama*, 73.

113. Department of Information and International Relations, *From the Heart of the Panchen Lama*, 71.

114. Dawa Lodro, personal communication, June 30, 2015.

115. Personal communication, Xining, June 29, 2015.

116. Personal communication, Latse Library, New York City, October 2009.

117. Personal communication, April 20, 2008.

118. Personal communication, April 20, 2008.

119. Personal communication, Latse Library, New York City, October 2009.

120. Personal communication, April 20, 2008.

121. Tsering Shakya, "The Development of Modern Tibetan Literature in the People's Republic of China in the 1980s," in *Modern Tibetan Literature and Social Change*, ed. Lauran Hartley and Patricia Schiaffini-Vedani (Durham, N.C. and London: Duke University Press, 2008), 66.

122. Personal communication, June 30, 2015.

123. Marielle Prins, "Toward a Tibetan Common Language: A mdo Perspectives on Attempts at Language Standardisation," in *Amdo Tibetans in Transition: Society and Culture in the Post-Mao Era*, ed. Toni Huber, PIATS 2000 Tibetan Studies Proceedings of the International Association of Tibetan Studies, Leiden 2000, 17–51 (Leiden: Brill, 2002), 34–49.

124. Gerald Roche and Lugyal Bum, "Language Revitalization of Tibetan," in *The Routledge Handbook of Language Revitalization*, ed. Leanne Hinton, Leena Huss, and Gerald Roche, e-book section 2.5 Asia, ch. 40 (New York: Routledge, 2018).

125. Gerald Roche and Lugyal Bum, "Language Revitalization of Tibetan."

126. Dmu dge bsam gtan, "Rang gsal A dar sha" [Luminous mirror], 1: 597; Lauran Hartley, "Contextually Speaking: Tibetan Literary Discourse and Social Change in the People's Republic of China (1980–2000)" (PhD diss., Indiana University, 2003), 167; Prins, "Toward a Tibetan Common Language," 32.

127. Dmu dge bsam gtan, "Rang gsal A dar sha" [Luminous mirror], 1: 600–601.

128. Hartley, "Contextually Speaking," 168.

129. Marielle Prins, Independent Scholar. *Trace Foundation*, http://www.trace.org/node/142.

130. Prins, "Toward a Tibetan Common Language," 40–49.

131. Dmu dge bsam gtan, "Rang gsal A dar sha" [Luminous mirror], 1: 601. See also Dhondup Tashi, "A Monastic Scholar Under China's Occupation of Tibet," 38–58; Hartley, "Contextually Speaking," 167–169.

132. Dmu dge bsam gtan, "Rang gsal A dar sha" [Luminous mirror], 1: 602.

133. "Academic seminar on the great scholar Mugé Samten Gyatso," Shang Shadur Gamal Monastery, August 26, 2016; accessed April 12, 2019, http://www.gamalgonchen.com/en/news/social-news /2016–08–26/20.html.

134. The only English-language translation that I have seen of this work is by the Tibetan historian Sam van Schaik, who translated the entry on Tibetan script in his blog: "Dungkar's Great Encyclopedia: The Tibetan Script," https://readingtibetan.wordpress.com/resources/dungkar/, accessed March 26, 2020.

135. The DungGar project was started by students at Minzu University to promote Tibetan language usage; see Miaoyan Yang, *Learning to Be Tibetan: The Construction of Ethnic Identity in China* (Lanham, Md.; Boulder, Colo.; New York; London: Lexington Books, 2017), 225–226.

136. The online dictionary is called "GoldenDict-BO" and includes other dictionaries besides Dungkar Rinpoché's encyclopedia. See "Sheep Brother's blog" (Yang Xiong *bókè*, 羊兄博客), accessed March 21, 2020, http://blog.tibetcul.com/home.php?mod=space&uid=9047&do=blog&id=187938.

137. Tshe tan zhabs drung, "Rna ba bdud rtsi" [Acoustic ambrosia], 1987, 1: 505. See chapter 1, note 8.

138. rab yangs mtha' bral nam mkha' skya sangs la| bgrang yas gza' skar 'bar bas 'phra btab ltar| rgya gar mkhas pas bsngags mdzad snyan ngag dpal| brgya phrag rgyan rnams 'bad pas 'chad la rangs| mtsho sngon mdo stod bod ljongs rong 'brog khrod| mi rigs spyi yis ci 'bri'i ming tshig bzhin| sdeb legs cher 'jebs dpe med mdzes byed de| myur 'khyugs smyu gus phul byung tshul du bskrun|

     Tshe tan zhabs drung, *Snyan ngag spyi don* [A general commentary on poetics] (Lanzhou: Gan su'u mi rigs dpe skrun khang, 1957 [2005 reprint]), 37. The grammar of the original leaves the main subject ambiguous; it could either be "nomads and farmers," as I translated, or an unstated "I." My translation is based on my understanding of the author's rhetorical strategy.

139. gzhan deng rabs dang mthun pa'i snyan ngag gi spyi don sdeb leg rig pa'i 'char sgo zhes bya ba|
     Tshe tan zhabs drung, "Rna ba'i bdud rtsi" [Acoustic ambrosia], 1987, 1: 778.

140. Tshe tan zhabs drung, *Snyan ngag spyi don* [A general commentary on poetics], 3–4. See chapter 3 and note 68.

141. Matthew Kapstein wrote, "Turning to his creative writing with these examples of his scholarship already in mind, I have been struck repeatedly by the constancy with which their author struggled to find a new voice not by rejecting Tibet's literary past, but by immersing himself within and revaluating it. If some conservative elements in the Tibetan community have taken offense at his sometimes derisive critiques of old ways, they have failed to recognize that here, at the same time, was a genuine voice of tradition." Matthew Kapstein, "Dhondup Gyal, the Making of a Modern Hero," *Lungta 12*: Contemporary Tibetan Literature (Summer 1999): 46.

142. Nancy G. Lin, "Dondrup Gyel and the Remaking of the Tibetan Ramayana," in *Modern Tibetan Literature and Social Change,* ed. Lauran R. Hartley and Patricia Schiaffani-Vedani (Durham, N.C.: Duke University Press, 2008), 97–105.

143. Lama Jabb, *Oral and Literary Continuities in Modern Tibetan Literature: The Inescapable Nation* (Lanham, Md. and Boulder, Colo.: Lexington Books, 2015), 10.

144. John Frederick Eppling, "A Calculus of Creative Expression: The Central Chapter of Dandin's *Kāvyādarśa*" (PhD diss., University of Wisconsin, Madison, 1989); on "svabhāvokti alaṃkāra," 345, 395–403.

145. The figure of speech called "expressing the inherent nature [of a referent]" is in Tibetan: *rang bzhin brjod pa'i rgyan;* Sanskrit: *svabhāvokti alaṃkāra.* There are four types of "expressing the inherent nature [of a referent];" the subtype used here is based on actions or functions (Tibetan: *bya ba;* Sanskrit: *kriya*). Tséten Zhabdrung describes this figure of speech as follows: "gsal ba| mtshon pa| 'gro ba lta bu'i gyi bya ba zhig brjod byas ted rang por brjod pa'i chas nas bya ba rang bzhin brjod pa ste|" "Expressing inherent nature through actions" is based on the accurate expression of a referent's action(s), e.g., "to go," "to indicate," "to clarify." Cf. Tshe tan zhabs drung, *Snyan ngag spyi don* [A general commentary on poetics], 39.

146. According to Tséten Zhabdrung's commentary, the seventeen suitable topics for poetry are: 1) cities, 2) oceans, 3) mountains, 4) seasons, 5) sunrises or sunsets, 6) moonrise or moon-sets, 6) sports or play in gardens or in water ,7) drinking alcohol, 8) sexual activities, 9) frustrations, 10) marriage, 11–13) youth, birth, growing up (of a prince), 14) debates on the future, 15) embassy, 16) wars, and 17) societal prosperity. See Tshe tan zhabs drung, *Synan ngag spyi don* [General commentary on poetics], 14–15.

147. nyin mtshan chu tshod nyer bzhi'i Ang grangs gsal| dgung zhogs nam phyed nyin gung ma nor mtshon| skad cig mi sdod dus kyi rjes 'gro ba'i| dus rtogs 'khor lo gdu bu'i dbyibs 'di rmad| Tshe tan zhabs drung, *Synan ngag spyi don* [A general commentary on poetics], 39.

148. Mugé Samten's text does not explicitly label this as an example of *rang bzhin brjod pa'i rgyan*.

149. glog skad la bstod pa|| spyi le 'bum phrag brgal ba'i yul dag tu|| rna skud yod med rkyen la ma ltos par|| gang 'dod gtam gyi sbyor ba skyel byed pa'i|| glog skad 'di yi thabs 'phrul blo las 'gongs||
     Dmu dge bsam gtan, "Bod kyi yi ge spyi rnam blo gsal 'jug ngogs" [Entryway to a clear mind: on Tibetan writing], in *Rje dmu dge bsam gtan rgya mtsho'i gsung 'bum* (Zi ling: Mtsho sngon mi rigs dpe skrun khang, 1997), 5: 246–247.

150. Pema Bhum, "Chö Jö/Expressions of Worship," in *Trace Foundation's Latse Library Newsletter* 5 (2007–2008): 36. Pema Bhum emphasized how unusual it was to use the religious genre of "offering" (*mchod brjod*) for praising the Communist Party. Lecture at the Tibetan and the Literary Workshop, Latse Library, New York City, May 2017.

151. I am grateful to Jonathan Gold, who expressed doubt that this was Sakya Pandita's claim during a "Tibet and the Literary" meeting in Toronto as part of the American Academy of Religion seminar. This inspired Rabsal's research on this, which was resolved in his publication. See Dge 'dun rab gsal, *Rig pa'i khye'u [Birth of the Arts]: English subtitle: Papers on the Arrival of the Literary Field of Knowledge in Tibet during the 13th Century and Beyond* (Dharamsala: Library of Tibetan Works and Archives, 2017), 199–201.

152. Tshe tan zhabs drung, *Snyan ngag spyi don* [A general commentary on poetics], 23–24.

153. Gedun Rabsal explained to me that *blang dor* is a common term in Buddhist ethics and involves a monastic cognitively making a behavioral choice, often concerning the observation of monastic vows. *Blang dor* takes on a different meaning in literary debates. Personal communication, February 20, 2020.

154. Translation by Nancy Lin, Lauran Hartley, and Pema Bhum, in Lin, "Dondrup Gyel and the Remaking of the Tibetan Ramayana," 96 n. 42, 110.

155. Lin, "Dondrup Gyel and the Remaking of the Tibetan Ramayana," 95; Hartley, "Contextually Speaking," 224.

156. Pema Bhum, "Heart Beat of a New Generation Revisited," in *Modern Tibetan Literature and Social Change*, ed. Lauran Hartley and Patricia Schiaffini-Vedani (Durham, N.C. and London: Duke University Press, 2008), 138.

157. Matthew Kapstein, "The Tulku's Miserable Lot: Critical Voices from Eastern Tibet," in *Amdo Tibetans in Transition: Society and Culture in the Post-Mao Era*, ed. Toni Huber, PIATS 2000 Tibetan Studies Proceedings of the International Association of Tibetan Studies, Leiden 2000, 99–111 (Leiden: Brill, 2002), 110.

158. Lama Jabb, *Oral and Literary Continuities in Modern Tibetan Literature*, 171.

159. Lama Jabb, *Oral and Literary Continuities in Modern Tibetan Literature*, 136; Tsering Shakya, "Literature or Propaganda, the Development of Tibetan Literature Since 1950," *Lungta* 12: Contemporary Tibetan Literature (Summer 1999): 63.

160. Yang, *Learning to Be Tibetan*, 232–233.

161. Yang, *Learning to Be Tibetan*, 232–233.

162. Lama Jabb, *Oral and Literary Continuities in Modern Tibetan Literature*, 237.

163. Xaver Erherd, "Review of Jabb, Lama: Oral and Literary Continuities in Modern Tibetan Literature. The Inescapable Nation," *Orientalistische Literaturzeitung* 114, no. 2 (2019): 85–87. https://doi.org/10.1515/olzg-2019–0055.

164. Toni Huber, "A mdo and Its Modern Transition," in *Amdo Tibetans in Transition: Society and Culture in the Post-Mao Era,* ed. Toni Huber, PIATS 2000 Tibetan Studies Proceedings of the International Association of Tibetan Studies, Leiden 2000, xi-xxii (Leiden: Brill, 2002), xx.

Bibliography

Akester, Matthew. "Obituary: Dungkar Losang Trinley." *Independent,* August 25, 1997.

Alonso, M. E., ed. *China's Inner Asian Frontier: Photographs of the Wulsin Expedition to Northwest China in 1923.* Cambridge, Mass.: Harvard University Press, 1979.

Archives of the Tibetan Autonomous Region (Xizang zizhiqu dang'an guan bian 西藏自治区档案馆编, Bod rang skyong ljongs khang gis rtsom sgrigs byas), compiler. *A Collection of Historical Archives of Tibet* (Xizang lishi dang'an huicui 西藏历史档案荟萃, Bod kyi lo rgyus yig tshang gces bdus), trilingual. Beijing: Cultural Relics Publishing House, 1995.

Aris, Michael, and Aung San Suu Kyi, eds. *Tibetan Studies in Honor of Hugh Richardson.* Bangkok: Orchid Press, 1980.

Arizago, Mara. "An Introduction to the Study of Bon in Modern China." *East and West* 59, no. 1/4 (2009): 327–35. Accessed April 1, 2020. www.jstor.org/stable/29757815.

Arjia Rinpoché. *Surviving the Dragon: A Tibetan Lama's Account of Forty Years Under Chinese Rule.* New York: Rodale, 2010.

Asad, Talal. *Formations of the Secular: Christianity, Islam and Modernity.* Stanford: Stanford University Press, 2003.

——. *Genealogies of Religion: Discipline and Reasons of Power in Christianity and Islam.* Baltimore, Md.: John Hopkins University Press, 1993.

Ashiwa, Yoshiko, and David L. Wank, eds. *Making Religion, Making the State: The Politics of Religion in Modern China.* Stanford, Calif.: Stanford University Press, 2009.

Atelier Golok. *Bod dang sa 'brel khag gi sa khra* [A map of Tibet and neighboring territories]. Dharamsala: Amnye Machen Institute, 1998.

Atwood, Christopher. *Encyclopedia of Mongolia and the Mongol Empire.* New York: Facts On File, 2004.

——. "The First Mongol Contact with the Tibetans." In *Trails of Tibetan Tradition: Papers for Elliot Sperling,* ed. Roberto Vitali, 21–45. Dharamsala: Amnye Machen Institute, 2014.

Avedon, John. *In Exile from the Land of Snows.* New York: HarperCollins, 1997.

Avishai, Orit. " 'Doing Religion' in a Secular World: Women in Conservative Religions and the Question of Agency." *Gender and Society* 22, no. 4 (August 2008): 409–433.

Barmé, Geremie, and Linda Jaivin, eds. *New Ghosts, Old Dreams: Chinese Rebel Voices.* New York: Times Books, 1992.

Barnett, Robert. "Beyond the Collaborator—Martyr Model: Strategies of Compliance, Opportunism, and Opposition Within Tibet." In *Contemporary Tibet: Politics, Development, and Society in a Disputed Region,* ed. Barry Sautman and June Teufel Dreyer, 25–66. Armonk, N.Y.: M. E. Sharpe, 2006.

Barnett, Robert, and Shirin Akiner, eds. *Resistance and Reform in Tibet*. New Delhi: Motilal Banarsiddass, 1994.

Beal, Samuel. *Chinese Accounts of India. Translation of Si yu ki: Buddhist Records of the Western World*, vol. 2. Calcutta: Susil Gupta, 1958.

——. *The Life of Hiuen-Tsiang. Translated from the Chinese of Shaman (monk) Hwui Li*. 1911; reprint, New Delhi: Munshiram Manoharlal, 1973.

Beckwith, Christopher. "The Chinese Names of the Tibetans, Tabghatch, and Turks." *Archivum Eurasiae Medii Aevi* 14 (2005): 5–20.

——. "A Study on the Early Medieval Chinese, Latin, and Tibetan Historical Sources on Pre-Imperial Tibet." PhD diss., Indiana University, 1977.

——. *The Tibetan Empire in Central Asia*. Princeton, N.J.: Princeton University Press, 1987.

Berger, Patricia. *Empire of Emptiness: Buddhist Art and Political Authority in Qing China*. Honolulu: University of Hawai'i Press, 2003.

Bertrand, Jacques, and André Laliberté, eds. *Multination States in Asia: Accommodation or Resistance*. Cambridge: Cambridge University Press, 2010.

Bhattacharya, J. N., and Nilanjana Sarkar, eds. *Encyclopedic Dictionary of Sanskrit Literature*. Delhi: Global Vision Publishing House, 2004.

Bielmeier, Roland, ed. *Linguistics of the Himalayas and Beyond*. Berlin, New York: Mouton de Gruyter, 2007.

Bikkhu Bodhi. "Spiritual Friendship." *Buddhist Publication Society Newsletter* 57 (2007).

Blakeslee, Joy. *Ama Adhe: The Voice That Remembers: The Heroic Story of a Woman's Fight to Free Tibet*. Somerville, Mass.: Wisdom, 1997.

Blo bzang lhun grub rdo rje. *Krung go'i bod brgyud dgon pa'i dkar chag las kan su'u glegs bam* [China's Tibet: a catalogue of Buddhist monasteries, their antiquities and liturgical objects, volume on Gansu province]. Lanzhou: Gansu minzu chubanshe, 2009.

Brag dgon pa Dkon mchog bstan pa rab rgyal. *Mdo smad chos 'byung*. [n.p.]: Rig gnas myur skyob dpe mdzod khang, [n.d.].

Bronner, Yigal, David Shulmann, and Gary Tubb, eds. *Innovations and Turning Points: Toward a History of Kāvya Literature*. Oxford: Oxford University Press, 2014.

Brox, Trine. "Changing the Tibetan Way: Contested Secularisms in the Tibetan Diaspora." In *Tibetan Studies: An Anthology, PIATS 6: Proceedings for the International Association of Tibetan Studies Konigswinter*, ed. Saadet Arslen and Peter Schwieger, 117–142. Andiast: International Institute for Tibetan and Buddhist Studies, 2010.

Bründer, Andreas. *Account of a Pilgrimage to Central Tibet*. Dharamsala: Tibetan Library of Works and Archives, 2008.

Bstan 'dzin dge legs. "Chos dung kar po'i rang mdangs/slob dpon chen mo dung dkar blo bzang 'phrin las mchog nub phyogs yul du snga phyir mjal ba'i bag chags rab rim." *Gtam tshogs* 37, no. 1 (July): 11–43. Dharamsala: Library of Tibetan Works and Archives, 2017.

Bstan 'dzin rgya mtsho. "Bka' 'bum rin po che par byang smon tshig." In *Jigs med dam chos rgya mtsho bka' 'bum* [Collected works of Jigmé Damcho Gyatso]. Vol. *pa*, folio 1. Printed form woodblocks at Reb gong Monastery, retrieved 2008.

Bu ston rin chen grub. *Bu ston chos 'byung*. Pe cin (Beijing): Krung go bod kyi shes rig dpe skrun khang, 1988.

——. *The History of Buddhism in India and Tibet*. Trans. E. Obermiller. Originally published as *Bu ston chos 'byung* [in Tibetan]. Delhi: Classics India Publications, 1999 [reprint].

Bubandt, Nils Ole, and Martijn van Beek. *Varieties of Secularism in Asia: Anthropological Explorations of Religion, Politics and the Spiritual*. New York: Routledge, 2012.

Butler, Judith. *Gender Trouble: Feminism and the Subversion of Identity*. New York and London: Routledge Classics, 1990.

Bynum, Caroline Walker. *Fragmentation and Redemption: Essays on Gender and the Human Body in Medieval Religion*. New York: Zone Books, 1991.

Cabezón, José Ignacio. *Buddhism and Language: A Study of Indo-Tibetan Scholasticism.* Albany: State University of New York Press, 1994.

——. *A Dose of Emptiness: An Annotated Translation of sTong thun chen mo of Mkhas grub dge legs pal bzang.* Albany: State University of New York Press, 1992.

——, ed. *Scholasticism: Cross-Cultural Perspectives.* Albany: State University of New York Press, 1998.

——. "State Control of Tibetan Buddhist Monasticism in the People's Republic of China." In *Chinese Religiosities: Afflictions of Modernity and State Formation,* ed. Mayfair Yang, 261–291. Berkeley: University of California Press, 2008.

Cabezón, José, and Roger Jackson, eds. *Tibetan Literature: Studies in Genre.* Ithaca, N.Y.: Snow Lion, 1996.

Caidan Xiarong 才旦夏茸 [Tshe tan zhabs drung]. *Zangzu shixue gailun* 藏族诗学 概论 (Snyan ngag spyi don) [General commentary on poetics], trans. He Wenxuan 賀文宣. Beijing: Minzu chubanshe, 2014.

Campany, Robert Ford. *To Live as Long as Heaven and Earth.* Berkeley: University of California Press, 2002.

——. "On the Very Idea of Religions (in the Modern West and in Early Medieval China)." *History of Religions* 42 (2003): 287–319.

Caple, Jane E. *Morality and Monastic Revival in Post-Mao Tibet.* Honolulu: University of Hawai'i Press, 2019.

Casanova, José. *Public Religions in the Modern World.* Chicago: University of Chicago Press. 1994.

——. "The Secular, Secularizations and Secularisms." In *Rethinking Secularism,* ed. Craig Calhoun, Mark Juergensmeyer, and Jonathan VanAntwerpen, 54–74. New York: Oxford University Press, 2011.

——. "Secularization Revisited: A Reply to Talal Asad." In *Powers of the Secular Modern: Talal Asad and His Interlocutors,* ed. David Scott and Charles Hirschkind, 12–30. Stanford, Calif.: Stanford University Press, 2006.

Chang, Yu-Nan. "The Chinese Communist State System Under the Constitution of 1954." *The Journal of Politics* 18, no. 3 (August 1956): 520–546.

Chattopadhyaya, Alaka. *Atisha and Tibet.* Trans. Lama Chimpa. Delhi: Motilal Banarsidass, 1996.

Chen Qingying 陈庆英. *Chen Qingying zangxue lunwenji* 陈庆英藏学论文集 [Chen Qingying's collected essays in Tibetology]. 2 vols. Beijing: Zhongguo zangxue chuban she, 2006.

Chou, Wen-shing. *Mount Wutai: Visions of a Sacred Buddhist Mountain.* Princeton, N.J.: Princeton University Press, 2018.

Chu skyes dge 'dun dpal bzang. *Reb gong yul skor zin tho* [Notes on Reb gong]. Lanzhou: Gansu minzu chuban she, 2007.

Cone, Margaret, and Richard Gombrich. *The Perfect Generosity of Prince Vessantara.* New York: Oxford University Press, 1971.

Covill, Linda, Ulrike Roesler, and Sarah Shaw, eds. *Lives Lived, Lives Imagined: Biography in the Buddhist Traditions.* Proceedings of the Conference held in Oxford, April 28–29, 2007. Boston: Wisdom, 2010.

Cui Naifu, ed. *Zhonghua renmin gonghe guo diming dacidian* [Toponym dictionary of China]. Beijing: Shangwu, 1998–2002.

Cüppers, Christoph, ed. *The Relationship Between Religion and State* (chos srid zung 'brel) *in Traditional Tibet.* Lumbini: Lumbini International Research Institute, 2004.

Dan dou si jian shi (*Dan tig dkar chag*) [A brief history of Dentik monastery]. Sections translated into English by Nicole Willock (rigs pa'i chos 'dzin; Ni ke). [n.p.]. Retrieved at monastery, 2008.

Dan zhu ang ben, Zhou Runnian, Mo Fushan, and Li Shuanglian, eds. *Zangzu da cidian* (*Bod rigs tshig mdzod chen mo*). Lanzhou: Gansu renmin chubanshe, 2003.

Davidson, Ronald. "The Litany of Names of Manjusri: Text and Translation of the Manjusrinamasamgiti." In *Tantric and Taoist Studies in Honour of R. A. Stein,* ed. Michel Strickmann, vol. xx, 1–69. Brussels: Institut Belge des Hautes Études Chinoises, 1982.

——. *Tibetan Renaissance: Tantric Buddhism in the Rebirth of Tibetan Culture*. New York: Columbia University Press, 2005.

Delehaye, Hippolyte. *The Work of the Bollandists Through Three Centuries 1615–1915*. Princeton, N.J.: Princeton University Press, 1922.

Department of Information and International Relations (DIIR). *From the Heart of the Panchen Lama*: *Major Speeches and a Petition 1962–1989*. Dharamsala: Central Tibetan Administration, 2003.

Dge bshes chos grags. *Brda dag ming tshigs gsal ba* [A comprehensive dictionary of the Tibetan language]. Dharamsala: Library of Tibetan Works and Archives, 1980.

Dge 'dun chos 'phel. *Deb ther dkar po*. Beijing: Minzu chubanshe, 2002.

Dge 'dun rab gsal. "Bstan rtsis kun las btus pa dang lo tshigs dwangs shel me long gnyis bsur ba'i dpyad zhib thor bu zhig" [Notes comparing 'A clear mirror: a chronology' and 'A comprehensive chronology']. *Tsanpo.com*, https://www.tsanpo.com/forum/21992.html.

——. *Rig pa'i khye'u: dus rabs bcu bsum par tha snyad rig gnas bod la ji ltar slebs pa las 'phros pa'i dbyad rtsom dang gzhan* [Papers on the arrival of the literary field of knowledge in Tibet during the thirteenth century and beyond]. Dharamsala: Library of Tibetan Works and Archives, 2017.

Dhondup Tashi. "A Monastic Scholar Under China's Occupation of Tibet: Muge Samten's Autobiography and His Role as a Vernacular Intellectual." MA thesis, University of British Columbia, 2019.

Diemberger, Hildegard. *When a Woman Becomes a Religious Dynasty: The Samding Dorje Phagmo of Tibet*. New York: Columbia University Press, 2007.

Dimitrov, Dragomir. *Mārgavibhāga: Die Unterscheidung der Stilarten, Kritische Ausgabe des ersten Kapitels von Daṇḍins Poetik Kāvyādarśa und der tibetischen Übertragung Sñan ṅag me loṅ nebst einer deutschen Übersetzung des Sanskrittexts*. Marburg: Indica et Tibetica Verlag, 2002.

Dmu dge bsam gtan rgya mtsho. "Bod du rig gnas dar tshul mdor bsdus bshad pa" [A concise history of dissemination of traditional fields of learning in Tibet]. In *Rje dmu dge bsam gtan rgya mtsho'i gsung 'bum*, vol. 3, 384–463. Zi ling: Mtsho sngon mi rigs dpe skrun khang, 1997.

——. "Bod kyi yi ge spyi rnam blo gsal 'jug ngogs" [Entryway to a clear mind: on Tibetan writing]. In *Rje dmu dge bsam gtan rgya mtsho'i gsung 'bum*, vol. 5, 1–304. Zi ling: Mtsho sngon mi rigs dpe skrun khang, 1997.

——. *Rje dmu dge bsam gtan rgya mtsho mi 'jigs dbyangs can dga' ba'i blo gros dpal bzang po'i gsung 'bum* [Collected works of Dmu dge bsam gtan, ocean of marvelous wisdom of the fearless *sarasvatī*]. 6 vols. Zi ling: Mtsho sngon mi rigs dpe skrun khang, 1997.

——. "Rtsom pa po rang gi byung ba brjod pa rang gsal A' dar sha" [Luminous mirror: the author's own telling what happened]. In *Rje dmu dge bsam gtan rgya mtsho mi 'jigs dbyangs can dga' ba'i blo gros dpal bzang po'i gsung 'bum*, vol. 1, 525–694. Zi ling: Mtsho sngon mi rigs dpe skrun khang, 1997.

Doboom Tulku. "The Lineage of the Panchen Lamas: A Brief History and Biographical Notes." *Lungta: The Lives of the Panchen Lamas* 10 (Winter 1996). Dharamsala: Amnye Machen Institute

"Document 19." Selected Documents of the Third Plenum of the Eleventh Party Congress, 1982. Trans. Janice Wickeri. In *Religion in China Today: Policy and Practice* by Donald MacInnis. Maryknoll, N.Y.: Orbis Books, 1989.

Don grub rgyal and Khrin Chin dbyin (Chen Qingying). *Btsan po khri sde srong btsan gyi lo rgyus mdo tsam brjod pa*. Pe cin: Mi rigs dep skrun khang, 1984.

Don rdor and Bstan 'dzin chos grags, eds. *Gangs ljongs lo rgyus thog gi grags can mi sna*. Lha sa: Bod ljongs mi dmangs dpe skrun khan, 1993.

Dreyer, June Teufel. *China's Forty Millions*. Cambridge and London: Harvard University Press, 1976.

Dreyfus, Georges. "Is Compassion an Emotion? A Cross-cultural Exploration of Mental Typologies." In *Visions of Compassion: Western Scientists and Tibetan Buddhists Examine Human Nature*, ed. Anne Harrington and Richard J. Davidson, 31–45. Oxford: Oxford University Press, 2002.

——. *The Sound of Two Hands Clapping: The Education of a Tibetan Buddhist Monk*. Berkeley: University of California Press, 2003.

Dreyfus, Hubert, and Paul Rabinow. *Michel Foucault: Beyond Structuralism and Hermeneutics* 2nd ed. Chicago: University of Chicago Press, 1983.

Dryburgh, Marjorie, and Sarah Dauncey, eds. *Writings Lives in China, 1600–2010: Histories of the Elusive Self.* New York: Palgrave Macmillan, 2013.

Duara, Prasenjit. "Knowledge and Power in the Discourse of Modernity: The Campaigns Against Popular Religion in Early Twentieth-Century China." *The Journal of Asian Studies* 50, no. 1 (February 1991): 67–83.

——. *Rescuing History from the Nation: Questioning Narratives of Modern China.* Chicago: University of Chicago Press, 1995.

Dunch, Ryan. "Christianity and 'Adaptation to Socialism.'" In *Chinese Religiosities: Afflictions of Modernity and State Formation*, ed. Mayfair Yang, 155–178. Berkeley: University of California Press, 2008.

Dung-dkar blo-bzang 'phrim-las. *The Merging of Religious and Secular Rule in Tibet.* Trans. Chen Guansheng. Beijing: Foreign Languages Press, 1991.

Dung dkar blo bzang 'phrin las. "Bod kyi chos srid zung 'brel gyi lam lugs la thog ma'i zhib 'jug byas pa'i shes tshor gnad bsdus" [Essential points on how research was conducted for the system of Buddhist governance in Tibet]. In *Mkhas dbang dung dkar blo bzang 'phrin las kyi gsung 'bum*, ed. Rnam rgyal ra 'phrin las rgya mtsho, vol. 4, 7–8. Beijing: Minzu chubanshe, 2004.

——. "Bod kyi chos srid zung 'brel skor bshad pa" [An explanation of the merging of religious and secular rule in Tibet]. Vol. 4, *Mkhas dbang dung dkar blo bzang 'phrin las kyi gsung 'bum*, ed. Rnam rgyal ra 'phrin las rgya mtsho. Beijing: Minzu chubanshe, 2004.

——. "Bod kyi dkar chag rig pa" [The science of Tibetan catalogues]. In *Mkhas dbang dung dkar blo bzang 'phrin las kyi gsung 'bum*, ed. Rnam rgyal ra 'phrin las rgya mtsho, vol. 2, 1–73. Beijing: Minzu chubanshe, 2004.

——. "Bod kyi chos srid zung 'brel skor bshad pa." In *Dung dkar blo bzang 'phrin las kyi gsung rtsom 'phyogs bsgrigs* [A collection of essays by Dungkar Lozang Trinle]. Beijing: Zhongguo zangxue chubanshe, 1997.

——. "Bod yig dpe rnying dpar skrun dang 'brel ba'i gnad don 'ga' zhig skor gleng ba" [A discussion of essential points related to the printing of ancient Tibetan texts]. In *Mkhas dbang dung dkar blo bzang 'phrin las kyi gsung 'bum*, ed., Rnam rgyal ra 'phrin las rgya mtsho, vol. 2, 74–120. Beijing: Minzu chubanshe, 2004.

——. "Deb ther dmar po'i nang gi gal che'i tshig 'grel gnad bsdus" [An explanation of select major terminologies in the *Red Annals*]. Vol. 6, *Mkhas dbang dung dkar blo bzang 'phrin las kyi gsung 'bum*, ed. Rnam rgyal ra 'phrin las rgya mtsho. Beijing: Minzu chubanshe, 2004.

——. *Dung dkar tshig mdzod chen mo* [Dungkar encyclopedia]. Beijing: Zhongguo Zangxue chubanshe, 2002.

——. *Mkhas dbang dung dkar blo bzang 'phrin las kyi gsung 'bum* [Collected works of the great polymath, Dungkar Lozang Trinlé]. Ed. Rnam rgyal ra 'phrin las rgya mtsho. 8 vols. Beijing: minzu chubanshe, 2004.

——. "Snyan ngag la 'jug tshul tshig rgyan rig pa'i sgo 'byed" [Gateway to the art of literary figures for writing poetry]. Vol. 1, *Mkhas dbang dung dkar blo bzang 'phrin las kyi gsung 'bum*, ed. Rnam rgyal ra 'phrin las rgya mtsho. Beijing: Minzu chubanshe, 2004.

Dung dkar 'jigs med. "Sprul sku nas slob dpon chen mo—nga'i A pha lags phyir dran byas ba" [From tülku to professor: in remembrance of my father]. *Krung go'i bod ljongs*, Zhongguo Xizang 中国西藏 [China's Tibet] 4, no. 27 (July 2014): 46–51.

Dung dkar tshig mdzod chen mo, eds. [n.a.]. "Rtsom pa po ngo spro mdor bdus" [A brief introduction to the author]. In *Dung dkar tshig mdzod chen mo*, 13–16. Beijing: Zhongguo Zangxue Chubanshe, 2002.

Dungkar Lozang Trinlé. "Tibetan Wood Block Printing: Ancient Art and Craft." Trans. Tsering Gonkatsang. *Himalaya* 36, no. 1 (Spring 2016): 163–171.

Eakin, Paul John. *How Our Lives Become Stories: Making Selves.* Ithaca, N.Y.: Cornell University Press, 1999.

Elverskog, Johann. *Our Great Qing: The Mongols, Buddhism, and the State in Imperial China.* Honolulu: University of Hawai'i Press, 2006.

Engels, Friedrich. "En ke si'i hphu lu hri rgyal po hphu li di li zhi wa'i len skye phreng bzhi." Translated into Tibetan from the Chinese by Rdo rje rab brtan. In *Mkhas dbang dung dkar blo bzang 'phrin las kyi gsung 'bum,* ed. Rnam rgyal ra 'phrin las rgya mtsho, vol. 4, 4–6. Beijing: Minzu chubanshe, 2004

Eppling, John Frederick. "A Calculus of Creative Expression: The Central Chapter of Daṇḍin's *Kāvyādarśa.*" PhD diss., University of Wisconsin, Madison, 1989.

Erherd, Xaver. "Review of Jabb, Lama: Oral and Literary Continuities in Modern Tibetan Literature. The Inescapable Nation." *Orientalistische Literaturzeitung* 114, no. 2 (2019): 85–87.

Farquhar, David M. "Emperor as Bodhisattva in the Governance of the Ch'ing Empire." *Harvard Journal of Asiatic Studies* 38, no. 1 (June 1978): 5–34.

Fisher, Gareth. "Mapping Religious Difference: Lay Buddhist Textual Communities in the Post-Mao Period." In *Recovering Buddhism in Modern China,* ed. Jan Kiely and J. Brooks Jessup, 257–290. New York: Columbia University Press, 2016.

Fletcher, Joseph. "A Brief History of the Chinese Northwest Frontier: China Proper's Northwest Frontier: Meeting Place of Four Cultures." In *China's Inner Asian Frontier: Photographs of the Wulsin Expedition to Northwest China in 1923,* ed. M. E. Alonso. Cambridge, Mass.: Harvard University Press, 1979.

Foucault, Michel. *The History of Sexuality. Vol. 1: An Introduction.* Trans. R. Hurley. New York: Vintage, 1978 [1990a].

——. "The Subject and Power." In *Michel Foucault: Beyond Structuralism and Hermeneutics,* ed. H. Dreyfus and P. Rabinow, 87–104. Chicago: University of Chicago Press, 1983.

——. *The Use of Pleasure. Volume 2: History of Sexuality.* Trans. R. Hurley. New York: Vintage, 1990b.

Gayley, Holly. *Love Letters from Golok: A Tantric Couple in Modern Tibet.* New York: Columbia University Press, 2017.

Gayley, Holly, and Nicole Willock. "Theorizing the Secular in Tibetan Cultural Worlds." *Himalaya* 36, no. 1 (Spring 2016): 12–19.

Geary, Patrick. *Living with the Dead in the Middle Ages.* Ithaca, N.Y.: Cornell University Press, 1994.

Gedun Rabsal and Nicole Willock. "Dictums for Developing Virtue." In *A Gathering of Brilliant Moons: Practice Advice from the Rimé Masters of Tibet,* ed. Holly Gayley and Joshua Schapiro, 83–96. Somerville, Mass.: Wisdom, 2017.

Geertz, Clifford. "Religion as a Cultural System." In *The Interpretation of Cultures: Selected Essays,* 87–125. New York: Basic Books, 1973.

Gendun Chopel. *In the Faded Forest.* Ed. and trans. Donald S. Lopez Jr. Chicago: University of Chicago Press, 2009.

——. *Grains of Gold: Tales of a Cosmopolitan Traveler.* Trans. Thupten Jinpa and Donald S. Lopez Jr. Chicago: University of Chicago Press, 2014.

——. *White Annals.* Trans. Samten Norboo. Dharamsala: Library of Tibetan Works and Archives, 1978.

Germano, David. "Re-membering the Dismembered Body of Tibet: Contemporary Tibetan Visionary Movements in the People's Republic of China." In *Buddhism in Contemporary Tibet: Religious Revival and Cultural Identity,* ed. Melvyn Goldstein and Matthew Kapstein, 53–94. Berkeley: University of California Press, 1998.

Germano, David, and Janet Gyatso. "Longchenpa and the Possession by the Ḍākinīs." In *Tantra in Practice,* ed. David Gordon White, 239–265. Princeton, N.J.: Princeton University Press, 2000.

Gerow, Edwin. *A Glossary of Indian Figures of Speech.* The Hague: Mouton, 1971.

Geshe Lhundub Sopa. *Steps on the Path to Enlightenment: A Commentary on Tsongkhapa's "Lamrim Chenmo."* Vol. 1: The Foundation Practices. Boston: Wisdom, 2004.

Geshe Sonam Rinchen. *The Three Principal Aspects of the Path.* Trans. Ruth Sonam. Ithaca, N.Y.: Snow Lion, 1999.

Gold, Jonathan. *The Dharma's Gatekeepers: Sakya Paṇḍita on Buddhist Scholarship in Tibet.* Albany: State University of New York Press, 2007.

Goldstein, Melvyn. "Change, Conflict and Continuity Among a Community of Nomadic Pastoralists: A Case Study of Western Tibet, 1950–1990." In *Resistance and Reform in Tibet*, ed. Robert Barnett and Shirin Akiner, 76–111. Delhi: Motilal Banarsidass, 1996.

——. "The Dragon and the Snow Lion: The Tibet Question in the 20th Century." *Tibetan Review* (April 1991): 9–26.

——. *A History of Modern Tibet, 1913–1951: The Demise of the Lamaist State.* Berkeley: University of California Press, 1989.

——. *A History of Modern Tibet, vol. 2: The Calm Before the Storm, 1951–1955.* Berkeley: University of California Press, 2007.

——. *A History of Modern Tibet, vol. 3: The Storm Clouds Descend, 1955–1957.* Berkeley: University of California Press, 2014.

——. "Introduction" and "The Revival of Monastic Life in Drepung Monastery." In *Buddhism in Contemporary Tibet: Religious Revival and Cultural Identity*, ed. Melvyn Goldstein and Matthew Kapstein, 1–14; 15–52. Berkeley: University of California Press, 1998.

——. *The New Tibetan-English Dictionary of Modern Tibetan.* Berkeley: University of California Press, 2001.

——. "Taxation and the Structure of a Tibetan Village." *Central Asiatic Journal* 15, no. 1 (1971): 1–27.

Goldstein, Melvyn, and Matthew Kapstein, eds. *Buddhism in Contemporary Tibet: Religious Revival and Cultural Identity.* Berkeley: University of California Press, 1998.

Goldstein, Melvyn, Ben Jiao, and Tanzen Lhundrup. *On the Cultural Revolution in Tibet: The Nyemo Incident of 1969.* Berkeley: University of California Press, 2009.

Goldstein, Melvyn, William Siebenschuh, and Dawai Sherap. *A Tibetan Revolutionary: The Political Life and Times of Bapa Phüntso Wangye.* Berkeley: University of California Press, 2004.

Goldstein, Melvyn, William Siebenschuh, and Tashi Tsering. *The Struggle for Modern Tibet: The Autobiography of Tashi Tsering.* Armonk, N.Y.: M. E. Sharpe, 1997.

Goossaert, Vincent, and David Palmer. *The Religious Question in Modern China.* Chicago: University of Chicago Press, 2012.

'Gos lo tsā ba gzhon nu dpal. *The Blue Annals (Deb ther sngon po).* Trans. Georges Roerich. Delhi: Motilal Banarsidass, 1996 [reprint].

——. *Deb ther sngon po* [The blue annals]. Chengdu: Si khron mi rigs dpe skrun khang, 1984 [reprint].

Grousset, Rene. *In the Footsteps of the Buddha.* New York: Orion Press, 1971.

Grushcke, Andreas. *The Cultural Monuments of Tibet's Outer Provinces.* 2 vols. Bangkok: White Lotus, 2001.

Gu Hua [=Hua Ku]. *A Small Town Called Hibiscus.* Trans. Gladys Yang. Beijing: China Publications Centre, 1983.

Gyatso, Janet. *Apparitions of Self: The Secret Autobiographies of a Tibetan Visionary.* Princeton, N.J.: Princeton University Press, 1999.

——. *Being Human in a Buddhist World: An Intellectual History of Medicine in Modern Tibet.* New York: Columbia University Press, 2015.

——. "Healing Burns with Fire: The Facilitations of Experience in Tibetan Buddhism." *Journal of the American Academy of Religion* 67, no. 1 (1999): 113–147.

——. "Moments of Tibetan Modernity: Methods, Assumptions, Caveats." In *Mapping the Modern in Tibet, PIATS 2006: Proceedings of the Eleventh Seminar of the International Association for Tibetan Studies. Königswinter 2006*, ed. Gray Tuttle, 1–44. Andiast: International Institute for Tibetan and Buddhist Studies (IITBS), GmBh, 2011.

Gyurme, Dorje. *Tibet: A Handbook.* Bath, UK: Footprint, 2004.

Haarh, Erik. *The Yar-lung Dynasty: A Study with Particular Regard to the Contribution by Myths and Legends to the History of Ancient Tibet and the Origin and Nature of Its Kings.* Copenhagen: G.E.C. GAD's Folag, 1969.

Harrell, Stevan. "Introduction: Civilizing Projects and the Reaction to Them." In *Cultural Encounters on China's Ethnic Frontiers*, ed. Stevan Harrell, 3–36. Seattle and London: University of Washington Press, 1995.

——, ed. *Cultural Encounters on China's Ethnic Frontiers*. Seattle and London: University of Washington Press, 1995.

Hartley, Lauran R. "Con**text**ually Speaking: Tibetan Literary Discourse and Social Change in the People's Republic of China (1980–2000)." PhD diss., Indiana University, 2003.

——. "Heterodox Views and the New Orthodox Poems: Tibetan Writers in the Early and Mid-Twentieth Century." In *Modern Tibetan Literature and Social Change*, ed. Lauran Hartley and Patricia Schiaffini-Vedani. Durham, N.C. and London: Duke University Press, 2008.

——. "Self as a Faithful Public Servant: The Autobiography of Mdo mkhar ba tshe ring dbang rgyal (1697–1763)." In *Mapping the Modern in Tibet, PIATS 2006: Proceedings of the Eleventh Seminar of the International Association for Tibetan Studies. Königswinter 2006*, ed. Gray Tuttle, 45–72. Andiast: International Institute for Tibetan and Buddhist Studies (IITBS), GmBh, 2011.

——. "Themes of Tradition and Change in Modern Tibetan Literature." *Lungta: Contemporary Tibetan Literature* 12 (Summer 1999): 29–44.

Hartley, Lauran R., and Patricia Schiaffini-Vedani, eds. *Modern Tibetan Literature and Social Change*. Durham, N.C. and London: Duke University Press, 2008.

Henrion-Dourcy, Isabelle. "A Look at the Margins: Autobiographical Writing in Tibetan in the People's Republic of China." In *Writing Lives in China, 1600–2010: Histories of the Elusive Self*, ed. Marjorie Dryburgh and Sarah Dauncey, 206–235. New York: Palgrave Macmillan, 2013.

Hess, Julia Meredith. *Immigrant Ambassadors: Citizenship and Belonging in the Tibetan Diaspora*. Stanford: Stanford University Press, 2009.

Holmes-Tagchungdarpa, Amy. *The Social Life of Tibetan Biography: Textuality, Community, and Authority in the Lineage of Tokden Shakya Shri*. Lanham, Md.: Lexington Books, 2014.

Hor tshang 'Jigs med, ed. *Mdo smad lo rgyus chen mo* [An extensive history of Mdo smad]. 6 vols. Dharamsala: Library of Tibetan Works and Archives, 2009.

Hualong xianzhi 化隆县志 [Hualong county gazetteer]. Xi'an: Shanxi renmin chubanshe, 1994.

Huber, Toni. *The Cult of Pure Crystal Mountain: Popular Pilgrimage and Visionary Landscape in Southeast Tibet*. Oxford: Oxford University Press, 1999.

——. *The Holy Land Reborn: Pilgrimage and the Tibetan Reinvention of Buddhist India*. Chicago: University of Chicago Press, 2008.

——. "Putting the gnas back into gnas-skor." In *Sacred Spaces and Powerful Places in Tibetan Culture: A Collection of Essays*, ed. Toni Huber, 77–104. Dharamsala: Library of Tibetan Works and Archives, 1999.

——, ed. *Sacred Spaces and Powerful Places in Tibetan Culture*. Dharamsala: Library of Tibetan Works and Archives, 1999a.

——. "Shangri-la in Exile: Representations of Tibetan Identity and Transnational Culture." In *Imagining Tibet: Perceptions, Projections, and Fantasies*, ed. Thierry Dodin and Heinz Räther, 357–371. Boston: Wisdom, 2001.

Information Office of the State Council of The People's Republic of China. *White Papers on Tibet* (Beijing, 1992).

International Campaign for Tibet. "Tibetan Refugees." Savetibet.org.

Ishihama, Yumiko. "The Notion of Buddhist Government (*chos srid*) Shared by Tibet, Mongol and Manchu in the Early 17th Century." In *The Relationship Between Religion and State (chos srid zung 'brel) in Traditional Tibet*, ed. Christoph Cüppers, 15–31. Lumbini: Lumbini International Research Institute, 2004.

Iwasaki, Tsutomu. "The Tibetan Tribes of Ho-hsi and Buddhism During the Northern Sung Period." *Acta Asiatica* 64 (1993): 17–37.

Jackson, David. *The Entrance Gate for the Wise Section III*. Wien: Arbeitskreis für Tibetische und Buddhistische Studien, Universität Wien, 1987.

Jacoby, Sarah H. *Love and Liberation: Autobiographical Writings of the Tibetan Buddhist Visionary Sera Khandro*. New York: Columbia University Press, 2014.

Jagou, Fabienne. *The Ninth Panchen Lama (1883–1937): A Life at the Crossroads of Sino-Tibetan Relations.* Paris: École Française d'extrême-Orient, 2011.

——. "A Pilgrim's Progress: the Peregrinations of the 6th Panchen Lama." In *Lungta: The Lives of the Panchen Lamas* 10 (Winter 1996). Dharamsala: Amnye Machen Institute.

——. "The Thirteenth Dalai Lama's Visit to Beijing in 1908: In Search of a New Kind of Chaplain-Donor Relationship." In *Buddhism Between Tibet and China,* ed. Matthew Kapstein. Boston: Wisdom, 2009.

Jampa Samten Shastri, ed. *Catalogue of the Library of Tibetan Works and Archives, Historical Works,* vol. 3. Dharamsala: Library of Tibetan Works and Archives, 1983.

'Jigs med chos 'phags, ed. *Mkhas dbang Tshe tan zhabs drung gi dpyad rtsom mkho bsdus* [A useful collection of essays by the great scholar Tshe tan zhabs drung]. Lanzhou: Gansu minzu chuban she, 1991.

——, ed. *Tshe tan zhabs drung rje btsun 'jigs med rigs pa'i blo gros mchog gi gsung 'bum* [Collected works of the great Tshe tan zhabs drung 'Jigs med rigs pa blo gros]. 13 vols. Beijing: Mi rigs dpe skrun khang (minzu chuban she), 2007.

'Jigs med dam chos rgya mtsho. *Bka' 'bum* [Collected works]. Woodblock print. Rongbo Monastery, Rebgong, retrieved 2008.

'Jigs med rigs pa'i blo gros gsung 'bum [Collected works of Tshe tan zhabs drung 'Jigs med rigs pa'i blo gros]. Woodblock print at Mthu ba Monastery, retrieved 2007.

'Jigs meds theg mchog. " 'Jam dbyangs bla ma rdo rje sems dpa'i ngo bo bka' drin mtshungs med rje btsun 'jigs med rigs pa'i blo gros dpal bzang bo'i rnam par thar ba bden gtam rna ba'i bdud rtsi zhes bya ba'i kha skong skal bzang me tog bzhad pa'i 'khri shing." In *Tshe tan zhabs drung rje btsun 'jigs med rigs pa'i blo gros mchog gi gsung 'bum,* ed. 'Jigs med chos 'phag. Beijing: Mi rigs dpe skrun khang, 2007.

Kagyu Thubten Chöling Publications Committee [Writers: Thomas Pardee, Susan Skolnick, Eric Swanson]. *Karmapa: The Sacred Prophecy,* with a foreword by His Holiness the Dalai Lama, ed. Willa Baker, Dr. Elisabeth Deran, Dr. Robert Kelly, and Jane Madill. Wappingers Falls, N.Y.: Kagyu Thubten Chöling Publications Committee, 1999.

Kapstein, Matthew, ed. *Buddhism Between China and* Tibet. Boston: Wisdom, 2009.

——. "Dhondup Gyal: The Making of a Modern Hero." *Lungta: Contemporary Tibetan Literature* 12 (Summer 1999): 45–48.

——. "The Indian Literary Identity in Tibet," In *Literary Cultures in History: Reconstructions from South Asia,* ed. Sheldon Pollock. Berkeley: University of California Press, 2003.

——. "A Pilgrimage of Rebirth Reborn: The 1992 Celebration of the Drigung Powa Chenmo." In *Buddhism in Contemporary Tibet: Religious Revival and Cultural Identity,* ed. Melvyn Goldstein and Matthew Kapstein. Berkeley: University of California Press, 1998.

——. *Tibetan Assimilation of Buddhism: Conversion, Contestation, and Memory.* Oxford: Oxford University Press, 2000.

——. "Tibetan Tibetology? Sketches of an Emerging Discipline." In *Images of Tibet in the 19th and 20th Centuries,* ed. Monica Esposito, vol. 2, 799–815. Paris: École française d'Extrême-Orient, 2008.

——. *The Tibetans.* Malden, Mass.: Blackwell, 2006.

——. "The Treaty Temple of the Turquoise Grove." In *Buddhism Between Tibet and China.* Boston: Wisdom, 2009.

——. "The Tulku's Miserable Lot: Critical Voices from Eastern Tibet." In *Amdo Tibetans in Transition: Society and Culture in the Post-Mao Era, PIATS 2000: Tibetan Studies Proceedings of the International Association of Tibetan Studies Leiden 2000,* ed. Toni Huber, 99–111. Leiden: Brill, 2002.

Karmay, Samten G. "Mountain Cults and National Identity in Tibet." In *Resistance and Reform in Tibet,* ed. Robert Barnett and Shirin Skinner, 112–120. Delhi: Motilal Banarsidass, 1994.

——, trans. *'Khrul ba'i rol rtsed. The Illusive Play: The Autobiography of the Fifth Dalai Lama.* Chicago: Serindia, 2014.

Karmay, Samten G., and Yasuhiko Nagano, eds. *New Horizons in Bon Studies.* Osaka, Japan: National Museum of Ethnology, 2000.

Karsten, Joachim. "A Study on the sKu-'bum/ T'a-erh ssu Monastery in Ch'inghai." PhD diss., Auckland University, New Zealand, 1997.

Kelsang Gyatso. *Universal Compassion*. London: Tharpa, 1997.

Khétsun, Tubten. *Memories of Life in Lhasa Under Chinese Rule*. Trans. and introduction by Matthew Akester. New York: Columbia University Press, 2008.

Ko zhul grags pa 'byung gnas and Rgyal ba blo bzang mkhas grub, eds. *Gangs can mkhas grub rim byon ming mdzod*, vol. 3. Lanzhou: Kan su'u mi rigs dpe skrun khang, 1992.

Kolås, Åshild, and Thowsen, Monika. *On the Margins of Tibet: Cultural Survival on the Sino-Tibetan Frontier*. Seattle: University of Washington Press, 2005.

Kwok, Daniel W.Y. *Scientism in Chinese Thought: 1900–1950*. New Haven, Conn. and London: Yale University Press, 1965.

La ke yi xi duo jie (拉科益西多杰). *Zangchuan fojiao gaoseng zhuanlüe* 藏传佛教高僧专列 [Eminent monks of Tibetan Buddhism]. Xining: Qinghai renmin chubanshe, 2007.

Lama Jabb. *Oral and Literary Continuities in Modern Tibetan Literature: The Inescapable Nation*. Lanham, Md. and Boulder, Colo.: Lexington Books, 2015.

Lama Zopa Rinpoché. *Extensive Offering Practice: A Practice to Accumulate the Most Extensive Merit with Lights and Other Offerings*. N.p.: Foundation for the Preservation of the Mahayana Tradition Education Services, 2003.

Lamrim Chenmo Translation Committee (LCTC). *Tsong-kha-pa. The Great Treatise on the Stages of the Path to Enlightenment*. Ithaca, N.Y.: Snow Lion, 2000.

Lejeune, Phillipe. *On Autobiography*. Minneapolis: University of Minnesota Press, 1989.

Lessing, Ferdinand. *Yung-ho-kung, an Iconography of the Lamaist Cathedral in Peking*. Stockholm: Sino-Swedish Expedition, Publication 18, VIII Ethnography 1, 1942.

Lhag pa phun tshogs. "Dung dkar rin po che'i dgongs pa shul 'dzin byas nas bod rig pa dar rgyas gong 'phel gtong dgos—mkhas pa'i dbang po dung dkar rin po che mchog la snying thag pa nas dran gso zhu" [Heartfelt commemoration of the venerable Dungkar Rinpoche: the need to set in motion the prosperity of Tibetan studies having inherited the legacy of Dungkar Rinpoche]. In *Mkhas dbang Dung dkar blo bzang 'phrin las kyi gsung 'bum*, ed. Rnam rgyal ra 'phrin las rgya mtsho, vol. 1, 1–20. Beijing: Minzu chubanshe, 2004.

Lha mo sgrol ma. "Mkhas dbang tshe tan zhabs drung gyi sku phreng rim byon gyi byung ba mdo tsham brjod pa" [A brief essay on the incarnation lineage of the polymath, Tshe tan zhabs drung]. *Zla zer* 46, no .2 (1994): 72–89.

Li Fang-kuei. "The Inscription of the Sino-Tibetan Treaty of 821–822." *T'oung Pao* 44 (1956): 1–3.

Li Fang-kuei and W. South Coblin. *A Study of the Old Tibetan Inscriptions*. Taipei: Academica Sinica, 1987.

Liebold, James. *Reconfiguring Chinese Nationalism: How the Qing Frontier and Its Indigenes Became Chinese*. New York: Palgrave MacMillan, 2007.

Lin Hongjie. "Lun minzu gainian de zhengzhi shuxing—cong Ouzhou weiyuanhui de xiangguan wenjian kan 'minzu' yu 'zuqun'" [On the political attributes of the concept of *minzu* ("ethno-nationality"): "ethno-nationality" and "ethnic group" in the relevant documents of the Council of Europe]. *Minzu yanjiu* 4 (2002): 11–20.

Lin, Nancy Grace. "Adapting the Buddha's Biographies: A Cultural History of the Wish-Fulfilling Vine in Tibet, Seventeenth to Eighteenth Centuries." PhD diss., University of California, Berkeley, 2011.

——. "Döndrup Gyel and the Ramayana." In *Modern Tibetan Literature and Social Change,* ed. Lauran Hartley and Patricia Schiaffini-Vedani, 86–111. Durham, N.C. and London: Duke University Press, 2008.

——. "Recounting the Fifth Dalai Lama's Rebirth Lineage." In *Revue d'Etudes Tibétaines,* special issue on reincarnation in Tibetan Buddhism, ed. Daniel Hirschberg, Derek Maher, and Tsering Wangchuk, 38 (Février 2017): 119–156.

Link, Perry. *The Uses of Literature: Life in the Socialist Chinese Literary System*. Princeton, N.J.: Princeton University Press, 2000.

Lipman, Jonathan. "Ethnicity and Politics in Republican China: The Ma Family Warlords of Gansu Province." *Modern China* 10, no. 3 (July 1984): 285–316.

——. *Familiar Strangers: A History of Northwest China.* Seattle: University of Washington Press, 1997.

Liu, Lydia. *Translingual Practice: Literature, National Culture, and Translated Modernity—China, 1900–1937.* Stanford, Calif.: Stanford University Press, 1995.

Lobsang Yongdan. "Precious Skin: The Rise and Fall of the Otter Fur Trade in Tibet." *Inner Asia* 20 (2018): 177–198.

Lopez, Donald S., Jr. *Buddhism and Science: A Guide for the Perplexed.* Chicago: University of Chicago Press, 2008.

——. *Prisoners of Shangri-la: Tibetan Buddhism and the West.* Chicago: University of Chicago Press, 1998.

——, ed. *Religions of Tibet in Practice.* Princeton, N.J.: Princeton University Press, 1997..

Lu Xinhua, Liu Xinwu, et al. *The Wounded: Stories of the Cultural Revolution.* Trans. Geremie Barmé and Bennett Lee. Hong Kong: Joint Publishing Company, 1979.

Lutz, Catherine. "Opening and Retrospectives: What Matters." *Cultural Anthropology* 32, no. 2 (June 2017): 181–191.

Ma Haiyun. "New Teachings and New Territories: Religion, Regulations and Regions in Qing Gansu, 1700–1800." PhD diss., Georgetown University, 2007.

Ma Rong. "A New Perspective in Guiding Ethnic Relations in the Twenty-first Century: 'De-politicization' of Ethnicity in China." *Asian Ethnicity* 8, no. 3 (October 2007): 199–217.

Ma Xueren, ed. *Hanzang duizhao foxue cidian* (汉藏对照佛学词典; Rgya bod shan sbyar sangs rgyas chos gzhung gi tshig mdzod) [Chinese-Tibetan bilingual Buddhist dictionary]. Lanzhou: Gansu minzu chubanshe, 2007.

MacFarquhar, Roderick, and John Fairbank, eds. *The People's Republic, Part 1: The Emergence of Revolutionary China 1949–1965.* Vol. 14, *The Cambridge History of Modern China.* Cambridge: Cambridge University Press, 1987.

MacInnis, Donald. *Religion in China Today: Policy and Practice.* Maryknoll, N.Y.: Orbis Books, 1989.

Maher, Derek F. "Translator's Introduction." In *One Hundred Thousand Moons: An Advanced Political History of Tibet* by Tsepon Wangchuk Deden Shakabpa, trans. Derek F. Maher. Leiden and Boston: Brill, 2010.

Mahmood, Saba. "Feminist Theory, Embodiment, and the Docile Agent: Some Reflections on the Egyptian Islamic Revival." *Cultural Anthropology* 16, no. 2 (May 2001): 202–236.

——. *Politics of Piety: The Islamic Revival and the Feminist Subject.* Princeton, N.J.: Princeton University Press, 2005.

Makley, Charlene. *The Battle for Fortune: State-led Development, Personhood, and Power Among Tibetans in China.* Ithaca, N.Y.: Cornell University Press, 2018.

——. *The Violence of Liberation: Gender and Tibetan Buddhist Revival in Post-Mao China.* Berkeley: University of California Press, 2007.

Mao Wujun and Ma Shilin, trans. *Anduo zhengjiao shi.* Gansu: Gansu minzu chubanshe, 1988.

Mao Zedong. "Guanyu xizang pingpan 关于西藏平叛" [On pacifying the rebellion in Tibet]. In *Maozhuxi xizang gongzuo wenxuan* 毛主席西藏工作文选 [A collection of working papers on Tibet by Chairman Mao], ed. the Chinese Communist Party Committee of the Tibetan Autonomous Region (中共西藏自治区委员会). Beijing: Zhongyang wenxian chubanshe, 2001.

——. *Mao' tse tung gi gsung rtsom gces bsdus* [in Tibetan]. Beijing: Beijing minzu chubanshe, 1992 [reprint].

Martin, Dan. "Indian Kāvya Poetry on the Far Side of the Himālayas: Translation, Transmission, Adaptation, Originality." In *Innovations and Turning Points: Toward a History of Kāvya Literature,* ed. Yigal Bronner, David Shulman, Gary Tubb, 563–608. Oxford: Oxford University Press, 2014.

——. *Tibetan Histories: A Bibliography of Tibetan-language Historical Works.* London: Serindia, 1997.

Masuzawa, Tomoko. *The Invention of World Religions, or How European Universalism was Preserved in the Language of Pluralism.* Chicago and London: University of Chicago Press, 2005.

McGranahan, Carole. *Arrested Histories: Tibet, the CIA, and Memories of a Forgotten War*. Durham, N.C. and London: Duke University Press, 2010.

McKay, Alex, ed. *Pilgrimage in Tibet*. Richmond, Surrey: Curzon Press, 1998.

——. *Tibet and Her Neighbors: A History*. London: Edition Hansjörg Mayer, 2003.

McMahan, David L. *The Making of Buddhist Modernism*. Oxford: Oxford University Press, 2008.

Mengele, Irmgard. *dGe-'dun-chos-'phel: A Biography of the 20th-Century Tibetan Scholar*. Dharamsala: Library of Tibetan Works and Archives, 1999.

Mgon po dbang rgyal. *Rgyal rabs lo tshigs shes bya mang 'dus mkhas pa'i spyi nor*. Beijing: Mi rigs dpe skrun khang, 2000.

Mi Yizhi. *Sa la zu shi* [History of the Salar]. Chengdu: Sichuan People's Publishing, 2004.

Muge Samten. *A History of Traditional Fields of Learning: A Concise History of Dissemination of Traditional Fields of Learning in Tibet (Bod du rig gnas dar tshul mdor bsdus bshad pa)*. Trans. Sangye Tandar Naga [bilingual edition, in English and Tibetan]. Dharamsala: Library of Tibetan Works and Archives, 2005.

Mullaney, Thomas. *Coming to Terms with the Nation: Ethnic Classification in Modern China*. Berkeley: University of California Press, 2011.

Nāgārjuna. *Tree of Wisdom (Shes rab sdong bu)*. Trans. W. L. Campbell. Calcutta: Calcutta University, 1919; reprint, Lexington, Ky.: Forgotten Books, 2007.

Nāgārjuna. *Nāgārjuna's Letter to a Friend with Commentary by Venerable Rendawa, Zhö-nu Lo-drö*. Trans. Geshe Lobsang Tharchin and Artemus B. Engle. Dharamsala: Library of Tibetan Works and Archives, 1979.

Nedostup, Rebecca. "Ritual Competition and Modernizing Nation-State." In *Chinese Religiosities: Afflictions of Modernity and State Formation*, ed. Mayfair Yang, 87–112. Berkeley: University of California Press, 2008.

——. *Superstitious Regimes: Religion and the Politics of Modernity*. Cambridge, Mass.: Harvard East Asian Monographs, Harvard University Press, 2009.

Negi, J. S., ed. *Tibetan-Sanskrit Dictionary (Bod skyad dang legs sbyar gyi tshig mdzod chen mo)*. Vol. 7. Varanasi: Dictionary Unit Central Institute of Higher Tibetan Studies Sarnath, 2001.

Ngag dbang blo bzang rgya mtsho. *'Khul ba'i rol rtsed. The Illusive Play: The Autobiography of the Fifth Dalai Lama*. Trans. Samten G. Karmay. Chicago: Serindia, 2014.

——. "Za hor gyi ban de Ngag dbang blo bzang rgya mtsho'i 'di snang 'khrul ba'i rol rtsed rtogs brjod kyi tshul du bkod pa du kū la'i gos bzang." In *Rgyal dbang lnga pa chen po'i gsung 'bum* [Collected works of the Fifth Dalai Lama], vol. 1. Dharamsala: Nam gsal sgron ma, 2007.

Nietupski, Paul Kocot. *Labrang Monastery: A Tibetan Buddhist Community on the Inner Asian Borderlands, 1709–1959*. Lanham, Md.: Rowman & Littlefield, 2011.

Nor brang O rgyan, ed. *Chos rnam kun btus*, vol. 2 (bar). Beijing: Krung go'i bod rig pa dpe skrun khang, 2008.

Padmakara Translation Group. *Nagarjuna's "Letter to a Friend."* With commentary by Kangyur Rinpoche. Ithaca, N.Y.: Snow Lion, 2005.

Palden Gyatso. *Autobiography of a Tibetan Monk*. Trans. Tsering Shakya. New York: Grove Press, 1997.

Palmer, David A. "Heretical Doctrines, Reactionary Secret Societies, Evil Cults: Labeling Heterodoxy in Twentieth-Century China." In *Chinese Religiosities: Afflictions of Modernity and State Formation*, ed. Mayfair Yang, 113–134. Berkeley: University of California Press, 2008.

Patrul Rinpoché. *Words of My Perfect Teacher*. Trans. the Padmakara Translation Group. New Delhi: Vistaar Publications, 1994.

Pelliot, Paul. "Quelques Transcriptions Chinoises de Noms Tibétains." *T'oung Pao* XVI (1915).

Pema Bhum (Pad ma 'bum). "The Dictionary of New Terms and the Chinese-Tibetan Dictionary." Trans. Lauran Hartley. *Trace Foundation's Latse Library Newsletter* 3 (Fall 2005): 13–25.

——. "The Heart-Beat of a New Generation: A Discussion of New Poetry." Trans. Ronald Schwartz. *Lungta: Contemporary Tibetan Literature* 12 (Summer 1999): 2–16.

——. "'Heartbeat of a New Generation' Revisited." In *Modern Tibetan Literature and Social Change*, ed. Lauran Hartley and Patricia Schiaffini-Vedani, 135–170. Durham, N.C. and London: Duke University Press, 2008.

——. "An Overview of the Life of Professor Dungkar Lozang Trinlé Rinpoché." *Trace Foundation's Latse Library Newsletter* 5 (2007–2008): 18–36.

——. *Six Stars with a Crooked Neck: Tibetan Memoirs of the Cultural Revolution* (dran tho smin drug ske 'khyog). Trans. Lauran R. Hartley [bilingual Tibetan and English]. Dharamsala: Tibet Times, 2001.

Penny, Benjamin, ed. *Religion and Biography in China and Tibet*. Richmond, Surrey: Curzon Press, 2002.

Petech, Luciano. *Aristocracy and Government in Tibet 1728–1959*. Roma: Istituto Italiano per il medio ed estremo Oriente, 1973.

——. "The Mongol Census in Tibet." In *Tibetan Studies in Honor of Hugh Richardson, The Proceedings of the International Seminar of Tibetan Studies, Oxford, 1979*, ed. Michael Aris and Aung San Suu Kyi. Warminster, England: Aris and Phillips, 1980.

——. "Tibetan Relations with Sung China and with the Mongols." In *China Among Equals: The Middle Kingdon and its Neighbors, 10th–14th Centuries*, ed. Morris Rossabi, 173–203. Berkeley: University of California Press, 1983.

'Phrin las, ed. *Mkhas dbang tshe tan zhabs drung 'jigs med rigs pa'i blo gros kyi gsung rtsom* [The collected works of the scholar Tshe tan zhabs drung 'Jigs med rigs pa'i blo gros]. 5 vols. Xining: Mtsho sngon mi rigs dpe skrun khang, 1987.

Pitkin, Annabella. "Lineage, Authority, and Innovation: The Biography of Khu nu bla ma Bstan 'dzin rgyal mtshan." In *Mapping the Modern, Proceedings from the International Association of Tibetan Studies Conference 2006 Konigswinter, Germany*, ed. Gray Tuttle, 173–203. Konigswinter: IITBS, International Institute for Tibetan and Buddhist Studies GmbH, 2011.

Pollock, Sheldon. *Literary Cultures in History: Reconstructions from South Asia*. Berkeley: University of California Press, 2003.

——. *A Rasa Reader: Classical Indian Aesthetics*. New York: Columbia University Press, 2016.

Powers, John. *The Buddha Party: How the People's Republic of China Works to Define and Control Tibetan Buddhism*. Oxford: Oxford University Press, 2017.

Press Trust of India. "127935 Tibetans Living Outside of Tibet." *Hindustan Times*, December 4, 2010.

Prins, Marielle. "Toward a Tibetan Common Language: A mdo Perspectives on Attempts at Language Standardisation." In *Amdo Tibetans in Transition: Society and Culture in the Post-Mao Era, PIATS 2000: Tibetan Studies Proceedings of the International Association of Tibetan Studies, Leiden 2000*, ed. Toni Huber, 17–51. Leiden: Brill, 2002.

Pu Wencheng. *Ganqing Zangchuan Fojiao Siyuan* 甘青藏传佛教寺院 [Tibetan Buddhist monasteries and temples in Gansu and Qinghai provinces]. Xining: Qinghai renmin chubanshe, 1990.

——. *Qinghai Fojiao Shi* 青海佛教史 [History of Buddhism in Qinghai province]. Xining: Qinghai minzu chubanshe, 2001.

——, trans. *Budun Fojiao shi* 布顿佛教史. Originally published as *Bu ston chos 'byung* [History of Buddhism by Bu ston rin chen grub]. Lanzhou: Gansu minzu chubanshe, 2007.

Pye, Lucien. "Reassessing the Cultural Revolution." *China Quarterly* 108, no. 12 (1986): 597–612.

Qinghai sheng ditu ce (青海省地图册) [Map of Qinghai province]. Zhongguo fensheng silie dituce [Map series of China's provinces]. Beijing: Huangqiu ditu chubanshe, 2008.

Quintman, Andrew. "Life Writing as a Literary Relic: Image, Inscription, and Consecration in Tibetan Biography." *Material Religion* 9, no. 4 (December 2013): 468–505.

——. *The Yogin and the Madman: Reading the Biographical Corpus of Tibet's Great Saint Milarepa*. New York: Columbia University Press, 2014.

Rgyal yab chen po Sun krung hran. *San ming khru'u yi: mi mang gi sgrig lam gsum* [Three Principles of the People]. Taipei: I the kung si krung hwa par khang, 1981.

Rgyal yongs mi dmangs 'thus mi'i tshogs chen thengs dang po'i gnas tshogs thog gros 'chams [Resolution at the first National People's Assembly]. Krung hwa mi dmangs spyi mthun rgyal khab kyi rtsa khrims

[Constitution of the People's Republic of China]. In Tibetan. Ch. Zhonghua renmin gongheguo xianfa, 1954. Private collection.

Rheinigans, Jim, ed. *Tibetan Literary Genres, Texts, and Text Types: From Genre Classification to Transformation.* Leiden, Boston: Brill, 2015.

Richardson, Hugh. *A Corpus of Early Tibetan Inscriptions.* London: Royal Asiatic Society, 1985.

Rijnhart, Susie. *With the Tibetans in Tent and Temple.* Edinburgh and London: Oliphant, Anderson & Ferrier, 1902.

Rinzang. "My Conversation with Akhu Yarphel." In *Conflicting Memories: Retellings of Tibetan History Under Mao,* ed. Robbie Barnett, Francoise Robin, and Benno Weiner. Trans. Gedun Rabsal and Nicole Willock from the Tibetan, 334–351. Leiden: Brill, Inner Asian Book Series, 2020.

Rnam rgyal ra 'phrin las rgya mtsho, ed. "Gangs can mkhas pa'i khyu mchog dung dkar blo bzang 'phrin las kyi mdzad rim" [A biographical timeline of Tibet's top scholar Dungkar Lozang Trinle]. In *Mkhas dbang dung dkar blo bzang 'phrin las kyi gsung 'bum,* appendix to vol. 4 and vol. 7, 1–7. Beijing: Minzu chubanshe, 2004.

Rnam rgyal tshe ring (Ch. An Shiying), ed., *Sam bod rgya gsum gshan sbyar gyi tshig mdzod* [Sanskrit, Tibetan, Chinese, trilingual dictionary]. Beijing: Mi rigs dpe skrun khang, 2005.

Roche, Gerald, and Lugyal Bum. "Language Revitalization of Tibetan." In *The Routledge Handbook of Language Revitalization,* ed. Leanne Hinton, Leena Huss, and Gerald Roche, e-book section 2.5 Asia, Ch. 40. New York: Routledge, 2018.

Roche, Gerald. "Articulating Language Oppression: Colonialism, Coloniality, and the Erasure of Tibet's Minority Languages." *Patterns of Prejudice* 53, no. 5 (2019): 487–514. https://doi.org/10.1080/0031322X.2019.1662074.

Roesler, Ulrike. "Between Self-Expression and Convention: Tibetan Reflections on Autobiographical Writing." *Life Writing* 17, no. 2 (2020): 163–186. DOI: 10.1080/14484528.2019.1620581.

——. "Classifying Literature or Organizing Knowledge? Some Considerations on Genre Classifications in Tibetan Literature." In *Tibetan Literary Genres, Texts, and Text Types: From Genre Classification to Transformation,* ed. Jim Rheinigans, 31–53. Leiden, Boston: Brill, 2015.

——. "Introduction." In *Lives Lived, Lives Imagined: Biography in the Buddhist Traditions,* ed. Linda Covill, Ulrike Roesler, and Sarah Shaw, 1–11. Boston: Wisdom, 2010.

Ruegg, David Seyfort. "Introductory Remarks on the Spiritual and Temporal Orders." In *The Relationship Between Religion and State (chos srid zung 'brel) in Traditional Tibet,* ed. Christoph Cüppers, 9–13. Lumbini: Lumbini International Research Institute, 2004.

——. "Preceptor-Donor Relations in Thirteenth-Century Tibetan Society and Polity: Its Inner Asian Precursors and Indian Models." In *The Tibetan History Reader,* ed. Gray Tuttle and Kurtis R. Schaeffer, 211–232. New York: Columbia University Press, 2013.

——. *The Symbiosis of Buddhism with Brahmanism/Hinduism in South Asia and of Buddhism with 'Local Cults' in Tibet and the Himalayan Region.* Wien: Verlag der Österreichische Akademie der Wissenschaften, 2008.

Samuel, Geoffrey. *Civilized Shamans: Buddhism in Tibetan Societies.* Washington and London: Smithsonian Institution Press, 1993.

Sautman, Barry, and June Dreyer, eds. *Contemporary Tibet: Politics, Development, and Society in a Disputed Region.* Armonk, N.Y.: M. E. Sharpe, 2006.

Schaeffer, Kurtis. *The Culture of the Book in Tibet.* New York: Columbia University Press, 2009.

——. *Himalayan Hermitess: The Life of a Tibetan Buddhist Nun.* Oxford and New York: Oxford University Press, 2004.

——. "Tibetan Biography: Growth and Criticism." In *Edition, éditions, l'écrit au Tibet, évolution et devenir,* ed. Anne Chayet, Cristina Scherrer-Schaub, Françoise Robin, Jean-Luc Achard, 263–306. München: Indus Verlag, 2010.

Schiaffani-Vedani, Patricia. "The 'Condor' Flies Over Tibet: Zhaxi Dawa and the Significance of Tibetan Magical Realism." In *Modern Tibetan Literature and Social Change,* ed. Lauran J. Hartley and Patricia Schiaffani-Vedani, 202–224. Durham, N.C. and London: Duke University Prss, 2008.

Schram, Louis. *The Mongours of the Kansu-Tibetan Frontier; Their Origin, History and Social Organiza-tion*. Philadelphia: The American Philosophical Society, 1954.

——. *The Mongours of the Kansu-Tibetan Frontier, Part II: Their Religious Life*. Philadelphia: The American Philosophical Society, 1957.

Schrempf, Mona, and Jack Patrick Haynes. "From Temple to Commodity? Tourism in Songpan and the Bon Monasteries of Amdo Shar Khog." In *Bon: The Everlasting Religion of Tibet, Tibetan Studies in Honor of David Snellgrove; East and West* 59, no. 1 (December 2009): 285–312.

Schuh, Dieter. "Srid ohne Chos? Reflektionen zum Verhältnis von Buddhismus und säkularer Herrschaft im tibetischen Kulturraum." In *The Relationship Between Religion and State (chos srid zung 'brel) in Traditional Tibet*, ed. Christoph Cüppers, 291–297. Lumbini: Lumbini International Research Institute, 2004.

——. *Untersuchungen zur Geschichte der tibetische Kalenderrechnung*. Wiesbaden: Franz Steiner Verlag Gmbh, 1973.

Schwartz, Ronald. *Circle of Protest: Political Ritual in the Tibetan Uprising*. New York: Columbia University Press, 1994.

Sde srid sangs rgya mtsho. *Dga' ldan chos 'byung baidurya serpo* [Yellow beryl]. Beijing: Krung go'i bod kyi shes rig dpe skrun khang, 1998 [reprint].

Seymour, James D., and Michael Anderson. *New Ghosts and Old Ghosts: Prison and Labor Reform Camps in China*. London and New York: Routledge East Gate Books, 1998.

Sha bo tshe ring. "Mkhas dbang dge 'dun chos 'phel dang khong gi snyan rtsom bshad pa lhag bsam 'o ma'i rdzing bu" [Pool of altruistic milk: on Dge 'dun chos 'phel and his poetry]. Vol. 3. *Bod kyi shes rig dpyad rtsom phyogs bsgrigs blo gsal bung ba 'dren pa'i dpyid kyi pho nya*. Beijing: Zhongguo zangxue chubanshe, 1992.

Shakabpa, Tsepon W.D. *One Hundred Thousand Moons: An Advanced Political History of Tibet*. Trans. Derek F. Maher. Leiden and Boston: Brill, 2010.

——. *Tibet: A Political History*. New Haven, Conn.: Yale University Press, 1967.

Shokdung. *The Division of Heaven and Earth: On Tibet's Peaceful Revolution*. Trans. M. Akester. Oxford: Oxford University Press, 2016.

Shushum Bhatia, Tsegyal Dranyi, and Derrick Rowling, "A Social and Demographic Study of Tibetan Refugees in India." *Social Science and Medicine* 54 (2002): 411–422.

Smith, E. Gene. *Among Tibetan Texts*. Boston: Wisdom, 2001.

Smith, Sidonie, and Julia Watson. *Reading Autobiography: A Guide for Interpreting Life Narratives*. Minneapolis: University of Minnesota Press, 2001.

Smith, Warren. *Tibetan Nation: A History of Tibetan Nationalism and Sino-Tibetan Relations*. Boulder, Colo.: Westview Press, 1996.

Smyer Yu, Dan. *Mindscaping the Landscape of Tibet: Place, Memorability, Ecoaesthetics*. Boston, Berlin: Walter de Gruyter, 2015.

——. *The Spread of Tibetan Buddhism in China: Charisma, Money, Enlightenment*. London: Routledge, 2011.

Snellgrove, David. *The Hevajra Tantra: A Critical Study: Part I: Introduction and Translation, Part II: Sanskrit and Tibetan Text*. London: School of Oriental and African Studies, 1959.

Sørenson, Per, trans. *Tibetan Buddhist Historiography, The Mirror Illuminating Royal Genealogies: An Annotated Translation of the XIVth Century Chronicle: rGyal-rabs gsal-ba'i me long* by Bsod rnams rgyal mtshan. Wiesbaden: Otto Harrasowitz Verlag, 1994.

Spence, Jonathan. *The Search for Modern China*. London: Hutchinson, 1991.

Sperling, Elliot. "Awe and Submission: A Tibetan Aristocrat at the Court of Qianlong." *International Review of History* 20 (1998).

——. "A Captivity in the Ninth Century." *The Tibet Journal* 4 (Winter 1979): 17–67.

——. "The Dalai Lama as Dupe." *Los Angeles Times*. https://www.latimes.com/archives/la-xpm-2008-apr -03-oe-sperling3-story.html.

——. "Did the Early Ming Emperors Attempt to Implement a 'Divide and Rule' Policy in Tibet?" In *Contributions on Tibetan Language, History, and Culture*, ed. Ernst Steinkellner and Helmut

Tauscher, 339–356. Wien: Arbeitskreis für tibetische u. buddhistische Studien, Universität Wien, 1983.

——. "The 5th Karma-pa and Some Aspects of the Relationship Between Tibet and the Early Ming." In *Tibetan Studies in Honour of Hugh Richardson. The Proceedings of the International Seminar of Tibetan Studies, Oxford, 1979*, ed. Michael Aris and Aung San Suu Kyi, 280–289. Westminster, England: Aris and Phillips.

——. "Orientalism and Aspects of Violence in the Tibetan Tradition." In *Imagining Tibet: Perceptions, Projections and Fantasies*, ed. Thierry Dodin and Heinz Räther, 317–329. Boston: Wisdom, 2001.

——. "Self-Delusion." *Tibet und Buddhismus* 109, no. 2 (May 2014). Info-buddhism.com.

——. "Tibet and China: The Interpretation of History Since 1950." *China Perspectives* 3 (2009): 25–37.

——. *The Tibet-China Conflict: History and Polemics*. Washington, D.C.: East-West Center Washington, 2004.

Stein, Rolf. *Recherches sur l'épopée et la barde au Tibet*. Bibliothèque de l'Institute des hautes études chinoises, vol. 13. Paris: Presses universitaires de France, 1959.

Steinkellner, Ernst. *Tibetan History and Language: Studies Dedicated to Géza Uray on his Seventieth Birthday*. Vienna: Arbeitskreis fuer Tibetische und Buddhistische Studien Universität Wien, 1991.

Stoddard, Heather. "The Long Life of rDo-sbis dGe-bšes Šes-rab rGya-mcho (1894–1968)." In *Tibetan Studies: Proceedings of the Fourth Seminar of the International Association of Tibetan Studies, Munich, 1985*, ed. Helga Uebach and Jampa L. Panglung, 465–471. Munich: Kommission für Zentralasiatische Studien, 1988.

——. *Le mendiant de l'Amdo*. Paris: Société d'ethnographie, 1986.

——. "Progressives and Exiles." In *The Tibetan History Reader*, ed. Gray Tuttle and Kurtis R. Schaeffer, 583–608. New York: Columbia University Press, 2013.

——. "Rekindling the Flame: A Note on Royal Patronage in Tenth Century Tibet." In *The Relationship Between Religion and State* (chos srid zung 'brel) *in Traditional Tibet*, ed. Christoph Cüppers, 49–104. Lumbini: Lumbini International Research Institute, 2004.

——. "Tibetan Publications and National Identity." In *Resistance and Reform in Tibet*, ed. Robert Barnett and Shirin Akiner, 138–139. Delhi: Motilal Banarsidass, 1994.

Strong, John. *The Legend of King Aśoka: A Study and Translation of the Aśokāvadāna*. Princeton, N.J.: Princeton University Press, 1983.

Sujata, Victoria. *Tibetan Songs of Realization: Echoes from a Seventeenth-Century Scholar and Siddha in Amdo*. Leiden: Brill, 2005.

——, trans. and photographer. *Songs of Shabkar: The Path of a Tibetan Yogis Inspired by Nature*. Cazedero, Calif.: Dharma Publishing, 2011.

Sum pa mkhan po ye shes dpal 'byor. *The Annals of Kokonor* (*Mtsho sngon lo rgyus tshangs glu gsar snyan*). Trans. Ho-chin Yang. Bloomington: Indiana University Publications, vol. 106, Uralic and Altaic Series, 1969.

Sun Yatsen. *San ming kru'u yi'i bsdus don* [Three principles of the people in Tibetan]. Trans. Yang Zhifu and Sherab Gyatso. Taipei, Taiwan: Meng Zang weiyuanhui, reprint 1971.

Swidler, Anne. *Talk of Love: How Culture Matters*. Chicago: University of Chicago Press, 2001.

Taikhang, T. Tsepal, comp. *Rare Tibetan Historical and Literary Texts from the Library of Tsepon W.D. Shakabpa Series 1*. New Delhi: Tsepal Taikhang, 1974.

Tambiah, Stanley Jeyaraja. *The Buddhist Saints of the Forest and the Cult of Amulets: A Study in Charisma, Hagiography, Sectarianism, and Millennial Buddhism*. Cambridge: Cambridge University Press, 1984.

Teeuwen, Mark. "Buddhist Modernities: Modernism and Its Limits." In *Buddhist Modernities: Reinventing Tradition in the Globalizing Modern World*, ed. H. Havnevik, U. Hüsken, M. Teeuwen, V. Tikhonov, and K. Wellens, 1–12. New York: Routledge, 2017.

Tenzin Monlam. "Tibetan Scholar Dungkar Rinpoche's 20th Death Anniversary." *Phayul*, July 24, 2017. http://www.phayul.com/news/article.aspx?id=39319&t=1.

Thanissaro Bhikkhu (Ajaan Geoff), trans. "Upaddha Sutta: Half of the Holy Life." Buddhasutra.com. Accessed April 12, 2019. http://buddhasutra.com/files/upaddha_sutta.htm.

Thuken Losang Chökyi Nyima. *The Crystal Mirror of Philosophical Systems: A Tibetan Study of Asian Religious Thought.* Trans. Geshé Lhundub Sopa. Ed. Roger R. Jackson. Boston: Wisdom, 2009.

Thupten Jinpa, ed. *Mind Training: The Great Collection.* Boston: Wisdom, 2006.

Thu'u bkwan blo bzang chos kyi nyi ma. *Grub mtha' she gyi me long.* TBRC W2124. Lanzhou: Gansu minzu chubanshe, [reprint 1984].

Tibet Information Network. *Background Briefing Papers: Documents and Statements from Tibet 1996–1997.* London: Tibet Information Network, 1998.

——. "Leading Scholar Dies, Cultural Criticism." August 4, 1997. https://www.columbia.edu/itc/ealac /barnett/pdfs/link2-dlt-obit.pdf.

Tibet Information Network/Robert Barnett. *A Poisoned Arrow: The Secret Report of the 10th Panchen Lama.* London: Tibet Information Network, 1997.

Tsepak Rigzin. *Tibetan-English Dictionary of Buddhist Terminology.* Dharamsala: Library of Tibetan Works and Archives, 1997.

Tsering Shakya. "The Development of Modern Tibetan Literature in the People's Republic of China in the 1980s." In *Modern Tibetan Literature and Social Change,* ed. Lauran Hartley and Patricia Schiaffini-Vedani, 61–85. Durham, N.C. and London: Duke University Press, 2008.

——. "The Development of Modern Tibetan Studies." In *Resistance and Reform in Tibet,* ed. Robert Barnett and Shirin Akiner, 1–14. New Delhi: Motilal Banarsiddass, 1994.

——. *The Dragon in the Land of Snows: A History of Modern Tibet Since 1947.* New York: Columbia University Press, 1999.

——. "The Emergence of Modern Tibetan Literature: Gsar rtsom." PhD diss., School of Oriental and African Studies, University of London, 2004.

——. "The Man Who Wasn't Allowed to Tell the Truth: The Seventh Panchen Lama." *Lungta: The Lives of the Panchen Lamas* 10 (Winter 1996): 24–29.

——. "Politicisation and the Tibetan Language." In *Resistance and Reform in Tibet,* ed. Robert Barnett and Shirin Akin, 157–165. London: C. Hurt & Co.; Delhi: Motilal Banarsidass, 1994.

——. "The Waterfall and Fragrant Flowers, Development of Modern Tibetan Literature." *Mānoa, A Pacific Journal of International Writings,* University of Hawaii 12, no. 2 (2000): 28–40.

——. "Whither the Tsampa Eaters?" *Himal* 6, no. 5 (1993).

Tsering Thar. *Nangshig: A Tibetan Bonpo Monastery and Its Family in Amdo.* Kathmandu, Nepal: Vajra Books, 2016.

Tseten Zhabdrung. "Research on the Nomenclature of the Buddhist Schools in Tibet." Trans. Tenzin Dorjee. *Tibet Journal* 11, no. 3 (Autumn 1986): 40–50.

Tshe ring dbang rgyal. *Tales of the Incomparable Prince.* Trans. Beth Newman. New York: HarperCollins, 1996.

Tshe tan zhabs drung 'Jigs med rigs pa'i blo gros. "Bod du dar ba'i nang ba'i grub mtha' so so'i ming 'dogs kyi dpya ba" [Research on the nomenclature of Buddhist schools and their transmission in Tibet]. *Sbrang char* [Spring rain] 1, no. 1 (1982): 54–64.

——. *Dag yig thon mi'i dgongs rgyan* [A Tibetan dictionary]. New Delhi: Tibet House, 1969.

——. "Dpa' bo gtsug lag 'phreng ba chos 'byung gi lo tshigs kyi dpyad pa" [An analysis of the historical dates in Dpa' bo gtsug lag 'phreng ba's *History of Buddhism*]." In *Mkhas dbang tshe tan zhabs drung gi dpyad rtsom mkho bsdus,* ed. Jigs med chos 'phags, 237–238. Lanzhou: Gansu minzu chubanshe, 1991.

——. "'Gos los [Gzhon nu dpal] lo tshigs bkod pa'i skor las 'ga' zhig nor ba'i dpyad pa" [An analysis of a few mistakes in 'Gos lo's historical dates]. In *Mkhas dbang tshe tan zhabs drung gi dpyad rtsom mkho bsdus,* ed. Jigs med chos 'phags, 232–233. Lanzhou: Gansu minzu chubanshe, 1991.

——. "Mdo smad grub pa'i gnas chen dan tig shel gyi ri bo le lag dang bcas pa'i dkar chag don ldan ngag gi rgyud mangs" [Zither of meaningful words: a catalogue of Dome's sacred place: Dentik, the Crystal Mountain, and its branch monasteries]. In *Tshe tan zhabs drung rje btsun 'jigs med rigs pa blo gros mchog gi gsung 'bum,* ed. 'Jigs med chos 'phags, vol. 3, 279–402. Beijing: Minzu chubanshe, 2007; In

'Jigs med rigs pa'i blo gros gsung 'bum [Collected works of Tshe tan zhabs drung 'Jigs med rigs pa'i blo gros]. Printed from woodblocks at Mthu ba Monastery, n.d.

——. "Mnyam med shAkya'i dbang bo'i rjes zhugs pa 'jigs med rigs pa'i blo gros rang gi byung ba brjod pa bden gtam rna ba'i bdud rtsi" [Acoustic ambrosia: a truthful telling of what happened by 'Jigs med rigs pa'i blo gros, a disciple of the powerful, matchless *shākya*]. In *Mkhas dbang tshe tan zhabs drung 'jigs med rigs pa'i blo gros kyi gsung rtsom,* ed. 'Phrin las, vol. 1, 500–801. Xining: Qinghai minzu chubanshe, 1987; In *Tshe tan zhabs drung rje btsun 'jigs med rigs pa blo gros mchog gi gsung 'bum,* ed. 'Jigs med chos 'phags, vol. 1, 39–279. Beijing: Minzu chubanshe, 2007; In *'Jigs med rigs pa'i blo gros gsung 'bum.* Woodblock print at Mthu ba Monastery, n.d.

——. "Mnyam med shAkya'i rgyal bo 'das 'khrungs kyi lo tshigs gtsor gyur pa'i bstan rtsis lo sum stong tsam gyi re'u mig gi rnam gzhag mthong tshad kun las btus pa" [A compilation of sources: an analysis of the chronology of three thousand years of history since the birth of the matchless Shākya, the victorious one]. In *Tshe tan zhabs drung rje btsun 'jigs med rigs pa blo gros mchog gi gsung 'bum,* ed. 'Jigs med chos 'phags, vol. 7, 1–320. Beijing: Mi rigs dpe skrun khang, 2007.

——. "Paṇ chen bsod [nams] grags [pa] kyi rgyal rabs 'phrul gyi lde mig deb dmar gsar ba'i lo tshigs kyi dpyad pa" [An analysis of historical dates in the *New Red Annals* by Paṇ chen bsod nams grags pa]. In *Mkhas dbang tshe tan zhabs drung gi dpyad rtsom mkho bsdus,* ed. Jigs med chos 'phags, 234–236. Lanzhou: Gansu minzu chubanshe, 1991.

——. "Pan chen thams cad mkhen cing gzigs pa chen po mdo smad 'khrungs gzhis phyogs su phebs pa'i legs mdzad cha shas tsam gyi ngo mtshar ba'i gtam gyi rtogs pa brjod pa dngul gyi me tog" [*Avadāna* of silver flowers: a wondrous account of the Panchen Lama's visit to Amdo, his birthplace]. In *Tshe tan zhabs drung rje btsun 'jigs med rigs pa'i blo gros mchog gi gsung 'bum,* ed. 'Jigs med chos 'phags, vol. 3, 263–278. Beijing: Minzu chubanshe, 2007; [partly published] In *Sbrang char* 16, no. 1 (1985): 29–30.

——. "Rgyal dbang lnga ba rin po che'i deb ther rdzogs ldan gzhon nu'i dga' ston gyi lo tshigs la dpyad pa" [An analysis of the historical dates in the Fifth Dalai Lama's *Feast of the Early Years of the Buddhist Era*]. In *Mkhas dbang tshe tan zhabs drung gi dpyad rtsom mkho bsdus,* ed. Jigs med chos 'phags, 239–245. Lanzhou: Gansu minzu chubanshe, 1991.

——. "Sde srid sangs rgyas rgya mtsho'i vaiḍūrya dkar po dang vaiḍūrya g.ya' sel sogs kyi lo tshigs la dpyad pa" [An analysis of historical dates in Regent Sde srid sangs rgyas rgya mtsho's works, including the *White Beryl* and *Corrections to the White Beryl,* etc.]. In *Mkhas dbang tshe tan zhabs drung gi dpyad rtsom mkho bsdus,* ed. Jigs med chos 'phags, 246–248. Lanzhou: Gansu minzu chubanshe, 1991.

——. *Snyan ngag spyi don* [A general commentary on poetics]. Lanzhou: Gan su'u mi rigs dpe skrun khang, 1957; 1982, 2005 [reprint].

——. "Sum pa ye shes dpal 'byor gyis bsgrigs pa'i lo tshigs la dpyad pa" [An analysis of historical dates in compositions by Sum pa ye shes dpal 'byor]. In *Mkhas dbang tshe tan zhabs drung gi dpyad rtsom mkho bsdus,* ed. Jigs med chos 'phags, 249–250. Lanzhou: Gansu minzu chubanshe, 1991.

——. *Thon mi'i zhal lung* [Thon mi's counsel]. Lanzhou: Gan su'u mi rigs dpe skrun khang, 2005 [reprint].

Tsongkhapa. *The Great Treatise on the Stages of the Path to Enlightenment.* Trans. Lamrim Chenmo Translation Committee (LCTC). Ithaca, N.Y.: Snow Lion, 2000.

Tucci, Giuseppe. *The Religions of Tibet.* Trans. Geoffrey Samuel. Berkeley: University of California Press, 1988.

——. *Tibetan Painted Scrolls.* Rome: La Libreria dello Stato, 1949.

——. *The Tombs of the Tibetan Kings.* Rome: Instituto Italiano per il medio ed estremo Oriente, 1950.

Tuttle, Gray. "Challenging Central Tibet's Dominance of History the Oceanic Book, a 19th Century Political-Religious Geographic History." In *Mapping the Modern in Tibet, PIATS 2006: Proceedings of the Eleventh Seminar of the International Association for Tibetan Studies. Königswinter 2006,* ed. Gray Tuttle, 139–176. Andiast: International Institute for Tibetan and Buddhist Studies (IITBS), GmBh, 2011.

——. "The Failure of Ideologies in China's Relations with Tibetans." In *Asian Nationalism Studies,* ed. Jacques Bertrand and André Laliberté, 219–243. Cambridge: Cambridge University Press, 2010.

——. "Local History in A mdo: The Tsong kha Range (ri rgyud)." *Asian Highlands Perspectives* 6 (2010): 23–97.

——, ed. *Mapping the Modern in Tibet, PIATS 2006: Proceedings of the Eleventh Seminar of the International Association for Tibetan Studies. Königswinter 2006.* Andiast: International Institute for Tibetan and Buddhist Studies (IITBS), GmBh, 2011.

——. "An Overview of Amdo (Northeastern Tibet) Historical Polities." *Tibetan and Himalayan Library.* www.thlib.org. http://www.thlib.org/about/wiki/An%20Overview%20of%20Amdo%20%28Northeastern%20Tibet%29%20Historical%20Polities.html

——. *Tibetan Buddhists in the Making of Modern China.* New York: Columbia University Press, 2005.

Tuttle, Gray, and Kurtis R. Schaeffer, eds. *The Tibetan History Reader.* New York: Columbia University Press, 2013.

Uebach, Helga. "Dbyar-mo-thang and Gong-bu-ma-ru: Tibetan Historiographical Tradition in the Treaty of 821/2." In *Tibetan History and Language: Studies Dedicated to Géza Uray on his Seventieth Birthday,* ed. Ernst Steinkellner. Wien: Arbeitskreis fuer Tibetische und Buddhistische Studien Universität Wien, 1991.

van der Kuijp, Leonard. "The Dalai Lamas and the Origin of Reincarnate Lamas." In *The Dalai Lamas: A Visual History,* ed. Martin Brauen. Zurich: Ethnographic Museum Zurich and Serindia, 2005; In *The Tibet History Reader,* ed. Gray Tuttle and Kurtis Schaeffer, 335–347. New York: Columbia University Press, 2013.

——. "Tibetan Belles-Lettres: The Influence of Daṇḍin and Ksemendra." In *Tibetan Literature: Studies in Genre,* ed. José Cabezón and Roger Jackson. Ithaca, N.Y.: Snow Lion, 1996.

van der Veer, Peter. "Embodiment, Materiality, and Power. A Review Essay." *Comparative Studies in Society and History* 50, no. 3 (2008): 809–818.

——. *Imperial Encounters: Religion and Modernity in India and Britain.* Princeton, N.J. and Oxford: Princeton University Press, 2001.

——. *The Modern Spirit of Asia: The Spiritual and the Secular in China and India.* Princeton, N.J.: Princeton University Press, 2013.

——. "Smash Temples, Burn Books: Comparing Secularists Projects in India and China." In *Rethinking Secularism,* ed. Craig Calhoun, Mark Juergensmeyer, and Jonathan Van Antwerpen. New York: Oxford University Press, 2011.

van Schaik, Sam. "Amdo Notes II." *Early Tibet* (blog). July 13, 2010. https://earlytibet.com/2010/07/15/amdo-notes-ii/.

——. "The Decline of Buddhism I: Was Lang Darma a Buddhist?" *Early Tibet* (blog), February 28, 2008. https://earlytibet.com/2008/02/28/lang-darma/.

——. *Tibet: A History.* New Haven, Conn. and London: Yale University Press, 2011.

Venturino, Steven. J. "Where Is Tibet in World Literature?" *World Literature Today* 78, no. 1 (Jan.–Apr. 2004): 51–56.

Vizenor, Gerald. *Fugitive Poses: Native American Indian Scenes of Absence and Presence.* Lincoln and London: University of Nebraska Press, 1998.

——. *Manifest Manners: Narratives on Postindian Survivance.* Lincoln and London: University of Nebraska Press, 1999.

Waddell, L. A. *Buddhism and Lamaism of Tibet: with Its Mystic Cults, Symbolism and Mythology, and in Its Relation to Indian Buddhism.* Jalandhar City, India: Gaurav Publishing House, 1978 [reprint].

Wallace, B. Alan, ed. *Buddhism and Science: Breaking New Ground.* New York: Columbia University Press, 2003.

Wang Furen and Suo Wenqing. *Highlights of Tibetan History.* Beijing: New World Press, 1984.

Wang Yao. "Hu Yaobang's Visit to Tibet May 22–31, 1980: An Important Development in the Chinese Government's Tibet Policy." In *Resistance and Reform in Tibet,* ed. Robert Barnett, 285–289. New Delhi: Motilal Banarsiddass, 1994.

Weber, Max. *The Protestant Ethic and the Spirit of Capitalism.* Trans. Talcott Parsons. Mineola, N.Y.: Dover, 2003 [reprint].

Wei Jingsheng. "Excerpts from Qincheng: A Twentieth-Century Bastille published in Exploration, March 1979." www.weijingsheng.org.

Welch, Holmes. *Buddhism Under Mao.* Cambridge, Mass.: Harvard University Press, 1972.

——. *The Buddhist Revival in China.* Cambridge, Mass.: Harvard University Press, 1968.

White, Hayden. *The Content of the Form: Narrative Discourse and Historical Representation.* Baltimore, Md. and London: John Hopkins University Press, 1997.

Willock, Nicole. "Rekindling Ashes of the Dharma and the Formation of Modern Tibetan Studies: The Busy Life of Alak Tseten Zhabdrung." *Trace Foundation's Latse Library Newsletter* 6 (2009–2010): 2–25.

——. "The Revival of the Tulku Institution in Modern China: Narratives and Practices." *Revue d'Etudes Tibétaines,* special issue on reincarnation in Tibetan Buddhism, ed. Daniel Hirschberg, Derek Maher, and Tsering Wangchuk, 38 (Février 2017): 183–201.

——. "A Tibetan Buddhist Polymath of Modern China." PhD diss., Indiana University, 2011.

Wu Zhenhua, ed. *Xizang diming* [Tibet toponyms]. Beijing: Zhongguo zangxue chubanshe, 1995.

Wylie, Turrell. *The Geography of Tibet According to the 'Dzam gling rgyas bshad.* Rome: Istituto Italiano Per Il Medio Ed Estremo Oriente, 1962.

——. "Reincarnation: A Political Innovation." In *Proceedings of the Csoma de Koros Memorial Symposium,* ed. L. Ligeti. Budapest: Akademiai Kiado, 1978.

Ya Hanzhang. *Biographies of the Tibetan Spiritual Leaders Panchen Erdenis.* Beijing: Foreign Languages Press, 1994.

Yang, Fengang. "The Red, Black, and Grey Markets of Religion in China." *Sociological Quarterly* 47 (2006): 93–122.

Yang, Mayfair Mei-hui, ed. *Chinese Religiosities: Afflictions of Modernity and State Formation.* Berkeley: University of California Press, 2008.

Yang, Miaoyan. *Learning to Be Tibetan: The Construction of Ethnic Identity in China.* Lanham, Md.; Boulder, Colo.; New York; London: Lexington Books, 2017.

Yeh, Emily. *Taming Tibet: Landscape Transformation and the Gift of Chinese Development.* Ithaca, N.Y.: Cornell University Press, 2013.

Yon tan rgya mtsho. *Chos sde chen po bla brang bkra shis 'khyil* [History of Labrang Tashikyil Monastery]. Paris: N.p., 1987 [scanned photocopy of dbu chen manuscript, held at TBRC].

You ning si jian jie mu lu (佑宁寺简介目录) [A brief catalogue to Youning (Dgon lung) Monastery], retrieved at monastery in 2008.

Yu, Xue. "Buddhist Efforts at Reconciliation of Buddhism and Marxism in the Early Years of the People's Republic of China." In *Recovering Buddhism in Modern China,* ed. Jan Kiely and J. Brooks Jessup, 177–215. New York: Columbia University Press, 2016.

Zhang Yisun, ed. *Bod rgya tshig mdzod chen mo* (Ch. 藏汉大词典) [Tibetan-Chinese encyclopedia]. Beijing: Mi rigs dpe skrun khang, 1985.

Zhongguo fojiao xiehui, 中国佛教协会, ed. *Xiandai foxue* (现代佛学) [Modern Buddhist studies]. Beijing: Zhongguo fojiao xiehui xuexi weiyuanhui 中国佛教协会学习委员会, 1954.

Index

CCP. *See* Chinese Communist Party

Central Nationalities Institute. *See* Minzu University

Central Nationalities Publishing House. *See* Minzu Press

Chekawa Yeshé Dorjé, 129

Chenpuk Monastery (Gcan phug) (Zhaomuchuan), 41

Chen Qingying, 180–181

China studies, modern, 18

China Tibetology Research Center (Krung go'i bod rig pa zhib 'jug lte gnas) (Zhōngguó zàngxué yánjiū zhōngxīn), 15, 32, 59

Chinese Communist Party (CCP), 12, 90; in civil war, 9–10, 198; "Document 19" issued by, 201; Dungkar Lozang Trinlé and, 57, 152–155, 160, 168, 174–175, 177, 181, 224, 283n150; Land Reform under, 13, 85, 94–97; Panchen Lama candidacy and, 205; on religion, discourse of, 171, 273n133; secularization and, 143–145; Strike Hard campaign of, 205–206, 279n79; Third Plenum of the Eleventh Chinese Communist Party National Congress, 14, 146, 204; on Tibet, historical status of, 161, 163–164, 166–168, 170, 271n96; Tibetan national identity under, 144–151, 160–163, 181, 218, 220–221, 227–229, 232–233, 266n24, 266n34

Chinese People's Political Consultative Conference (mi dmangs tshogs pa) (rénmín zhèngxié) (人民政协) (CPPCC), 12, 14, 150, 198, 238n51, 275n3

Chinggis Khan, 163–164, 271n104

Chökyi Gyeltsen (Chos kyi rgyal mtshan), Tenth Panchen Lama, 54, 109, *202*, 208, 214; in *Acoustic Ambrosia*, 98–99, 197–198, 204; arrest, incarceration of, 146, 150, 198; "*Avadāna* of Silver Flowers" and, 30, 199–200, 207, 279n83; Mao and, 94, 98, 149–150, 198, 203, 220; reincarnate lama institution and, 184, 186, 201, 203–204, 206; 70,000 Character Petition of, 149–150, 198, 203, 220; Tséten Zhabdrung and, 13, 17, 30, 47, 82, 94, 98–99, 184, 186, 196–197, *197*, 198–200, *200*, 201, 204, 207, 275n3, 279n83; *yang-dar* and, 68, 249n130

chöluk (*chos lugs*), 177, 273n126, 273n128; Dungkar Lozang Trinlé on, 145, 158–160, 171–173, 175; in Seventeen Point Agreement, 174

chö-sī zung-drel (*chos srid zung 'brel*) (merging of religious and secular rule), 171, 180; in *The Merging of Religious and Secular Rule in Tibet*, 157–161; Tibetan exiles on, 173

Chos kyi rgyal mtshan. *See* Chökyi Gyeltsen, Tenth Panchen Lama

chos lugs. See chöluk

chos srid zung 'brel. See chö-sī zung-drel

Chronicle of Labrang Monastery (Yontan Gyatso), 88

chu lha (Varuṇa), 115, 260n6

civil war, Chinese, 9–10, 198

collaborator: Dungkar Lozang Trinlé as, 145–146, 152–153, 267n44; resistance fighter and, binary model of, 6–7, 19

Collected Topics (bsdus grwa), 41, 50, 244n16

Collected Works (Dungkar Lozang Trinlé), 16, 24, 31, 60; biographical details in, 32, 54, 155; "Essential Points Reflecting on Initial Research for the System of Merging the Religious and Secular in Tibet" in, 159, 269n63; *The Merging of Religious and Secular Rule in Tibet* in, 155; "Terminologies in the Red Annals" in, 169

Collected Works (Jigmé Damchö Gyatso), 43, 100–101

Collected Works (Mao): *chos lugs* and translation of, 273n128; Mugé Samten, Tséten Zhabdrung translating, 13–14, 52, 75, 101–102, 196, 257n106

Collected Works (Mugé Samten), 16, 24, 27, 49, 54, 176

Collected Works (*sung-bum*) (*gsung 'bum*), 24–25

Collected Works (Tséten Zhabdrung), 16, 31, 40, 43, 82; *Acoustic Ambrosia*, addendum to, in, 278n55, 279n85; *Acoustic Ambrosia* in, 27, 241n88; calligraphy in, 44; printing of, 24–25, 100

Collection of Dungkar Lozang Trinlé's Essays, A (Dungkar Lozang Trinlé), 151–152

Collection of Historical Archives of Tibet, A, 107, 109, 257n111

Commentary on the "Mirror of Poetics" (Tséten Zhabdrung). *See General Commentary on Poetics, A*

Communists, Chinese. *See* Chinese Communist Party

Concise Explanation of the Traditional Fields of Learning in Tibet, A (Mugé Samten). *See History of Traditional Fields of Learning, A*

Constitution of the People's Republic of China: promulgation of, 98, 109; Tséten Zhabdrung translating, 74–75, 98, 174, 196, 198